Canadian Handbook of Flexible Benefits

Robert J. McKay
Editor

Hewitt Associates

JOHN WILEY & SONS

New York • Chichester • Brisbane • Toronto • Singapore

In recognition of the importance of preserving what has been written, it is a policy of John Wiley & Sons, Inc., to have books of enduring value published in the United States printed on acid-free paper, and we exert our best efforts to that end.

Library of Congress Cataloging-in-Publication Data:
Canadian handbook of flexible benefits / Robert J. McKay, editor.
    p. cm.
  Includes bibliographical references and index.
  ISBN 0-471-52262-7
  1. Cafeteria benefit plans—Canada—Handbooks, manuals, etc.
  2. Cafeteria benefit plans—Law and legislation—Canada—Handbooks,
  manuals, etc. I. McKay, Robert J.
  HD4928.N62C2213 1990
  658.3'25'0971—dc20   90-42189

Printed in the United States of America

10 9 8 7 6 5 4 3 2 1

Foreword

F lexible benefits are transforming the delivery of employee compensation and benefits in Canada. The thrust for this transformation is the dramatic change in the demographics of the Canadian workforce. Traditional employee benefit programs no longer meet the needs of today's workforce. In their place, flexible benefit programs are expected to grow exponentially during the 1990s. This book explores the impetus, the elements, and the issues behind flexible benefits in Canada.

Traditional employee benefit programs have been designed for a family unit typically consisting of working male, homemaker female, and two children. The reality is that the traditional family represents only 17 percent of today's workforce, compared to 65 percent of the workforce in the 1960s. Today, almost 60 percent of women are in the workforce, and more than 50 percent of families have dual incomes. Almost 15 percent of families have one parent. More than 80 percent of these one-parent families are women and more than 60 percent of single parents work outside the home. Clearly, the traditional employee benefit program cannot adequately cater to the changing needs of our workforce. Because these needs change over time, an effective employee benefit program should adjust for these changes.

The first flexible benefit programs were introduced in Canada in the early 1980s. Those who introduced the pioneer programs faced uncertainties regarding the possible risks of anti-selection by employees against the programs (which would have resulted in rising costs), lack of software to offer alternatives to in-house administration, lack of clarity regarding the taxation implications, and skepticism by some critics that flexible benefits would not prove popular in Canada. These fears have proved groundless. As of this writing, more than 50 flexible benefit programs have been implemented and the prognosis is for dramatic growth. Indeed, a *Benefits Canada* survey of Canadian employers on the shape of employee benefit programs now and by the year 2000 indicates that 85 percent of the Canadian companies surveyed predicted an increase in the use of flexible benefits by the year 2000.

The emerging practice of flexible benefits is about much more than choices among benefits. It is a new delivery system for total compensation. The plan sponsor decides each year how much to allocate to the program—the amount and timing of the financing is under the control of the plan sponsor. The plan members decide how to allocate their allowance so as to create a configuration of benefits that best suits their needs. It is this equation that offers the plan sponsor the potential for controlling benefit costs, while better satisfying employee needs.

This book has been written by authors who are expert in the subject matter and have worked together on more than 100 flexible benefit programs. Its purpose is to inform the reader on the origins, structure, and technical issues surrounding the design and implementation of flexible benefit programs. The book is not intended as the final authority on this matter, since flexible benefit programs, by their nature, are continually changing shape and expanding.

It is hoped this book will prove invaluable to the reader by creating a better understanding of this new form of employee compensation and by serving as reference material.

FRANK LIVSEY

Willowdale, Ontario
August 1990

Editor's Note: Frank Livsey is a partner of Hewitt Associates and consulted on the first Canadian flexible benefit programs.

Preface

This book was written to serve as a comprehensive reference on flexible benefits—one of the fastest growing design approaches for the delivery of employee benefits and compensation.

The book is intended to be useful to both the novice and the expert in employee benefit matters. Within the text are answers to some of the most frequently asked questions about flexible programs. For example, what alternatives exist for the design of a flexible program? In which benefit areas is choice making most often introduced? How can the cost impact of a flexible program be measured? Also included is detailed treatment of the more technical activities involved with a flexible program implementation—the generating of flexible credits and the pricing of benefit options, establishing the administrative apparatus for individual elections, and designing a plan that meets Revenue Canada's requirements.

The book is organized in seven parts. Part One provides an overview of flexible benefits, including discussion of the major forces influencing the growth and development of flexible programs, review of the alternatives available for flexible program design, and a summary of the steps involved in starting a program.

Part Two focuses on the design of flexible programs. The section is organized by benefit area—health (including medical, dental, vision, and hearing); death and disability coverages; flexible expense accounts; vacation and other time off with pay arrangements; retirement options and newer, emerging benefits.

Part Three concentrates on the legal and regulatory environment. Included is background on the legal and tax frameworks for employee benefits and how they apply to flexible programs. This section also looks at potential discrimination issues with provincial human rights legislation.

Part Four examines the structure and financing of flexible programs in terms of options and prices. Also included is a discussion of the insurance and risk aspects of flexible program choices.

Parts Five and Six explain the steps involved in communicating and administering flexible benefit programs.

Part Seven focuses on the experience under flexible programs. Chapter Twenty-One provides a financial analysis of flexible programs, including a model for performing a cost/benefit analysis of a proposed program. The final chapter, Chapter Twenty-Two, includes case studies of several organizations that have introduced flexible benefits to their employees.

Readers who are unfamiliar with benefit terminology may wish to refer to the Glossary that follows Part Seven.

It should be noted that throughout this book, the text refers to *flexible benefits*. Some readers may question whether the reference ought to be *flexible compensation*. Flexible benefits was chosen because it has become the accepted term in Canada. In fact, flexible compensation more accurately describes the scope of flexible plans. Benefits represent a form of compensation, even though provided to the employee indirectly in the form of employer contributions for medical or other coverage, pension benefits, and the like. Moreover, given the significant sums involved—approaching 40 percent of payroll in some organizations—the direction today is toward increased recognition of employee benefits as a component of total compensation. Finally, choice-making programs further blur once-distinct lines between benefits and compensation as employees often are able to convert unused benefits to cash, or conversely, to divert a portion of pay to the purchase of benefits.

In compiling this book, the editors have drawn on the accumulated experience of numerous consultants at Hewitt Associates. The contributors were invaluable in sharing both their technical knowledge and practical insights into the many different aspects of flexible program operation. They included Kristine Gordon, Frank Livsey, Sandra Reid, and Paul Russell.

In addition to these contributors, the editor would like to acknowledge and thank the contributors to the U.S. version of this book, *Fundamentals of Flexible Compensation*. In particular, the coordination and editing of that book by Christine Seltz and Dale Gifford made the preparation of this Canadian version far easier.

Ruta Skelton and Jean Campbell provided significant assistance in editing the manuscript for this book. The book would never have been published without the effort of the support staff of Hewitt Associates. Lynette Bruce, Dorothy Klubal, Senja Tate, and Helen Wilkie bore most of the burden of typing the manuscript. Finally, thanks to Bill Scott, Christopher Newton, Mike Forsberg, and Janice Munro who helped research many of the issues covered in this book. Hewitt Associates as a whole was most gracious in its support of the time devoted to developing the manuscript.

ROBERT J. MCKAY

Toronto, Ontario
August 1990

About the Editor

Robert J. McKay is an actuary and partner with Hewitt Associates. Hewitt Associates pioneered the concept of flexible benefits in Canada and the United States and is one of the world's largest management consulting firms specializing in employee benefits and compensation.

Mr. McKay has designed and implemented flexible benefit programs for a wide variety of employers in both Canada and the United States. He is a frequent speaker on the topic of flexible benefits and is acknowledged as Canada's leading practitioner in the field.

Contents

PART SEVEN   EXPERIENCE

Part One

Overview

One

Origins and Objectives

Not long ago, the concept of flexible benefits was viewed as a leading-edge approach to delivering benefits and compensation. Proponents touted employee involvement in compensation and benefit decisions as the way of the future. Detractors proclaimed the notion right for academic discussion, but unfit for practical application. Until recently, management held back, uncomfortable with an idea that was both novel and innovative.

Today all of that has changed. As Figures 1.1 and 1.2 illustrate, more than 50 Canadian organizations and more than 1,200 major employers in the United States—representing most industries and all employer sizes —have implemented flexible benefit programs, with most of the activity occurring in recent years. More significantly, evidence is mounting that choice making will replace fixed approaches as the "norm" for delivering employee benefits and compensation in the future.

For many years, the concept of choice has existed within benefit programs. For instance, employees have long had the opportunity to purchase supplemental life insurance beyond employer-provided levels or to pay higher contributions for more valuable medical coverage. The essential difference between that type of choice and the creation of a *choice-making* program, however, is that employees have the opportunity to determine (within certain limits) how employer dollars for benefits are spent on their behalf. Conceptually, a flexible approach

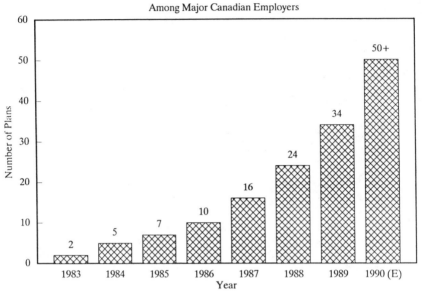

Figure 1.1
Prevalence of Flexible Benefit Plans
Among Major Canadian Employers

Source: Hewitt Associates

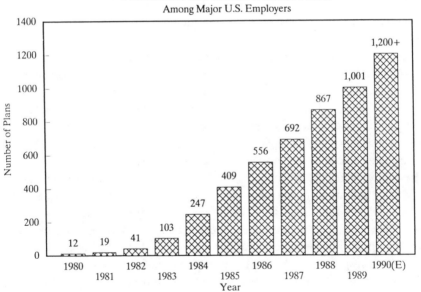

Figure 1.2
Prevalence of Flexible Benefit Plans
Among Major U.S. Employers

Source: Hewitt Associates

recognizes that a certain portion of total compensation will be provided by the employer in the form of employee benefits, but how that pool of funds is spent—in terms of types and levels of benefits—is essentially up to the individual to determine. These are largely the types of programs tabulated in the preceding figure.

§ 1.1   ENVIRONMENT FOR FLEXIBLE BENEFITS

Why has interest in flexible benefits increased, particularly in the latter part of the 1980s?

Changes in employee benefits do not occur in a vacuum. Instead, change occurs in response to specific stimuli. In the case of flexible benefits, the environment for employee benefits was turned upside down by developments in the 1980s. Among major employers, who tend to set the pattern, employee benefits had evolved to a point of maturity. The demographics of the workforce had changed dramatically from decades earlier when benefit programs still were in their infancy. At the same time, major employers in the United States successfully introduced flexible programs, in part because a major recession focused attention on finding ways to control costs. Meanwhile, the same pressures that led to a fundamental rethinking of benefit programs stimulated developments on two other fronts—namely, in Ottawa, where Revenue Canada's advance rulings on a number of proposed flexible plans enhanced the ability of employers to offer employee choice, and in computer technology, making it easier to administer programs with choices.

Understanding the environment for flexible programs makes it easier to see that these arrangements developed more as a rational response to complex, emerging issues, than as a gimmick of the 1980s.

(a)   EVOLUTION OF EMPLOYEE BENEFITS

Employee benefits in Canada came into existence when the country shifted from an agricultural to an industrial society in the late nineteenth century. As workers migrated to the cities and broke up the traditional extended family support system, people began looking to government and private employers for social security. Prior to the establishment of security plans, responsibility for meeting security needs rested with the individual.

By 1900, the federal civil service, railways, and a few large financial institutions had introduced pension plans for their employees.

That was the first step. The majority of Canadians still paid for their health care benefits as they needed them. Free wards in hospitals, public clinics, sanitoria, and charitable hospitals provided care for those who could not afford to pay. During the 1920s and 1930s, interest in benefit plans began to surface with the introduction of the Old Age Pensions Act (1927) and a proposal by the Canadian Medical Association for a national health insurance plan. However, the Depression of the 1930s halted most efforts by private companies to introduce employee benefit plans. As the economy revived during the Second World War, employers once again began introducing benefit plans. Most were contributory, since the government considered them to be less inflationary.

In 1945, the federal government proposed a comprehensive health insurance plan, but then postponed it because the provinces would not transfer certain taxing authority to the federal government.

The present health care system in Canada had its beginning in the Hospital Insurance and Diagnostic Services Act of 1957 and the Medical Care Act of 1966. Under these Acts, provinces complying with established federal standards became entitled to annual subsidies from the federal government amounting to approximately one-half the cost of providing hospital and medical benefits.

Consequently, provinces control the health care system, but receive federal subsidies if they comply with federal conditions.

The Hospital Act required the provinces to satisfy four conditions:

- The health insurance plan must be administered on a non-profit basis by a public authority appointed by the government of the province.
- No minimum residence requirement or waiting period in excess of three months is allowed.
- Provinces must provide insured services on uniform terms and conditions to all residents.
- The percentage of insurable residents must be at least 90 percent at the start of the plan and 95 percent after three years.

By January 1961, all of the provinces had established hospital insurance plans, and by April 2, 1962, they each had medical care plans.

The Canada Health Act of 1984 replaced both the Hospital Act and the Medical Care Act. The government had become concerned that the principles of the medical care legislation were being eroded.

Physicians were and are predominantly paid on a fee-for-service basis. The payment schedule is negotiated each year between the provincial government authority and the physicians' organization. Likewise, hospitals negotiate their operating budgets each year.

By the early 1980s, the federal government found its universality principle was eroding, because some hospitals were charging extra user fees for hospital beds, and some physicians were extra-billing above the scheduled fees. As a result, the Canada Health Act outlawed extra-billing and user fees. It also reiterated the principles of the Hospital Act, extended coverage to 100 percent of a province's residents, and ensured portability between provinces.

Today, provincial governments administer the health insurance plans and are responsible for any costs beyond those subsidized by the federal government. Provincial funding arrangements vary, including premiums charged to residents, employer payroll taxes, and financing from general tax revenues.

Retirement benefits also expanded in the 1950s and 1960s. By 1970, there were 16,000 private and public pension plans—up from 2,000 in 1945.

The Old Age Security (OAS) Act of 1952 introduced a basic flat-rate benefit to most residents. The Canada Pension Plan (CPP)--in Quebec, the Quebec Pension Plan (QPP)—of 1966 began providing an earnings-related benefit to those people who contribute to the plan during their working lives. The retirement pension from the C/QPP is equal to 25 percent of the contributor's adjusted average earnings. The program also provides disability pensions, survivor's pensions, orphan's benefits, and death benefits. In addition, the Guaranteed Income Supplement, payable under the Old Age Security Act, supplements retirement income if an individual's pension falls below a specified threshold. All federal programs are then supplemented by various provincial guaranteed income plans to assist low-income pensioners.

Canada experienced a major shift in responsibility for security and health care needs in the post-Second World War period. Canadians came to view security benefits and health care as fundamental needs and rights, like education.

They were willing to meet those needs collectively and pay for them through taxes. The result is that, today, the lion's share of these needs are met through government programs. Private employers offer a variety of benefits, but most of these supplement government programs. The most notable exceptions are dental care and group life insurance.

Recently, however, the concept of universality has been brought into question. The federal government, faced with large budget deficits, has considered universal Old Age Security and Family Allowance payments as candidates for cutbacks. (The Family Allowances Act of 1973 provided payments to families with children under age 18.) Effective in 1989, individuals with income over $50,000 are required to repay all or a portion of their OAS or Family Allowance benefits. This payment takes the form of a special tax calculated on their personal tax returns.

The result of these changes was a major shift in responsibility for security from the individual to the government and to the employer, resulting in the widespread availability of employee benefit coverage. By the 1970s, large corporations typically provided a final-average-pay pension plan, with many also offering a supplemental savings plan. Medical coverage included semi-private hospitalization and major medical coverage with a small deductible and 80 to 100 percent coinsurance. Company-paid life insurance provided at least one year's salary. Long-term disability benefits replaced 60 percent of pay, inclusive of Canada or Quebec Pension Plan (C/QPP) benefits.

Today, the configuration of employee benefit programs is even more complete. Among almost 300 major employers surveyed in 1989, the prevalence and characteristics of benefit programs for salaried employees include:

- 92 percent maintain a *defined benefit pension plan* that typically bases benefits on the employee's highest five-year earnings and requires no employee contributions.

- 60 percent offer one or more *defined contribution* vehicles that enable the employee to accumulate capital, usually as a supplement to retirement income. The most common defined contribution arrangements include company savings plans (41 percent of employers) that typically match 50 cents on each dollar contributed by the employee up to certain limits; deferred profit sharing plans (4 percent of employers); and money purchase pension plans (10 percent of employers).

- 99 percent of the surveyed employers provide *supplemental medical* coverage. Deductibles usually apply, but the amount generally is limited to $25 or less. Employees also generally pay up to 20 percent of the remaining costs through the coinsurance feature in the plans. Employee premiums are required in only 24 percent of the plans.

   In addition, 98 percent of employers provide *dental* coverage, 53 percent provide *vision* care, and 49 percent cover *hearing* expenses.

- The vast majority of employers also offers protection in the event of death or disability. *Group life insurance* is universally provided, with one to two times pay provided on a company-paid basis, and as much as four to five times pay provided in total from company-paid and contributory coverage. In addition, half of the surveyed companies make life insurance for dependents of an employee available.

Again, disability coverage is universally provided. On *short-term disability*, majority practice is to continue all or a portion of salary for some period of time, such as six months, before commencement of long-term disability benefits. In the event of *permanent disability*, companies replace typically 60 percent or more of salary, inclusive of Canada or Quebec Pension Plan disability benefits, with the income usually continuing until retirement.

- All companies provide paid *vacations* and *holidays*. Vacation time usually relates to the employee's length of service—for example, two weeks off after one year and three weeks after three years, grading up to five or more weeks after 20 years of service. In addition, most companies provide 10 to 12 paid holidays per year.

(b) CHANGES IN DEMOGRAPHICS

Changes in the demographics of the workforce have been well documented. Today, more women are entering and remaining in the workforce. The proportion of "traditional" households—employed males with dependent spouse and children—is declining. The proportion of single and dual-income households is increasing.

Greater diversity in the workforce has created significant pressure on employers to recognize and accommodate the variety in employee needs for benefits—both today and tomorrow, as those needs change over time (Figure 1.3).

For example, child care represents one of the newer areas of need for many employees. Fewer households today—whether supported by one income or two—have the family network in place to care for young children. As a result, many employers are feeling increased pressure to "do something" to accommodate the needs of working parents. However, under sustained pressure to control benefit costs, few have been willing to shoulder the entire obligation for another new—and expensive—coverage area.

Another issue arising out of the change in demographics is an increase in the number of households with duplicate sources of employee benefit protection. Many employers—as well as employees—question the usefulness of two sources of coverage (for example, dental), or high levels of

Figure 1.3
Labour Force Participation of Canadian Families

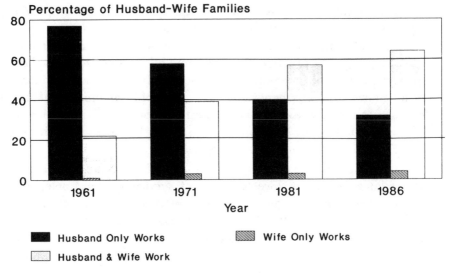

Percentage of Husband-Wife Families

Source: Census of Canada

protection when the need for such coverage may be minimal (as may be the case with death benefits for households without dependents).

Related to the issue of diversity within the workforce is growing recognition that the needs, priorities, and values people have for benefits change over time. The need for security coverages, for example, tends to be high during the child-rearing years, but less so once children are grown. Retirement income is an important priority—but usually later in a working career. Life events such as marriage, saving for the purchase of a home or education of children, loss of employment by a spouse, and so on are occasion for re-evaluation of benefit coverages. In effect, these differences set up a sort of "moving target" for employee benefit programs to meet.

(c) RISE IN COSTS

As the prevalence of benefit plans has grown, so too has the cost. According to statistics compiled by the Conference Board of Canada, employee benefit costs (including pensions and government benefits), as a percent of total compensation, have increased at an average annual rate of 2.7 percent per year between 1966 and 1985. These increases have not been uniform over the years, however. Substantial increases occurred in Canada in 1974, 1976, and 1981. Benefit cost increases have varied because of changing attitudes toward benefits as a part of total compensation (resulting in improvements and new plans), increasing coverage requirements, and the periodic introduction of regulatory legislation (Figure 1.4).

Two factors account for the recent slowdown in cost increases. One has been recognition by employers that benefits had reached a saturation point. Security needs were already being met—or exceeded—for many employees, particularly in the larger organizations. Second, the early 1980s represented a period of severe recession for many employers and underscored the need to slow the rate of escalation, or in some cases, to actually cut benefit costs. As a result, many employers started to cut back some benefit areas or otherwise halt "improvements." This contributed to the slowdown in aggregate cost increases.

Today, cost containment is becoming an increasing concern. Health and Welfare Canada statistics show that total health care spending increased from $47.8 billion in 1987 to $52 billion in 1988—an increase

Figure 1.4
Employer Payments for Benefits as a
Percentage of Total Compensation

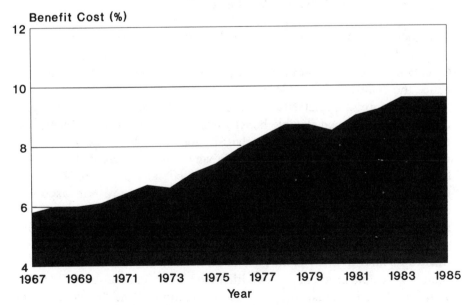

Source: Conference Board of Canada, Report 28–88.

of 9 percent—exceeding 1988's inflation rate of 4.1 percent. This trend is expected to continue throughout the 1990s.

Higher rates of utilization and the aging population, in addition to the rising cost of medical services, are driving the upward escalation in health care costs. Simply stated, more people are making more use of more medical services. As a result, high growth rates have occurred in annual expenditures for health care.

In 1989, people over 65 made up 11 percent of the Canadian population. By the late 1990s, this population is expected to double. The Canadian Medical Association predicts a 75 percent increase in the health care costs of the elderly over the next 20 years. The aging population will put pressure on government, employers, and employees, through increased costs for post-retirement health care plans and higher medicare costs.

The combined effect of these changes is larger health care costs to government and employers. Although few employers will be able to exert much control over external factors such as the cost of medical technology, many will be attempting to influence internal factors such as utilization. Influencing utilization through plan design and employee communication, for example, holds significant potential for helping to curb the rate of escalation in an employer's health care costs.

(d) REGULATORY ENVIRONMENT

Although the basic framework of rules and regulations for employee benefits has been in place for a long time, only recently has Revenue Canada confirmed certain interpretations of the Income Tax Act to enhance the viability of flexible programs.

The interpretations clarified that *constructive receipt* does not apply to properly developed flexible benefit programs. Constructive receipt is a doctrine developed through British and Canadian court rulings, whereby individuals are taxed on company expenditures, if they could have taken the payment in cash, but elected not to do so. Revenue Canada ruled that members of flexible benefit plans are not taxed on company contributions to flexible plans (typically called flexible credits) merely because one of the options—cash—is taxable. Instead, each individual is taxed based on how he or she decides to use the credits. This is illustrated later in this chapter, where an employee is given the choice of spending flexible credits on group life (taxable) or on other benefits such as health care (non-taxable). Because no section of the Act deals with flexible benefit plans, this confirmation was crucial to the growth of such programs in Canada. This evolution differs from that in the United States where two changes had significant impact on the environment for flexible benefits.

The first change involved legislative amendment of the United States tax code to permit choice making in benefits involving taxable and non-taxable options. It was the Revenue Act of 1978 that created the "twin pillars" of flexible benefits—Section 401(k) and Section 125. Section 401(k) permitted trade-offs between cash and deferral of compensation into a retirement income vehicle. Section 125 permitted choice making between taxable and non-taxable benefits. Psychologically, the legislation had a major impact on the growth in flexible programs in that a previously "gray area" within the tax code was clarified, providing a firm legal basis for choice-making programs. The increased prevalence of flexible benefits in the United States provided a stimulus for the development of flexible programs here in Canada.

The second change arose through regulation. In 1981, the IRS issued implementing regulations for Section 401(k) arrangements. Included within the regulations was a key provision permitting *individuals* to decide if they wanted to defer a portion of salary into a retirement income vehicle. Shortly after release of the Section 401(k) regulations, salary reduction also came to be used for the purchase of other employee benefits. In effect, employee contributions for benefits were treated as *employer* payments, and escaped federal income and most state and local taxes. The result was that for the first time, employees had a *tax-efficient* means of paying for benefits. Later, the Tax Reform Act of 1986 confirmed, through legislation, the use of salary reduction for benefit purchases. Although Revenue Canada maintains that salary reduction is prohibited in Canada, many tax lawyers argue that employees can trade off income to which they are not yet entitled, and receive a corresponding increase in company-paid benefits. Such income could include a salary increase or a performance bonus.

(e)   ADMINISTRATIVE SOLUTIONS

Another factor influencing the environment for flexible benefits has been the relatively recent advent of computerized solutions to handle day-to-day flexible program operation. Many aspects of conventional employee benefit administration have been automated for some time. However, accommodation of choice-making programs, with their individual elections, annual re-enrollments, and often special claims and payment record-keeping requirements, has placed new demands on administrative systems and procedures. Until the early 1980s, the obstacles associated with administering a flexible program were largely viewed as insurmountable—unless an employer was willing to commit significant resources to the design and programming of an internal system.

Eventually, however, demand led to the proliferation of automated solutions developed specifically for flexible program administration. Today, personal computer systems, mainframe software, time-sharing services, and third-party approaches to administration are readily available from consulting firms, insurers, third-party administrators, and software vendors. Even though some organizations may still choose to develop administrative and record-keeping systems in-house, alternative software solutions are available to meet the needs of both large and small organizations.

§ 1.2 KEY PURPOSES FOR FLEXIBLE BENEFITS

The first flexible benefit programs were introduced in the United States in the early 1970s under relatively unusual circumstances. In 1973, a West Coast division of TRW, Inc. adopted a choice-making arrangement for the principal purpose of meeting diverse employee needs. The division employed a large group of highly educated engineers and technicians who wanted more control over benefit decisions. TRW implemented a program that permitted employees to opt up or down from previous life and medical coverages. If the employee chose less valuable coverage, the difference was paid in cash. If the employee elected more valuable coverage, the difference in price was paid through payroll deductions.

At about the same time, Educational Testing Service (ETS) in Princeton, New Jersey, adopted a different type of flexible approach. A benefit study indicated that ETS lagged behind other organizations in the competitiveness of their program. The organization decided to enrich its program—but allow employees to decide individually how the new funds should be spent on various benefit options.

These earliest social experiments proved tremendously successful. Employees appreciated the opportunity to make benefits more useful, and the employers received high marks (and considerable outside interest) for innovating on essentially a new frontier. However, both situations were pigeonholed as small and unique employee environments. Not until 1978, when the former American Can Company (now known as Primerica) implemented a flexible program, did the barrier to the broader business community collapse.

American Can's primary interest in flexible benefits was to find a means of slowing the rate of growth in benefit costs and breaking a lock-step with union-driven benefits. The company also was in the process of diversifying its business and needed to be able to compete more effectively for talented employees. American Can set up a program that carved the existing package into two pieces. The first layer represented a cutback to a core level of benefits uniformly applicable to all employees. The next layer provided the flexible benefit options. Employees could arrange the flexible options to suit individual circumstances.

The American Can experience represented a breakthrough in several ways. First, the company demonstrated that a flexible approach could work in a large company environment. Second, their experience showed that an existing program could be split so that choice making need not be an add-on or require additional employer funding. Finally, American Can introduced the concept that a flexible approach contained the potential to control future increases in benefit costs. By dividing an existing program into core and options, some of the built-in escalation in benefit costs could be curbed. If the cost of the flexible options increased, the company could make a conscious decision to add more money, or pass along the cost to employees in the form of higher price tags.

The Canadian breakthrough into flexible benefits occurred when Cominco, a major West Coast mining company, introduced a flexible benefit plan for its 2,000 salaried employees in March 1984. Like American Can, Cominco split its benefit package into a core level of benefits provided to all employees and several levels of options providing benefits greater than the core. The cost savings anticipated by Cominco, because the core benefits were less rich than the previous program, were given back to employees as flexible credits. Employees received sufficient credits to buy back their previous program if they wished. Employees who wanted more coverage could supplement their credits through payroll deductions. Employees needing less coverage could direct excess flexible credits to the Cominco savings plan or could take them in taxable cash.

There were two major reasons why Cominco pioneered flexible benefits in Canada. First, Cominco wanted an attractive, innovative benefit package to appeal to the varying needs of its diverse employee group—employees ranging from corporate staff in Vancouver to salaried employees at Cominco's remote mines in Western Canada, including its Polaris mine located in the Northwest Territories, less than 100 kilometres from the magnetic North Pole. Second, Cominco wanted to reward its staff employees, who had borne the brunt of salary freezes in the early 1980s. The communication campaign for Flex-Com, as the Cominco program was called, emphasized that "flex" was a special privilege only extended to salaried employees.

Flex-Com was extremely well received, and more than 75 percent of employees chose a different plan than they had before the introduction of flexible benefits. Cominco did not ignore the plan once it had been introduced. Cominco discovered that a flexible benefit program is dynamic and ever-changing. Since 1984, a number of new benefits have been added to the employee's "menu."

Other Canadian flexible pioneers include:

- **American Express Canada, Inc.** In 1988, American Express Canada introduced the first flexible benefit plan in the financial sector. "Express Yourself" was also the first plan in Canada to use the opt-up-or-down structure, instead of the core-plus-option approach. See § 2.2(a) for a discussion of these approaches.)
- **BP Canada.** This was the first program developed to merge two traditional benefits plans.
- **Carder-Gray Advertising DDB Needham Inc.** In 1985, Carder-Gray introduced a flexible plan for its 75 employees, making it the first broad plan covering fewer than 100 employees.
- **Hewitt Associates.** Canada's first health care expense account was developed in 1980.
- **Lipton's Fashion Ware.** Canada's first (and, to date, only) "modular" type flexible program was introduced in the mid-1980s.
- **PCS Inc.** The union representing Rocanville, Saskatchewan hourly-rated employees of the world's largest producer of potash negotiated a flexible program for its members in 1989, following the successful introduction of flexible benefits to staff employees.
- **Prudential Insurance Company of America.** The first flexible program at an insurance company came into effect on January 1, 1989.

Although considerable refinement has occurred since then, much about these early programs looks familiar in flexible program practices today.

(a) APPEAL TO DIVERSE EMPLOYEE NEEDS

Fundamentally, flexible benefits is an alternative *delivery* mechanism for compensation and benefits. Under a conventional program, an employer provides a package of benefits to all employees. Little discretion exists for the individual to shape or re-arrange coverage levels to suit individual needs or circumstances.

In contrast, the distinguishing characteristic of a flexible approach is the opportunity for the individual to make choices about the uses of employer-provided benefit funds. Under a flexible program, the employee decides among *types* of benefits and *levels* of coverage. In addition, the employee determines the *form* of compensation in terms of whether to spend the employer contribution on benefits, to receive some portion of the allocation in cash, or to save some or all of the allocation for use at a later date (such as retirement). In effect, a flexible approach recognizes the different needs employees have for benefits at different points in time.

But the appeal of a flexible program is not entirely one-sided; the employer gains from the process as well. From the employer perspective, choice making is an opportunity that employees appreciate, which leads to raised perceptions of a benefit program, even in the absence of higher employer contributions for benefits or the introduction of new plans. Moreover, benefit options generally must include some recognition of "price" for employees to review and compare in making choices. Assigning a price tag to a benefit tends to give it a value that employees previously may not have recognized. Finally, to make choices, employees must understand their benefits. The process of becoming more familiar with benefits creates an active—rather than passive—interest in benefit coverages.

(b)   CONTROL BENEFIT COSTS

A flexible approach allows an employer to set in place a more clearly defined mechanism for controlling costs over the long term. With a conventional program, cost management can be achieved, but largely in terms of cutting back coverages or passing along higher costs to employees. A flexible approach introduces a third option—namely, allowing employees to trade off among coverages. Consider some examples.

First, if an employer needs to reduce benefit costs immediately (as many United States employers did in the 1980s), a flexible program can be introduced to soften the blow to employees. Perhaps the prior rich coverages are made available, *if* employees are willing to pay a larger proportion of the cost or to accept lower benefits in another area. Perhaps another less rich level of coverage is made available at little or no employee cost. Instead of a unilateral decision either to reduce coverage or to increase contributions, the employer allows individual employees to decide how the necessary cost-containment efforts will affect them.

Second, a flexible program can provide employees with incentive to select lower levels of coverage—even in the absence of a reduction in employer contributions. Medical and dental plans that require *more* employee cost sharing in the delivery of services (for example, deductibles and copayment amounts) tend to experience *lower* utilization. When the employee must pay a higher proportion of the cost of services, smarter health care utilization tends to result.

Finally, a flexible approach allows the employer to separate decisions on the *cost* of compensation from decisions on the *form* of compensation. The employer determines each year how much funding should occur in the benefit program. Employees then determine how that amount should be allocated among the various options available.

This enables the employer to avoid the automatic, inflation-driven escalation characteristic of conventional programs. In effect, the employer has introduced a *defined contribution* approach to paying for coverage. For example, if the cost of medical options rises faster than the employer's willingness to spend, employer contributions to the program can be held at a predetermined level. In this case, employees will be required either to pay more for the same level of coverage or to select a lower-valued option. Again, the employer keeps costs at acceptable levels while individual employees determine how limitations on the benefit dollar will affect them.

(c) DELIVER COMPENSATION TAX-EFFECTIVELY

Tax efficiency can be introduced into a flexible program to take advantage of differing treatment of benefit plans under the Income Tax Act. Section 18(1)(a) of the Act specifies that employer contributions for medical and dental plans are tax-deductible to the employer, while Section 6(c) states that the contribution is not taxable income to the employee.

Similar treatment applies to company-paid group life coverage under $25,000; however, the cost of any coverage in excess of $25,000 is a taxable benefit to the employee. Benefit payments for company-paid long-term disability coverage, on the other hand, are taxable to the employee who becomes disabled. However, the premium payment for LTD coverage is not taxable to the employee. By allowing the employee to decide which benefits to purchase with employer dollars and which to purchase with payroll deductions, a flexible plan can tailor an individual's benefit to meet his or her tax needs.

The situation can best be illustrated by an example. The ABC company provides company-paid LTD (60 percent), medical, dental, and group life benefits (two times pay) and would like to offer some choice in its program. Consider an employee, Pat Doe, earning $50,000 per year. Assuming that the cost of group life coverage is $3.60 per year per $1,000 of benefit, Pat has a taxable benefit equal to the cost of $75,000 of insurance ($100,000 total coverage less $25,000 provided tax-free). The taxable benefit equals $3.60 × 75 or $270. So Pat pays $121.50 tax on this $270, assuming a marginal rate of 45 percent.

ABC can introduce choice into the program with or without using a flexible structure. Without the flexible benefit framework, ABC could offer Pat the ability to purchase more medical and dental benefits through payroll deductions. Assuming the richer medical plan costs $70 per year more than the current plan, while the richer dental plan costs $200 more per year, ABC would collect $270 out of Pat's pay to cover the additional cost of these coverages. Since these contributions are after tax, Pat would have to earn $491 to pay the premiums. So under non-flexible choice making, there would be two tax consequences—Pat would purchase the optional benefits with after-tax payroll deductions and would pay tax on the group life premiums on coverage over $25,000.

How can a flexible benefit structure improve Pat's tax situation? The answer is by reversing who purchases the coverage to maximize the tax-effective use of ABC's benefit expenditures. A flexible plan could allow Pat to pay the $270 cost of group life over $25,000 through payroll deductions and direct ABC's savings of $270 to buy upgraded medical ($70) and dental ($200). Pat is still paying $270 in payroll deductions; however, ABC's expenditure no longer causes a taxable benefit to Pat. This is summarized in the following table:

	Tax Consequences	
Benefit	Non-Flexible Program	Flexible Program
Medical	$70 cost paid with after-tax payroll deductions	$70 cost paid with pre-tax credits (no taxable benefit)
Dental	$200 cost paid with after-tax payroll deductions	$200 cost paid with pre-tax credits (no taxable benefit)
Group Life	$270 taxable benefit ($121.50 tax)	$270 cost paid with after-tax payroll deduction

So Pat pays $121.50 less tax under the flexible benefit structure for exactly the same coverage.

Another tax advantage is available in long-term disability. If Pat becomes disabled, the 60 percent benefit will be taxable income because

ABC paid the LTD premium. Under a flexible benefit plan, Pat could be given the choice of maintaining a company-paid LTD plan or paying the premium with after-tax payroll deductions. In the latter case, the 60 percent benefit would be tax-free if Pat became disabled. Pat could direct the LTD premium that ABC would otherwise have paid to purchase another benefit such as additional vacation.

(d) MEET COMPETITIVE PRESSURE

Organizations implementing flexible programs tend to be regarded as "innovative," "responsive," or "leading-edge" employers. Indeed, some companies are beginning to view flexible benefits as a means of differentiating themselves, particularly in markets such as Southern Ontario, where there is strong competition for highly qualified employees.

To some extent, as well, flexible programs have moved sufficiently into the mainstream of employee benefits to set the standard for "competitive practice." Increasingly, flexibility is being regarded as a "benefit"—the lack of which can work to lower the perceived value of even a generous conventional program.

§ 1.3 EMERGING OBJECTIVES FOR FLEXIBLE BENEFITS

The major movement toward flexible benefits in the 1980s was born of the need to contain costs and supported by the logic of meeting diverse employee needs, maximizing the perceived value of benefits, and delivering compensation tax effectively. Certainly these objectives will remain important long into the future.

But some newer objectives are emerging today that will expand the uses for flexible benefits. Consider come examples.

- **Merging benefit programs.** Flexible benefits provide a mechanism for combining benefit programs of merged or acquired organizations. Instead of continuing separate programs (thereby facilitating ongoing comparison of the different structures) or merging programs into a whole (which often leads to "cherry picking" the richest plans from each entity), a flexible approach allows the employer to offer benefit options that may resemble, but not duplicate, prior coverages. That way, employees can come close to reconstructing earlier coverages without saddling the employer with a prior program.

- **Allowing cost variations by geographic location or business unit.**
  Even companies with a common benefit structure across the organization may want to introduce company cost variations. The reason
  may be to reflect differences in cost by geographic location or differences in acceptable overhead among various lines of business within
  the organization. For example, a diversified company may need to
  maintain lower compensation costs in labour-intensive operations
  (such as restaurant operations), but have a competitive need to maintain high benefit levels in other businesses. Such an employer may be
  able to maintain an identical flexible program for all business units,
  while varying the flexible credit allowance (or option price tags)
  based on the business unit's cost constraints.

- **Varying benefit contributions based on business performance.**
  Many organizations need to minimize their fixed costs, while being
  able to tolerate greater fluctuations in variable costs. Their inclination
  would be to spend labour dollars in ways that will motivate employees
  to be more productive. These management needs have resulted in recent revisions to direct pay systems—more emphasis on incentives,
  such as bonuses and restructuring of salary programs, so that performance becomes a more important factor. To a certain extent, fixed
  cost constraints have also affected the retirement area, with some employers shifting new money *away* from defined benefit pensions and
  into capital accumulation vehicles that do not represent the permanent, fixed commitment of a pension plan.

  A few employers also are exploring the use of flexible benefits to
  allow variations in the funding of benefit plan coverages based on
  company performance. Certainly, none are suggesting that an employee's entire benefit allocation should be subject to the whims of
  profitability. However, some employers are investigating the possibility of providing a fixed credit amount that will purchase a safety net of
  coverage as well as providing an additional variable contribution determined each year based upon business performance. Employees can
  use the variable amount to purchase benefits, defer the amount into a
  tax-favoured savings plan, or take the amount as taxable cash.

- **Reducing compensation inequities.** Most organizations currently
  pay some employees more than others through the benefit program.
  For example, employees who cover dependents in a group health
  plan typically receive more value, in the form of a higher employer
  subsidy, than employees with no dependents. Moreover, older employees receive more value from a life insurance program than

younger employees. To some organizations, these additional subsidies are appropriate and consistent with long-term security goals for employees. Others, however, have concluded that this differentiation by employee—driven not by performance or service, but by the life circumstances of the employee—is no longer appropriate.

A few employers are using flexible benefits to reduce or eliminate differences in treatment among employees, either immediately upon introduction of the program or gradually over a period of years. The objective is to equalize employer-provided contributions for benefits, regardless of the employee's age or number of dependents.

- **Encouraging a total compensation perspective.** Such motivations as changing the fixed nature of employer contributions for group benefits, introducing performance-based contributions maximizing employee perceptions of benefits, and reducing compensation inequities often reflect a more fundamental objective: to promote a total compensation perspective among employees, so benefit dollars appear more similar to direct pay and therefore more "real" to employees. By expressing employer contributions for benefits as dollars and allowing employees to decide how those dollars are to be spent, the line between direct pay and benefits becomes less distinct. Employees see their compensation as one amount in pay and another in flexible credits plus any other non-flexible benefit amounts—the entirety of which represents *total compensation.*

From management's perspective, the total compensation viewpoint also reinforces the concept that benefit costs, like direct pay costs, can and should be controlled.

Two

Elements of Flexible Benefits

§ 2.1 INTRODUCTION

A flexible approach involves opening up a benefit and compensation program to individual choice. However, the degree of flexibility offered varies substantially, depending on the type of program adopted. For example, a program allowing employees to purchase optional benefits with payroll deductions provides limited flexibility. In contrast, a choice-making program that permits employees to decide among types of benefits, levels of coverage, and forms of compensation (cash, savings, or benefit purchase) provides a relatively high degree of flexibility. In the medium range are health care expense accounts, which offer employees the opportunity to pay for certain expenses on a tax-efficient basis. In practice, however, the different approaches overlap, with many companies combining some or all of these elements.

§ 2.2 CHOICE MAKING

(a) IN GENERAL

Choice making continues to be the principal design approach for a flexible benefit program. In allowing employees to trade off among benefits, employers can accommodate diverse employee needs, offer greater variety in benefits, and increase the perceived value of benefit expenditures. Although the approaches used to introduce choice making vary considerably from one employer to the next, conceptually, the funds used to drive a choice-making system are generated in three ways: rearrangement of existing benefit dollars, cutback from existing levels, or introduction of new money. These employer funds are frequently referred to as *flexible credits*.

The *rearrangement* or *opt-up-or-down* approach allows employees to reduce or increase coverage levels in various benefit areas. By electing coverage levels lower than current company-paid levels, company funds or flexible credits are generated for use in other benefit areas. Election of higher-than-current coverage in one area requires trading down in another benefit area or increased employee contributions.

The *cutback* or *core plus credits* approach is useful when current benefits are more valuable than all employees need (or the employer can afford to support). The employer may offer lower or *core* levels of benefits, or even permit employees to waive coverage entirely in some areas. All or a portion of the difference in value between current benefit levels and the core benefit levels would provide the funds or flexible credits for employees to construct a new program or to buy back the former coverages, if desired. In practice, although a buy-back option is psychologically appealing, few employees actually reconstruct the prior arrangement.

The last approach relies on the introduction of *new money*, either employee or employer money. Employee money is introduced through payroll deductions and is used to provide additional funds in a flexible program. Employer money can be introduced and used to fund a flexible program in several ways: a percentage of the employee's pay, a flat-dollar amount, or a combination of these two approaches. Flat-dollar allocations have the advantage of not inflating with increases in pay, and any change in the flat-dollar allocation can be communicated as a benefit improvement. Sometimes a credit formula is based on service. Employers need not lock in to an allocation of additional employer dollars each year. A profit-related or gain-sharing technique can also be used to provide additional flexible credits based on financial performance of the employer. Such an approach reduces fixed costs, because additional allocations are made only in years when the allocation can be justified by performance.

The differences between the three approaches—rearrangement, cutback, and new money—are illusory at best. Most plans incorporate elements of each approach in the over-all design of the program. For example, cutting back to a core level of coverage might be coupled with trade-offs permitted across certain benefit areas.

(b) PRE-TAX FLEXIBLE CREDITS VERSUS AFTER-TAX PAYROLL DEDUCTIONS

Flexible credits are more powerful than payroll deductions. Payroll deductions are taken off an employee's pay after tax has been withheld; so to contribute $100 to buy a benefit with deductions, the employee might have had to earn $150 or $175. Flexible credits, on the other hand, are not taxed until after they are spent, and their tax treatment depends on how they were spent. Revenue Canada treats flexible credits as employer benefit premiums, not employee earnings. Therefore, they are taxed according to how they are used by the employee. For example, credits used to purchase supplemental medical or dental benefits are never taxed. This is because any company contribution to a private health services plan such as supplemental medical or dental is not considered income to the employee. In addition, the credits are a tax-deductible business expense to the employer. The net result is that the employee can purchase $100 of coverage with $100 in credits, which is more advantageous than purchasing it with $100 of payroll deductions.

The tax advantage of flexible credits does not apply to all benefits; for example, any credits used to purchase dependent life insurance are taxable income to the employee. Chapter Eleven discusses the tax treatment of flexible benefits and credits in detail. Some of the major observations in the chapter are summarized in Table 2.1.

The different tax treatment of benefits offers major opportunities for employees under a flexible plan. For example, an employee with a 60 percent company-paid long-term disability benefit before the introduction of flexible benefits might prefer to pay the premium using after-tax payroll deductions and direct the company contribution to purchase an improved dental plan. In that way, any long-term disability benefit payout would be tax-free to the employee. And the company contribution used to purchase extra dental coverage is not taxable to the employee. The opportunity to use the different tax treatments also presents a challenge. Employees

Table 2.1
Tax Treatment of Flexible Benefits and Credits

Benefit Type	Employer Contribution Tax-Deductible	Tax Treatment of Employer Contributions (Including Flexible Credits) to Employee	Tax Treatment of Benefit Payouts
Supplemental Medical	Yes	No taxable benefit	Not taxable
Dental	Yes	No taxable benefit	Not taxable
Vision	Yes	No taxable benefit	Not taxable
Health Care Expense Account	Yes	No taxable benefit	Not taxable
Employee Group Life	Yes	No taxable benefit on first $25,000 of benefit. Cost of excess coverage taxable to employee	Not taxable
Employee Accidental Death and Disability (AD&D)	Yes	No taxable benefit	Not taxable
Dependent Life	Yes	Cost of coverage taxable benefit to employee	Not taxable
Long-Term Disability	Yes	No taxable benefit	Taxable income
Cash	Yes	N/A	Taxable income

must be educated in the subtleties of the Income Tax Act as it applies to benefits. This requires an extensive communication effort. Also, the administration of the program is complicated by tracking benefits purchased by two types of dollars—company credits and employee deductions.

(c) AREAS OF CHOICE

Certain benefits accommodate choice making better than others. Defined benefit pension plans represent an area where choice making is not easily introduced, because the value of any benefit trade-off varies significantly by the age and pay of the employee. Still, as will be discussed in a subsequent chapter, some employers have accomplished a measure of choice making in the retirement area, even though the actual design may exist outside the flexible program.

The areas that more readily accommodate choice making include indemnity plan coverages (health care, group-term life insurance, and disability) and time off with pay. Each of these areas, however, presents unique challenges.

In health care, most companies structure options around a supplemental medical plan, with differences occurring only in areas such as the deductible, coinsurance and maximum payment amounts. Items such as covered expenses usually are kept constant from option to option.

Key issues to settle in medical and dental will include the appropriate levels of deductibles, coinsurance and out-of-pocket limits, the minimum level of required coverage (if any), and the degree to which employer subsidies of dependent coverage should continue.

Within group-term life insurance, there are several key considerations related to the degree of choice to be offered. For example, in addition to deciding what total amounts of insurance to offer, an employer must also decide the increments of coverage (for example, multiples of $10,000 or multiples of pay). Existing practice, as well as administrative convenience, will usually influence this decision. Moreover, the employer must decide the method of credit generation and the price tags to be used—age-sex-and-smoker-related (which reflects true cost) or a flat rate to all employees. Finally, decisions also must be made regarding the levels of coverage an employee may pay for with before-tax dollars, recognizing that employees are taxed on the value of amounts in excess of $25,000, if paid for by the company or through flexible credits.

Structuring appropriate levels of choice in the long-term disability area can be challenging as well. Some employers offer employees only an in-or-out decision. Others offer several alternative pay replacement levels or benefit duration periods or options which provide an inflation-protected benefit. The key issues in the disability area include the appropriateness of letting employees waive coverage, the impact of company versus employee contributions on the taxability (and resulting adequacy) of disability income, and the most appropriate levels of pay replacement, if options are offered.

Finally, the area of time off with pay will require some special decisions. Increasingly, employers are including vacation time as a choice area within a flexible program, offering employees both the buying and selling aspects of a vacation choice. But some organizations limit the choice to a one-way decision. For example, some organizations limit employee choice to the *selling* of vacation days only, that is receiving more pay in return for fewer vacation days. Within these organizations, concern often centres on the potential for scheduling conflicts when employees are permitted more time off. Other employers offer employees only the choice of *buying* vacation days, that is, receiving less pay in return for more vacation days. Existing carry-over policies and the potential impact on cash flow are key influences on decisions to include buying and/or selling of vacation time. As with most areas of flexible benefits, there are no right or wrong approaches. Each design area needs to be evaluated against the employer's own circumstances and environment.

In terms of the over-all design of a choice-making program, many employers initially are tempted to restrict the types and levels of choice offered as a means of simplifying decisions for employees. Experience shows, however, that employees feel comfortable with even the most complex flexible program—provided the choices are communicated well. Conversely, even the simplest program can generate confusion if the communication effort is slighted. So although there are often good reasons to restrict choice—to provide minimum levels of protection or to minimize adverse selection—concern about employee understanding of a flexible program need not dictate the degree of choice available.

(d) SPECIAL CONSIDERATIONS

Two topics related to choice making have yet to be discussed: adverse selection and waivers of coverage. Like other aspects of choice making, these two topics are complex and will be dealt with in greater detail in other chapters. To round out this discussion, however, brief mention will be made here.

(1) Adverse Selection

All voluntary benefit plans contain an element of employee selection. Employees participate because they know they will use the benefit (such as dental) or because they know they will need the benefit if an unforeseen event occurs (medical emergency, death, or disability).

Adverse selection occurs when employees can accurately anticipate their use of benefits and choose the option that provides the most coverage at the least cost. For example, an employee facing orthodontic expenses for a child knows that the highest level of dental coverage is a good buy, even if the benefit price tags are high. In most situations, however, employees cannot accurately project their benefit use, particularly for a family. In fact, many employees will choose the highest available level of medical and dental coverage, just in case a major expense occurs.

The potential for adverse selection can be controlled through the design of a flexible program. Various techniques enable employers to offer a wide range of choices without running much risk of greater-than-expected claims. These techniques will be discussed at length in a subsequent chapter. In brief, however, the approaches include:

- Restricting the employee's ability to increase coverage levels dramatically from one year to the next
- Subsidizing the price tags for certain options to encourage broad participation
- Providing a less-than-full-value rebate to employees waiving coverage
- Grouping coverages for more predictable expenses (for example, prescription drugs) with less predictable expenses (for example, other health care)
- Encouraging use of health care expense accounts as an alternative to insuring more predictable types of expenses (for example, vision).

Each of these techniques can help control adverse selection. The price that an employer pays by utilizing some of these techniques, however, is reduced choice making to the employee. The practitioner needs to recognize that the objectives of maximum flexibility in choice making and elimination of adverse selection are often in conflict.

(2) Waivers of Coverage

Some plans allow employees to elect no coverage in certain benefit areas, which constitutes a waiver of coverage. Whether such a waiver is allowed, and in which benefit areas, is a matter of employer discretion—and different employers will decide the issue in different ways. Some will refuse to allow employees to elect coverage below certain minimal core levels.

Others will permit waivers only in certain benefit areas. Still others are comfortable allowing employees the complete freedom to opt out entirely.

Employers often are more concerned about employees going without supplemental medical and disability income benefits than dental coverage, for example. However, experience has shown that employees who waive supplemental medical coverage are not going bare. Instead, they typically have health coverage from another source, such as their spouse's employer. And even if they do not have other supplemental coverage available, they still are covered for most major expenses through their provincial health plan.

Like adverse selection, restrictions on an employee's ability to waive coverage can often conflict with the objective of providing maximum flexibility through choice making.

§ 2.3   HEALTH CARE EXPENSE ACCOUNTS

(a)   IN GENERAL

A health care expense account is an individual employee account that provides reimbursement of eligible health care expenses. At the start of the plan year, the employee determines whether or not to establish an account and how many flexible credits to allocate to it. When an expense is incurred, the employee submits a request for reimbursement to the employer who issues payment from the account. Payments from the account represent non-taxable income to the employee, just as though he or she had incurred a medical claim. To preserve the favourable tax status of the account, employees cannot direct payroll deductions to it—funds must come from employer flexible credits.

The only catch with a health care expense account is that expenses must be anticipated very carefully. Under the Revenue Canada rules for health care expense accounts, any monies left on deposit at year-end can either be rolled forward into next year's account or they can be cashed out. However, the employee must decide whether to use the cash-out or roll-over approach prior to the beginning of the plan year.

Despite this minor handicap, health care expense accounts represent a versatile and popular element in flexible benefit programs. Companies offering a choice-making program often include a health care expense account as another benefit option. But an account can also be adopted on a stand-alone basis in the absence of any other choices within an employer's benefit program.

The popularity of this element of a flexible program is attributable to several motivations, including:

- Expanding the types of benefits offered employees with little or no additional employer cost (such as vision care)
- Encouraging employees to self-insure predictable or budgetable expenses that are subject to adverse selection (such as vision care)
- Delivering compensation tax effectively.

(b) SOURCES OF FUNDS

Health care expense accounts attached to a choice-making program are more apt to be funded from two sources—employer contributions and dollars freed up from trade-offs in other benefit areas. In contrast, stand-alone accounts are funded by employer contributions only.

Deposits normally are spread proportionately throughout the year. This avoids a major drain on the employee's income at any one point during the year. Alternatively, they may be deposited in blocks (for example, at the end of each quarter or at the beginning of the year) to reduce the record-keeping effort.

(c) TYPES OF BENEFITS

Under a health care expense account, employees can be reimbursed for health-related expenses not covered by the employer's other medical and dental plans. In general, any health-related expense which could be used to meet requirements for deductibility on an employee's income tax return is eligible for reimbursement. For example, deductible and copayment amounts may be reimbursed for both medical and dental benefits, along with the cost of procedures not covered by the underlying medical and dental plans (such as drugs which have been prescribed, but which are also available over the counter, vision care expenses and orthondontic work).

(d) MECHANICS OF THE PROCESS

The mechanics of the election/enrollment process and the reimbursement of expenses are fairly straightforward.

Employees decide whether to deposit funds in the account at the *beginning* of a plan year. These funds may arise from any of the sources identified earlier. They also decide whether or not to have any unused funds at year-end cashed out or rolled over to the subsequent year's account.

Once made, the elections cannot be changed for any reason during the year, unless the employee has a *change in family status*. Addition or loss of a dependent and a change in a spouse's employment status are examples of family status changes that generally would allow an employee to change elections during the year.

With the elections in place, the employer creates individual book accounts for the health care expense account in which the employee has elected to participate. No formal segregation of assets takes place, and no monies are deposited in trust. Instead, the accounts are carried on the books of the employer who tracks both debits (reimbursements) and credits (accruals).

When an employee incurs an eligible expense under the account, the employee completes a reimbursement claim form and submits it along with a copy of the bill or proof of payment (such as, a cancelled cheque) to the plan administrator for reimbursement. The administrator, after reviewing the claim, reimburses the employee with a cheque for the amount of the claim.

After the end of the year, employers typically allow employees a few months to submit claims incurred during the prior plan year. Once this process is completed, all unused deposits are either forfeited, cashed out, or forwarded to next year's account, depending upon the design of the plan. (In practice, most employees take care to estimate expenses with enough precision to avoid forfeiture or forwarding of account balances.) Disposition of forfeitures is a matter of employer discretion. Some reallocate funds to participants on a per capita basis (that is, unrelated to the employee's actual amount of forfeiture). Some use forfeitures to reduce employer benefit costs in a subsequent year. A few have adopted practices unrelated to the benefit program, such as donating the funds to charity.

Three

Starting a Flexible Program

The impetus to investigate flexible benefits can originate within an organization in any number of ways. Employees may have lobbied the employer for greater involvement in benefit decisions or for expansion of the existing program into new benefit areas. A comparative analysis might have revealed disparities in the current program significant enough to warrant management concern over trailing competitive practice. Business conditions might be such as to require a cutback in employee benefit costs or significant levelling of the rate of escalation in costs. The employer may be having trouble recruiting employees in a competitive labour market. Whatever the motivations, the next step involves determining whether a flexible program would meet the needs of the organization, and if so, what type of program would make the most sense, and then developing a strategy to implement the program.

The purpose of this chapter is to provide a framework or model for organizing the start-up effort and to preview the steps involved in implementing a flexible program. Many of the functions that are involved are technical or substantive in nature and are dealt with at length in subsequent chapters of this book. This material focuses on the process for launching the start-up and implementation effort.

§ 3.1 OVERVIEW OF THE PROCESS

One of the few universal truths about a flexible benefit project is that it usually is broader in scope and reach than almost any other modification an organization might make to the structure and nature of compensation and benefits. As a result, most organizations set high expectations for the outcome of a flexible program—and expect to achieve them, or few would commit the energy and resources necessary to set a program in place.

The complexity of the undertaking stems largely from the multidisciplinary nature of the effort. For example, employees are asked to make decisions in areas where they previously had little involvement, so communication plays a more extensive role than it would in almost any other type of benefit change. The choice-making mechanism requires tracking of individual elections and/or accounting for the flow of funds under health care expense accounts. So administrative considerations exert considerable influence on the feasibility and type of flexible program an employer decides to adopt. In many organizations, a decision to go with a flexible approach hinges on cost considerations so that, in a sense, a flexible program is more price-sensitive than a conventional program. Careful attention is paid to establishing the financial structure of a flexible program to achieve the organization's objectives in the first and subsequent years of operation.

Figure 3.1 provides a model of the process many organizations have followed for moving a flexible program from inception through implementation. Most organizations find it useful to divide the development process into two phases. One is creating the preliminary design, determining its feasibility, and generally planning the steps involved in an implementation. The other is actually executing the plan: finalizing the program design and cost structure, developing the communication materials, building an administration system or selecting a vendor to handle the administration, and otherwise readying the program for first-time enrollment of employees.

Although the figure separates the various activities into distinct stages, in reality, many of the steps overlap. For example, design of the program rarely occurs independently of the pricing of options or the determination of systems constraints. The primary purpose of the figure is to illustrate the different types of functions that need to be performed to launch a program; only secondarily is it to show the progression or order of the various steps.

The time frame for implementing a flexible program varies by employer. A few organizations have installed full choice-making programs

Figure 3.1
Steps in Starting a Flexible Program

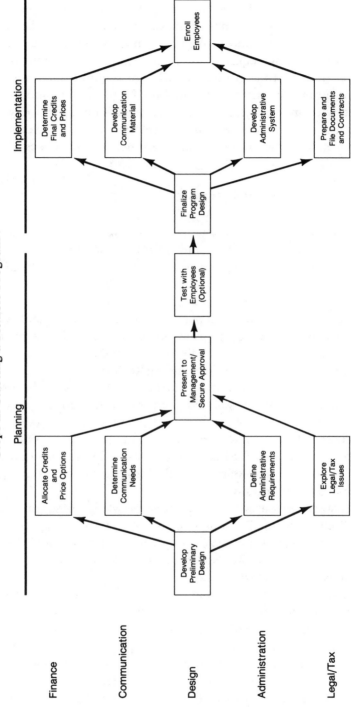

in as short a period as four months. In general, however, implementation time schedules range from six to eighteen months. The systems effort usually is the most time-consuming aspect, with an average of six to eight months required for implementation of administrative software. (Longer time frames usually are required for internal development of an administrative solution.) Employee communication ranks next, with an average of two to four months needed for development of communication materials. After development, most organizations allow between four and six weeks for enrollment of employees.

§ 3.2 GETTING STARTED

One of the first steps an organization usually takes is assembling a project team for development and installation of the program. The core team normally consists of a project leader and others from within human resources or the benefit department. An effective step to take early in the process, however, is expansion of the team to include input or representation from other parts of the organization that will be most affected by a flexible program. In some cases, this is primarily staff roles—namely, systems or internal administration, corporate communication (sometimes also including training or public relations), finance, legal counsel, and so forth. In other cases, the project team includes line managers to add perspective and another view of benefits and compensation issues.

There are several reasons for seeking early input from these other areas. One is to surface any constraints or limitations that could hamper or impede development of the program later, particularly in the area of administration.

Another reason is to broaden the knowledge base for decisions that will need to be made about a flexible program. Participation from those closest to a particular issue will yield better and more informed judgements on the numerous aspects of a flexible program where few right or obvious answers exist.

Finally, expanding the composition of the project team promotes consensus building along the way and a sense of ownership or responsibility for the outcome. Involvement in the process produces not only better decisions, but a broader group of people who understand the reasons and rationale underlying the decisions. That shared understanding will help increase the sense of purpose people feel when carrying out the developmental tasks required to unveil a new program—and will produce substantial dividends when many of these same specialists later are called upon to explain the merits of the new approach to employees.

No magic combination exists for either the size or composition of the project team. In general, a two- or three-person team may be too small to assure adequate input, while 15 to 20 may impede effective decision making. Depending on the size of the organization, six to eight members may constitute a workaۡ le project team—large enough to ensure breadth of perspective, while small enough to facilitate decision making.

Within the special project team, it often makes sense to combine doers and decision makers. For example, an over-all project leader might have day-to-day responsibility for coordinating the specialized tasks that need to be performed and for keeping the team on its assigned time schedule. Meanwhile, senior decision makers, with an otherwise full schedule, would be freed to concentrate on policy issues or to steer the process through appropriate channels within the organization.

Many organizations use people outside the company (or the benefit area), both in the preliminary planning and later stages of implementation. The role performed may be that of serving as a technical resource (for information on what can be done, how other organizations have handled a similar matter, the impact of particular decisions, etc.); as a process facilitator (to identify key issues, bring the project team to consensus, etc.); or as organizers (to scope out what needs to be done, advise on efficient means of accomplishing a particular task, etc.). This type of assistance may come from an independent consulting firm, a brokerage or insurance company consultant, or even from another internal person operating in the capacity of advisor or consultant.

§ 3.3   PLANNING THE PROGRAM

The sample framework described here for planning the program includes: (1) determining the preliminary design (benefit areas to be included, development of specific options, decisions on option prices and credit allocation, and over-all cost impact); (2) analyzing the implementation effort (required tasks, potential constraints, likely alternatives, budget and staffing requirements); (3) securing management approval to proceed and, as an optional, but often useful, step; (4) testing the proposed program with a sample of employees. Although the model incorporates all of these steps under the planning phase of the program, in some instances the steps are viewed as covering two phases: preliminary design (including management approval and employee testing) and planning for implementation.

Regardless of how the effort is categorized or how formal or informal the process is, the following steps generally are taken when planning a flexible benefit program.

(a) DEVELOP PRELIMINARY DESIGN

Each organization is unique. Organizations vary by the size and characteristics of the employee workforce, the provisions of the current benefit program, the objectives for exploring a flexible benefit program, the financial and administrative constraints, and the current employee relations environment. Combined with the viewpoints of those responsible for benefit and compensation planning, all of these differences come together as input into designing a program that is the best fit for that organization. In the same way that no two traditional benefit programs are exactly alike, no two flexible programs are identical.

The project team can use a number of approaches to narrow the wide range of available design alternatives and, ultimately, to determine the most appropriate program design. An approach that has worked well for many firms, however, involves three components: data collection, objective setting, and development of design. Following this progression produces an approach that has a high likelihood of reflecting the uniqueness of the organization, its attitudes, and its employees, and of meeting the organization's objectives (i.e., being viewed as successful by management and employees).

- **Data collection.** The data collection substep ensures that the project team knows as much as it can before starting to design the program. Although what is needed and what level of depth is required will vary considerably, the following list may be helpful:

  - Employee data (number, types, demographic characteristics)
  - Current benefits (types, eligibility requirements, benefit levels, employee contributions)
  - Current benefit costs (costs by benefit area—per employee, as a percent of pay, per $1,000 of coverage—broken down as appropriate or available)
  - Employee attitudes concerning benefits (an optional—but often helpful—step, undertaken either through a survey or a more informal collection process)
  - Competitive benefit information (another optional—but generally helpful—step as competitive positioning is often important)

- Flexible benefit approaches and issues (what can be done, what others are doing, etc. in order to bring the project team to a common level of knowledge).

- **Objective setting.** The design process is typically streamlined by identifying at the front end how management views certain key issues. Examples of the types of issues helpful to identify, discuss, and reach consensus on can include:

  - What are the primary objectives for considering the implementation of a flexible benefit program?
  - What are the financial goals and/or constraints for the program?
  - How should responsibility for the financial security of employees be allocated between the organization and the employee?
  - What minimum level of coverage (if any) should be required of employees in each benefit area?
  - Should benefits be viewed primarily as a source of protection or as a part of total compensation?
  - Should (or must) the current plan be maintained as an option in each benefit area?
  - What concerns or problems exist with the current benefit plans (from the company or employee perspective)?

- **Development of design.** With the foundation of knowledge gained from the data-collection stage and the objective-setting process, the project task force is prepared to develop alternative design approaches, consider the relative merits of each, and select the design that best fits the organization.

  The types of decisions which need to be made in this stage include:

  - Which general structure should be used?
    - The common *core plus credits* approach where the employee is given company credits to spend on a range of options
    - The *rearrangement* or *opt-up-or-down* approach where the employee restructures benefits within an existing plan by taking more coverage in some areas (opting up) and less coverage in other cases (opting down)
    - The *modular* approach where the employee chooses from three or four packages or modules. Each module contains a predetermined level of medical, dental, life and possibly disability benefits.
    - A *combination* of the above approaches.

- Which benefit areas should be opened to employee choice?

supplemental medical	spousal life	vacation
dental	accidental death	home and auto
vision	long-term disability	other
group life	pension	

- What range of choice is appropriate (from low option to high option)?
- How many options should be made available?
- Which design features should vary between the options?
- Should a health care expense account be introduced?

The project team will generally be able to reach a consensus on most issues, but it may decide to leave open one or two difficult decisions for additional input from a group such as senior management. For example, should employees be permitted to opt out of medical? Or, should vacation choices be incorporated into the program?

(b)   ALLOCATE CREDITS AND PRICE OPTIONS

Once the basic design structure of the flexible program has been determined, an organization needs to analyze the expected impact on company and employee costs to develop the approximate level of flexible credits (if credits are to be an element of the program), the approach for allocating these credits to individual employees, and the prices which will be assigned (or charged to employees) for the various options.

The desired short-term impact on company costs will typically be discussed in the objective-setting phase. Often, the objective is to maintain the same level of cost which would have been produced by the prior program in the initial year of the flexible program, but gain added control over the rate of increase in future years. In some U.S. programs, the objective is to produce an immediate short-term savings in benefit costs. This may be defined as a specific dollar amount, a specific percentage of medical costs or over-all benefit costs, or an amount of savings resulting from a particular aspect of the new program. This immediate cost-savings objective is rarely, if ever, present in a Canadian flexible plan. Decisions on the amount of credits and the option prices in combination with other aspects of the program will determine the resulting impact on the organization's costs.

The intended impact on employee costs will also help dictate the decisions on credit amount, credit allocation, and option pricing. In some situations, all employees must be allowed to buy back their previous coverage with no change in net contributions (prices less credits). In other cases, prices are being modified—for example, to move from a flat-rate basis to an age-related basis in group life, or to increase medical contributions—thereby creating an expectation that the implementation of the new program will create some winners and losers among employees. An analysis of these winners and losers under alternative credit and pricing strategies is typically an important aspect of decision making in this area.

(c) DETERMINE COMMUNICATION NEEDS

Introduction of any flexible benefit program requires explanation of the decisions employees will be asked to make. However, the context of the basic communication message (concept and mechanics of choice making) will be influenced by the specific circumstances of the employer. For example, is the new flexible program primarily a good news message for employees—that is, nobody loses under the program, company costs will remain the same at least in the first year, and/or significant new benefit opportunities are being incorporated? Or does the flexible program represent a vehicle for accomplishing certain other employer objectives, such as some immediate reduction in costs, or phaseout of dependent or other subsidies? Most flexible program introductions contain elements of each; however, how much of each will be a critical influence on the tone, themes, and messages used in the communication effort.

This contextual backdrop will largely have been established in the preliminary design and financial structuring discussions, but the viewpoint reflected so far has been primarily that of the company. The next step involves working with the tentative program design and structure to gauge how the program will play with employees.

Here environment plays a critical role. For example, have employees been lobbying for changes in benefits, so that even a cutback in certain areas would be viewed as a reasonable trade-off for the opportunity to exercise choice elsewhere in the program? What is the general mood or trust level in the employer? For example, have employees experienced changes in other areas so that the timing of a flexible program implementation might raise suspicions? What are employee perceptions of the business conditions of the employer, and how might these perceptions influence the packaging or look of communication materials?

Once the context has been established, the specifics of the communication effort need to be defined at least in enough reasonable detail to develop preliminary budgets for implementation. Also, the project team needs to focus on the assignment and staffing of communication responsibilities: How much and which elements of the communication effort can be accomplished internally? In terms of developing the preliminary communication plan, consideration should focus on the following kinds of issues:

- Types of communication channels through which to reach employees (newsletters, booklets, audiovisual presentations, mailings to the employee's home, etc.)
- Quantity and quality of communication materials
- Characteristics of the work force or environment that might require special attention (for example, diverse education levels, English- and French-speaking employees, work areas with limited space for storing materials)
- Logistics of distributing and receiving communication materials
- Timing of the release of information to employees, including the staffing of training sessions, benefit hotlines, and so forth.

It also may be helpful to review communication samples from other organizations where flexible programs have been introduced. However, although useful for the gleaning of ideas, few prototypes exist for adoption by other organizations. Every flexible program is different—the communication materials will reflect those differences as well as the unique environment of the particular employer introducing the program.

(d) DEFINE ADMINISTRATIVE REQUIREMENTS

Basically the objective of this step is to determine what needs to be done to administer the flexible program and to identify how administration will be accomplished. Much of the project team's efforts in this area will focus on information gathering: assessing current capabilities, defining new requirements of the flexible program, and evaluating alternatives for handling administration.

In this regard, it is often most useful to begin with an audit of existing systems and procedures. How well (or poorly) is benefit administration currently accomplished? What is the capability of existing payroll and human resource information systems? What computer and people resources presently are available? Part of the audit process might also involve uncovering any plans for upgrading or modifying existing systems and procedures. Looking forward a few years may aid the project team in evaluating whether any present constraints are likely to pose a temporary versus more permanent barrier to either the flexible program's design or administration.

Next, most organizations develop a checklist of administrative requirements. The focus here is on identifying which procedures and tasks already are being performed, as well as what new requirements will be needed to accomplish flexible program administration, such as calculating individual credits and prices, or processing health care expense account contributions and reimbursements. Definition of systems requirements establishes criteria for determining the direction to take for flexible program administration.

A subsequent step usually involves evaluating externally developed administrative solutions. Here the project team is concentrating on narrowing the range of possibilities: internal development, installation of a software package, or third-party administration. Even if an organization has available the resources and capability to develop its own system, a review of the systems alternatives available on the outside may be a useful part of the process. Flexible programs require unique and specialized knowledge within the area of benefits and human resource information management. So interviewing technical specialists from provider organizations often will yield helpful information.

Another step involves exploring staffing considerations and planning the training of flexible program administrators. Depending on the type of flexible program under consideration, the administrative workload may be handled with existing resources or may require some additional staffing. Either way, however, the people responsible for administering the program on an ongoing basis will need training in the requirements and operation of the new system.

Once these steps have been completed, the project team will be in a reasonably good position to determine the magnitude of the effort and costs involved in implementing an administrative system. At this point, however, the cost figures remain preliminary in that finalization of certain details of the program design may yet influence the ultimate cost of administration.

(e)   EXPLORE LEGAL AND TAX ISSUES

As soon as preliminary design has been established, many organizations involve their legal counsel or tax experts to research or investigate any potential legal issues. No specific legislation or regulations exist concerning flexible benefit programs. The legal guidance for those plans comes from sections of the Income Tax Act dealing with employee benefits and corresponding Revenue Canada Interpretation Bulletins. Because the Act and Bulletins do not specifically address flexible plans, a few gray areas still exist. Management may want to have an opinion from legal counsel before proceeding, even though most questions have been clarified over the past few years. An organization's legal counsel may also seek additional guidance or input from outside lawyers specializing in employee benefit and pension issues.

(f) PRESENT TO MANAGEMENT/SECURE APPROVAL

By this point in the process, the project team has completed the staff work necessary to enable management to make an informed go/no-go decision. How formal or informal the decision-making process is depends on the organization and the extent of management involvement in the developmental phases of the program. Although a flexible program is not generally viewed as requiring approval of the board of directors, most organizations take measures to inform at least the compensation committee of the board of the status of a flexible program undertaking.

One of the reasons formalized management approval occurs at this stage of the process (rather than earlier) is to minimize the possibility of making decisions based on insufficient information. The project team needs to make sufficient progress in the areas identified earlier to provide management a complete grasp of the issues involved—impact on company cost, impact on employees, time frame, administrative ramifications, and so forth. Also, until this point, the project team has committed largely time (rather than significant dollars) to determining the feasibility of a flexible program. From this point forward, the organization usually will be committing hard dollars to the implementation effort, and the budgets usually need to be established and approved in advance.

In presenting the program to management, organizations typically include information on the following:

- Objectives for the program
- Scope and design of the flexible program
- Cost/benefit analysis
- Communication considerations
- Administrative and systems considerations

- Legal and tax issues
- Timetable for implementation
- Implementation budgets and costs.

(g) TEST WITH EMPLOYEES

While not a mandatory step in a flexible program implementation, many organizations find it useful to gather employee input. Some of the reasons for pretesting a program with employees include the following:

- To collect employee reactions and attitudes toward the concept of flexible benefits and the specifics of the particular flexible program design
- To test the types of choices employees will be likely to make, and as a result, identify whether assumptions about option pricing, adverse selection, and so forth, are on target
- To identify any differences in attitudes or information needs by employee subgroups
- To test the content or approach to be used in the communication effort
- To build some employee ownership into the flexible program.

§ 3.4 IMPLEMENTING THE PROGRAM

The following framework or model focuses on completing the steps involved in a flexible program installation: finalizing the program design and financial structure, developing communication and enrollment materials, building or implementing an administrative system, as well as developing day-to-day operating procedures and completing the necessary legal documents or insurance contracts.

Note that one of the most important steps the project team can take is to assign responsibilities and completion dates for each of the various tasks and then monitor progress against the over-all time schedule. All of the different subgroups will be working on separate tasks within the implementation effort, but the whole needs to come together at the end for enrollment of employees. Coordination becomes critical, because not one of the subgroup's undertakings is an optional part of the implementation. Delay (or derailment) of any one of the independent tasks will affect (or postpone) the outcome of the entire project.

(a) FINALIZE PROGRAM DESIGN

The preliminary program design might undergo some changes (either modest or substantive) as a result of management input received during the approval stage, or as a result of employee feedback if the program was tested with employees.

Irrespective of these changes, however, the preliminary design needs to be brought to a finer level of detail. This level of detail generally is not required earlier in the process (to evaluate the over-all impact on company or employee costs, administrative requirements, and so forth), but it is necessary at this point to develop the actual administrative system and employee communication materials. Here the project team will be concentrating on issues such as the following:

- How (if at all) will pay changes during the year affect coverage amounts and/or employee contributions?
- What is the minimum claim amount that can be submitted for the issuing of a reimbursement cheque from the health care expense account?
- When does an employee transferring from one division to another become eligible to make elections?
- How long does coverage continue after an employee terminates?

(b) DETERMINE FINAL CREDITS AND PRICES

The option prices and flexible credit allowances developed for the preliminary design may have been based on sketchy cost data or tentative decisions on allocation methodology to minimize the investment of time and effort required in the early stages of developing the program.

However, once the program has been approved and final design decisions made, it is typical practice to reevaluate the pricing and credit structure. Additional (and more current) experience data may be available. Given the passage of time, an organization's insurer or third-party administrator may be able to produce a better breakdown of recent claims. The new data will be helpful for taking a second look at the impact of the proposed financial structure.

In many cases, the prices for certain options will be identical to the rates charged by the carrier. However, a change in carriers usually will result in some last minute pricing changes.

(c) DEVELOP COMMUNICATION MATERIAL

The reason for developing communication material is essentially two-fold: to help employees understand the nature of the flexible program and options available to them; and to enroll employees in the program—preferably with as few errors as possible. To accomplish these goals, different types of communication materials are needed.

One type of material is largely informational. This includes: announcement brochures; special newsletters or mailings; articles in company magazines or newspapers; audiovisual, videotape, or overhead presentations; and descriptive booklets or handbooks. How elaborate the communication effort is depends on the organization and the circumstances surrounding the flexible program introduction. Some organizations have chosen to create a splash with the new program, complete with a name and special logos, high-quality graphics and paper stock, and numerous collateral materials (buttons, pins, coffee mugs, posters, tent cards, and so on). Others have adopted a more low-key approach. Regardless of production values or the extent of collateral materials, most organizations find that communicating using a variety of media is necessary to ensure a high level of employee understanding.

Another type of material concentrates on getting employees enrolled in the flexible program. Enrollment material generally includes a booklet or folder describing the program, some type of worksheet or workbook for employees to use in making their elections, and an election form that, once completed, will be used by administrators to enroll employees in the program. Some organizations have provided employees with sophisticated tools to make their elections: personalized statements showing available options, option price tags, and credit allowances, or even computer programs to allow employees to model their elections under various scenarios. To aid in the enrollment process, many organizations also produce confirmation statements that recap employee elections before the options become effective.

A different aspect of the communication process is aimed at meeting leaders and flexible program administrators. These people usually are involved in employee meetings or other one-on-one interfaces with employees. It is often most helpful if they can have available to them meeting leader guides, training programs, and so forth, that prepare them for the roles they will play in the unveiling and eventual operation of the flexible program.

(d) DEVELOP ADMINISTRATIVE SYSTEM

Procedures and record-keeping systems will need to be developed to handle administration of the program. The degree to which the system is automated depends on the size of the employee group, the nature and structure of the program, and the computer and personnel resources available. In general, administrative systems and procedures need to be able to accomplish the following:

- Determine participant eligibility
- Compute flexible credit allowances and option price tags (if credits and prices are part of the design)
- Enroll employees in their benefit choices (including editing employee elections)
- Process interim coverage for new employees (if appropriate), and coverage changes for employees with a change in family status during the year
- Maintain health care expense account balances and process claims (if this is part of the program)
- Report to management (and/or carriers and administrators) on various aspects of the program, such as use of flexible credits or payroll deductions, enrollment in each benefit area, utilization by coverage category, and so forth.

To avoid any last-minute surprises, most organizations work into the implementation timetable a period for testing the administrative system before the initial enrollment. That way, any potential problems can be corrected before the flood of first-time enrollments.

(e) PREPARE DOCUMENTS AND CONTRACTS

No formal legal document is required to establish the flexible program. However, depending on the design of the program, it may be necessary to modify other plan documents. The savings plan, for example, may need to clarify that unused credits may be transferred into the plan.

Insurance contracts and administrative service agreements will have to be developed, in the case of a new insurance carrier, or extensively rewritten, in the case of an existing carrier.

§ 3.5 ENROLLING EMPLOYEES

At this point, everything the project team has worked so hard to accomplish will come together. Employees will understand the new flexible program and make choices based on individual needs. The administrative system will record the elections and be ready to handle the activities involved in ongoing administration. And the project team will feel a tremendous sense of accomplishment over a job well done.

After the pace of the initial enrollment has subsided, the project team usually reassembles for a debriefing. The purpose is to incorporate any lessons learned from the first enrollment into planning for subsequent years. This might involve identifying areas on the election form where employees or administrators had difficulty entering elections, or uncovering common themes in the questions employees asked about the program that might be addressed in subsequent communication. It might also involve re-evaluating any options that were elected by only a very small percentage of employees and generally looking for ways to streamline or improve any aspect of the flexible program's operation in later years.

Part Two

Design

Four

Coverage and Eligibility

The purpose of Part Two is to provide a benefit-by-benefit guide to the design of a flexible benefit program. Regardless of the components of the structure, however, an organization ultimately will need to determine which employee groups are to be covered under the program and what, if any, special requirements should apply for certain groups.

For many organizations, the coverage and eligibility determination will largely represent an extension of current practices. For example, if all employees are currently covered under a common benefit program, the flexible program typically would cover the same employee group, subject to any eligibility or other requirements currently in place. Similarly, groups presently excluded from coverage (such as part-time employees) or covered under separate arrangements (such as members of a collective-bargaining unit, or retired employees) might remain outside the flexible program.

For other organizations, different issues may arise. Large or diverse organizations may already operate multiple employee benefit programs based on cost or other considerations relating to the different business units or operating entities. In these instances, coverage decisions might be influenced by the type of benefits or the financing structure already in place. There also may be other considerations, such as the employee relations environment or the compatibility of administrative systems and procedures.

A separate issue for flexible programs is coverage of new employees—those who join a company sometime before the next annual enrollment. Organizations often establish a waiting period before eligibility for flexible program participation begins, but practices vary in terms of the types of coverage offered in the interim.

The purpose of this material is to examine the issues relating to coverage of different employee groups under a flexible program.

§ 4.1 TYPES OF COVERAGE CATEGORIES

(a) SALARIED EMPLOYEES

Flexible benefit programs originated within the salaried employee population. To date, all Canadian flexible programs cover full-time salaried employees. In general, few employers impose eligibility restrictions on active employees other than they must be regular, full-time salaried employees. (See also the later discussion of coverage for new employees.)

Occasionally, however, organizations impose eligibility requirements by employee group or by benefit area. For example, a one- to three-year waiting period might apply for long-term disability coverage for certain employees, such as those outside management ranks. All other flexible program choices would be available, but disability coverage as an option would not be available until an employee satisfied the service requirement. (Alternatively, the employee might receive no employer credits for disability, but still could purchase the coverage.)

(b) HOURLY EMPLOYEES

To date, flexible benefit programs have emerged much more slowly within the hourly workforce, particularly among union members. Only 7 percent of flexible benefit programs in existence in Canada cover non-union, hourly employees. The few employers who do sponsor programs for this group are typically those whose non-union employees were previously covered under the same program as salaried employees. Very few programs cover union employees.

As flexible benefit programs continue to evolve in Canada, it is likely that employers will begin to include hourly employees. This has already happened in the United States, where 64 percent of the programs now cover non-bargaining hourly employees. Of those U.S. organizations with bargaining groups, 41 percent extend the flexible programs to some or all bargaining employees.

The emergence of flexible programs for hourly employees has trailed salaried employee practices for several reasons. One is the strong influence of the collective-bargaining process on the determination (or shaping) of benefits for hourly employees. Flexible benefits has been pegged within the labour environment as essentially a technique for shifting a greater proportion of the cost of benefits (particularly supplemental medical and dental) to employees. Recognition that the primary thrust of flexible programs among salaried employees is to permit the tailoring of benefits to individual needs has been slow to gain acceptance.

Another factor frequently is deep-seated union concern about the ability of members to make benefit decisions. A perception often exists that benefit decisions somehow are more complicated than other personal financial decisions an employee might make, and that the penalty for a wrong election is severe (for example, high medical expenses should the employee waive coverage). In general, familiarity with risk-reducing features such as stop-loss limits and core coverages is low.

To some extent, the concept of flexible benefits with its emphasis on individual determination of benefit needs also runs counter to the basic principle of collective bargaining. Providing choices to individual members has the potential to diminish the role of the union. While certainly not an overt consideration, shades of this reasoning may underlie general labour reaction to choice-making approaches. (In reality, bargaining on employer contributions to a flexible program, in terms of credits and prices, would be little different from negotiating benefit schedules and flat-dollar amounts for which a union currently is able to "take credit" with constituents.)

The first plan for unionized employees in Canada was introduced in Saskatchewan in July of 1990. The union representing employees at the Rocanville mine of the Potash Corporation of Saskatchewan Inc. negotiated a flexible benefit plan patterned after the successful plan covering salaried employees.

(c) PART-TIME EMPLOYEES

Part-time employees represent a growing segment of the workforce, with part-time employment participation increasing from 12 percent in 1976 to 15 percent in 1989. About two million people work part-time and 70 percent of these are women. The highest concentration of part-timers is in service industries, financial institutions, and hospitals.

Part-time benefits vary substantially among employers. In industries where part-time employees comprise a significant portion of the regular work-force, part-timers generally are extended benefit coverage, but only infrequently at the same level of employer subsidy as the full-time employee population. In other industries where part-time employment is less common, few, if any, benefits are provided. Another important consideration in part-time employee benefit coverage is the number of hours worked. Part-time employees working at least 30 hours a week typically receive benefits (in over half of the cases in a recent study). Employees working fewer than 20 hours generally receive no benefits beyond provincially mandated coverage such as vacation and pensions.

Table 4.1 illustrates coverage of part-time employees under flexible programs. In brief, about three-quarters of employers with part-time employees include part-timers in the program. Only 10 percent include all part-time employees under the flexible program. Of the balance, the majority base coverage on hours worked.

Of those employers including part-time employees under the program, one quarter provide the same benefits and employer subsidy, regardless of employment status. Where distinctions exist, the employer either provides fewer credits to part-time employees, charges higher price tags for benefit options, or offers fewer benefit areas to part-time employees. Some of these employers use more than one of these approaches.

Where the level of employer subsidy is based on hours of employment, an issue sometimes arises over the determination of hours worked. Most employers use scheduled, rather than actual, hours for determining the employer subsidy. However, inequities could result when actual hours vary substantially from scheduled hours of employment—either significantly higher or lower. Some employers have remedied the problem by using an alternative definition, such as actual hours of employment during the previous quarter.

Table 4.1
Eligibility Requirements for
Part-Time Employees

Eligibility	Percent of Programs
All part-time employees	10
17 1/2 or 20 hours of employment (weekly)	32
Other restrictions	32
Not eligible	26

Source: Hewitt Associates 1989 Survey of Canadian Flexible Benefit Programs and Practices.

(d) RETIRED EMPLOYEES

Very few Canadian employers extend flexible benefits to retirees. The vast majority of flexible programs (93 percent) cover retired employees under a separate non-flexible retiree arrangement. Approaches that could introduce limited flexibility to retirees may become more popular in the next decade. They include: constructing a comparable flexible program (usually for health benefits, or health and death benefits only); or permitting the employee to make a one-time election of preretirement flexible program coverage and allowing that coverage to remain in force throughout retirement.

There are a number of reasons why most employers have not offered flexible options to retirees. These include:

- A belief that retirees are more homogenous than workers and their needs do not vary significantly. (In fact, the demographic and lifestyle differences among retirees can be even more dramatic than among active employees. For example, the benefit needs of a 55-year-old retiree with a working spouse and children in university are very different from those of an 80-year-old widow or widower living in Florida for six months of the year.)
- Difficulty in communicating with retirees. The communication approaches used for active employees, such as videotapes, sound/slide presentations and employee meetings cannot be used in a retiree program.
- The sense among employers that some of the key motivations for introducing flexible benefits to the active workforce do not apply to retirees. Specifically, increasing employee awareness of benefits, attracting and retaining employees, and being competitive are not applicable to retirees.
- A greater concern about adverse selection, because retirees with chronic diseases would elect options with maximum medical coverage. This would drive costs up in future years.

Despite these reasons, flexible benefits for retirees will likely grow over the next decade. The impetus will come from several directions, including:

- Flexible benefit plans have a good track record for active employees; as employees retire they will pressure their employers to continue offering choice.

- The increasing cost of retiree benefits may encourage employers to adopt a defined contribution funding approach. Under this approach, employers would agree to pay a specified number of dollars per retiree. Any additional costs would be paid by the retiree.

  Retiree medical costs may go up even faster than active employee costs, as people live longer and technology keeps advancing. The possibility that provincial health insurance plans will try to pay less of the medical bills for the elderly is also a concern—for example, provinces that pay prescription drugs for residents over age 65 would like to pass the cost back to the private sector when insurance is available.

- "Retiree flex" allows employers to reward career employees. Instead of giving retirees all or nothing, based on their attaining 10 years of service by retirement age, the emphasis may switch to looking at employer contributions that vary by service. Employees would earn the right to retiree supplemental medical, dental and life insurance benefits, much the same way they now earn pensions over their full careers. To accomplish this, the employer could tie the flexible credits to service at retirement and grant each retiree $25, say, in credits for each year of service.

§ 4.2 COVERAGE FOR NEW EMPLOYEES

Most organizations take considerable care to communicate flexible benefit programs so employees will have enough information to be able to evaluate their choices and make decisions. A new employee must make the same kinds of decisions—but often without the same level of support from the communication effort. Although the company can share the same communication materials with new employees and provide resources to answer any questions, most employers still are uncomfortable with new employees making decisions immediately upon employment—especially changes that are irrevocable until the next enrollment or a change in family status. Nevertheless, almost half of flexible programs permit immediate participation in a full choice-making program, while another quarter allow immediate participation in only certain benefit areas.

For those employers having a waiting period for enrollment in the full choice-making program, the coverage provided in the interim varies. Some (19 percent) provide no coverage until the end of the waiting period (usually organizations with shorter waiting periods). Others (26 percent) provide standard coverage in the interim. In these cases, the employee enrolls in the full choice-making plan following a waiting period ranging from 30 days up to the date of the next annual enrollment.

§ 4.3 COVERAGE BY BUSINESS UNIT

In general, most organizations cover all employees under a common flexible program structure, except where it is more appropriate to develop separate programs, such as union-negotiated arrangements. In addition, the culture of an organization most likely will influence the appropriateness of developing different flexible programs for separate employee groups, or excluding certain groups from coverage.

In some organizations, a flexible approach provides the opportunity to unify benefit structures across business units or entities. This can reduce or minimize the cost and administrative effort involved in operating separate programs or enhance the ability to transfer employees among operations. Coverage decisions occasionally hinge on the compatibility and flexibility of administrative systems and procedures. (For example, where employees are on different payroll systems, the administrative system for the flexible program needs to be able to accept multiple sources of employee data and produce output for these same employee groups.)

Conceptually, however, what the employer is doing is creating a common flexible program "umbrella" for all employee groups. Within the umbrella program, certain design specifics may vary. For example, employees in Alberta and British Columbia may have the option of selling the employer payment of the provincial medicare premium for additional flexible credits. This would not be available in other provinces, because there is no employee medicare premium. The credit formula and option price tags might be set to reflect geographical differences or the cost structure of the business unit. The essential framework, however, is in place to house all employees across the organization under a common benefit structure.

Five

Health Care

§ 5.1 INTRODUCTION

Choice in health care benefits is usually a cornerstone of a flexible benefit program—a "natural" for employee choice making. Health benefits are among the most visible, highly perceived, and frequently used of all employee benefits. The high cost (and value) of health care benefits, as well as concern over the potential for large unexpected expenses, means that employees will seriously consider which choices are best for them. The frequent availability of coverage through alternative sources, particularly the spouse's employer, dramatically increases employee interest in choice.

Before analyzing how health care benefits can be incorporated into a flexible benefit plan, it is necessary to review how employer-sponsored health benefits coordinate with Canada's universal health care system. Each province and territory has a health insurance plan providing 100 percent payment of most medical and hospital services for individuals who have been residents for at least three months. Although the provincial plans differ in some details, they all pay for the following services:

- Physicians' and surgeons' fees
- Hospital room and board at ward rates
- Hospital miscellaneous expenses
- Expenses incurred out of the province, up to the same amount that would have been paid in the province.

A detailed summary of the provisions of the provincial plans is included in § 5.8.

Several provinces also pay for certain dental expenses. Details are also included in § 5.8.

Supplemental medical plans "top up" benefits provided under the provincial health insurance plans. According to Hewitt Associates Spec-Book,™ 99 percent of major employers provide supplemental plans to their employees.

Supplemental plans generally cover services such as:

- Hospital room and board at semi-private and, in some cases, private rates;
- Prescription drugs;
- Private duty nursing;
- Emergency medical expenses incurred out of Canada in excess of the amount paid by the provincial health insurance plan;
- Medical devices and equipment such as wheelchairs, artificial limbs and orthopedic shoes;
- Ambulance services.

Most supplemental medical plans pay 100 percent of any semi-private hospital expenses and cover all other expenses with a modest annual deductible (frequently $25 per individual and $50 per family). The supplemental plan typically reimburses between 80 percent and 100 percent of expenses in excess of the deductible up to a maximum payment. Typical maximum benefits are $25,000 per person per year; $50,000 per person every three years; or $100,000 per person's lifetime. Frequently the plan also has internal maximums that apply to certain services, such as private duty nursing ($5,000 or $10,000 per person per year) and vision care ($150 every 24 months). The cost of most supplemental plans is fully paid by the employer. Only 24 percent of plans require employee premiums and 12 percent of these charge a premium only for dependents.

All of the attention paid to health care in the past several years reflects the state of transition within the industry and in the approaches employers are utilizing to provide health care benefits to employees. Several developments demonstrate this transition:

- Consistently high cost increases over the past few years have grabbed the attention of employers and forced more active involvement in attempting to improve the management of medical and dental costs.

- Alternative dental care delivery systems, such as capitation programs, are now being offered by most major insurance companies.
- There has been some interest in medical provisions that encourage the use of generic drugs.

These and other factors highlight the fact that a great deal is happening in the health care benefit arena apart from the trend toward flexibility. Often it is extremely difficult to separate the design of health care choices from many of the other design challenges facing employers. In fact, introduction of a flexible program is usually viewed as an opportunity for an organization to step back from day-to-day operations and rethink over-all employee benefit strategy (whether specific to flexibility or not) in health care. Frequently, a number of changes unrelated to a flexible approach are packaged with the introduction of choice making in health care.

§ 5.2 OBJECTIVES FOR CHOICE MAKING IN HEALTH CARE

The objectives an employer has for health care choices typically are consistent with those that apply to the over-all flexible benefit program. Frequently, the major objectives relate to appealing to diverse employee needs and controlling benefit costs. Although these and other objectives were discussed in Chapter One, some aspects of each are particularly applicable to health care benefits.

- **Appeal to employees.** Providing an employee with choices in health care recognizes that a single plan cannot best meet everyone's needs. There is a diversity of needs within any workforce—due to the number and characteristics of dependents, the availability of coverage from other sources, anticipated utilization, financial resources (to pay premiums and claims), tolerance for risk, and so forth. Moreover, the needs of an individual are likely to change over time. Providing choices to employees responds to this diversity and gives employees greater control, with the net result being enhanced awareness and perhaps greater appreciation of the coverage.
- **Control benefit costs.** The employer's objective to control or manage benefit costs better is usually strongest in health care—because costs have typically escalated much more rapidly than in other benefits. In addition to seeking greater control over increases in future costs, an organization may wish to find ways of encouraging more

cost-efficient employee utilization of health care services (either less expensive providers or fewer unnecessary services).

- **Deliver tax effectiveness.** Within the health care portion of a flexible benefit program, tax efficiencies for the employee arise primarily through the use of company-provided flexible credits to purchase enhanced coverage.
- **Merge different programs.** When two companies or two programs within a single company are being merged, it is sometimes very sensitive to require one group to give up their medical plan and move to the other group's plan. Under a flexible program, both plans may be left as options (at least for the first year or two) as a way of smoothing the transition.
- **Emphasize value.** Many employers believe that employees do not fully understand or appreciate the real value (cost) of their health care benefits. Through giving employees choices and presenting them with the prices of each option, it is possible to enhance employee appreciation of the true value of these benefits.

§ 5.3 TYPES OF HEALTH CARE CHOICES

Choices can be provided in any health care benefit. However, it is almost universal to introduce employee choice in supplemental medical benefits and only slightly less common to allow choices in dental benefits (although the range of choice usually is not as great). About half of the plans offer options in vision or hearing benefits. Although the subject is covered in depth in a later chapter, it should be noted that many flexible benefit programs also include a health care expense account allowing for pretax reimbursement of medical, dental and vision and hearing expenses not covered by an employer's other plans.

Among those organizations included in a recent survey of choice-making programs, the following percentages allowed choices in company-sponsored health care plans:

Benefit Area	Percent of Companies
Medical	89
Dental	81
Vision	52

(a) PROVINCIAL HEALTH INSURANCE PREMIUM REIMBURSEMENT

Employers operating in Alberta or British Columbia frequently include provincial health insurance plan premium reimbursement under their flexible plans. These two provinces have the only remaining employee premiums for provincial coverage. All other provinces fund their programs out of general revenue or a special employer payroll tax.

In early 1990, the monthly premiums were:

	Single	Couple	Family
Alberta	$19.75	$39.50	$39.50
British Columbia	31.00	55.00	62.00

(For couples and families, either the husband or wife, but not both, elects to pay the premium.)

Although this is an employee premium, 91 percent of major employers reimburse all or part of the premium as an employee benefit. Employers who do reimburse the premium can offer two choices under the flexible benefit plan:

- Option 1: have the company pay the premium; or
- Option 2: have the spouse's employer pay the premium (if the spouse's employer is among the 91 percent that do pay). Employees who elect this opt-out option will receive extra flexible credits that can be used to purchase other benefits. Typically the credit given to employees will be less than the actual premium, producing a potential employer cost savings.

(b) SUPPLEMENTAL MEDICAL

As the previous table indicated, supplemental medical is the single most common area for choice in flexible programs. Its costs are rising more rapidly than other employer-provided benefits, it is highly visible, and usually a substantial percentage of employees have the opportunity to be covered under a working spouse's supplemental plan.

In terms of design characteristics, a choice of two to four supplemental medical plans generally is offered to employees. The primary variations in the options are the size of deductible, the coinsurance level, and possibly the services covered. Employees may be allowed to select no coverage as an option, although a minimum level of coverage is often required.

(c) DENTAL

Less of a pattern exists in the design of dental options. In some plans the employee is offered a yes or no choice—either to elect dental or take no dental coverage at all. In other situations, there is a choice of two or three different plans—with the plans providing different coverage levels across all types of expenses (diagnostic and preventive, restorative, reconstructive, orthodontic, and so on) or one plan having a different emphasis in coverage (such as substantial coverage for diagnostic and preventive services, but little or no coverage for major services).

(d) VISION AND HEARING

It is relatively infrequent to have vision benefits, hearing benefits, or both as stand-alone options within a flexible program. When provided as an option under a program, they are most often combined with a supplemental medical selection, primarily to minimize the potential for substantial adverse selection. Alternatively, they may be excluded from the supplemental medical plan altogether and covered under a health care expense account.

§ 5.4 GENERAL HEALTH CARE DESIGN CONSIDERATIONS

Many design considerations relate specifically to medical, dental, or vision and hearing. However, a number of design issues cross the full spectrum of health care benefits. Such issues include the determination of the sources of coverage, the coverage tiers, whether employees should be allowed to opt out of coverage, the sources of funds to pay for the benefits, the relationship with a health care expense account, and the over-all appeal or attractiveness of the options to employees. The general considerations that cross health care areas are addressed in this section, with greater detail provided in each of the specific benefit design sections.

(a) SOURCES OF COVERAGE

The principal sources of health care coverage are discussed below.

- **Group plans.** Traditional employer-sponsored plans are the primary source of supplemental medical, dental, and vision and hearing coverage for most organizations. These plans may be fully insured, partially insured, or self-insured, but the company determines the coverage levels to be provided, and the participant generally determines which service providers (hospitals, pharmacists, dentists, and so on) are to be utilized.

- **Dental capitation plans.** A capitation plan is a dental plan sponsored by an organization that, for a fixed prepaid monthly fee will provide a broad range of dental care services as needed by the participant. These services are provided by a specified group of dentists. Such organizations are sometimes referred to as dental maintenance organizations (DMOs) or managed dental care networks. The network of dental providers agree to discount their normal fees in return for an anticipated increase in volume.

- **Health care expense accounts.** HCEAs will be discussed extensively in Chapter Seven, but they should be considered as a third source of health care coverage, because an HCEA reimburses the participating employee for certain health care expenses. Moreover, an employee's decisions on health care options are likely to be influenced by the existence of an HCEA as a pretax source of reimbursement for out-of-pocket expenditures.

In most cases, group plans and an HCEA will be incorporated as sources of coverage within a flexible benefit program. Dental capitation plans are rarely included.

(b) COVERAGE TIERS

The majority of health care plans have some features that reflect the number or types of individuals covered under the plan—either in program design or in pricing or in both. When designing health care options, it is important to consider these features and whether each option should use the same approach.

The most common plan design features that relate to the number of individuals covered under an employee's election are family maximums on deductibles and stop-loss limits. For example, a supplemental medical plan may have a $50 annual deductible for an individual, but may provide that after three members of a family have each incurred their $50 individual deductible. Alternatively, after all family members in total have incurred $150 in deductibles, no more deductibles would be charged the family that year. Such a plan may also have a family stop-loss limit (the maximum paid by the employee in a year), which is three times the individual stop-loss limit. For example, once the individual or family has satisfied the deductible, coinsurance charges on remaining expenses will not exceed $250 per person or $750 per family.

Family maximums on deductibles and stop-loss limits—especially those that are three or more times the individual amounts—usually add very little to the cost of an option (frequently, less than one or two percent). Often, the added security provided through these family limits will significantly exceed the incremental cost. This comfort factor may be particularly important in a flexible option with a large deductible and a high stop-loss limit. Even though the advantage is more significant in high-deductible plans, typically all supplemental medical options within a flexible program will have parallel features in this area.

On the pricing side, the family-coverage issue is of greater significance. Although it is rare for a contributory plan to use a one-tier pricing approach, a completely non-contributory plan effectively has a one-tier price structure—the same price regardless of number or type of dependents. Plans with very low employee contributions have often utilized a two-tier pricing approach—one cost for employee-only coverage and a higher cost for family coverage, regardless of the number of dependents. As employee contributions for family coverage increase, the incentive grows to subdivide the family category to reflect the expected cost impact of varying the numbers or types of dependents. Subdividing by size of the family unit also helps minimize equity concerns in terms of the employee covering only one dependent paying the same amount as an employee covering several dependents. In these situations, three- and four-tier pricing approaches are most common. The most typical breakdowns include:

- Employee-only, family
- Employee-only, employee-plus-one, employee-plus-two-or-more dependents
- Employee-only, employee-plus-spouse-or-children, employee-plus-spouse-and-children
- Employee-only, employee-plus-spouse, employee-plus-children, employee-plus-three-or-more-dependents.
- Employee-only, employee-plus-one, employee-plus-two, employee-plus-three-or-more-dependents.

The approaches that distinguish between types of dependents (spouse versus children), rather than simply number of dependents, tend to favour single parents with more than one child, by allowing them to pay less than the full-family rate. This approach may also be somewhat more equitable in that an average child tends to generate significantly lower claims than an adult—especially for medical benefits.

A more extensive discussion of pricing and credit allocation issues by family status is included in Chapter Thirteen.

(c) OPT-OUT CHOICE

The issue of whether employees should be permitted to opt out of health care coverage has the potential of being one of the most emotionally charged subjects in the design of a flexible benefit program. Whether or not it actually becomes a major issue is often more related to pre-flexible program practice than to an organization's underlying philosophies.

For instance, many organizations currently have contributory supplemental medical plans with a small monthly contribution for employee coverage and a higher contribution level if dependents are covered. In such an environment, a small percentage of employees typically decide not to pay the contribution, however modest, and therefore have effectively opted out of medical coverage. Presumably these employees—or almost all of them—have supplemental medical coverage from another source, although the employer usually has no verification of other coverage. An employer with this type of situation may be uncomfortable with employees forgoing coverage under a flexible program, but in reality, that "bridge has already been crossed" and minimum medical coverage usually is not required.

In other situations, waivers of coverage may not be permissible. This occurs frequently when the prior medical plan was non-contributory for all employees and their dependents. In such a case, neither employee nor employer is accustomed to choice and may be particularly wary of an opt-out alternative. The mandatory nature of provincial health insurance plans, however, minimizes this problem. Even if employees opt out of the supplemental program, they are still covered for most medical expenses through the provincial plan. Because of this, most flexible benefit plans (65 percent) permit opting out of supplemental medical. In some of these cases, they communicate the provincial program as the core.

Although the concern over an employee electing to forgo medical coverage is usually related to the potential for a large uninsured claim, different issues arise in the area of dental, because a catastrophic dental claim is extremely unlikely. If an organization has a significant concern over employees opting out of dental coverage, it usually is related to the potential for adverse selection and the ability of an individual to defer necessary dental treatment from a period without coverage to a period with coverage. This type of manipulation will lead to higher rates for all plan participants. Most employees and plan sponsors view this as unfair to participants who remain in the plan year after year. Requiring a minimum level of coverage may reduce the individual's ability or incentive to select against the plan. (See Chapter Fourteen for a discussion of adverse selection issues.)

If, under a flexible benefit program, an employee is allowed to opt out of health care coverage, three significant issues need to be addressed. First, should the employee be required to provide some evidence of other coverage, particularly for supplemental medical? Based on a recent survey of flexible programs, 65 percent allow opting out of medical, but about one-sixth of those require some proof or certification of other coverage. Sometimes this process is as simple as signing a statement on the annual enrollment form, while in other cases, more extensive documentation is required.

Second, should some restrictions be placed on the options that are available during subsequent enrollment? About two-thirds of flexible program employers include restrictions for both medical and dental re-enrollment. Another 20 percent of the programs have restrictions only for dental plans. Although re-enrollment restrictions reduce the potential for adverse selection, they also diminish the attractiveness of the no coverage choice for an employee who is uncertain about future years' needs.

Third, if the flexible program provides credits to employees, how many credits should be given to an employee opting out of medical? Out of dental? Out of vision and hearing? The amount should be sufficient to make it worth considering for employees with other coverage, but not so high as to exceed the expected reduction in claims for those who opt out. (In general, those who are in a position to consider dropping health coverage are likely to generate lower-than-average claims cost. For more complete discussion of credit determination, see Chapter Thirteen on Prices and Credits.)

(d) SOURCES OF FUNDS

It is quite rare for health care options to be paid either fully by the plan sponsor or completely by the employees. Generally, the employer will provide a significant subsidy, and the participating employee will pay the additional cost required to select the desired options. The employer's subsidy may differ for medical, dental, and vision and hearing benefits; it may vary by the number of family members covered (either explicitly in the credits or implicitly in subsidized prices); and it may be the same as or different from the subsidy in the pre-flexible program. Determining the plan sponsor's subsidy and how that subsidy is reflected in the pricing and credit structure is covered in Chapter Thirteen.

In nearly all flexible programs, any employee contributions for health care benefits are paid on a pretax basis using employer-provided flexible credits. Where credits are not sufficient to buy the desired level of coverage, they can usually be supplemented by trading off other benefits. Paying for health care benefits in this manner does not generate a taxable benefit (as does group life insurance on amounts exceeding $25,000) or change the tax treatment of benefit payments (as does long-term disability benefits paid for by the employer).

(e) HEALTH CARE EXPENSE ACCOUNTS

A health care expense account (HCEA) will allow for reimbursement of health care expenses not paid by an employee's choice of medical, dental, or vision and hearing options. The existence of an HCEA may not have a dramatic effect on the design of the health care options, but there may be certain decisions that are influenced by the HCEA.

The most dramatic example might be the complete elimination of a stand-alone vision plan and its replacement by a credit allocation (equal to the company cost of the vision plan) which, along with credits generated from other benefits, can be deposited in the HCEA for vision and other health care expenses. This might be appropriate in a situation where the vision benefits are so low as to be viewed by employees as more of an irritant than a significant benefit and where the administrative expenses are disproportionately high relative to the benefits provided.

In other situations, employee pressure for increases in certain special benefits may be better handled by adding an HCEA than by increasing benefits under the health care options. This is particularly true for quite predictable benefits that are very important to a subgroup of employees, but of minimal interest to the vast majority of employees. A prime example is orthodontia, which is usually paid at 50 percent, up to a specified dollar limit under the dental plan. The uninsured 50 percent and any amount over the lifetime maximum could be paid out of the HCEA.

(f) OPTION ATTRACTIVENESS

The detailed design considerations relating to each type of health care benefit will be covered in the next sections of this chapter. However, after all of the individual health care options are designed, it usually makes good sense to review the over-all design from the employee's perspective.

For example, the options should be attractive to employees. In general, simplicity in option design strengthens a positive employee response. There are sufficient complexities within a flexible program without introducing health care options that have a great number of minor and difficult-to-understand differences. A parallel structure among the options with only two or three key elements varying (such as deductibles, coinsurance and stop-loss limits) enhances employee understanding and appeal. If practical, it is also beneficial to have this parallelism apply not only within a benefit area, such as medical, but across all health care options. For example, it may be appropriate for a program with a four-tier pricing structure in medical also to use a four-tier structure in dental, even though the dental prices alone might not seem to justify so fine a breakdown of employee contributions.

The options also should be reviewed to ensure a reasonable spread of employee value and cost. If there are many options with only minor differences in provisions and prices, employees may struggle with adequately differentiating between the options. If there are few options with wide gaps between them, employees may feel uncomfortable with moving away from their comfort zone of current benefits. A reasonable middle ground should be struck.

An organization may have an objective of encouraging employees to select certain options—for example, a medical option with a deductible and coinsurance instead of the prior no deductible, 100 percent coinsurance medical option. This can be aided by adding certain attractive features to the preferred option (e.g., higher maximum plan payments), by subsidizing the prices of that option, or by the manner in which the program is communicated (including how the options are named).

Although certain options may not appeal to a broad group of employees and, therefore, participation is anticipated to be low, keeping these options may be very appropriate. Some options may be important because they meet the needs of a small, but significant, subgroup of employees. For example, a large-deductible catastrophic medical plan may be just the right fit for employees covered under their spouse's medical plan. Another may be useful for filling in the gaps in a series of options.

During the election process, employees will, to varying degrees, scrutinize the option features and the price differentials to determine which option best meets their needs. The employer should anticipate this employee scrutiny and test the design and pricing to ensure that the options make sense. Options with higher price tags should provide extra coverage commensurate with the added cost.

§ 5.5 DESIGN OF SUPPLEMENTAL MEDICAL

(a) IN GENERAL

For the same reasons that medical is usually considered to be the best candidate for choice making within a flexible benefit program, the design of supplemental medical choices is typically the most time-consuming aspect of developing the flexible program. There are numerous challenging issues surrounding the development of medical choices (for example, how many and in what ways should they differ, how should adverse selection be minimized), and decisions are most often complicated by other types of medical design changes also under consideration (for example, addition of vision coverage, increase in deductible levels). The pages that follow address the considerations applicable to these design issues, with an emphasis on those aspects that are unique to or accentuated by the introduction of medical choice making.

(b) STRUCTURE OF OPTIONS

Detailing the design features of each medical option usually begins with an outline of the basic structure of medical choices. How many options should be made available to employees? Will the current plan be offered as an option? What will be the lowest option? How will the supplemental medical options differ?

(1) High Option

Employees often have a love-hate relationship with their supplemental medical coverage. While they may sometimes complain about what the plan fails to cover and how long it takes to get a claim paid, they tend to react with great concern if the plan is cut back or restructured.

Therefore, the current medical plan is almost always offered as one of the supplemental medical options and, in most cases, it is the high option. Occasionally, some tinkering is necessary to make it parallel to the other options or to modify certain features for cost-management purposes. Keeping the current plan as one of the options can help smooth the transition to the flexible program and soften any employee concerns that might arise. This may be especially important for an organization that has undergone a great deal of turmoil or whose employees are particularly suspicious or where other employee groups (such as union employees) are covered under a similar supplemental medical plan.

Often employees would welcome an option that is even richer than the existing plan, and would be willing to pay the added cost. This is particularly true where the current plan has significant employee co-payments through coinsurance and deductibles, or does not cover certain expenses, such as vision, at adequate levels. However, if offered, such an option typically will result in high claims experience and ultimately higher prices in subsequent years. Therefore, the plan designers must weigh the employee demands for a top-notch medical plan against the potential negative reaction when prices rise in the future.

Determination of the level of coverage that is appropriate for the high supplemental medical option will usually be based on a number of considerations, including:

- Provisions of the pre-flexible supplemental medical plan
- Medical benefits for other employee groups within the organization
- Employee relations environment
- Employer financial objectives
- Competitive practice.

(2) LOW OPTION

In many situations, the low supplemental medical option is defined by whether employees should be allowed to opt out of medical coverage. If employees are allowed to waive coverage, the lowest option is no coverage. If not, the provisions of the low option need to be established.

Most often, the lowest plan option is viewed as a catastrophic-protection or safety-net option. An individual covered under this option would have virtually no protection from the higher-frequency, lower-cost claims such as prescription drugs. But in the event of a major unexpected medical problem generating a large claim, this option would serve to protect the individual from high expenses.

Defining the level of expense that a typical employee could absorb in this type of situation is quite subjective. However, the considerations include:

- What portion of the employee group is likely to have coverage available through a working spouse? This is probably the subgroup with the lowest need for protection.

- How much can the typical employee afford to pay in supplemental medical expenses in a particular year? Although this may be difficult to define, the answer is largely a function of pay level. An investment banking firm with an average income of $60,000 will likely come to a very different conclusion from a retailer with an average pay of $20,000.
- What responsibility does the organization assume to protect employees from the risk of making poor decisions? If concern is high, the spread between the highest and the lowest options should be narrowed.

Typically, the lowest available option has a substantial up-front deductible (often $250), 80 percent payment of remaining expenses, and a stop-loss limit (sometimes as high as $1,000). In some cases, the deductible may be significantly lower (for example, $100 for a relatively low-paying organization) or substantially higher (for example, $500 for a high-paying organization that almost decided to allow employees to opt out completely).

Most often the option has family deductible and stop-loss limits of two or three times the individual amounts. However, as the individual deductible and stop-loss limits become larger, organizations sometimes reduce the family maximum to minimize some of the risk involved. At the extreme, for a very large deductible option (for example, $500), the only deductible and stop-loss limit may be per family amounts. This adds very little extra cost to the option because it is unlikely that a family selecting such a low option, would have more than one individual with very major expenses in a single year.

(3) OTHER OPTIONS

Once the highest and the lowest supplemental medical options are defined, other options can be created to fill in between the extremes. How much filling in is appropriate depends a great deal on how wide the gap is. If the richest plan is the prior high-value medical plan and the lowest option is no coverage, there is a wide gap. Therefore, a greater need exists for intermediate options. In contrast, if the richest and the lowest options both provide 80 percent coverage with deductibles of $0 and $100, respectively, less need exists for intermediate options.

Today, in a typical situation, employees are offered three or four choices, with all of the options structured in a fairly parallel manner in terms of reasonable progression in deductible amounts, coinsurance percentages, and stop-loss limits. Sometimes, however, the options also differ in the expenses that are covered. Frequently, certain expenses that are covered, such as semi-private hospital coverage and vision care, are excluded from the lowest option to help differentiate it from the other plans.

If the prior supplemental medical plan is maintained as the high option, but the organization wishes to encourage employees to select or at least seriously consider the lower plan options, placing higher lifetime maximums or lower stop-loss limits on the lower options could help to accomplish that result. In practice, however, different lifetime maximums on the options may not be particularly meaningful under a program in which employees have the opportunity to make annual changes in their coverage choices.

An example of a fairly common supplemental medical option structure is illustrated in Example 5.1.

(c)   COORDINATION WITH OTHER PLANS

All supplemental medical plans, whether flexible or not, need to have clearly defined rules that outline what is paid in the event an individual incurring medical claims is covered by two employer plans. One of the plans will be primary (i.e., paying first) and the other will be secondary (i.e., paying second). When only one plan is involved (or the plan is the primary payer), the benefits to be paid are clear—that is, whatever the primary (or only) plan normally would provide. With two employer plans involved, the issues become more complicated. Which plan is the primary versus the secondary payer? And what benefits will the plan pay, if it is determined to be secondary?

Guidance on these issues which was provided several years ago by the provincial Superintendents of Insurance received broad approval

Example 5.1
Typical Supplement Medical Options

Option	Deductible (Individual/ Family)	Plan Payments	Stop-Loss (Individual/ Family)	Hospital	Vision
Premium	None	100%	None	Semi-private/ private	$180
Standard	$25/$50	90%	$250/$500	Semi-private	$120
Catastrophic	$100/$200	80%	$500/$1,000	Not covered	Not covered

by the Canadian Life and Health Insurance Association (CLHIA). (Technically, Superintendents' guidelines apply to insured plans only, although uninsured plans generally follow insured plan conventions.) The guidelines move employers away from an approach that automatically designated the father's plan as primary payer for a child (when plans of both the father and the mother covered the child). Under the revised approach, the sex of the parent is ignored, and instead, the plan covering the parent with the earlier birthday in the calendar year becomes the primary payer.

In the United States, the National Association of Insurance Commissioners (NAIC) adopted similar guidelines to those described above; however, they went further with another recommendation (introduced but subsequently withdrawn) that would have permitted employers to provide less-than-full reimbursement of medical claims for employees with duplicate coverage. Traditionally, coordination has meant that employees with dual coverage could receive *no less* than 100 percent payment of covered expenses. A secondary plan was required to pay its regular benefits, but to no more than the amount necessary to pay the full amount of the claim in combination with the primary plan. The situation is in direct conflict with the goals most employers have for encouraging employees to reduce medical utilization, and often believed to be unfair to other employees with only one source of coverage. As a result, some self-insured plans ignored the traditional approach to coordination of benefits and provided less-than-full payment in duplicate coverage situations through alternate methods of coordinating payments between plans. The revised NAIC guidelines would have given this same flexibility to insured plans. To date, this approach has not been seen in Canada; however, it could be introduced in the 1990s.

One of the most common alternative coordination techniques currently used in the United States is known as maintenance of benefits or benefits-less-benefits. Under this approach, the deductibles and copayment amounts are preserved when the plan is secondary, because the secondary plan defines its payment as the *difference* between what it would normally pay if it were the sole plan, and what the other plan actually pays. Thus the covered individual does not receive full payment from the combination of the two plans.

Consideration of a maintenance of benefits (or some other intermediate) approach to handling two-plan coverage is particularly appropriate when introducing a flexible program with choices in medical. Under the traditional coordination of benefits method, the individual covered under two plans would often receive full payment of any claim, regardless of the option selected. Using the maintenance of benefits approach would retain a difference in payments between the options when the flexible program is secondary (as is the case in the absence of another plan) and avoid providing full payment of the total claim (as is also the case in the absence of another plan). With more two-income families and double-digit increases in supplemental medical plan costs, Canadian employers may also want to consider alternatives to 100 percent payment of covered expenses.

(d) SPECIAL CONSIDERATIONS

- **Employment of couples.** Sometimes, a significant number of married couples work for the same organization. When both the husband and the wife are employed at the same organization, the supplemental medical and other health care plans need to specify any special rules. For example, can an employee be covered both as an employee and as a dependent? Should one employee elect family coverage and the other elect no coverage? Do the same coordination of benefits provisions apply to an individual covered twice under the plan, as would apply to an individual covered by different employer plans?

  These issues have typically been resolved under the prior medical plan, and often parallel decisions are appropriate when moving into a flexible program. The subject should be re-addressed, however, particularly if there are significant changes in pricing (either level or structure of employee contributions) or coordination of benefit provisions (which may eliminate any incentive to be covered twice by the same plan).

  If the flexible program specifically identifies credits for employees from the medical plan, and these credits vary by family status or number of covered dependents, this issue becomes more complex. Do both employees receive the same credits they would have received had their spouse been employed elsewhere? This may seem to be the most equitable (especially to employees), but could significantly increase the organization's cost, because both employees do not receive the full medical value in a traditional plan. Should each employee be allowed to cover himself or herself and only one be allowed to cover the children? Can the organization even adequately identify where these situations exist?

- **Default coverages.** In the initial year of a flexible program, all employees are encouraged and expected to submit a completed enrollment form, indicating their coverage choices. Reminder notices and contact with supervisors should produce close to a 100 percent response. However, it may be necessary to assign default coverages to some employees who simply fail to complete and return the form.

The default coverage could be any option, but might be determined as the option closest to the employee's prior coverage, the non-contributory option (if one is available), the lowest option, or no coverage. The default with respect to the family members covered might be the coverage category in effect most recently or employee-only coverage. In subsequent years, the default coverages most often duplicate the prior year's election (both regarding type of option and covered dependents).

Decisions as to default coverages (what they should be and whether they should be explicitly communicated to employees) typically reflect the employer's attitudes on responsibility for protecting employees.

§ 5.6 DESIGN OF DENTAL

(a) IN GENERAL

More than 80 percent of the organizations with flexible benefit programs include dental choices as an element of the program. The attractions for the employer and for the employee are quite similar to those which make medical the most prevalent area for choice making. The plan design process is typically less complex for dental benefits than for medical benefits.

(b) STRUCTURE OF OPTIONS

The design decisions in dental relate primarily to the number and type of options to be made available to employees.

(1) Types of Options

As discussed earlier, employees are most frequently allowed to opt out of dental coverage within flexible programs, because the risk to the employee of doing so is modest. In such a program, the lowest option has already been defined as no coverage.

Usually the organization introducing the flexible program already has a dental plan in place which is operating reasonably successfully, and the employer is experiencing little pressure to modify it. When this is the case, it is often an easy decision to maintain the existing dental plan as an option.

In some cases, the employer provides two options in dental, the current plan or no coverage. This is essentially a yes or no choice. However, if there are concerns about the current dental plan, these might be addressed in one of three ways under the flexible program:

- **Modify the existing plan.** For example, the existing plan might be quite satisfactory except that the annual maximum is less than competitive or the deductible might require updating. Either change could be made with essentially the same plan offered under the flexible program.

- **Add one or two options.** Possibly the existing plan provides maximum benefits or a dental fee guide that have not been updated in some time or simply pays benefits that are lower than many employees believe is competitive. In such a case, the current plan could be maintained as an option and a new plan introduced which meets the needs for increased coverage. Or the current plan might require a high level of employee contributions and a lower coverage option (either free or with lower employee contributions) might prove attractive.

- **Drop dental coverage.** If a plan has generated a great deal of employee dissatisfaction (either due to low benefit levels or poor claims handling), and if the plan sponsor is concerned over the level of administrative cost and effort to maintain the plan, one alternative might be to terminate the dental plan, convert the prior company cost into credits for employees, and simply allow employees who expect to have dental expenses to use these credits in a health care expense account for health care. Those who do not expect significant dental expenses could use their credits for other purposes.

There are both broad and detailed design issues that need to be addressed when designing a new dental plan or creating additional options. These include: size and type of deductible; whether the deductible should be waived for certain types of expenses; plan payment levels for various types of expenses (diagnostic and preventive, restorative, major, orthodontic, etc.); and maximums (annual and lifetime). These are important subjects for the design of dental plans generally, but they will be addressed here only in the context of choice-making programs.

If alternative dental plans are to be offered, the alternatives can be designed to provide higher (or lower) coverage across most types of expenses. The differences in benefits and prices should be sufficient to provide employees with meaningful choices.

Often the across-the-board difference in benefit levels does not apply to orthodontic benefits. Orthodontic expenses are very substantial, generally quite predictable, and typically somewhat deferrable. Plan benefits for orthodontia are also usually subject to a separate lifetime maximum, such as $1,000 or $1,500. To reduce the potential for employee manipulation (that is, making a selection based on what is known to be an upcoming expense) and because of the problems associated with different lifetime maximums under a program with choices, each dental option will usually have the same lifetime orthodontia maximum.

Alternatively, one option may be designed to emphasize diagnostic and preventive expenses with marginal (or no coverage) for major expenses. This may be a replacement for the no-coverage option in order to encourage continuing visits to the dentist for exams, X-rays, and cleanings.

(2) Capitation Options

Approximately 25 percent of flexible benefit sponsors include a capitation plan as an option under their programs. The employer's considerations regarding whether or not to have a capitation plan include:

- Does the prior dental care program include a dental capitation choice? If employees are accustomed to the option and it is working well, there is little related to the introduction of more employee choice which would suggest dropping or modifying this choice.
- What advantages do alternative providers create for participating employees or the organization sponsoring the flexible program? The level of protection and the cost of the coverage should be compared to the group plans to determine if adding capitation options is attractive.
- What is the track record of the provider? To be attractive, capitation plans should be financially sound, produce relatively stable costs, have a history of honouring commitments, and be able to attract and retain quality dentists.
- Does the plan have adequate administrative capabilities? Day-to-day operations should be handled efficiently, and the organization should be able to respond adequately to the employer's requests for information.
- Does the provider offer services in all locations in which the plan sponsor operates?

(3) Number of Options

The predictability of dental expenses makes it important to achieve a high level of participation in each plan option to minimize adverse selection concerns. Adequate participation is achieved partially by minimizing the number of plans, but also by pricing approaches and restrictions on changes in coverage. (See also Chapter Fourteen for discussion of approaches to minimizing adverse selection.) Therefore, one or two options is the norm, with plans rarely offering more than three.

(c) COORDINATION WITH OTHER PLANS

As is the case with medical, dental plans need to be structured to coordinate with other employers' plans. But the scope of the issue is much narrower in dental for several reasons. First, situations with duplicate coverage are less frequent. Many employers (especially smaller employers) do not provide dental insurance to their employees, and those that do often require contributions for participation. Second, for many claims, each plan may pay less than 50 percent of the submitted claim, due to deductibles, employee copayments (which may be as high as 50 percent for major expenses), and expenses exceeding the applicable fee guide. So, the total frequently does not exceed 100 percent—the point at which most traditional coordination of benefits provisions become effective.

(d) SPECIAL CONSIDERATIONS

- **Anticipatory behaviour.** Under a flexible program, the communication with employees usually starts at least three months before the new benefits become effective. Changes in benefits being provided by the plans may encourage an acceleration (if benefits are being reduced) or a deferral (if benefits are being increased) of visits to the dentist. This may not be a significant problem, but probably merits consideration, both when designing the options and when discussing the timing of the communication steps.
- **Adverse selection.** The opportunity for an employee to select against the plan is much greater in dental than in medical. The impact of this adverse selection can be moderated by effective plan design, pricing, and restrictions on changes. This subject is dealt with extensively in a separate chapter.

§ 5.7   DESIGN OF VISION AND HEARING

About half of the organizations with flexible programs include any vision and/or hearing choices under the program. Where a choice does occur, it is generally part of another health care plan (medical or dental). Occasionally, a stand-alone plan is offered. Normally, the benefit available is usually a continuation of the plan that was provided prior to the introduction of flexibility.

If there is currently no vision or hearing plan and employees are interested in such coverage, the typical decision is to include vision and hearing as an eligible health care account expense. Normally, an employer would not create a separate option to provide such benefits.

If there is an existing plan that is generating problems or concerns over the value provided, relative to the expense and administrative effort, there is an alternative. The employer terminates the vision or hearing plan, converts the employer contribution into flexible credits, and positions the health care expense account as an alternative means of covering these expenses.

§ 5.8   PROVINCIAL HEALTH INSURANCE PLANS

(a)   OVERVIEW

All 12 provinces and territories sponsor health insurance for their residents, with hospital and medical insurance plans. The plans came into existence as a result of the federal Hospital Insurance and Diagnostic Services Act of 1957 and the federal Medical Care Act of 1966. The agreements specified that the federal government would pay approximately 50 percent of the cost of the plans.

In 1984, the Canada Health Act replaced these statutes and set out the current prerequisites for federal contributions to provincial health service plans. Provinces complying with the Canada Health Act are entitled to a transfer of federal tax revenues and a per capita cash payment that escalates with the growth in the Gross National Product (GNP). Since the cost of health care services has increased faster than the increase in the GNP, federal support has slipped from the initial 50 percent.

The Canada Health Act establishes the following criteria for federal-provincial co-operation:

- **Public administration.** The plan must be administered on a non-profit basis by a public authority appointed by and accountable to the government of the province.
- **Comprehensiveness.** The plan must insure all medically necessary services provided by doctors, hospitals, and dentists.
- **Universality.** The plan must entitle all residents in the province to all insured services on uniform terms and conditions. Exceptions to this include members of the Canadian Forces covered under the National Defence Act, and Royal Canadian Mounted Police officers of rank covered under the RCMP Act.
- **Portability.** When a person takes up residence in another province, coverage must continue during the minimum waiting period of the new province. Insured persons temporarily absent from their home province must be eligible for coverage at the rate payable by the plan of the host province; where the services are provided outside Canada, coverage shall be at the rate payable for similar services provided in the province. In cases of referral, where services are unavailable in Canada, prior approval from the provincial authorities is generally required.
- **Accessibility.** Insured health services must be available on uniform conditions and on a basis that includes no direct or indirect impediments to reasonable access.

Extra billing and most user charges are prohibited. The *Canada Health Act* provides for a reduction in federal funding in the event of extra billing or prohibited user charges.

(b) CONTROL STRUCTURE

There are essentially three areas of control in the health care system: the federal government, the provincial government, and the medical profession.

(1) Federal Government

The federal government controls the supply of medical practitioners by:

- Limiting the number of immigrant doctors
- Setting regional quotas of specialists
- Offering practice incentives for under-served areas.

The federal education minister is responsible for the university grants to medical schools and thus controls the supply of medical graduates.

(2)   Provincial Governments

Provincial governments regulate the supply of facilities, and expenditures and they set quality controls. Provincial health ministers have the following responsibilities under the hospital insurance plans:

- Setting the hospitals' annual operating budgets
- Controlling all hospital residency training
- Setting ceilings on specialists in training
- Controlling the supply of beds, equipment and new services
- Conducting quality inspections
- Monitoring utilization and costs.

Under the medical insurance plan, the health minister and a commission share the following responsibilities:

- Negotiating fee schedules and income ceilings
- Conducting claims review
- Constructing profiles of procedures performed by each physician
- Verifying physicians' billings
- Recommending physicians for prosecution.

(3)   Medical Profession

The medical profession regulates medical quality, expenditure, and fraud controls through the health professions board and the College of Physicians and Surgeons. As such, it is responsible for:

- Medical licensing and discipline
- Standards, inspection of doctors' office records, and practices
- Investigating complaints over fees.

(c)   FUNDING

The provincial governments are responsible for any costs remaining after the federal subsidy.

In Newfoundland, Prince Edward Island, Nova Scotia, New Brunswick, Saskatchewan, the Northwest Territories, and the Yukon, the hospital and medical plans are funded by general operating revenue alone.

The other five provinces collect additional funds beyond general operating revenue. Three provinces levy a payroll tax on employers:

- Ontario—0.98 to 1.95 percent of payroll, depending on payroll size
- Quebec—3.45 percent of payroll
- Manitoba—0 to 2.25 percent of payroll, depending on payroll size.

The provinces of Alberta and British Columbia require residents covered by the plan to pay premiums. Special exemptions are made for low-income residents in both provinces and for persons over age 65 in Alberta. In 1990, monthly premiums in these two provinces are as follows:

- Alberta—single, $19.75
  —family, $39.50
- British Columbia—single, $31.00
  —couple, $55.00
  —family, $62.00.

In British Columbia, the premiums are applicable to the medical services plan only; no premium is payable for hospital services.

(d)   COVERAGE RULES

(1)   Eligibility

All residents, regardless of health, age, or financial status, are eligible for benefits. This is a prerequisite under the agreement between the federal and provincial governments. A "resident" means a person lawfully allowed to be and remain in Canada, who is ordinarily present in the particular province or territory. By definition, this excludes tourists, transients, and visitors.

Coverage is compulsory in some provinces and not in others. However, all provinces require individuals to enroll or register in the program.

(2)   Effective Dates of Coverage

The normal residency period that must be established in each province is three months for persons moving from province to province in Canada. A person leaving one province to establish residence in another province is usually covered for the three-month period by the plan in the province of prior residence.

Students attending school outside their home province are generally considered to be residents of their home province for purposes of their hospital services plan.

People establishing residence in a province, who previously lived outside Canada, are normally considered residents on the date of their arrival. The spouse and dependent children of a resident are insured as a family unit. The head of the family is required to register all members of the family.

Age limits on dependent children vary somewhat. However, most provinces define dependent children as under age 19 or under age 21 if they are full-time students. Handicapped dependents are eligible with no age limit.

(e)   INSURED HOSPITAL SERVICES

(1)   Basic Services

The following basic services are covered by all provinces when medically necessary in the diagnosis and treatment of illness or injury, on an in-patient basis:

- Accommodation and meals at the standard public ward level
- Necessary in-hospital nursing services
- Laboratory, X-ray, and other diagnostic procedures
- Drugs, biological, and related preparations administered in a hospital
- Use of operating room, case room, and anesthetic facilities, including necessary equipment and supplies
- Routine surgical supplies
- Use of radiotherapy facilities
- Services rendered by employees of the hospital.

(2)   Other Services

Other types of hospital services are offered by various provinces as follows:

British Columbia
- Physiotherapy facilities on an in-patient basis
- Active treatment of certain types of chronic illnesses or disability in a general, rehabilitation, chronic or convalescent hospital

- Emergency out-patient treatment within 24 hours of an accident; and
- Out-patient treatment for narcotic addiction.

Alberta

- Semi-private or private accommodation, if medically required
- Diagnostic laboratory and radiological procedures on an out-patient basis
- Emergency and out-patient services
- Physiotherapy, occupational, and speech therapy
- Psychiatric therapy on an out-patient basis
- Ultra-violet light therapy for psoriasis.

Saskatchewan

- Treatment of tubercular patients
- Medically required out-patient services, including X-ray and laboratory procedures, physiotherapy and occupational therapy services.

Manitoba

- Physiotherapy, occupational therapy, speech therapy, and psychiatric care in hospitals designated by the Commission
- Medically required out-patient services, including diagnostic X-rays and laboratory work, operating room and anesthetic facilities, necessary nursing, medical and surgical supplies, and necessary prescribed drugs.

Ontario

- Semi-private or private accommodation when necessary and certified in writing by the attending physician
- Use of respiratory equipment in-hospital
- Use of home renal dialysis and of home hyperalimentation equipment, supplies and medications where available in an Ontario hospital and prescribed by a staff physician of that hospital
- Occupational therapy, speech therapy, and physiotherapy in approved Canadian hospitals when prescribed by a physician as a medically necessary course of treatment (physiotherapy also in approved private non-hospital facilities in Ontario)
- Laboratory, radiological, and other diagnostic procedures on an out-patient basis
- Use of diet counselling services when prescribed by a physician
- Meals required during a treatment program on an out-patient basis.

Quebec

- Prostheses and orthopedic devices that can be implanted in the body on an in-patient basis
- Use of physiotherapy facilities on an in-patient basis
- Medically required out-patient services including electric shock treatment, insulin treatment, behaviour therapy, emergency care, minor surgery, diagnostic services, ergotherapy, inhalation therapy, hearing and speech therapy, orthoptic treatment of visual defects, clinical psychiatric services, services and examinations required under Quebec law, to obtain and keep employment.

New Brunswick

- Use of physiotherapy facilities on an in-patient basis
- Available out-patient services when prescribed by a physician for the purpose of maintaining health, preventing disease and assisting in the diagnosis and treatment of an injury, illness or disability.

Nova Scotia

- Use of physiotherapy facilities on an in-patient basis
- Extensive out-patient procedures including emergency diagnosis and treatment within 48 hours of an accident.

Prince Edward Island

- Use of physiotherapy facilities on an in-patient basis;
- Medically required out-patient services including necessary meals and nursing services, laboratory, radiological and other diagnostic procedures, drugs, biologicals and related preparations when used for emergency diagnosis and treatment, use of operating room and anesthetic facilities, routine surgical supplies, use of radiotherapy and physiotherapy facilities where available.

Newfoundland

- Electrocardiographs and electroencephalographs on an in-patient basis
- Use of physiotherapy facilities on an in-patient basis
- Medically required out-patient services including laboratory and radiological procedures, use of radiotherapy and physiotherapy facilities, where available.

Northwest Territories

- Use of physiotherapy facilities on an in-patient basis, where available
- Emergency and out-patient treatment within 24 hours after an accident.

(3)   User Fees

Some provinces continue to charge user fees for specified hospital services in spite of the reduction in federal funding. The insured resident is required to pay this fee when receiving such services from hospitals.

The following is a summary for those provinces where a user fee is charged for hospital services:

British Columbia
- $16.70 per day in a chronic/extended care hospital, if the individual is over 18 years of age.
  Note: Newborns, persons admitted involuntarily to a psychiatric unit under the Mental Health Act, and individuals who are involuntarily undergoing treatment for tuberculosis are excluded from these charges.
- $5 per visit for physiotherapy, chiropractic, massage therapy, podiatric, and naturopathic services.

Alberta
- Auxiliary Hospital Charges
  —Private room up to 60 days $ 6.25
  —Hospital charge beginning with 61st day $14.00
  —Private room beginning with 61st day $20.25
- Mental Health Hospitals
  —Daily hospital charge (for voluntary
  patients) beginning with 61st day $14.00

Manitoba
- The standard ward charge of $20.20 also applies in a hospital where an individual has been medically discharged, but remains in hospital.

Ontario
- Chronic care and extended care patients age 18 and over pay $23.51 per day after the first 60 days.

New Brunswick
- A charge of $13.70 per day after the first 60 days applies where an individual has been medically discharged, but remains in hospital.

(f)   INSURED SERVICES OF MEDICAL PRACTITIONERS

(1)   Basic Services

The following basic health services are covered in each province:

- Medically required services of general practitioners and specialists reimbursed at an approved schedule of fees, including:

  —The diagnosis and treatment of medical disabilities and conditions
  —Surgical services
  —Maternity services
  —Anesthesia services
  —X-ray, laboratory, and other diagnostic procedures
  —Inoculations, vaccinations, and routine physical examinations;
  —Specialists' services upon referral.

- Oral surgical services provided by a dentist in hospital including:

  —Maxillo-facial surgery required as a result of accidents
  —Orthodontic care of a cleft palate
  —Surgical extraction of impacted teeth.

In certain provinces, the services of other medical practitioners are covered, as discussed next.

(2) Optometrists

All provinces, other than Prince Edward Island, cover the services of optometrists for eye examinations, but not for the fitting or cost of lenses.

(3) Chiropractors

Services of chiropractors are covered in the following provinces:

British Columbia
  - Under age 65: one initial and 11 subsequent office visits per year
  - Age 65 and over: one initial and 14 subsequent office visits per year.
Alberta
  - Services to a maximum of $12 per visit
  - Limit of $300 per benefit period per individual
  - X-ray provision of $19.90 for each disability.
Saskatchewan
  - Visits and X-rays for which payment is based on a fee schedule established by the provincial Commission and the Chiropractors Association of Saskatchewan.

Manitoba
- Insured services covered to a maximum of $158 per person per year
- $10.65 for initial and all subsequent visits.

Ontario
- Maximum allowance in a 12-month period beginning July 1 is $220 (including $40 for X-rays).
- The rate allowed is $11.75 for the initial visit, $9.65 for each subsequent visit and $12 for a home visit.
- The payment for X-rays ranges from $8 to $35 for different X-rays defined in the plan.

New Brunswick
- No coverage, except under the Seniors' Health Benefits Program
- Limited to eight visits in a calendar year at 80 percent of the cost, to a maximum of $12 per visit.

Yukon
- No coverage, except for services performed in hospital.

(4)　Podiatrists

Services of podiatrists are covered in the following provinces:

British Columbia
- Coverage is limited to an annual maximum of $150 per patient.

Alberta
- Services and appliances are limited to $300 per yearly benefit period per person.

Saskatchewan
- Community Health Services Branch provides chiropody services to all residents at no charge.

Ontario
- Maximum allowance in a 12-month period beginning July 1 is $125 (excluding X-rays).
- The rate allowed is $15.20 for the initial visit, $10.75 for each subsequent visit, $14 for a home visit and $7 for a visit if the patient is institutionalized.
- Payment for X-rays ranges from $5.50 to $11 for different specified X-rays to a maximum of $30 per 12-month period.

New Brunswick
- No coverage except under the Seniors' Health Benefits Program
- Limited to five visits in a calendar year at 80 percent of the cost to a maximum of $16 per visit.

(5) Physiotherapists

Services of physiotherapists are covered in the following provinces:

British Columbia
- For patients under age 65, 12 visits per benefit year to a maximum of $157.15.
- For patients age 65 and over, 15 visits per benefit year to a maximum of $194.95.

Alberta
- $300 per benefit period per individual.

Saskatchewan
- Services are covered if performed in a hospital or accredited facility or if performed by physiotherapists under contract with the hospital.

Ontario
- Services provided by physiotherapists who work in facilities approved and listed in Schedule 9, attached to the Ontario Health Insurance Act when established in 1975. (Note: No new physiotherapists or facilities have been or will be added to the schedule.) Office visits are payable at $11.50 per visit, home visits at $23 per visit.

(6) Naturopaths

Services of naturopaths are only covered in British Columbia:

- For patients under age 65, 12 visits per benefit year to a maximum of $155.55
- For patients age 65 and older, 15 visits per benefit year to a maximum of $193.

(7) Osteopaths

Services of osteopaths are covered in the following provinces:

British Columbia
- Osteopaths are considered and reimbursed the same as physicians.

Alberta
- $300 per individual per benefit year.

Ontario
- Maximum of $155 per person in a 12-month period beginning July 1 (including $25 for X-rays).
- The rate allowed is $12 for the initial visit, $9 for each subsequent visit and $15 for a home visit.

(g) INSURED MEDICAL SERVICES

In addition, the following medical services are provided in the indicated provinces:

(1) Ambulance

British Columbia
- Service is provided through a separate provincial agency—Emergency Health Services Commission. The patient charge is $37 for the first 40 kilometres, then $.40 per kilometre, to a maximum of $227.

Alberta
- Only the cost of transportation between hospitals located in the same city of Alberta is covered.

Ontario
- Medically necessary: the insured resident is required to pay a fee of $22 for land or air ambulance use (use of air ambulance requires prior approval from Ontario Emergency Health Services).
- Not medically necessary: the insured resident is required to pay a fee of $44 plus $1.10 for each kilometre travelled in excess of 40 kilometres.

    Note: Fees do not apply to transportation between one hospital and another.

Quebec
- Coverage is provided to persons age 65 and over, and to social aid recipients.
- Service for victims of road accidents is paid by the Régie de l'assurance automobile du Québec.

New Brunswick
- No coverage except through the Interhospital Transfer Program; 50 percent of the cost is covered with the patient paying a maximum of $50. The program also pays for all ambulance mercy flights.

Nova Scotia
- The Ministry of Health sponsors an Ambulance Subsidy Program for eligible residents with no private or third-party insurance.

Newfoundland
- The Provincial Ambulance Program provides (i) land ambulance service at $40 for 80 kilometres or less, $50 over 80 kilometres, plus $25 escort fee, if required; (ii) air ambulance service of $55 plus $25 escort fee.

Northwest Territories
- The plan will reimburse the amount spent on air transportation from any point in the Territories that is in excess of:
  —The return fare between Yellowknife and Edmonton
  —The one-way regular air fare between Yellowknife and Edmonton for any one-way journey required
  —Two return fares from Yellowknife to Edmonton for medically required transportation for any one family unit within any 12-month period.

(2) Special Nursing

Special nursing services are only provided in the following provinces:

British Columbia
- Services of a Registered Nurse, including the cost of board, up to $40 per year per patient are covered only when recommended by a physician.
- Services of the Victorian Order of Nurses acting with or under an attending physician will be covered at $2 net per visit to a yearly maximum of $40 per patient. (This limit does not apply to the administration of injection on physician's instructions.)

Yukon Territory
- Services of a Registered Nurse or Certified Nursing Aide are covered up to $250 per year upon the written referral of a medical practitioner to residents age 65 and over, or at least age 60 whose spouse is at least age 65.

(3) Nursing Homes/Homes for the Aged

Nursing home care is provided in the following provinces:

Alberta
- Residents must have resided in Alberta for three consecutive years prior to application for services and must require continuous nursing service and regular medical supervision in a participating nursing home. Services include accommodation, meals, laundry, personal services, special diets when necessary and routine drugs and dressings ordered by the attending physician.
- Residents pay the following daily charges:

—$14 for standard ward accommodation

—$16.50 for semi-private accommodation

—$20.25 for private accommodation.

Saskatchewan

- The Health Department provides Continuing Care to residents of licensed special care homes requiring specific levels of care.
- The patients' charge is $657 per month, adjusted quarterly.

Manitoba

- Personal Care Homes and Hostels for residents requiring nursing care provide the following services: accommodation at standard ward level; meals including special and therapeutic diets; necessary nursing services; routine medical and surgical supplies; prescribed drugs and related preparations; physiotherapy and occupational therapy; routine laundry and linen services.
- Residents pay the following daily charges:

—$20.20 for standard ward accommodation

—$25 for semi-private accommodation

—an amount the Commission considers reasonable for private accommodation.

Ontario

- When regular medical supervision, nursing and personal care are required on a 24-hour basis, the patient pays $16.08 or $24.08 per day depending on the facility and the plan pays the balance of the standard ward costs in a licensed nursing home.

Northwest Territories

- Nursing home care services are provided within approved facilities.

Yukon

- The plan provides standard ward accommodation, necessary personal, para or nursing services and drugs, biologicals, and related preparations when administered in the nursing home facility. Any government income security payments received by a patient must be used to pay room and board. However, a patient is allowed to retain $75 per month as a "comfort" allowance.

(4)   Chronic Care

Chronic care coverage is provided in the following provinces:

British Columbia

- Coverage is provided to patients requiring 24-hour-a-day skilled nursing services and regular medical attention in an extended-care unit of an acute hospital. Also, in a separate chronic or convalescent hospital or in the following residential facilities: personal care homes; intermediate care facilities; mental health boarding facilities; private hospitals; and extended care hospitals. Services provided include: standard ward accommodation; necessary nursing; drugs, biologicals and related preparations; laboratory and radiological procedures and the necessary interpretations.

- Patients in an extended/chronic care hospital who are over 18 years of age pay $16.70 per day.

Alberta
- Coverage is provided to residents in an auxiliary (long-term or chronic illness) hospital. Patients pay the basic daily charge of $14 after the first 120 days.

Manitoba
- Coverage is as described for Personal Care Homes under Nursing Home Care.

Ontario
- Chronic care hospital care is available when long-term illnesses or disabilities cannot be treated at home.
- Patients occupying chronic care beds for longer than 60 days pay $23.51 per day unless they are under age 18 or qualify for exemption.

Northwest Territories
- Chronic care services are provided within approved facilities.
- Patients make a daily co-payment for room and board depending on age, such as:

—under age 16: $10

—age 16–18: $10–$19 depending on ability to pay

—age 19–64: no co-payment unless the patient is receiving a disability pension which is the used for room and board costs, less $75 per month the patient keeps as a "comfort allowance."

(5)   Home Care

Home care coverage is provided in the following provinces:

British Columbia
- Residents aged 19 and up, who are unable to function independently due to chronic health problems receive the following services through the Long-Term Care program:

—Visiting in-home nursing services;

—In-home physiotherapy, and speech therapy;

—Adult day care

—Homemaker services.

Alberta
- There is no provincial in-home care. However, residents from age 65 and Widows' Pension recipients are covered at no cost by a Supplementary Alberta Blue Cross program. The Plan provides home nursing care to $200 per family unit per benefit year.

Saskatchewan
- There is no provincial in-home care. However, non-profit associations provide Visiting Home Care services to residents with a physician's referral. Funding is received from clients and Health Department grants.

Ontario
- With a physician's referral, the following visiting in-home health care services are provided:
  - Nurse, physiotherapist, occupational therapist, speech therapist, social worker, nutritionist, or a homemaker for up to 80 hours per disability.
  - Provision for dressings and medical supplies, diagnostic and laboratory services, hospital and sick room equipment.
  - Transportation to and from home to a hospital, health facility, or attending physician's office.
  - Use of respiratory equipment whenever a nurse or therapist is present.

Quebec
- There is no provincial home care program. However, the Centre local de services communautaires (CLSC) provides services of visiting nurses, social workers, etc. at no charge to the patient.

New Brunswick
- Assistance of a general nature in the performance of the personal functions and activities necessary for daily living that a person is unable to perform adequately by reason of age, infirmity or mental or physical disability.

Newfoundland
- There is no provincial home care program. However, some regional programs are funded by the Hospital Services Division of the Health Department Visiting Services and some equipment and supplies are available to the chronically disabled and elderly who meet certain eligibility requirements.

(h) VISION CARE

The following provinces provide vision care coverage over and above diagnostic services for eye examinations.

Manitoba
- The initial fittings of contact lenses following congenital cataract surgery (including the cost of lenses and service for the first six months): the plan pays $380. Also, the Manitoba Eyeglasses Program for seniors aged 65 or older provides benefits based on a schedule for dispensing fees, frames, and lenses.

Ontario
- The Assistive Devices Program pays 75 percent of the cost of visual aids (excluding ordinary contact lenses and eye glasses) for residents with long-term physical disabilities.

Quebec
- The Ocular Prosthesis Program reimburses $200 on the purchase and fitting of one ocular prosthesis per eye every five years, plus $15 annual allowance for upkeep and repair.
- In addition, the "Functional Aids Program for the Visually Handicapped" offers mechanical, electronic, optical, and other devices on loan to visually handicapped residents under age 36 and those over 36 who received functional aid under the program. Guide dogs, white canes and some writing aids are available to all visually handicapped residents, regardless of age.

New Brunswick
- The Seniors' Health Benefits Program provides eyeglass lenses or contacts (excluding frames) once every two calendar years (80 percent coverage to a maximum of $40) and low vision aids for seniors whose corrected vision is less than 20/70 (80 percent coverage to a maximum of $60 per calendar year).

Yukon
- For residents 65 or over and spouses over 60 years, the plan pays for one pair of lenses and $50 toward the cost of frames in any two-year period. The plan also pays for contact lenses provided after cataract surgery.

(i) MISCELLANEOUS INSURED SERVICES

The following provinces provide additional miscellaneous services and are listed by province:

British Columbia
- Orthoptic treatment, limited to $50 per patient per year when referred by a medical practitioner.

Alberta
- The Aids to Daily Living Program provides aids for disabled, chronically or terminally ill residents (wheelchairs, some medical aids, dressings, supplies, braces, artificial limbs, etc.).
- The Extended Health Benefits Program for Senior Citizens and Widows/Widowers is available to residents 65 years or older and their spouses, and Alberta Widows' Pension recipients aged 55 to 64. Benefits cover dental care, eyeglasses, hearing aids and certain medical/surgical supplies and rehabilitation equipment.
- Alberta Blue Cross Non-Group Membership provides coverage through Alberta Health Care on an individual basis at special rates to residents otherwise unable to obtain group coverage. Coverage includes:
  —Hospital differential charges for semi-private and private room care (no longer available to seniors)
  —Ambulance services
  —Prescription drugs
  —Appliances, home nursing, clinical psychological services
  —Dental care due to accidental injury
  —Coverage is at no cost to seniors and Alberta Widow's Pension recipients.

Saskatchewan
- Saskatchewan Assistance Plan Supplementary Health Benefits: the Medical Services Division of the Public Health Department pays part or all of the cost of health services for those granted assistance.
- Hearing Aid Plan—hearing aids are available to residents of all ages at wholesale cost. All assessments are covered under the hospital plan.
- Saskatchewan Aids to Independent Living Program (SAIL): provides aids and appliances to the physically handicapped including:
  —For paraplegics with a specialist's referral, drugs and supplies, grants for lifts, ramps, car hand controls
  —50 percent reimbursement for ostomy supplies
  —Oxygen
  —Drugs for chronic end-stage renal disease

—Drugs and food supplements for cystic fibrosis

—Artificial limbs and prosthesis, including myoelectric prostheses;

—Medical supplies for hemophiliacs

—Travel and sustenance for residents with congenital abnormalities

—Some assistance for other food supplements.

- Saskatchewan Abilities Council: This is a non-government association that provides a variety of mobility aids for residents to stay at home instead of in hospital—for example, wheelchairs, walkers, funds for CNIB visual programs, etc.

Manitoba

- Prosthetic and Orthotic Devices: when prescribed by a physician— artificial limbs, certain limb and spinal braces.
- In some cases, the plan provides post-mastectomy breast forms and brassieres, orthotic shoes for children under 18, hearing aids prescribed by an octologist or an audiologist for children under 18, and telecommunication devices for the profoundly deaf.

Ontario

- Assistive Devices Program: pays 75 percent of the approved cost of eligible devices for residents with long-term physical disabilities including: hearing aids, visual and communication aids, incontinence supplies, orthotic devices, ostomy supplies, prosthetic devices, respiratory equipment, seating systems, wheelchair and mobility aids.

Quebec

- Program covering prosthetic, orthopedic and other devices and supplies: for permanently disabled residents, purchases, repairs, etc., of medically necessary:

—Artificial limbs

—Back or leg braces

—Canes or crutches

—Wheelchairs, walkers, etc. (wheelchairs are not covered outside Quebec).

- Hearing Aid Program: The Régie covers the cost of buying, adjusting, repairing or replacing one hearing aid per ear for residents that meet the hearing impairment criteria. Lost or stolen hearing aids cannot be replaced under this program.
- Post-Mastectomy Breast Form Program: The Régie reimburses $50 per breast form and allows two breast forms per breast every two years.

- Ostomy Program: Quebec residents with a permanent colostomy, ileostomy, or ileal conduit receive $300 a year per ostomy to cover part of the cost of buying or replacing ostomy appliances and accessories.

New Brunswick

- Seniors' Health Benefits Program: Resident seniors over 65 are eligible for the following, with some restrictions:
  - —Injection supplies for self-administered medications (80% covered)
  - —Diabetic testing supplies (80% covered to a maximum of $320 per calendar year)
  - —80 percent coverage for ostomy supplies
  - —Eye exams (once every two calendar years, exams following cataract surgery also allowed)
  - —Eyeglass lenses or contacts (frames are not covered) once every two calendar years (80% coverage to a maximum of $40)
  - —Low vision aids
  - —Hearing aids, once every five calendar years
  - —Foot care
  - —Chiropractic treatments, not X-rays
  - —Limb prostheses, including maintenance and repair
  - —Breast prostheses
  - —Orthotics
  - —Tracheotomy supplies.

Nova Scotia

- Medical Services Plan (MSI) Prosthetic Services Program—artificial limbs and eyes, with prior approval.

Newfoundland

- Non-Emergency Medical Transportation Program reimburses residents 50 percent of expenses associated with approved medical transportation exceeding $500 in any 12-month period.

Yukon

- Hearing aids supplied for children under 16 years and seniors. Other appliances, prostheses, orthopaedic shoes to children under 16 are also available with approval from the Plan.

Northwest Territories

- Extended Medical Benefits: Coverage for medically required prosthetics, orthotics, wheelchairs, and so on for 14 listed diseases. Residents must claim through their group plan first.

- Airfare Assistance Plan: Coverage is available only to residents who must travel for medical treatment and do not have a private group travel benefit. Residents with coverage through their employer must apply for this benefit.

(j) PHARMACARE

Pharmacare benefits vary from province to province. Some cover only the cost of prescribed drugs, others extend to other types of medical supplies. Also, in some cases, there are deductible amounts and copayment features where residents bear responsibility for a portion of their drug costs.

The following is a summary of the benefits available under the existing pharmacare programs, universal as well as those for senior citizens by province.

British Columbia
- Residents under age 65 must satisfy a $300 annual deductible per family unit and pay 20 percent of all charges up to a maximum annual payment of $2,000. B.C. Pharmacare pays the remaining expenses at 100 percent.
- Residents over age 65 are required to pay 75 percent of the dispensing fees to an annual maximum of $125 per person.
- Residents who are handicapped, on social assistance or living in licensed care facilities receive full benefits.
- The plan covers:
  —Drugs prescribed by a doctor, dentist or podiatrist
  —Ostomy supplies
  —Designated permanent prosthetic appliances
  —Insulin, syringe and needles for diabetics.

Alberta
- Senior citizens are sent a Blue Cross Drug card upon reaching age 65 and this entitles them to receive prescribed drugs and medicines for 20 percent of their cost. The remaining 80 percent is reimbursed to the pharmacist by the provincial plan.

Saskatchewan
- All residents receive 80 percent reimbursement for all covered prescription drugs after the annual deductible is satisfied, as follows:

—Single seniors age 65 or over: $50

—Senior families (at least one member age 65 or over): $75

—All other families and single residents: $125.

- Social assistance recipients, licensed special care home residents and Saskatchewan Aids to Independent Living Program residents for chronic end-stage renal disease, cystic fibrosis and paraplegia pay a per prescription charge of $3.95.

Manitoba

- All residents are reimbursed 80 percent of the cost of allowable prescription drugs after satisfying a calendar year deductible of:

—$150 per family for residents under age 65

—$85 per family for residents age 65 and over.

Ontario

- Residents age 65 and over who have been resident in Ontario for at least one year are eligible for coverage under the Ontario drug program.
- Individuals receiving federal guaranteed income supplement or Ontario GAINS or family benefit supports are also eligible.
- Prescription drugs and medications are eligible for 100 percent re-imbursement, providing they are purchased in Ontario and are listed in the Ontario Drug Benefit Formulary.

Quebec

- Residents age 65 and over and individuals who qualify for a spouse's allowance under the Old Age Security Act are eligible.
- Only drugs listed in an official drug list are covered by the Plan and pharmacists are reimbursed directly by the provincial plan.
- In some cases, the pharmacist may require the resident to pay a deterrent fee if:

—The cost of the drug is in excess of the usual price for such substances

—The resident refuses to accept a generic substitute which may cost less where the prescribing physician has indicated that sub-stitution is allowed.

New Brunswick

- Prescription drug coverage is available to the residents who:

—Are 65 or over

—Have cystic fibrosis

—Reside in a licensed nursing home

—Have undergone organ or bone marrow transplants and require cyclosporin. (These individuals are covered for that drug only.)

- Residents age 65 and over pay a maximum dispensing fee of $6.45 per prescription. Low-income seniors who receive the Guaranteed Income Supplement are reimbursed by the Prescription Drug Program for any fees in excess of $120 per calendar year.
- Nursing home residents, cystic fibrosis patients and transplant recipients do not pay the fee.

Nova Scotia

- Residents age 65 and over are eligible under the program which reimburses pharmacies directly.
- The Plan pays for the cost of prescription drugs, ostomy equipment and diabetic supplies.

Prince Edward Island

- Residents age 65 and over are eligible.
- The individual pays the dispensing fee and $4 toward the total cost of the drug ingredient; the program pays the remaining ingredient cost.
- The pharmacist has a list of approved benefits.

Newfoundland

- Residents age 65 and over are covered under the Newfoundland and Labrador Prescription Drug Program.
- The program reimburses pharmacists directly for the drug ingredient cost; the individual is responsible for the dispensing fee.
- The program covers drugs which by law require a prescription and a small number of items which do not require a prescription.

Northwest Territories

- Residents age 65 and over are eligible.
- The Plan covers the total cost for: (i) products on the N.W.T. Formulary for non-native and Metis seniors; and (ii) products that, by law, require a prescription and are listed in the Compendium of Pharmaceuticals and Specialties for status Indians and Inuit seniors.

Yukon

- Residents age 65 and over, or at least age 60 whose spouse is age 65 or over are eligible.
- The territorial Pharmacare Plan covers 100 percent of the cost of all prescription drugs.
- The Chronic Disease Program also covers prescription drugs and medical supplies for residents with one of 45 listed chronic diseases.

(k) DENTAL

The range of dental services provided to eligible residents varies from province to province. In those provinces where senior citizens are beneficiaries of the program, the in-office dental plan provides for coverage of major restorative services such as dentures. In those provinces where children are the beneficiaries, the emphasis is on preventive and basic restorative services.

The following is a description of the types of dental services provided under each program by province:

British Columbia
- The British Columbia Dental Care Plan was suspended September 1, 1982, for the duration of the restraint period. Welfare recipients continue to receive dental care through the Ministry of Human Resources. (At the time of writing, the program had not been resumed.)

Alberta
- Residents age 65 or over and their dependents are covered for goods and services provided by a dental surgeon or dental mechanic, subject to the following limitations:
  —The benefit for a complete denture or reset of a complete denture in a given arch will be paid no more frequently than once every five years
  —The benefit for a partial denture in a given arch will be paid no more frequently than once every five years
  —The benefit for relines and rebase of dentures will be paid no more frequently than once every two years
  —Benefit payments will not exceed $1,200 for any two consecutive calendar years
  —Benefits for major orthodontics will be paid only if prior approval has been given by the Minister of Health after consultation with the Alberta Dental Association.

Saskatchewan
- Children from age 5 to and including age 13 are covered for the following services when performed by a dentist employed by the Denticare program:
  —Examinations and diagnostic services, including X-rays
  —Fillings of teeth with amalgam or composite materials

—Periodontal services for treatment of diseased gums

—Extraction of teeth

—The provision of certain prosthetic and orthodontic appliances as approved by the program

—Necessary drugs and medicines required for a dental condition.

Manitoba

- Children ages 6 to 14 in rural school areas and ages 6 to 10 in the district school areas of Mystery Lake and Portage La Prairie are covered for the following dental services:

—Cleaning and scaling of teeth (prophylaxis)

—Topical fluoride applications

—Oral hygiene instruction

—Examinations and diagnostic services including X-rays

—Amalgam and composite fillings

—Crowns, including stainless steel

—Periodontal services for the treatment of diseased gums

—Extraction of teeth

—Endodontic services such as root canal therapy, pulpotomy, etc.

—Minor orthodontics

—Space maintainers and cross bite correction.

   Note: Coverage terminates at the end of the year a child reaches the limiting age.

- The Plan excludes from coverage cephalometric X-rays, gold restorations, and major orthodontics and prosthodontics except in special circumstances.

Quebec

- Children up to age 12 are covered for the following specified services:

—Preventive-prophylaxis, fluoride

—Diagnostic—exams and X-rays

—Restorative—fillings and stainless steel crowns

—Endodontics—root canals, pulpotomics

—Extractions and oral surgery.

- Children ages 13 to 15 are covered for the following:

- —Preventive
- —Diagnostic
- —Oral surgery.
- Social aid recipients receive the same services as children less than 13 years old, excluding root canal treatment, but including:
  - —One complete or partial upper and lower denture every five years
  - —Repairs, relining and replacement of dentures, subject to certain conditions.

Nova Scotia
- All children born on or after January 1, 1967, and who have not reached age 16 are covered for the following services:
  - —Oral exams and bite-wing X-rays once every 12 months
  - —Prophylaxis, fluoride, and counselling once every 12 months
  - —Space maintainers, retainers, and cross bite correction
  - —Fillings and crowns (excluding gold crowns)
  - —Root canal therapy and other endodontic services
  - —Periodontal services; periodontic surgery is covered only if done in a hospital
  - —Oral surgery
  - —Lab services in connection with the above dental services.

Prince Edward Island
- Children from ages 3 to 17 are eligible subject to an annual registration fee of $10 per child to a maximum of $25 per family. The program covers the following services:
  - —Exams, X-rays
  - —Prophylaxis, fluoride treatment
  - —Fillings
  - —Endodontics and periodontal services
  - —Oral surgery.

Newfoundland
- Children up to and including age 12 are covered for the services listed below, subject to a co-payment of $5 per service (other than X-rays, examinations and fluoride treatment). Children of social aid recipients are covered up to age 18.
  - —Examinations and X-rays

—Prophylaxis and fluoride treatment

—Cross bite correction

—Amalgam and composite fillings

—Replacement of missing anterior teeth

—Extractions

—Endodontics such as root canals, pulpotomics.

Yukon

- Residents age 65 and over and spouses age 60 married to a 65-year-old resident are covered under the Yukon dental program subject to a maximum of $1,200 for any two consecutive years. Eligible services include:

—Diagnostic exams and X-rays

—Fillings and other restorations

—Dentures

—Preventive services.

(I)   OUT-OF-PROVINCE COVERAGE

All provincial plans provide coverage for residents in need of emergency care and treatment while temporarily absent from their home province. "Temporarily absent" is normally defined as absence for up to one year. The plans usually pay expenses whether they are incurred inside or outside Canada. When a resident leaves his or her province and relocates to another province, home-province coverage is continued for two months after the month of arrival in the new province, plus in some cases, time spent in transit. Coverage in the new home province commences three months after arrival. Some provinces also continue coverage for up to three months when residents leave the province to establish permanent residence outside Canada.

Out-of-province medical and hospital expenses incurred while temporarily absent are paid at the host province rate. Outside Canada, dollar limits based on home rates are usually applied.

Note that out-of-province coverage generally applies only to emergency treatment required when a resident is absent from the province. Elective treatment received outside the province is either not covered, or covered at lower rates than the rates that apply in the event of an accident or unexpected illness.

(m) COORDINATION OF PRIVATE INSURANCE WITH
PROVINCIAL PLANS

Generally speaking, private insurance cannot duplicate provincial plan coverage. Some provinces specifically prohibit private insurers from providing benefits covered by the provincial programs. In others, although no prohibition exists, a resident is not able to receive duplicate reimbursement.

On the other hand, services over and above those provided by the provincial plan can usually be insured. Examples of this would be the differential between semi-private or private accommodation and ward-level coverage in a hospital or, in Ontario, any charges made for chiropractic services after the yearly maximum has been reached. One major exception to this rule is that the cost of physicians' services above the provincial fee guide cannot legally be insured in most provinces.

Six

Death and Disability

§ 6.1 INTRODUCTION

Death and disability coverages often are included as choice areas within flexible programs. These benefits may not be as highly utilized or as visible as medical and dental benefits, for example, but they do serve a most valued function: providing protection to employees and their dependents from the loss of income due to accident, injury, or illness. Because death and disability premiums are not escalating as rapidly as medical and dental premiums, cost control usually is not a major design consideration. However, a host of other factors create different kinds of design challenges for the structuring of death and disability benefit options.

Designing choices in death benefit coverage can become complex because of the many types of group life insurance available. In addition to deciding what form or forms of death benefits to offer, an employer will need to address various other issues. For example, what levels of coverage should be made available? How should the options be priced? Who should pay for the coverage? Should flexible credits be used to allow pre-tax premium payment? Answers to these questions are not always easy or obvious. The design of death benefit choices must take into account the employer's objectives and employee needs as well as tax requirements.

Although the design of disability benefit choices often is viewed as less complex than that of other benefits, there are a number of issues unique to disability. For example, in the area of short-term disability, the

111

primary issue is whether to offer choices at all, given the extent of coverage already provided through an employer's underlying sick leave or salary continuation program. In long-term disability benefits, a major design issue relates to determining the appropriate level(s) of pay replacement to ensure that the choices are distinct and different, and yet provide an adequate, but not excessive, benefit amount to employees. Another consideration is whether to use flexible credits for pre-tax premium payment in light of benefit taxation rules.

§ 6.2   DEATH BENEFITS

Group life insurance is a natural benefit area to include in a choice-making program, because death benefit needs vary dramatically over an employee's lifetime. For example, the needs of a middle-aged employee with a spouse at home, children, and a mortgage will be much greater than those of a young, single employee. In contrast, an older employee nearing retirement with neither children to support nor mortgage payments—but drawing a career-high income—will have still other needs.

In addition, an employee may have various sources of death benefits outside the group life plan, such as the Canada/Quebec Pension Plan, retirement plans, or individual life insurance policies. Providing choices in group life enables employees to select the level of coverage that best meets individual needs and coordinates with other sources of coverage.

(a)   TYPES OF GROUP LIFE INSURANCE

Group-*term* life insurance is the only form of life insurance typically included in a flexible program. Whole life and universal life policies are generally not included, because these forms of insurance allow cash value buildup and, therefore, do not receive the same tax treatment as group term insurance. Some employers, however, offer whole life or universal life (on a group or individual basis) within the flexible program, as long as the coverage is purchased with after-tax payroll deductions— not flexible credits. (Universal life is covered in detail in Chapter Ten.)

(1)   Employee Life Insurance

Employee life insurance provides a lump-sum benefit to a designated beneficiary upon the death of the employee. The primary intent is to ease the financial strain on a family resulting from the loss of an income provider. Employers may provide a maximum of $25,000 of coverage to employees on a non-taxable basis. The cost of amounts in excess of $25,000 is a taxable benefit for employees. A benefit purchased with flexible credits is considered an employer-provided benefit subject to the $25,000 limit.

In a typical flexible program structure, an employer provides a certain core level of coverage and offers various options to supplement basic coverage amounts. Levels of coverage typically are based on multiples of pay (such as one times pay, two times pay, and so on), although occasionally flat-dollar amounts (such as $10,000, $20,000, and so on) are offered. Many companies place a dollar cap on the total benefit payable.

Employers may charge all employees a flat rate per $1,000 of coverage or assign risk-related rates, which reflect the true cost of the coverage. For example, older, higher risk employees may pay more than younger, lower risk employees. Some plans also consider gender and smoker status in setting the rates, with males paying more than females and smokers paying more than non-smokers.

(2)   Accidental Death and Dismemberment

Accidental death and dismemberment (AD&D) coverage provides additional benefits if an employee's death occurs as the result of an accident. The plan also may pay benefits—usually stated as a fraction of the policy's face value—in the event of accidental dismemberment.

Some employers structure AD&D coverage exactly the same as employee life insurance, so the benefit for an accidental death simply would be double the benefit paid for death by other causes. In these cases, the cost of employee life and AD&D coverage usually is bundled into a combined rate. Other employers construct a separate AD&D plan with different levels of coverage and separate premiums. AD&D coverage is typically quite inexpensive, and the cost usually does not vary by age, sex or smoker status. So unless AD&D is tied to employee life (and the combined rate is age/sex/smoker graded), AD&D typically is priced as a flat amount per $1,000 of coverage, applicable to everyone.

(3)   Dependent Life Insurance

Dependent life insurance provides a lump-sum benefit to a beneficiary (typically the employee) upon the death of a spouse or child. Coverage for a spouse and children may be packaged as one election or offered separately as independent options. The coverage usually is offered in flat-dollar amounts, typically providing higher benefits for a spouse (say, $10,000) than for a child (for example, $2,500). Until recently the coverage amounts available for dependent life were generally much lower than for employee life. This was due to the belief that the death of a dependent generally had less impact on a family's financial status than the death of the employee.

Recently, however, many flexible programs have begun offering significant amounts of spouse's group life insurance—up to $100,000 or even more in some cases. This level of benefit can meet the needs of many types of employees. For example, the "traditional" male employee with a wife and children at home might purchase $100,000 of spouse's life insurance to pay for child care, if his wife died. A two-income family would also find large amounts of spouse's insurance attractive if the premium is less than the cost of employee insurance offered by the spouse's employer.

Dependent life usually is available on a contributory basis only. The cost may be either a flat-dollar amount or a graded rate (often based on the age of the employee and the sex and smoker status of the spouse) per $1,000 of coverage.

(4)   Survivor Income

Survivor income plans are designed to provide a continuing stream of payments (usually paid monthly) to an employee's surviving spouse and/or child(ren). Survivor income benefits may be based on a percentage of the employee's pay (such as 25 percent of salary) or may provide a flat-dollar amount (such as $350 per month). The plan often provides one amount for a surviving spouse plus another amount for children.

Sixty percent of employers offering survivor income benefits provide coverage on a contributory basis. Where the employee is required to contribute, premiums usually are based on pay, age, or a combination of pay and age.

(b)   DESIGN CONSIDERATIONS

Designing group life insurance options within a flexible program requires consideration and analysis of various factors—including an employer's objectives, the needs of employees, and income tax requirements. Coverage provided under the prior plan also is a consideration in terms of evaluating whether to continue or modify current practice.

(1) Areas of Choice

A fundamental design decision is whether to offer group life insurance in a flexible program. Since employers typically offer some degree of choice in existing employee life plans, most flexible programs (81 percent) include employee life insurance as a choice-making area. In cases where employee life insurance choices did not previously exist, many employers view introduction of a flexible program as an opportunity to offer group life choices because employees generally perceive choice making as a benefit enhancement. Many employers also offer choices in AD&D (81 percent) and dependent life (78 percent). About half of the employers offer dependent AD&D. These benefits are popular with employees and often can be included as options in a flexible program at little or no company cost.

Inclusion of AD&D within a flexible benefit program touches on a moderately gray area within the Income Tax Act. Long-standing practice among employers is to treat AD&D as a non-taxable accident and sickness lump-sum benefit, excluding the cost of the coverage from the employee's taxable income. However, Revenue Canada has questioned this interpretation in a couple of situations, particularly where family AD&D benefits are provided. Because it is an unclear area, some employers offer AD&D choices only on an after-tax payroll deduction basis to avoid any potentially negative ramifications to the flexible program.

Employers may not provide dependent life coverage on a non-taxable basis—any company-paid coverage generates a taxable benefit to the employee equal to the employer's cost. As a result, some employers offer dependent life coverage choices on an after-tax payroll deduction basis only.

Very few flexible programs (seven percent) offer survivor income choices. (Even among non-flexible programs, survivor income plans are relatively rare.) These plans tend to be moderately expensive and often difficult to price, because benefits usually are payable for an indefinite period of time (for example, until the spouse's death or remarriage). Moreover, survivor income plans have not been as popular with employees as other types of life insurance, probably because the payment mechanism (a portion of the employee's earnings paid out over a period of time) is more difficult to understand and holds less appeal than a lump-sum payment (as is the case with life insurance).

(2) Structure of Options

Some of the key issues employers need to address in determining the structure of death benefit options are discussed next.

(i) High Option. Determining the high death benefit option usually is a function of various factors. These include employee needs and the presence of other death benefits, such as survivor income plans and pension plans. In addition, underwriting considerations will affect the maximum benefits permissible in a flexible program. (For more complete discussion of this issue, see Chapter Fifteen.)

For employee life and AD&D, a high-end option of four, five or six times pay is usually considered adequate to meet almost all employees' needs. Separately, some employers impose an over-all plan maximum (in terms of a dollar limit), usually for underwriting reasons.

For dependent life, employers usually limit the "richest" option to $50,000 or $100,000 for spouse coverage (although a growing number are using $250,000 or more), and $5,000 or $10,000 for children.

For survivor income, the high-end option usually is no greater than 50 percent of the employee's pay for the surviving spouse plus an incremental amount such as five percent of pay per child, to a maximum of 15 percent of pay for children.

(ii) Low Option. The fundamental issue related to the lowest death benefit option is whether to require employees to take a minimum level of protection—or to allow employees to opt out of coverage completely. Most employers feel a sense of obligation to ensure that all employees have at least a core level of life insurance. The most common minimum benefit amount is one times pay (67 percent). Minimums also may be based on estimated burial expenses, competitive practice, past benefit levels, or a combination of these factors.

Since AD&D, survivor income, and dependent life generally are supplemental death benefits (with little or no company subsidy), employees typically have the option to decline coverage.

(iii) Increments of Coverage. Common practice for employee life and usually AD&D is to establish incremental levels of coverage based on multiples of pay, rather than flat-dollar amounts. Tying coverage to pay is based on the premise that life insurance is generally intended to replace the breadwinner's income, so the level of coverage should bear some reasonable relationship to an employee's earnings. Among employers with options offered as multiples of pay, the most common increment of coverage is a full multiple of pay—such as one times pay, two times pay, and so forth. In some cases, employers also offer half multiples—for example, 0.5 times pay, 1.5 times pay, and so forth. This is frequently found where the plan's rules allow the employee to increase coverage one level a year without medical evidence. The half multiple reduces the insurer's risk.

Only a minority of employers base levels of employee coverage on flat-dollar amounts, with the most common increments being $10,000 or $20,000. Employers who use flat-dollar amounts believe they allow employees to choose a benefit level that precisely meets their needs.

Dependent life is almost always offered in flat-dollar increments, usually at lower levels than employee life. Survivor income typically is offered in increments of the employee's pay, such as 10 percent to 50 percent, sometimes to a flat-dollar maximum on the monthly benefit payable. Less frequently, the increment is a flat-dollar amount (such as $100 to $1,000) payable monthly.

(iv) Number of Options. An employer may offer any number of options to employees. But among employers who provide choices in the various group life areas, the average is five options in employee life, six in AD&D, one in survivor income, and six in dependent life. Conceptually, the employer's goal is to offer enough choices to provide a reasonable degree of flexibility to employees, but not so many choices as to cause confusion or unnecessary administrative complexity.

Generally, the number of options offered is a function of other decisions concerning the range of options—such as the spread between the highest and lowest levels of coverage, the increments of coverage, and the ease of plan administration.

(3)   Source of Funds

(i) Employee Life Insurance. The funding of employee group life options in a flexible program often mirrors the funding approach used for the prior basic-plus-supplemental group life plan. In other words, under a flexible program, an employer typically funds a basic level of coverage—either by attaching a $0 price tag or by providing employees with enough credits to purchase the basic coverage. Employees have the option of purchasing additional levels of coverage using remaining flexible credits or their own contributions.

Another design issue related to funding is whether to permit employees to use flexible credits to pay the group life premium either to supplement after-tax payroll deductions or to replace the deductions. Under Income Tax Act Section 6(1), the cost of employer-provided group life insurance in excess of $25,000 is taxable income to the employee. Coverage paid for with employer flexible credits is considered employer-provided. Thus, allowing employees to pay for amounts in excess of $25,000 with credits creates an additional taxable benefit. As a result, some employers have concluded that group life insurance should only be purchased using payroll deductions. Others have permitted credits to be used to purchase group life; in these cases, the employers advise the employees to spend credits in areas such as medical, dental, and health care expense accounts first, since they do not generate a taxable benefit. If any credits are left over, they could be spent on group life.

Unless the employee premium rates for group life coverage are the same for everyone, certain employees will notice a tax savings by purchasing group life with flexible credits, while others will notice a tax disadvantage. This complication occurs because the employee pays tax based on a taxable benefit calculation as prescribed by Revenue Canada. The taxable benefit is the "cost" of company-paid life insurance in excess of $25,000; and the cost is based on the average premium rate paid by the company. Employees whose actual premium is higher than the average cost will reduce their taxes by paying with credits, while those with a lower premium will see a tax increase. This is illustrated through the following example:

> Assume the average cost for company-paid basic and optional life insurance at a company is $0.25 per month per $1,000 of coverage, based on all participating employees. Consider an employee—a 50-year-old male smoker—who has $25,000 company-paid life insurance coverage and purchases an additional $100,000 at a monthly premium rate of $.60 per $1,000 or $60 per month. This individual pays $720 per year for the coverage. If the benefit is purchased with payroll deductions, he would need to earn $1,359—assuming a 47 percent tax bracket—to pay the premium of $720. If, on the other hand, he pays the premium with $720 in flexible credits, his taxable benefit is $25 per month ($0.25 per $1,000 average cost times $100,000), or $300 per year. His tax would be $141 (47% of $300), so he is much better off using credits instead of deductions.
>
> A younger, female non-smoker, with a premium of $0.05 per month per $1,000 would be better off using deductions. In the previous example, the premium would be $5 per month or $60 per year. If the coverage were purchased with credits, the taxable benefit would still be based on the $0.25 average cost and would be $25 per month or $300 per year.

Employers considering allowing coverage to be purchased using flexible credits should review the additional communication and administrative requirements before making a decision.

(ii) Dependent Life Insurance. Dependent life typically is paid for solely by the employee. Here again, the issue is whether to require after-tax premium payment using deductions or allow pre-tax payment through credits.

Dependent life falls under Section 6(1)(a) of the Income Tax Act and the $25,000 income tax exclusion for employee life insurance does not apply. Therefore the value of all employer-provided dependent life (which would include coverage paid for with flexible credits) is taxable to employees. Since the cost of dependent life is relatively inexpensive and there are no major tax advantages to using flexible credits to purchase dependent life benefits, many employers simply require employees to pay the contributions in after-tax payroll deduction dollars.

(4) Option Pricing/Credit Allocation

The primary design issue facing employers in the area of pricing group life options is whether to charge a flat rate to all employees or graduated rates based on age and other risk factors. Although prior practice will have some bearing on the decision, other design objectives may make it appropriate to consider a change.

For employee life, risk-graded rates (reflecting age and possible gender and/or smoker status) are much more consistent with actual cost than flat rates for all employees, considering the relationship between the factors and the probability of a claim. Moreover, employers run the risk of adverse selection under a flat-rate scheme, since a flat rate typically is less expensive for older, male smokers (which encourages plan participation), and more expensive for younger, female non-smokers (which provides an incentive to seek coverage elsewhere).

In situations where age-graded rates represent a departure from prior practice, employers need to be sensitive to what might be perceived as a "take-away" by some employees. In these cases, employers may want to consider offering the lowest level of coverage (such as one times pay) to all employees at a flat rate, and price higher coverage options on a graded basis. This dual price structure adds an element of complexity from both a communication and an administration perspective, but may be appropriate in some situations.

Credit allocation for a graded pricing structure is another design issue when credits are based on a cutback from prior coverage levels. Employers who provide all employees the same percent-of-pay credit allocation, in essence, make lower-cost employees (who pay less for coverage) winners, and higher-cost employees (who pay more) losers. Another alternative is to age-grade the credit allocation structure so it correlates directly with the pricing structure. This approach may raise a question about equity (since older employees receive more credits than younger employees), but it does eliminate the concern over winners and losers. Some employers partially address the equity issue by narrowing the spread—making age differences in the credit allocation less extreme than age differences in the prices. Theoretically, employers could grade the credits to reflect gender and smoker status. However, few, if any, employers would want to allocate more credits to smokers and males than to non-smokers and females. (See Chapter Twelve for a complete discussion of the relevant human rights issues involved.)

In general, graded rates based on the dependent's age, gender and smoker status are impractical for smaller amounts of dependent life—especially covering children. Some employers, however, grade the rates for spouse coverage based on the spouse's or employee's age and if appropriate, the spouse's gender and smoker status. This is most common when substantial amounts of coverage are available.

(5) Enrollment/Reenrollment Restrictions

Most employers attempt to limit the potential for adverse selection in life insurance by implementing enrollment and/or reenrollment restrictions. About two-thirds of employers (65 percent) place restrictions on first-year elections, if employees elect higher than previous levels of coverage. For subsequent enrollments, most employers (92 percent) place some restrictions on an employee's ability to elect more coverage—21 percent of employers allow the employee to increase one level of coverage with no evidence, while 71 percent require proof of insurability for any increase. (See also Chapter Fifteen on Insurance Considerations.)

§ 6.3 DISABILITY BENEFITS

Disability income plans protect employees against the loss of income due to illness or injury. Disability benefits—particularly short-term disability—are not as commonly included under flexible programs as many other group benefits (such as medical, dental, and life insurance). About three-quarters of flexible plans offer choices in disability to expand the scope of choices offered, to provide benefits on a more tax-efficient basis, to offer cost-of-living protection or to fill in any gaps in other employer-provided coverages.

(a) TYPES OF DISABILITY COVERAGE

Both short- and long-term disability income benefits may be offered under flexible programs.

(1)   Short-Term Disability

Short-term disability (STD) options are designed to replace a portion of a sick or injured employee's income after expiration of a company's underlying sick leave or salary continuation benefits (such as 30 or 60 days), but before commencement of long-term disability benefits (usually five or six months). Many sick leave or salary continuation plans provide full or partial pay replacement for an extended period of time, often related to the employee's length of service. For shorter-service employees, however, a gap in coverage may exist.

Options in the short-term disability area often are intended to allow employees to fill in the gap, usually on an employee-pay-all basis. Benefit amounts typically match the levels of pay replacement offered under options in the long-term disability area.

(2)   Long-Term Disability

Long-term disability (LTD) plans provide income to employees unable to work for an extended period of time, due to illness or injury. LTD benefits typically commence after a 17-week or 6-month waiting period, and continue until retirement age or until the employee recovers. LTD benefits are designed to replace a portion of an employee's income—typically 50 to 70 percent generally integrated with benefits from other sources (such as the Canada/Quebec Pension Plan and Worker's Compensation).

(b)   DESIGN CONSIDERATIONS

As with other benefit areas, offering disability choices in a flexible program requires consideration of a variety of factors based on employer objectives and employee needs.

(1)   Areas of Choice

A fundamental decision in the design of a flexible program is whether to include choices in disability.

Short-term disability represents an emerging coverage area under flexible programs. Very few flexible programs offer STD choices. Typically, the chief design consideration on whether to include short-term disability choices under the flexible program relates to the employer's existing sick leave or salary continuation practices. If the employer already provides full or partial pay replacement to employees for the entire LTD waiting period, the need for STD choices may be absent. However, if salary continuation or sick leave benefits are service-related or dependent upon an employee's employment classification (such as hourly, salaried, and management), STD choices may represent an appropriate choice area under a flexible program.

Long-term disability benefit choices are offered in three-quarters (74 percent) of flexible programs. For employers with previously contributory coverage (which employees could decline to take), inclusion of LTD under a flexible program represents an extension of current practice. For other employers with non-contributory coverage, inclusion of LTD under the flexible program may provide employees an opportunity to upgrade existing benefits on an elective (versus company-paid) basis. As an alternative, they may elect lower coverage or none at all and use the savings for other choices.

(2) Structure of Options

Following are key issues employers need to address in determining the structure of options in the area of disability.

(i) High Option.   Generally 70 percent pay replacement is the highest LTD benefit option made available. Replacement of more than 70 percent of pay may create insufficient incentive for an employee to seek rehabilitation and return to work. If the LTD plan is employee-paid, the high option may be less than 70 percent, because the payout is non-taxable. For STD, a high option of between 70 and 100 percent is usually provided.

Underwriting restrictions may dictate a maximum on monthly benefits payable—which may cap the benefit received by employees at higher pay levels.

(ii) Low Option.   An employee's choice in STD benefits often is simply whether to purchase coverage to fill any gap between the end of sick leave or salary continuation and the beginning of LTD coverage. Thus, the low-end option is, in essence, no coverage.

Among flexible programs offering LTD choices, only a few have no coverage as the low-end option. An employer's decision about whether to allow employees to waive LTD coverage is often influenced by various factors. One is that Canada/Quebec Pension Plan disability benefits provide, in a sense, a core level of protection. So employees waiving coverage have available at least one alternate source of protection if a disability is serious enough to satisfy C/QPP criteria. Another factor is an employer's sense of responsibility to provide all employees with some level of additional protection. In addition, concern over adverse selection (i.e., the likelihood that high-risk employees will be more inclined to elect coverage) also may cause an employer to require at least a minimum level of disability coverage.

Generally, 50 to 60 percent of pay replacement is the minimum benefit option offered. Less than 50 percent of pay replacement typically is viewed as too low to allow the employee to maintain an adequate standard of living. Moreover, at lower levels of pay replacement, a large proportion of the benefit typically would be eliminated through integration with government benefits, particularly at lower income levels. (This would be of particular concern where employees had been contributing for coverage and then received little benefit from the LTD plan due to integration with C/QPP or other plans.)

(iii)   Number of Options.   Unlike many other benefit areas included in a flexible program, most employers with disability options limit the number of choices, offering an average of one option in short-term disability and three options in long-term disability.

The typical objective of disability benefits is to allow an employee to maintain an adequate standard of living during a period of disability. The range of pay replacement generally considered appropriate for this purpose is relatively narrow.

For long-term disability, 50 to 70 percent pay replacement is usually considered adequate. Although employers could offer multiple options within that range, the difference in cost (and benefit dollars) is fairly small. Some employers provide two clear-cut choices in LTD—options of one-half and two-thirds pay replacement. Other employers might provide a non-contributory core benefit with a relatively modest dollar maximum (such as $1,500 per month) or a low limit on covered pay (such as $2,000 per month) and allow employees who are affected by these limits to select higher options (at their cost).

Although LTD plans only provide two or three levels of benefit, an increasing proportion of plans double the number of choices by allowing the employee to purchase an inflation-protected LTD benefit with a higher premium. An employee would, therefore, have two choices to make: first what initial level of benefit is appropriate (say, 50, 60, or 70 percent); and second, whether or not the benefit should be indexed. Few, if any, plans have full inflation protection. Instead, they protect a percentage of the full increase in the Consumer Price Index (60 or 75 percent is typical) and limit the annual increase to five percent. The cost-of-living increases normally occur once a year, starting 12 months after the first LTD payment. Some plans delay the COLA adjustments until two or five years after LTD payments begin to limit costs.

Where STD is included in a flexible program, an employee's choices often parallel the pay replacement amounts available under the LTD plan. On the other hand, the choice may be to extend the duration of benefits to fill any gap between STD and LTD. Choices of this nature are especially important to short-service employees who may not have accrued enough days to cover the LTD waiting period.

(3) Sources of Funds

Funding approaches for disability benefits vary. For short-term disability, most employers continue to provide salary continuation to currently eligible employees on a fully company-paid basis. However, inside the flexible program, the options for employees with a gap in coverage usually are provided on an employee-pay-all basis.

For long-term disability, funding approaches differ. Basically, the approaches available include continuing to provide fully company-paid coverage, providing a core level of coverage and allowing employees to purchase higher coverage levels, or requiring employees to bear the full cost of coverage. Many employers choose to fund LTD under the flexible program at the same level, as was the case under the prior program.

A decision on whether to use flexible credits or payroll deductions to purchase options under the program is often complicated. Under the Income Tax Act, benefits paid for by payroll deductions on an after-tax basis are non-taxable to an employee who becomes disabled. Benefits attributable to flexible credits are treated as employer-provided and, therefore, are taxable when paid. Some employers require the use of credits for premium payment on the grounds that credits represent a more cost-efficient means of paying for the coverage, since the probability of disability occurring is relatively low and, therefore, the tax consequences of receiving disability benefits will affect relatively few employees. Moreover, in most cases, the marginal tax rate for employees receiving disability benefits is considerably lower than for active employees making contributions. This is due to the reduction in income from full salary to partial pay replacement.

Other employers take the opposite view. They believe their employees are better served by paying the premium with after-tax payroll deductions. In these cases, the benefit is received tax-free by disabled employees.

A third group of employers believes there is no right or wrong answer to the credit versus payroll deduction debate. So, they allow the employee to decide how to pay the premium and, therefore, whether or not the benefit would be taxable. Some experts have argued that this complicates LTD choices so much that most employees will not understand the program—employees have two or even three choices to make (level of benefit, how to purchase it and possibly whether or not to buy inflation protection). Despite the skeptics, a number of flexible plans do allow employees the choice to pay premiums with credits or payroll deductions. And these plans have been very successful, despite the extra administration and communication required. Cominco implemented the first such plan. Prior to introducing flexible benefits in 1984, LTD was company-paid. Now, more than 50 percent of employees elect the payroll deduction option and direct their former company LTD subsidy elsewhere.

A plan offering the choice between payroll deductions and credits must carefully structure the insurance arrangements. Separate contracts and policies must be established and no company contribution can directly or indirectly go to the employee-paid plan, or else Revenue Canada would treat the benefit as taxable. Revenue Canada has given written confirmation, however, that where the contracts are separate, employees can be given the choice as to how to pay for the benefit.

(4)   Option Pricing/Credit Allocation

Under a flexible approach, employers must decide how to price options and allocate credits. Typically, the credit allocation and price tags are expressed as a percentage of pay (such as one-half of one percent of pay), since the benefits are based on pay. Employers who fund one or all disability option(s), usually attach a $0 price tag to the option(s) or provide flexible credits equal to the cost of the coverage. Option price tags usually represent the expected true cost of disability coverage based on insurance carrier rates. Since the range of coverage is limited to 50 to 70 percent pay replacement, the difference in the cost of various options is usually modest. Although not a common practice, some employers use age-graded prices, since the probability of a long-term disability varies substantially by age.

The cost of adding inflation protection to an LTD benefit is also relatively modest. A 5 percent cost-of-living feature might increase LTD premiums by 25 percent.

Seven

Flexible Expense Accounts

§ 7.1 INTRODUCTION

The flexible expense account concept provides considerable versatility to both employer and employee. Through a flexible expense account, a special pool of funds is created from which the employee draws to pay certain expenses—often on a tax-favoured basis. Unlike indemnity plans, in which the employee is purchasing protection in case an event occurs, a flexible expense account exists to be used.

A flexible expense account most commonly serves as a means of paying for health-related expenses. If the account is structured properly, these payments are not taxable to the recipient. Accounts can also provide for payment of other benefit expenses that are either taxable or, if they are eligible expenses under the Income Tax Act, non-taxable. Reimbursement of these other expenses can be attractive even if the benefits are treated as taxable to employees. Where the employer wishes to reimburse both health and non-health expenses, separate accounts are typically set up to cover the health-related expenses (*health care expense account*) and the non-health-related expenses.

The legal framework or set of rules within which a flexible benefit program must operate is discussed in Chapter Eleven. The main sources of reference are the Interpretation Bulletins on the meaning of private health services plans, employee fringe benefits, and employee counselling.

The rules governing health accounts are particularly important. To qualify for tax-favoured treatment, a health care expense account needs to be structured as a *private health services plan*. Generally, coverage under the plan must be for health care expenses, which would otherwise have been deductible under the Income Tax Act without reference to the 3 percent-of-net-income threshold specified in the Act. It is not necessary for a trust to be established. Once these and other requirements discussed later in this chapter are met, payment of eligible expenses is deductible by the employer and is not taxable to the employee.

There are several reasons why flexible expense accounts are attractive to employers and employees. For some employers, expense accounts are a simple way of testing the appeal of flexible benefits, without committing to a broad-based, full-choice program. For others, a flexible expense account provides a convenient vehicle to offer new benefits to employees, such as reimbursement of vision, dental, or other health-related expenses. Yet, the employer is neither locked in to a potentially expensive coverage area, nor committed to covering a benefit that might appeal to only a small segment of the employee population. Such a vehicle may be attractive in bargaining situations. For example, the employer and union may negotiate that part of the settlement be allocated to a flexible expense account to provide employees with more benefit flexibility on a tax-favoured basis. Finally, a health care expense account provides a way to soften the impact of higher employee cost-sharing through deductibles and co-payment amounts.

§ 7.2 PLAN STRUCTURE

A flexible expense account is an individual employee account funded by employer contributions that provides reimbursement of certain eligible benefit expenses—medical or other (usually non-taxable) benefits. The employer decides whether to offer a health account, a non-health account, or both. Employees decide whether to participate and how many credits to allocate to each account. When an expense is incurred, the employee submits a request for reimbursement to the employer or administrator who verifies the expense is eligible, checks there are sufficient funds in the account, and then issues payment from the account.

Payments from the health care expense account represent non-taxable income to the employee, just as though he or she had incurred a claim through a traditional medical or dental plan. The tax status of payments from the non-health account will depend on the type of expense. For example, payment of legal expenses will be taxable while payment for a subsidized mortgage may be tax-free.

A major consideration with flexible expense accounts is that expenses must be anticipated carefully or the employee will have an unused account balance at year-end. There are three ways of handling the year-end balances, according to Revenue Canada:

- The plan could specify that excess amounts are forfeited. (Until recently, Revenue Canada required health care accounts to have this feature, commonly known as *use-it-or-lose-it.*)
- The plan could *roll over* this amount to the following year's account, with no tax consequences to the employee. On termination, unused balances are forfeited.
- The balance could be paid in cash (taxable) to the employee at the end of the year. (Revenue Canada has only recently indicated that this option is acceptable.)

Health care expense accounts must incorporate one of these three approaches. It is possible to offer the employee the choice between the rollover and cash-out alternatives. However, in this case, each employee must elect which approach to use *before the beginning* of the plan year.

Flexible expense accounts represent one of the most versatile elements within a flexible benefit program. Companies offering a choice-making program can include one or more types of expense accounts as another benefit option. But flexible expense accounts also can be adopted on a stand-alone basis in the absence of any other choices within an employer's benefit program.

The popularity of flexible expense accounts can be attributed to several motivations. The most common are:

- To expand the types of benefits offered to employees with little or no additional employer cost (for example, orthodontia and vision care)
- To encourage employees to self-insure predictable or budgetable expenses that are subject to adverse selection (for example, vision care and basic dental care)
- To deliver compensation tax-effectively.

(a) SOURCES OF FUNDS

Flexible expense accounts must be employer-funded—this is typically accomplished by asking employees to indicate how many flexible credits to allocate to the plan. (Employees may not supplement the flexible credit pool with payroll deductions, because these are after-tax dollars.) Flexible expense accounts within full choice-making programs are apt to be funded from two main sources—direct employer contributions and dollars freed up from trade-offs in other benefit areas. In contrast, stand-alone expense accounts are funded by direct employer contributions only.

There are many possible sources of company contributions to a flexible expense account. If accounts are being offered as a new benefit in addition to the existing program, an employer may have the resources to channel new money into the accounts. If the flexible accounts are part of a full-choice flexible benefit program, the plan design usually dictates how many credits each employee will be able to spend for the whole program. By choosing lower cost options where available, flexible credits are freed up and may be directed to the expense accounts. The employer need not make a specific allocation of funds to the account; each employee is expected to be able to determine the mix of benefits and expense account amounts that best fits his or her particular needs.

Some employers have introduced a flexible expense account as a way to ease the blow of reduced medical benefits. Part of the employer's savings from adopting a less valuable plan might be contributed to employee accounts.

How the employer contribution is communicated to employees is an important consideration in implementing an account. If there is no guarantee that employer contributions will continue at the same level, or if the first contribution is "seed money" not to be repeated in future years, this should be made clear in the initial communication to employees. If the contribution is tied to savings in other parts of the benefit program, employees may expect information on how well costs have been controlled.

Employer contributions and benefit trade-off dollars may be deposited uniformly throughout the year or in blocks (for example, at the end of each quarter) to reduce the record-keeping effort.

(b)　TYPES OF ACCOUNTS

Expense account funds may be used to pay eligible expenses in several benefit areas. Typically, one account would be established for health care expenses and another account for other benefits. The purpose of a separate account for health care expenses would be to ensure that it is considered a private health services plan by Revenue Canada. A brief summary of the characteristics of each type of flexible expense account follows.

(1) Health Care Expense Account

Under a health care expense account, employees can be reimbursed for health-related expenses not covered by provincial health insurance or the employer's other health plans. In general, any health-related expense that could be used to meet requirements for deductibility on an employee's income tax return is eligible for reimbursement. For example, deductible and co-payment amounts may be reimbursed for both medical and dental benefits, along with the cost of procedures not covered by the underlying medical and dental plans (cosmetic surgery, orthodontia, and so forth). Benefits exceeding the maximum limits under the underlying plans can also be reimbursed.

Eligible expenses include:

- Medical practitioners' fees—acupuncturists, chiropractors, speech therapists, and so forth
- Dental expenses
- Health care facilities—nursing homes, institutions, and so on
- Medical devices and supplies—artificial limbs, walkers, hearing aids, and so forth
- Other expenses such as ambulances and seeing-eye dogs.

An extensive list of eligible expenses is contained in § 7.7.

(2) Other Expense Accounts

A wide range of "other benefit" expenses could be considered for reimbursement in a separate account, including:

- Group home/auto insurance
- Group mortgage
- Group legal
- Financial counselling
- Fitness club
- Sabbatical leave
- Subsidized parking
- Registered education savings plan.

This type of account might also be considered for the perquisites portion of executive compensation, in which case eligible expenses might include:

- First-class air travel
- Club memberships
- Spousal travel, if business-related.

The range of benefits that can be considered under the "other benefits" category is virtually unlimited. If the benefit is non-taxable, it is particularly attractive for including in an account. But even if the benefit is taxable to the employee, it may still be attractive, since an employer-paid taxable benefit is less costly to the employee than if the employee pays directly with after-tax dollars.

If the taxation treatment of a benefit area under consideration is uncertain, the employer may wish to obtain an unbinding opinion or a binding ruling from Revenue Canada before proceeding with the program. When both taxable and non-taxable benefits are included in the plan, it may be appropriate to set up two sub-accounts—one to cover non-taxable payments and the other to reimburse taxable expenses. If this is not done, Revenue Canada could rule that the doctrine of constructive receipt applies, in which case all payments would be taxable.

7.3 REQUIREMENTS FOR FLEXIBLE EXPENSE ACCOUNTS

The mechanics of the election/enrollment process and the reimbursement of expenses are fairly straightforward.

Originally, Revenue Canada indicated that health care expense accounts were acceptable, as long as there was an element of risk to the operation of the accounts. Employees did not have the opportunity to recoup unused funds during the year. Instead, funds held in health care expense accounts were subject to a risk of loss, just as premiums paid for insurance coverage might never be recovered if the insured risk never occurs. So, Revenue Canada's initial view on health care expense accounts was that any unused balance should be forfeited by the employee at year-end.

More recently, these requirements have been softened—now, unused funds may be rolled over to the next year's account or paid out in cash at the end of the year. Employee choice between these alternatives would be acceptable as long as the employee elected which option he or she preferred before the beginning of the year. To date, no plan has been structured to allow a cash-out option. Although Revenue Canada has not ruled on non-health care expense accounts, it is likely similar requirements would be imposed if the benefit were non-taxable.

Revenue Canada has imposed three major restrictions on health care expense accounts to incorporate the insurance risk idea and to prevent abuses of the accounts. First, employees may designate how much money will be contributed to their accounts only once a year. Second, the plan must have a roll over or cash-out feature to dispose of any unused account balance at the end of the year. Third, plans must incorporate the use-it-or-lose-it feature for terminating employees.

(a) ANNUAL ELECTIONS

Employees can generally predict some expenses for the coming year. For example, the amount they will need for basic dental care or the price of a new pair of eyeglasses can be determined quite easily. Certain other expenses, though, may be difficult to foresee when employees make their annual elections.

Yet, effective communication and planning tools, to help employees predict expenses in a coming year, can make the annual election requirement less onerous than it appears at first glance. In fact, for some employers, the annual election requirement has been an administrative boost, since practically all account changes are now legally restricted to once a year.

After an employee designates funds to any of the accounts, the decision is irrevocable—unless there is a change in the employee's family status. This could be a marriage or divorce, the birth or death of a family member, or the spouse's loss of employment.

(b) ROLL OVER OR CASH OUT

The term *roll over* describes the element of insurance risk imposed on expense accounts by Revenue Canada. It reflects the requirement that funds allocated to a health care expense account must be used to reimburse expenses incurred during the year, or the funds will be rolled over to the next year's account. As mentioned earlier, Revenue Canada has indicated it would accept the pay out of unused balances in taxable cash as an alternate to the roll-over requirement. This would be acceptable as long as the employee chose the cash-out option instead of the roll-over option before the beginning of the plan year.

(c) USE IT OR LOSE IT

As mentioned earlier, an element of risk must be incorporated into a health care expense account. Revenue Canada, therefore, requires that when an employee terminates, any remaining money in the health care expense account must be forfeited. However, according to Revenue Canada, any funds attributable to the current year may be cashed out, if the cash option is in place.

§ 7.4 MECHANICS

Employees decide whether to deposit funds in each type of flexible expense account prior to the beginning of a plan year. These funds may arise from any of the sources identified earlier. The category of benefit for which the funds will be used must be identified at the start of the year. Typically, a *health care expense account* would be established as a minimum. An *other benefits expense account* might also be established—it might be subdivided into a taxable and non-taxable benefits account. Funds may not be transferred from one type of account to another during the plan year.

(a) CREATION OF ACCOUNTS

With the elections in place, the employer creates individual book accounts for each flexible expense account in which the employee has chosen to participate. No formal segregation of assets takes place, and no monies are deposited in trust. Instead, the accounts are carried on the books of the employer, who tracks both debits (reimbursements) and credits (accruals).

(b) PAYMENT OF EXPENSES

When an employee incurs an eligible expense under one of the expense accounts, he or she completes a reimbursement claim form and submits it along with a copy of the bill or proof of payment (for example, a cancelled cheque) to the plan administrator for reimbursement. The administrator, after reviewing the claim, reimburses the employee with a cheque for the amount of the claim. The payment process is illustrated in Figure 7.1.

Care should be taken in allocating credits. If the credits are allocated in full at the beginning of the plan year, the employer is at financial risk if an employee is reimbursed in full and then terminates. For this reason, many accounts are credited on a monthly basis. In these cases, reimbursements are only made up to the amount credited in the account and any excess claim is carried forward and reimbursed from future additional credits to the account.

Figure 7.1
Health Care Expense Account Claims

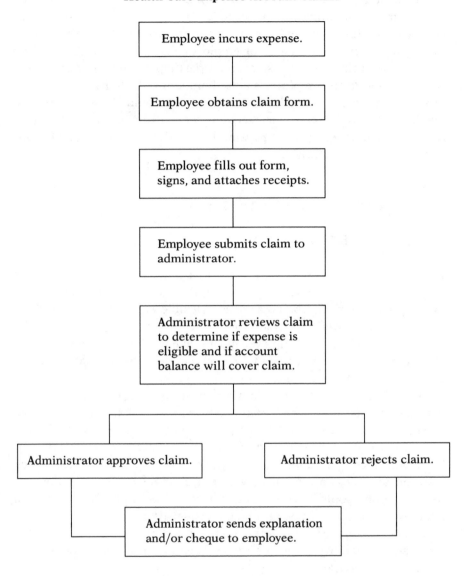

(c)   END OF YEAR

After the end of the year, employers typically allow employees a few months to submit claims incurred during the year. Once this process is completed, all unused deposits or accruals for active employees are either forfeited (if the plan is designed this way), rolled over (if elected in advance) to the next year, or paid out to the employee (as taxable cash). Any unused deposits or accruals for terminated employees are forfeited and revert to the employer. (In practice, most employees take care to estimate expenses with enough precision to avoid forfeiture.) Disposition of forfeitures is a matter of employer discretion. Funds could be reallocated to flexible expense account participants on a per capita basis (unrelated to the employee's actual amount of forfeiture).

If the plan design includes forfeitures, they could be used to reduce employer benefit costs in a subsequent year. A further alternative (unrelated to the benefit program) would be to donate the forfeited funds to a charitable organization.

§ 7.5 DESIGN CONSIDERATIONS

(a) TYPE OF APPROACH

Flexible expense accounts may serve as the cornerstone of a flexible benefit program or exist as another option within a broader choice-making arrangement. The appropriate flexible expense design will depend on an organization's objectives.

The first decision the employer must make is whether or not to introduce a flexible expense account. The second decision is what type(s) of account(s) should be included.

An important consideration in whether or not to introduce an account is the amount of funds which could be directed to the account. If an employee could allocate only $100 or $200 at most, it may not be worth the administrative and communication effort to install an account. However, if the employee could direct $500, say, from other benefit areas, selling vacation and, possibly, from new employer money, then a flexible expense account would be an attractive, viable benefit plan. Also, internal administrative capabilities may be a consideration in whether or not to include an expense account, although this is a diminishing issue with the increased availability of outside record-keeping firms and computerized administrative packages.

Virtually all employers offering an expense account have a health care expense account—these accounts are simple to understand, tax-effective, and complement the other health care plans sponsored by the employer. The growth of health care expense accounts has been dramatic; over one-third (37 percent) of employers with flexible programs now include an account in their program. Fewer employers provide an "other expense account." The "other benefits" provided through such an account can usually be offered as stand-alone options within a flexible benefit plan.

However, an important advantage of including another expense account is that the employee does not need to decide how to spend the funds in the account before the plan year. An account can also be a simple, effective way of communicating these benefit options.

(b)   IMPACT ON OTHER BENEFIT CHOICES

The tax-effective advantage of paying for deductibles, co-payment amounts, and other non-reimbursed expenses on a pre-tax basis exists only through a health care expense account. In a sound choice-making program, those employees who expect to have few expenses in a particular coverage area may be encouraged to choose a lower-cost option or opt out of a benefit entirely, if they know the expenses they do incur can be reimbursed from their flexible expense account. For example, employees who anticipate minimal routine dental expenses may choose to opt out of a dental program entirely, using freed-up credits for another benefit package, while any dental expenses that do occur could be reimbursed through a health care expense account. Another example would be where an employee decides to elect a low-value (high-deductible) medical care plan, using freed-up credits to purchase additional long-term disability coverage, while expenses toward the high deductible can be reimbursed from the health care expense account.

(c)   FUNDING

A number of decisions must be made in determining how to fund flexible expense accounts. The employer must decide where the funds should come from (new money or dollars freed-up from benefit trade-offs), how much is available, whether any limits on accounts should be imposed, and how to handle any forfeitures.

(d)   LIMITS

Another plan design decision is whether there should be any limits on how much an employee can dedicate to the flexible expense account. A reason for placing a ceiling on contributions is to limit the risk of substantial individual forfeitures or roll overs. In practice, very few plans have such a limit.

(e) REIMBURSEMENT REQUIREMENTS

Another factor in flexible expense accounts is the incorporation of features that will facilitate administration. Generally, a limit on how often reimbursement may be received (for instance, once per month) and a minimum total of expenses that should be submitted (say, $25 or $50) will ease the task of the plan administrator.

(f) DISPOSITION OF FUNDS AT YEAR-END

The plan design must include a method of disposing of left-over funds in an employee's account at year-end. Of the three approaches described earlier (forfeiture, roll-over, cash-out), the easiest to administer is the forfeiture. If the forfeited funds revert to the employer, it is also the most cost-effective. However, employees would prefer that the excess funds are either rolled over or cashed out. Both approaches are easy to communicate and administer. The most attractive design, from the employees' perspective, is to offer a choice between roll-over and cash-out. However, the extra administrative and communication requirements may make this structure unacceptable to the employer unless the potential amount of left-over funds is significant.

§ 7.6 AN EXAMPLE

Under an actual case example, employees are provided with flexible credits of $120. After completing two full years of service, an additional $120 is provided for each year of service, up to 10 years. An employee with 10 or more years of service, therefore, receives flexible credits of $1,320. The company-paid credits may be supplemented by credits generated from other benefits. For example, employees can direct the employer's LTD premium to the account and pay for LTD themselves with after-tax dollars. Prior to the beginning of the year, the employee elects how many credits should be directed to the account. Any "left-over" credits are either paid in cash at year-end or transferred to the firm's profit-sharing plan, depending on the employee's prior election.

The plan does not pay the employee's bills for health care directly. Instead, it reimburses expenses incurred by the employee (and/or dependents), that are not reimbursed under any other employer-sponsored plan.

Health care expenses that may be reimbursed under the plan include:

- Amounts not paid by the basic medical plan, such as the deductible and coinsurance
- Deductibles and coinsurance for other health, dental, or vision plans under which the employee or dependents are covered
- Virtually all dental expenses (if the employer does not have a traditional dental plan)
- Virtually all vision expenses
- Hearing expenses
- Psychiatric or psychological counselling
- Transportation expenses to receive medical care
- Miscellaneous expenses including birth control pills, cosmetic surgery, stop-smoking, or weight-loss programs prescribed by a physician.

The plan operates on a calendar-year basis. Prior to each calendar year, employees receive a statement showing the number of flexible credits available. During the year, employees may submit a claim once a month for reimbursement if the claim exceeds $25 and if there is a balance remaining in the health care expense account.

Any unused credits at the end of a year are carried forward to next year's account.

To illustrate how the plan operates, consider how the account activity for Pat, a four-year employee, might change during the year. Based on the company's credit formula, Pat received $600 worth of credits on January 1.

Date	Claim	Remaining Balance
January 1	—	$600
March 10	$110 (dental check-up)	490
June 26	$250 (glasses)	240
August 8	$100 (medical deductible)	140
November 15	$115 (dental check-up)	25
December 31	—	25 (roll over to next year)

§ 7.7   ELIGIBLE EXPENSES FOR HEALTH CARE EXPENSE ACCOUNTS

The usefulness of a health care expense account is very broad. The eligible expenses are those that would be tax-deductible and are listed in the Income Tax Act. Taxpayers can claim deductions of eligible expenses for tax purposes for themselves, their spouses, or any dependents for whom they may be claiming a tax deduction that year.

In addition to deductibles and coinsurance amounts, the expenses covered by the account could include the following items, as long as no other provincial health insurance or private health care plan covers them:

(a)   PRACTITIONERS

- Acupuncturists
- Chiropodists (podiatrists)
- Chiropractors
- Christian Science practitioners
- Naturopaths
- Nurses
- Occupational therapists
- Optometrists
- Osteopaths
- Physiotherapists
- Practical nurses
- Psychoanalysts
- Psychologists
- Speech therapists
- Therapeutists.

(b)   DENTAL EXPENSES

- Preventive, diagnostic, restorative, orthodontic, and therapeutic care.

(c)   FACILITIES

- Alcoholism or drug addiction treatment centres, including meals and lodging
- Care in a nursing home
- Care in a self-contained domestic establishment (e.g., in own home)
- Care of a person who has been certified to be mentally incompetent
- Care in a special school, institution or other place for a mentally or physically handicapped individual
- Care in an institution
- Care of a blind person

- Full-time attendants or care in a nursing home (for confinement to a bed or wheelchair)
- Payments to a licensed private hospital
- Semi-private, preferred, or private charges in a hospital.

(d) DEVICES AND SUPPLIES

- Artificial eye
- Artificial limbs
- Crutches
- Device or equipment, including a replacement part, designed exclusively for use by an individual who is suffering from a chronic respiratory ailment to assist breathing, but not including an air conditioner, humidifier, dehumidifier, or air cleaner
- Device or equipment designed to pace or monitor the heart of an individual who suffers from heart disease
- Device designed to assist a crippled individual in walking
- Device designed exclusively to enable an individual with a mobility impairment to operate a vehicle
- Device or equipment, including a synthetic speech system, Braille printer and large print-on-screen device, designed exclusively to be used by a blind individual in the operation of a computer
- Device to decode special television signals to permit the vocal portion of the signal to be visually displayed
- Device designed to be attached to infants diagnosed as being prone to sudden infant death syndrome in order to sound an alarm if the infant ceases to breathe
- Device designed to enable diabetics to measure blood sugar levels
- Drugs, medications or other preparations or substances prescribed by a medical practitioner or dentist
- Electronic speech synthesizer that enables a mute individual to communicate by use of a portable keyboard
- External breast prosthesis that is required because of a mastectomy
- Hearing aids
- Hospital bed, including attachments to it that may have been included in a prescription
- Ileostomy or colostomy pads

- Insulin
- Iron lung
- Kidney machines
- Laryngeal speaking aids
- Limb braces
- Mechanical device or equipment designed to be used to assist an individual to enter or leave a bathtub or shower, or to get on or off a toilet
- Needle or syringe
- Optical scanner or similar device designed to be used by blind individuals to enable them to read print
- Orthopedic shoe or boot, or an insert for a shoe or boot, made to order for an individual in accordance with a prescription to overcome a physical disability of the individual
- Oxygen tent or equipment
- Power-operated lift designed exclusively for use by disabled individuals to allow them access to different levels of a building or assist them to gain access to a vehicle, or to place wheelchairs in or on a vehicle
- Spinal braces
- Teletypewriter or similar device, including a telephone ringing indicator, that enables a deaf or mute individual to receive telephone calls
- Walkers
- Wheelchairs
- Wig made to order for an individual who has suffered abnormal hair loss owing to disease, medical treatment, or accident.

(e)   OTHER

- Ambulance fees for transportation
- Cosmetic surgery
- Cost of arranging and having a bone marrow or organ transplant
- Costs of medical services and supplies out of the province of residence
- Electrolysis or hair removal performed by a licensed technician
- Hearing expenses, including hearing aids and hearing ear dogs
- Laboratory, radiological, or other diagnostic procedures or services
- Modifications to a home for persons confined to a wheelchair
- Preventive diagnostic, laboratory, and radiological procedures

- Surgical hair transplant performed by a physician
- Transportation expenses to receive medical care:

  —Cost of using public transportation or private vehicle if not available, for distances of 40 kilometres or greater.

  —Cost of meals and accommodation if travel distance is at least 80 kilometres.

  —Reasonable transportation, meals and accommodation for one accompanying person, if doctor certifies that a person is not capable of travelling alone.

- Vision expenses including eyeglasses, contact lenses, and seeing-eye dogs

- Weight-loss or stop-smoking program prescribed by a doctor for a specific ailment.

Eight

Time Off with Pay

§ 8.1 INTRODUCTION

Benefit programs include several different variations of time off with pay from vacation through holidays and sick leave to a variety of leaves of absence (such as jury duty and maternity leave). Some of these types of time off, such as vacation, tend to be taken largely at the employee's election. Most holidays are fixed on particular dates, although employers frequently allow a few holidays to float, permitting the employee discretion over when to take the day(s). Sick leave is intended to be used only when the employee is legitimately ill. Leaves of absence, on the other hand, although technically a type of time off, usually are excluded from a flexible program, largely because leaves tend to last an extended period of time and typically require management approval.

An emerging development in the area of time off with pay is the combining of all the different types of paid time off (excluding leaves) into a single umbrella category, personal days or personal time. The employee receives a specified allotment of days and determines how to use the time—whether for vacation and sometimes holidays or for illness. The umbrella category also helps minimize the burden to employers of having to police the separate types of time off. The employee recognizes that excessive sick days erode the time available for vacation and vice versa.

§ 8.2 OBJECTIVES FOR CHOICE MAKING IN TIME OFF

Time off with pay is becoming an increasingly popular option within flexible programs. Today almost three in five (59 percent) of flexible

145

programs offer vacation buying, vacation selling, or both. Among these companies, 25 percent permit both buying and selling, while 19 percent permit buying only and 56 percent permit only the selling of vacation days.

One of the chief reasons employers include time off in a flexible program is that the trading of vacation time is popular with employees. In fact, time off typically ranks at (or near) the top of the list of benefit changes employees would like to see incorporated under a flexible approach.

For example, buying usually holds considerable appeal for younger employees with shorter service, since vacation schedules usually relate to length of employment. Also, shorter-service employees are more likely to be part of a dual-income household where flexibility in matching vacation schedules is likely to be important. (For example, the employee might be eligible for two weeks, while the spouse may receive three to four weeks elsewhere). These employees tend to be interested in trading other benefits (for example, supplemental medical when coverage is available through the spouse's employer) for additional time off. Buying of vacation time also may appeal to some longer service employees who have sufficient vacation for normal needs, but periodically might be interested in an extended vacation.

The opportunity to sell time off tends to appeal to older, longer-service employees, and often higher-paid employees. Frequently, these employees currently may be using only a portion of their scheduled vacation time and may be forfeiting the rest in organizations without carry-over provisions. Also, these employees tend to place greater priority on security coverages and may want to use the dollars freed from vacation time to pay for coverages in other areas, particularly in organizations implementing age-related premiums (for example, for life insurance).

Among organizations that permit both buying and selling, the buyers tend to be younger, shorter-service, and lower-paid employees. However, the sellers tend to be somewhat higher-paid employees, most likely those with sufficient seniority to have extra unused days. The net effect of buying and selling between these two groups tends to come close to a wash from the standpoint of cost.

Beyond offering a popular option to employees, employers often have other reasons for including time off in a flexible program. Other objectives include:

- **Expansion of vacation schedules.** When competitive or other pressures cause an employer to consider extending vacation (or other time-off programs), a flexible approach can enable liberalization without commensurate cost to the employer. An organization may offer employees the option to buy more time without a blanket increase in vacation days for everyone. If an employer wants to pay a portion of the cost, an extra contribution for all employees can be added to the flexible credit pool.

- **Increase in flexible credits.** Vacation selling can be used to enrich the credit pool for a flexible program. Selling five days of vacation time (1/52 of a year) can add almost 2 percent of pay to the credit total. This may be an attractive way to allow employees to expand the credit formula on an optional basis for purchase of other benefits without a blanket increase in employer contributions.

- **Transition from a banking system.** Historically, many employers have allowed employees to bank unused vacation time for use at a later date. However, the potential for large, unfunded liabilities to accumulate on a company's books often makes vacation banking an unattractive system. To some extent, introduction of a flexible program, including the opportunity to buy or sell vacation days, may provide the motivation or rationale for cutting back or eliminating an existing banking system. As will be discussed later, the carrying forward of unused vacation time is considerably more difficult to accommodate under a choice-making program.

§ 8.3 TYPES OF TIME-OFF CHOICES

Conceptually, an employer could allow choice making in any time-off area. In practice, however, the buying and selling of time off is most common in the vacation area. Inclusion of holidays as a choice area usually is more prevalent in industries that operate each day of the year (such as hospitals and airlines). Sick leave is only rarely included under a flexible program, except to the extent an employer has consolidated (or intends to consolidate) the various types of time off into a personal leave or paid time-off umbrella. (See also Chapter Six on disability for discussion of short-term disability under flexible programs.) Other special-purpose types of time off (such as leaves of absence) almost always are left outside flexible program structures.

(a) VACATION

Vacation is the type of time off most frequently included in flexible programs. Typically, employers retain the pre-flexible vacation schedule and permit the buying of additional days beyond that point or the selling of days within the existing schedule. Key issues relating to designing a vacation option include:

- **Number of days.** Companies tend to limit the number of days that may be traded for several reasons. One reason is to limit the magnitude of the amount of soft-dollar expense from time off that can be converted into hard-dollar cost (i.e., converting unused days to flexible credits or cash, if the plan permits). Another reason is that limiting the number of days that can be bought or sold to a set number helps minimize potential scheduling problems, particularly in situations where the employee would need to be replaced during the vacation.

- **Units of time.** Conceivably, organizations could permit the buying or selling of vacation in any increment of time. In practice, most organizations use either days or weeks. Denominating time off in days—rather than a block of time, such as a week—tends to provide employees greater flexibility, especially with the fairly high price of purchasing a full week of vacation (usually about two percent of annual pay). On the other hand, blocks of time may be easier to track, particularly in organizations with non-standard work weeks (such as 10- or 12-hour shifts). Denominating time off in units of less than a day tends to be relatively rare.

- **Pricing of time.** The pricing of time off raises issues relating to economics versus perception. From an economic standpoint, a case could be made that the value of a day (or week) of time is higher than the actual daily (or weekly) rate for buying purposes and lower for selling purposes. That is, both the cost of employee benefits and the value of unused vacation time currently donated to the employer (that does not allow vacation banking) should be factored into the arithmetic. Only rarely, however, are employers able to calculate the true value of time off with such precision—or convince employees of the logic of such an approach. As a result, most flexible programs price time off at 100 percent of the daily or weekly rate of pay.

  Occasionally, a dollar maximum is placed on the price assigned to a day of vacation, especially for selling days, in order to limit the hard-dollar exposure from highly paid employees.

(b) HOLIDAYS

The inclusion of holidays in a choice-making program usually is based on the employer's business. Some organizations operate every day of the year (for example, hospitals), so the buying or selling of holidays can be treated much the same as vacation time. In fact, at these organizations, vacation and holiday time frequently are treated as like entities and continue as such under a choice-making program.

At most organizations, however, practical barriers prohibit the inclusion of holidays. If an organization is closed on designated holidays (for example, national or provincial holidays), allowing sale of the day makes little sense. Many organizations make available additional floating days that employees may take largely at their discretion (much like vacation). It is the floating, rather than fixed, holidays that become eligible for trade under the choice-making program.

Floating days also may work well as options in an organization that wants to provide time-off flexibility but is constrained by a vacation banking system. Floating days usually are not subject to banking in the same way as vacation days. Outside the flexible program, the employer might retain banking of vacation days, while inside the program, only the floating days are permissible as a choice area.

(c) PERSONAL DAYS

In general, few organizations include sick leave or initial illness days as a choice area within a flexible program. (Typically, sick leave policies provide full or partial salary continuation for a period of time, such as 30 days or a period related to the employee's length of service.) Companies tend to have more difficulty with the abuse of sick leave than almost any other benefit area. It is a difficult management problem to control, with major cost implications, when employees treat accrued sick time as though it were vacation. (See also Chapter Six on disability for discussion of options in short-term disability, which usually commences after expiration of an initial period of salary continuation.)

Instead, some organizations have opted to consolidate vacation, holidays (all or only the floating days) and sick leave into an umbrella of paid time off. The idea is to move away from the traditional concept of special-purpose types of time off and into an environment that delineates a total number of days with pay and permits employees to determine how to use those days—whether for vacation or illness. The total number of days off may remain the same, or the sick days may be reduced, but the

point is to create awareness that only a certain number of personal days
will be allotted each year. A flexible approach simply allows employees
to buy or sell days above or below their specified allotment.

§ 8.4   RESTRICTIONS ON TIME-OFF CHOICES

Time off is unlike almost any other benefit area that could be included
under a flexible program. Outside a flexible program, an employee who
has earned time off often has a choice to take that vacation now or later
or to carry over unused time, generally without application of any special rules. Based on discussions with Revenue Canada, however, that
same time-off choice in a flexible program could trigger special rules—
namely, the prohibition against deferral of compensation except as allowed under Section 248(1) of the Income Tax Act.

(a)   REVENUE CANADA'S POSITION

Revenue Canada has recently reviewed its position concerning the buying and selling of vacation time. Its current opinion is that purchased
time off generally should not be carried forward from one year to the
next—the reason being that the only deferral of compensation permissible is specified in Section 248(1) of the Income Tax Act.

A plan sponsor wanting to minimize the risk of a Revenue Canada
challenge could split vacation days into two types—*regular* and *purchased* days. Regular vacation should be used first. Purchased vacation
would only be used after all regular vacation has been used. To prevent
any employee from using a vacation-buying feature to build up large
amounts of untaxed deferred compensation, the plan would require that
any unused purchased vacation be cashed in at the end of the year.

For example, assume a pre-flexible program entitled an employee to
four weeks of vacation, and the new flexible program permits the employee to buy five additional days. If that employee elects to buy a week,
for a total of five weeks of vacation, then the employee's purchased days
are the extra five days in excess of four weeks. If the employee uses all
five weeks of vacation, no days are cashed out. But, if the employee
uses only four weeks, the five purchased days cannot be banked—they
must be cashed in.

The rules are different for regular days. From the preceding example,
suppose the employee uses only three weeks of vacation. The five unused, regular days would be eligible to be carried forward for use in the

subsequent year. However, the five unused, purchased days would still have to be cashed in.

Most companies encourage employees to use vacation days—whether regular or purchased—in the current year to avoid loss of unused vacation time. Alternatively, some organizations will cash-out any unused purchased days before the end of the year. That way, the employee avoids being in the position of deferring compensation to a subsequent tax year.

The rules outlined above describe Revenue Canada's position on avoiding the abuse of vacation-buying options. Revenue Canada has expressed this position on an ad hoc basis in response to inquiries and, so far, not in published form. Other approaches may, therefore, also be viable. For example:

- The program could allow limited banking, say, up to five days of purchased vacation, and prohibit any cashing out of these days. This would avoid the deferred compensation concern.
- The administrator could analyze the utilization of the buying option. If the results showed that vacation buying is widely used at all pay levels and the vast majority of employees take the vacation in the year purchased, this would demonstrate that the option was not being abused.
- The plan might only allow vacation to be purchased with employer-provided flexible credits. In this case, the employee would be unable to defer any salary.

An employer considering deviating from the requirement of forfeiting unused purchased vacation should consult legal counsel.

To date, Revenue Canada has been concerned less with vacation-selling options under flexible programs. A possible reason for this could be that the use of this option frequently increases tax revenue. Consider, for example, an individual earning $52,000 per year who sells one week of vacation for $1,000 in additional flexible credits. Revenue Canada will still collect tax on $52,000 of earnings; and, if the individual takes, say, $500 of the credits in cash and $500 in non-taxable benefits, Revenue Canada will collect tax on an additional $500 of income.

(b)   PROVINCIAL LABOUR STANDARDS

Labour Standards Acts or similar legislation can restrict vacation selling within a flexible program. Each province and territory has an Act giving minimum vacation requirements for employees under its jurisdiction. For

Table 8.1
Minimum Vacation Entitlement in Each Province

Jurisdiction	Annual Vacation	Vacation Pay (as % of annual earnings)
Alberta	2 weeks	4%
	3 weeks after 5 years	6% after 5 years
British Columbia	2 weeks	4%
	3 weeks after 5 years	6% after 5 years
Federal	2 weeks	4%
	3 weeks after 6 years	6% after 6 years
Manitoba	2 weeks	4%
	3 weeks after 5 years	6% after 5 years
New Brunswick	2 weeks	4%
Newfoundland	2 weeks	4%
Northwest Territories	2 weeks	4%
	3 weeks after 6 years	6% after 6 years
Nova Scotia	2 weeks	4%
Ontario	2 weeks	4%
Prince Edward Island	2 weeks	4%
Quebec	2 weeks	4%
	3 weeks after 10 years	6% after 10 years
Saskatchewan	3 weeks	5.77%
	4 weeks after 10 years	7.69% after 10 years
Yukon Territory	2 weeks	4%

federally regulated industries, the Canada Labour Code has similar requirements. The minimum vacation entitlements are summarized in Table 8.1.

§ 8.5 DESIGN CONSIDERATIONS

(a) TYPE OF APPROACH

One key consideration is whether to allow choices in the area of time off. As mentioned in § 8.4, the banking of purchased time off under a flexible program is risky. Therefore, organizations with extensive banking arrangements already in place either would need to modify current practices or retain vacation banking outside the flexible program, while permitting more limited choices (such as floating holidays or purchase of additional non-bankable vacation days) within the flexible program.

Other considerations relate to the areas of scheduling (for buying) and hard-dollar cost (for selling). Allowing employees to buy extra time off raises the potential for scheduling conflicts—or greater costs if the employee who buys extra vacation must be replaced at a higher rate. As a result, most organizations are careful to communicate that purchased time off requires the same scheduling and coordination with management or supervisory staff as regular vacation. (In fact, some organizations require a supervisor's approval before the employee may even purchase additional days.)

The selling of time involves conversion of soft-dollar expense to hard-dollar cost, particularly among employees who previously failed to use their entire allotment. In practice, however, most companies find that even among senior (higher-paid) employees, vacation remains a valuable benefit, so the amount of time actually sold has a relatively modest impact on costs. Further, where vacation buying is also allowed, more employees tend to purchase vacation time, so the net cost effect tends to be minimal.

For employers interested in offering flexibility in time off, the trend in recent years has been to combine opportunities, rather than allow only buying or selling. The combined offering tends to mitigate the cost effect of allowing selling only and provides the broadest flexibility to employees.

(b) AREAS OF CHOICE

Majority practice is to restrict time-off choices to vacation only. Sometimes employers will include holidays—usually only the days that float. The exception is industries that operate each day of the year so that the trading of holidays represents a practical option. Sick leave is eligible for trading only to the extent that an organization already has converted to an umbrella time-off program that treats all time off as personal days, regardless of reason.

(c) LIMITS ON CHOICE

Most programs place some limits on the trading of time off. Usually the limits take the form of a maximum number of days that may be bought or sold—typically five days either way. Most organizations set a price for days bought or sold at 100 percent of pay. Only a minority of organizations limit their exposure by capping the dollar amount on days sold (such as, actual pay to no more than $200 per day). Separately, most organizations require employees to take some vacation time (for example, minimum of two weeks or the provincial standard, if greater) at least partly to restrict the potential for abuse in terms of allowing employees to cash out vacation and then use the time anyway.

(d) DIFFERENT VACATION AND FLEXIBLE PLAN YEARS

Most flexible programs that allow buying and selling of vacation ensure the vacation year is the same as the flexible plan year. For example, an organization with a calendar year vacation accrual system would likely enroll employees for a calendar-year under the flexible plan. If the years are different, the flexible program can be difficult to administer without jeopardizing its tax-favoured status. The problem is ensuring that an employee who sells vacation does not sell current vacation, but, instead, sells future entitlement to vacation.

For example, an employee enrolling for 1991 under a flexible plan entitled to four weeks' vacation from July 1 to June 30 each year might be eligible to sell one week, say, of the July 1, 1991 to June 30, 1992 vacation. The July 1, 1990 to June 30, 1991 vacation should not be exchanged for 1991 benefits. Otherwise, Revenue Canada's doctrine of constructive receipt may be applied, because the employee made the decision after becoming entitled to the vacation benefit, not before.

(e) DIFFERENT CALENDAR AND FLEXIBLE PLAN YEARS

Revenue Canada's opinion that unused, purchased vacation days be cashed out before the end of the calendar year is impossible to administer where the flexible plan year does not end December 31. For example, consider a flexible plan where employees might select benefits for the period April 1 to March 31. Since the flexible year is only three-quarters completed by December 31, the plan administrator does not know which purchased days will be used by March 31. In this case, a reasonable application of Revenue Canada's position would require the unused, purchased days to be cashed out by the end of the *following* calendar year. At most, a few employees would have a one-year deferral of a fraction of their compensation.

(f) ADMINISTRATION OF CHOICES

To some extent, an organization's level of comfort with vacation choices may hinge on the systems and procedures already in place to monitor time-off recording. At issue is the potential for abuse—allowing employees either to cash out a portion of time off and use the days anyway or to take more time than even an additional purchased allotment. Different organizations decide the issue in different ways. Some have adequate controls in place to monitor time reporting accurately. Others have only limited concern over the potential of employees abusing time-off policies, irrespective of controls. In any event, administration may loom as an issue that inclines an organization one way or the other on inclusion of time-off choices in a flexible program.

Nine

Retirement

---

§ 9.1 INTRODUCTION

Flexibility in retirement benefits is not a new concept. However, to date, few employers have included retirement choices as specific options within flexible programs. For an employer to offer true choice making in the retirement area, the goal would be to allow employees to: (1) reduce retirement benefits in exchange for cash or credits that could be used for other benefit purposes; or (2) apply credits from other areas to the purchase of additional retirement benefits. Structuring retirement plans in this manner raises a host of technical (and practical) issues that employers need to address, if they wish to include retirement options in their flexible programs.

This chapter discusses how retirement options conceptually could be included within a flexible program. In general, defined contribution plans can be integrated into a flexible program more readily than defined benefit plans.

§ 9.2 OBJECTIVES FOR CHOICE MAKING IN RETIREMENT

The reasons for wanting to include retirement choices in a flexible program generally parallel the motivations for offering choice in other benefit areas, with a few differences. As in the case of other benefits, one reason for offering choice is to meet employee needs and preferences, particularly in cases where the employer is unwilling (or unable) to raise retirement benefits on a company-paid basis. Retirement may also be an area that holds significant appeal to only a minority of the employee population, while the majority has greater interest in other benefit areas. Providing choices enables employees to meet their own special needs (such as permitting earlier retirement, making up for a short career with the current employer, or otherwise supplementing existing retirement benefits).

Another motivation for including retirement as a choice area is to provide an additional option for unused flexible credits (amounts remaining after the purchase of medical, dental, life insurance, and other coverage). Some employers are concerned about employees cashing out employer-provided benefit dollars, yet they recognize that cash represents an attractive flexible program option to employees. In these cases a Registered Retirement Savings Plan (RRSP) or Deferred Profit Sharing Plan (DPSP) can serve as an alternative to cash.

A different motivation for reviewing the retirement area while designing a flexible program is to determine whether it could be a potential source of credits for the flexible program. This approach may have merit in creating additional credits where the trimming back of a high-value pension plan would do little to diminish either employee security or the employer's competitive position.

§ 9.3   DEFINED BENEFIT PLANS

The reasons few employers have included defined benefit retirement choices as specific options within choice-making programs include:

- The nature and structure of defined benefit plans which are the primary source of retirement income for the majority of employees. Most pension plans are geared to providing benefits based on the employee's final average earnings and years of service at retirement. This makes it difficult to set an accurate price tag on increments of pension very far in advance of the employee's actual retirement date (or at least without knowledge of the intended retirement date).
- The rising stock and bond markets have boosted pension fund investments in recent years, thereby reducing (or even eliminating) current pension costs for many employers. As a result, employer attention to cost control has been diverted from pensions to other benefit areas (primarily health care).

- The complexity of the various plans and pension benefit legislation has caused many employers to avoid further complicating their plans.
- By establishing Group RRSPs, employers have been able to meet employee needs for additional retirement income in a simple way, as well as provide a tax-favoured vehicle for employee contributions.

(a) DEFINED BENEFIT PLANS AS A SOURCE OF CREDITS

Conceptually, an employer with a rich defined benefit plan may allow employees to cut back their future service benefits and receive credits that may be used to purchase additional benefits in other areas or taken in cash. (The cutback is limited to future service benefits, because a cutback in previously accrued benefits is generally prohibited by law.)

All, or a portion, of the savings attributable to the reduction in future service benefits may be used as a credit generator within the flexible program. Employees would be able to use those funds inside the flexible program—possibly with an option to retain the retirement aspect of those funds through deposit in a companion DPSP or money purchase pension plan.

There are, however, difficulties in determining the appropriate credits and the possibility of anti-selection against the employer. Consider a final average earnings pension plan. Anti-selection will occur if the credits derived from future service benefits are based on assumed pay increases and the employee leaves in the next few years. In this case, employer costs will be higher than would otherwise be the case.

Although used infrequently in recent years, the approach of releasing credits as a funding source for the flexible program could have merit in certain situations. An employer may already be considering the consolidation of different pension plans (such as after a merger or acquisition) or generally re-evaluating the structure of a pension plan that provides higher benefits than may be necessary for competitive reasons.

(b) DEFINED BENEFIT PLANS AS AN OPTIONAL BENEFIT

In theory, a plan sponsor with a defined benefit pension plan could establish a core (basic) benefit and allow employees to buy larger benefits using credits from other benefit areas or payroll dollars. For example, the core benefit might be a future service benefit for each year of service equal to one percent of pay with the option to buy an additional 0.5 or one percent of pay using flexible credits or payroll deduction dollars. The employee could make a different election each year.

In practice, fewer employers structure pension options *within* choice-making plans in this manner. (However, such options are quite common *outside* of choice-making plans, where individual equity in price tags is not as important.) The unpopularity of this approach within a flexible plan stems primarily from:

- Difficulty in determining price tags, especially for a final average earnings plan
- Possible risk in terms of the potential for subsidization of employee choices
- Difficulty in complying with regulatory requirements of federal and provincial authorities
- Additional plan administration.

Another problem is that the plan will incur extra costs if an employee buys additional benefits with today's dollars and receives higher pay increases than assumed in the calculation of price tags.

Because of this risk and the difficulty in setting price tags, an employer may wish to allow employees the option of only buying/selling units of pension based on current pay. For example, this could be 0.5 percent of current pay or units of $10 per month.

The pricing and funding of the defined benefit pension options can occur in one of two ways. One way would be through the existing pension trust. This approach offers the most latitude for design and pricing of the options, because the employer can decide how aggressive to be in setting the actuarial assumptions used to determine the price tags. However, the employer is required to stand behind the benefit promise and, if the aggressive assumptions were not realized, the employer would be responsible for any shortfall.

The other alternative would be to purchase annuities from an insurance company. This alternative provides the greatest financial protection to the employer, but it occurs at the expense of flexibility in pricing the options for employees. Another potential concern, however, is that design may be limited by underwriting restrictions of the carrier.

§ 9.4 DEFINED CONTRIBUTION PLANS

A few employers have begun to explore using a defined contribution plan as an additional funding source for a flexible program. And, many employers allow employees to direct any unused credits to an RRSP or DPSP.

(a)   DEFINED CONTRIBUTION PLANS AS A SOURCE OF CREDITS

For a defined contribution pension plan, a portion of employer monies could be made available for employee elections within the flexible program. A money purchase pension plan, for example, may require an employer contribution of 5 percent of pay. The employer could introduce flexibility by allowing employees to elect some percentage of pay, say 2 percent, that could be used as a source of credits for the flexible program, instead of having this money flow into the pension plan.

Similarly, part or all of the employer matching contributions under a savings plan or a portion of the annual allocation in a profit sharing plan could be made available to employees for use in the flexible program.

This type of approach tends to have appeal in situations where an employer's objective is to focus employee attention on the total compensation aspect of pay and benefits. Alternatively, a savings or profit sharing plan may be very rich and employer credits in the flexible program may be insufficient for employees to cover their benefit needs. However, whether savings or profit sharing monies should be used as a funding source in the flexible program depends on employer objectives in the retirement area and the level of retirement income already provided through other retirement plans.

(b)   DEFINED CONTRIBUTION PLANS AS AN OPTIONAL BENEFIT

The complexity of determining price tags is not an issue in the case of a defined contribution pension plan. Employees could be offered a range of options based on different contribution levels. Unused credits could be deposited in one of various vehicles, including a registered pension plan, RRSP or DPSP. Although it is not typical practice, an employer could decide to grant a matching contribution for unused credits in order to promote saving for retirement. Alternatively, incentives might include matching on a profit- or performance-related basis, or purely discretionary matching. It should be noted that any unused credits or additional matching contributions applied in this manner would not create any additional tax room for the employee—they would be counted toward the aggregate tax limits allowed by Revenue Canada.

Another consideration is the treatment of unused credits in a savings plan. That is, will excess credits be eligible for employer matching funds? Should matching still occur if unused credits represent the employee's only contribution in the plan? Finally, will unused credits be made available under the same terms and conditions that apply for withdrawal of other savings plan funds?

§ 9.5   ISSUES TO BE CONSIDERED

(a)   LEGISLATIVE ISSUES

Care must be taken to ensure the retirement options within a flexible plan conform to the requirements of the various pension benefit acts across Canada. In particular, accrued benefits may not be reduced and the 50 percent cost-sharing rule must be followed. In addition, employers need to consider the effect of any indexing rules.

(b)   TAX ISSUES

Similarly, retirement plans must recognize the rules on maximum tax deductibility of retirement contributions. In June, 1990, the House of Commons passed legislation to amend provisions of the Income Tax Act that govern tax assistance for savings in pension and retirement savings plans.

The amendments affect employer-sponsored registered pension plans (RPPs), DPSPs, and RRSPs.

The new system provides equal treatment for savers, whether they save through RPPs, DPSPs, or RRSPs. It sets a uniform limit on tax-assisted savings of 18 percent of earnings to a dollar maximum. The dollar maximum will be phased in over a period ending in 1994 for RPPs and DPSPs, and 1995 for RRSPs. At the end of the phase-in period, the dollar limit on contributions will be $15,500 for RPPs and RRSPs, and $7,750 for DPSPs. After that, the limits will be indexed to the growth in the average national wage. The limits are shown in the table at the top of page 163.

To implement the new comprehensive limit, employers who sponsor RPPs or DPSPs will be required to report a pension adjustment (PA) for each plan member during each year. The PA, which reflects the benefits a plan member has earned during the year under employer-sponsored plans, is subtracted from the member's comprehensive contribution limit. This determines the maximum RRSP contribution the plan member may make the *following* year.

Year	Money Purchase RPP Limit	DPSP Limit	RRSP Limit
1991	$12,500	$6,250	$11,500
1992	13,500	6,750	12,500
1993	14,500	7,250	13,500
1994	15,500	7,750	14,500
1995	15,500*	7,750*	15,500
1996	15,500*	7,750*	15,500*

* To be indexed to the growth in the average wage. Indexing to commence in 1995 for money purchase RPPs and DPSPs and in 1996 for RRSPs.

For DPSPs, the PA will simply be the total of the employer's contributions in respect of the employee and forfeited amounts (and related investment earnings) that are allocated to the employee. For money purchase plans, the PA will be the total of the employer's contributions in respect of the employee, plus any contributions by the employee plus forfeited amounts (and related earnings) and amounts of surplus that are allocated to the employee. For defined benefit plans, the PA will be determined directly from the benefit formula and, where applicable, the employee's pensionable earnings in the year.

To the extent that flexible credits are released from retirement benefits as a funding source for non-retirement benefits, an employee gains tax room for retirement saving, subject to the above rules. On the other hand, to the extent that unused credits are applied to purchase additional pension benefits or allocated to the DPSP portion of a savings plan, available tax room is reduced.

(c) ADMINISTRATIVE ISSUES

Special procedures will be necessary to administer the pension options. Any pension benefits purchased by employees using flexible credits must be fully vested. Therefore, it is necessary to keep track of these benefits separately from the benefits that are subject to the normal vesting requirements of the pension plan. Tracking of benefit amounts could be complex. For example, some benefits may be based on final average earnings, while other benefits may be of a fixed-dollar nature.

One consideration in including defined contribution plans as an option in a flexible plan may be the compatibility of the employer's payroll and record-keeping systems. Most defined contribution plans are designed to accept employee contributions in the form of a percentage of pay. Under a flexible program, unused credits usually would be dispersed to employees as a specific dollar amount (paid out each pay period or on a one-time basis at the end of the year). The record-keeping system for the plan needs to be able to accept specific dollar amounts—a modification to the system may not be worth the administrative effort involved if both the number and dollar amount of deposits are expected to be low. (On the other hand, funds flowing out of the retirement plan to the flexible plan usually are easier to accommodate since credit allocations to employees typically are based on a combination of a percentage of pay plus a flat-dollar amount.)

Employees would need careful explanation regarding the rights attached to the pension options.

(d) OTHER ISSUES

For most employers, the level and structure of existing retirement plans will exert primary influence on any decisions relating to the flexible program. For example, an employer with an already rich defined benefit pension plan may have little incentive to offer more under a flexible approach. Instead (and depending on other considerations), introduction of a flexible program may provide the impetus for a cutback in that plan—assuming a substantial portion of the cost savings would flow through to employees in the form of higher credits or expanded benefit options under the flexible program.

However, the majority of employers may find themselves in other situations—for example, recognizing that employees would welcome an additional opportunity to supplement pension income; and (perhaps) to seek an additional source of credits for the flexible program. In these situations, the following checklist of considerations may prove helpful:

- Would enough employees elect retirement choices to justify any added administrative expense? (For example, would it be worthwhile to develop pension options, or modify record-keeping systems to accept the flow of funds between the flexible benefit plan and the defined contribution plan—or both?)
- Given the expected flexible program credit structure, what is the likely amount of deposits—to either arrangement?
- How much tax room exists in an RRSP or DPSP plan to accept an additional source of contributions?

- How important is a cash option to employees?
- Where does the pension plan rank relative to competitive norms?
- How well understood is the existing pension plan?
- What parallelism (if any) in terms of matching, withdrawal, and so forth, will be accorded unused credits deposited in the DPSP—versus regular amounts?
- How would pension options be funded? How much risk is the employer willing to bear in terms of the potential for future subsidization?

§ 9.6 RETIREMENT CHOICES OUTSIDE THE FLEXIBLE PROGRAM

To complete the discussion of retirement plans as an option, mention should be made of options that do not fall into the category of "pure" flexible options. That is, they are not of equivalent value and do not allow employees the opportunity to use credits in other benefit areas. They are optional retirement programs and can take several forms. For example:

- An employee may be given the choice of: (1) electing membership in a non-contributory defined benefit pension plan providing a benefit equal to, say, 1 percent of pay for each year of service; or (2) joining a contributory pension plan which provides a benefit equal to 2 percent of pay for each year of service, toward which the employee contributes 5 percent of pay each year. (Despite the difficulties with this approach, which are similar to those outlined in § 9.3(b), about one in 10 employers have such a plan outside a choice-making program.)
- A defined contribution plan (such as a savings plan) may allow employees to contribute 1 to 6 percent of their pay. The company matching contribution may be $0.50 for each $1 contributed by the employee.
- A hybrid plan may be offered. For example, employees may automatically be covered by a non-contributory defined benefit pension plan that provides a benefit of 1 percent of pay for each year of service. In addition, there may be a voluntary supplemental defined contribution plan under which employees can contribute in multiples of 1 percent of pay with a dollar-for-dollar employer match, up to a maximum employer contribution of 3 percent of pay.
- A choice may be given between a defined benefit option and a defined contribution option. For example, an employee may be covered under a defined benefit pension plan and a savings plan. The

employee may be given the choice of forgoing the company match in the savings plan in exchange for a higher benefit under the defined benefit pension plan.

Although these optional retirement programs are not "pure" flexible options, they do offer interesting alternatives. Care must be taken, however, in the design of these programs to protect the employer from anti-selection by employees.

§ 9.7 SUMMARY

To date, few employers have introduced true choice making along the lines outlined in this chapter. In large part, employers have had concerns regarding the complexities involved in determining appropriate pricing strategy and the issues involved in administering the pension options and complying with the requirements of the regulatory authorities. Nevertheless, the area of retirement benefits could be the subject of experiment in second and subsequent generations of flexible benefit programs.

Ten

Emerging Benefits

§ 10.1 INTRODUCTION

Flexible benefit programs usually allow employees to select the appropriate level of coverage within traditional benefit areas, such as medical, dental, life insurance, and disability. Options need not be limited to traditional programs, however. The flexible structure allows employers to add new benefits to the range of employee choices, and it allows the employer to decide whether or not to subsidize the cost of the benefits.

Although employees are very creative when asked what other options should be added to a flexible benefit program, not all of their suggestions are feasible or appropriate. Among the characteristics that would make a benefit an attractive choice within a flexible benefit program are:

- **Group purchasing power.** Employees may be able to pool their resources and negotiate better rates than they could individually receive.
- **Risk sharing.** The basic principle of insurance applies where an individual may not be able to absorb the cost of a catastrophic event, such as a fire or an accident. In this case, each member of the group bears a small, acceptable portion of the risk.
- **Company selection of provider.** Individuals are faced with an overwhelming array of providers for insurance (such as home and auto) and investments (such as RRSPs). By selecting a provider, the employer provides a valuable service to the employee.

However, this factor works both ways. Many employers are reluctant to introduce certain benefits (such as home and auto insurance), because of the implied endorsement of the provider. Negative reaction from one employee, because of a disputed claim, could overwhelm the good publicity from introducing the plan.

- **Payroll deduction convenience.** Most benefits discussed in this chapter may be purchased using payroll deductions. Since most payroll systems can handle multiple payroll deductions, the administrative cost to the employer to introduce a new benefit is minimal.

- **Fill gaps in other company plans.** Traditional benefit plans provide coverage against the financial risk of many contingencies. However, there are some gaps in the coverage. A health care expense account is an example of an emerging benefit that fills such a gap. The account covers health care expenses not reimbursed under traditional benefit plans. (Chapter Seven has been devoted to expense accounts.)

- **Tax advantages.** Some benefits may be provided on a more tax-effective basis by an employer than the employee could receive by purchasing it outside the group plan. This occurs where part or all of the premium or cost paid by the employer does not generate a taxable benefit for the employee. Group mortgage plans are an example. Under a flexible program, the employee could direct flexible credits to pay part of the mortgage. As discussed later, this may not produce a taxable benefit for the employee.

- **Exchange for unwanted benefits.** A new benefit may be very attractive to the employee, if it can be exchanged for an unwanted benefit.

The balance of this chapter discusses emerging benefits in three general categories: work and family benefits; financial benefits; and "other" benefits.

§ 10.2 WORK AND FAMILY BENEFITS

(a) SABBATICAL LEAVE PLANS

For many years, teachers and other educators have had the ability to take periodic paid sabbaticals away from work. In 1986, employees in other occupations became eligible to defer a portion of their salary (and taxes) until they take a sabbatical. This occurred when Section 248(1) of the Income Tax Act was amended to restrict tax advantages enjoyed by many employees, who, in the past, elected to defer the receipt of a portion of their salaries. However, sabbatical plans were specifically exempted from these Section 248(1) salary deferral rules.

Under a sabbatical plan, an employee is entitled to defer a portion of salary for a limited period of time on a tax-neutral basis. The deferred salary is not taxable until the employee actually receives it. However, any investment income earned must be paid out to the employee each year. All earnings paid to the employee are taxable in the year.

(1)   Design Features

In order to be accorded favourable tax treatment, sabbatical plans must meet certain criteria. These are contained in Regulation 6801 to the Income Tax Act and are discussed next.

- **Eligibility and enrollment.** The regulations specify that a sabbatical plan must be "an arrangement *in writing* between an employer and the employee." Therefore, to enroll in the plan, each member must sign an agreement. The agreement may be quite brief—similar to an enrollment form that refers to the plan and sets out the employee's percentage of salary deferred, deferral period, and sabbatical period.
- **Amount of deferral.** An employee may defer up to 33-1/3 percent of salary each year. Employees may be given the option of deferring a range of percentages of salary, say, any multiple of 3 up to 33 percent.
- **Election to defer.** The election to defer must be made prior to the beginning of each calendar year. The election should be made far enough in advance of the next year to allow the payroll department enough time to make the necessary adjustments.

  For administrative simplicity, employees should not be entitled to make more than one election per year. However, employers may find it prudent to allow an exception in cases of financial hardship.
- **Deferral period.** The maximum deferral period is *six years*. The deferred salary must be received in income no later than in the seventh year.

  An employer's staffing requirements will dictate the degree of flexibility permitted as to the selection of an employee's sabbatical deferral period. A cushion at the end of the deferral period may be used to avoid complications arising from unforeseen changes in staffing needs. For example, if an employee's deferral period is limited to five years, an employer may reserve the right to extend the employee's deferral by up to one year, in the case of internal staffing complications.

A typical design may be to allow for a deferral of 20 percent of salary each year for five years, with the sixth year being the sabbatical period at 100 percent of pay. Universities frequently have "four over five" programs. Four years of contributions are made, at 20 percent of pay, with the applicant living on 80 percent of normal salary in the fifth year.

- **Sabbatical period.** The length of the sabbatical period must be *no less than six consecutive months,* commencing immediately after the deferral period. The only other requirement is that the employee return to employment after the sabbatical period for a period at least as long as the sabbatical period. For example, if an employee's sabbatical period is one year, the member must return to work with the employer for at least a year.

  A situation might arise where a employee decides not to return to the employer following the sabbatical. Revenue Canada would likely reassess the individual's tax returns for the years the salary was deferred.

- **Pay during sabbatical period.** The Income Tax Regulations stipulate that no salary or wages be paid to an individual while on sabbatical leave, apart from the accumulated deferred earnings. However, reasonable fringe benefits, usually provided to employees, may continue to be offered.

- **Restitution.** Plans need to allow for employees who are partway through the sabbatical plan and then terminate employment, become disabled, or die. The employee's accumulated deferred salary typically would be refunded to the employee or his/her estate.

- **Funding of the plan.** The plan may be either funded or unfunded. Under the funded approach, the employee's deferred salary would typically be contributed to a trust fund or other interest-bearing account. With the unfunded approach, a book reserve would be established to keep account of the employees' deferred salaries. Income would not ordinarily be credited.

  The funded approach is normally preferable. It provides employees with greater security. Employees also get full value for their contributions, because income is credited. A slight disadvantage of the funded approach is administrative complexity. However, the financial institution (trust company or insurance company) holding the funds ordinarily would be responsible for administration.

- **Pension and benefit issues.** Employers must decide how to treat pension and group insurance benefits under a sabbatical program. The central issue concerning benefits is whether pension and group benefits are based upon an employee's actual earnings (salary less deferral) or upon nominal earning (full earnings, disregarding deferred salary).

    The employer can decide which earnings should be used to calculate the employee benefits such as life and disability insurance. However, there is no such latitude for registered pension plans. Under a registered pension plan, Revenue Canada requires that the pension benefit be based on actual earnings. Because of this, employers either advise employees not to reduce their salary in anticipation of a sabbatical if they intend to retire within a few years of returning from the sabbatical, or they agree to make up any pension shortfall through a supplemental, non-registered plan.

(2)   A Typical Sabbatical Plan

- **Funding.** Employees are eligible to apply employer credits from their flexible expense account toward the sabbatical plan. In addition, they may elect to take a reduction in their current salary to fund their sabbatical leave.

- **Eligibility.** Typically, employees must have a minimum of two years of service. The arrangements must be in writing between the employee and the company.

- **Deferral maximum.** The usual maximum is 33 percent of salary each year (in multiples of 3 percent). The maximum deferral period is five years. The company reserves the right to delay an employee's sabbatical by up to one year, because of internal staffing needs.

- **Sabbatical period.** Typically, plans specify a one-year maximum, with a six-month minimum.

- **Sabbatical period compensation.** Only the deferred money accumulated to date may be paid in compensation. An employee may not receive any other pay or compensation. If an employee leaves the employer, becomes disabled, or dies, the accumulated deferred salary is refunded to the employee or his/her estate.

- **Funding of the plan.** Deferred salaries are physically put aside into a trust. Any income the deferred funds earn must be taken as taxable income in the year it is earned.

(b) LONG-TERM CARE

An attractive benefit that may become popular in the 1990s in Canada is long-term care coverage. This coverage provides financial support for elderly individuals, who can no longer take care of themselves. Hospitalization and rehabilitation usually are not features of the coverage. The most obvious example of a long-term care facility is a nursing home. Although provincial health insurance plans cover a portion of the cost, the individual may be left paying a significant amount.

For example, in Ontario, the cost of a private room in a nursing home is $2,350 a month. The province pays $1,350 of this, leaving a $1,000 cost to the individual. Long-term care coverage can supplement this provincial subsidy.

Nursing homes can provide different levels of care:

- Skilled nursing, for persons requiring constant supervision and treatment by a Registered Nurse under the direction of a doctor
- Intermediate care, for persons requiring part-time services of skilled medical personnel
- Custodial care, which requires the services of an individual who can assist in dressing, walking, eating, and other daily activities.

Other types of long-term care that may be available include:

- Home care, which can be skilled or unskilled care, provided in the individual's or a relative's home
- Adult day care, providing custodial care services given outside the individual's home
- Respite care, which refers to temporary services provided to relieve the person who normally assumes primary care responsibility.

Long-term care may become a popular benefit, because of demographic changes, changes in family structures, and changes in work patterns.

- **Demographic changes.** The elderly population is the fastest growing segment of our population. With better health care and medical technology, people are living longer. With increased longevity, the risk of needing long-term care increases as well. Life expectancy beyond age 60 is increasing rapidly, as shown in Table 10.1.

  Due to increased life expectancy, people aged 85 and over have become the fastest growing segment of our aging population. Meanwhile,

Table 10.1
Canadian Life Expectancy at Age 60

Year	Male	Female
1921	16.6 years	17.1 years
1941	16.1	17.6
1961	16.7	19.9
1971	17.0	21.4
1981	18.0	22.9
1987	18.4	23.2

Source: Statistics Canada

the baby boom generation is becoming more interested in how to provide care for parents.

- **Changes in family structures.** Although families have historically been the main providers of long-term care for their elderly members, migration and lifestyle patterns have increased the need for others to care for elderly parents.

- **Changes in work patterns.** Women have traditionally been the caregivers for parents and parents-in-law. As more women have entered the work force, their ability to be providers of long-term care to their elderly relatives has diminished.

(1) Inadequacy of Current Forms of Care

Because they are living longer, the elderly have become more susceptible to chronic health conditions, and, as a result, require more assistance over longer periods. Current safety nets are becoming inadequate to deal with such health and custodial needs. Residential living communities, while highly touted as a solution, are often too expensive and built in insufficient numbers to solve long-term care needs.

Provincial plans only cover a portion of nursing home costs and do not always cover other types of long-term custodial care services.

(2) Insurance Product Features

Perhaps the most viable option for long-term care is in the form of a group insurance policies. More than 70 U.S. insurers now offer long-term care products; however, to date, few, if any, Canadian policies are available. In the United States, basic plan design typically includes the following features:

- **Covered providers.** Expenses for nursing care, home care, adult care, and respite care are typically covered.
- **Benefits.** Usually a set dollar amount, such as $100 per day, is established in the policy. The daily dollar benefit may vary, depending upon the facility (skilled nursing facility, custodial nursing home, and so forth). Any charges in excess of the daily benefit are paid by the insured.
- **Contributions.** A group long-term care plan is generally 100 percent employee contributory through after-tax payroll deductions. (Revenue Canada has not ruled on whether or not long-term care services are "qualified" medical expenses.)
- **Eligibility.** One, some, or all of the following group classifications may be covered in a given policy: employees, retirees, spouses, and parents.
- **Maximum benefit periods.** These typically range from 3 to 10 years. The longer the benefit period, the higher the premium for the policy. Policies that do not have benefit periods will use over-all dollar maximums.
- **Inflation protection.** This is an option that can increase the daily fixed benefit by a certain percentage (usually 3 to 5 percent) for a specified number of years.
- **Portability.** If the employee terminates employment or divorces, or the group plan is discontinued, the employee can continue with an individual policy.
- **Waiver of premium.** This feature eliminates premiums once the benefits received equal a specified number of days of nursing home benefits.
- **Age at entry-level premiums.** This refers to the "employee pay all" premium, which generally is fixed and based on age at the time of the initial purchase. Table 10.2 outlines typical premium rates for U.S. policies.

Along with these features, group long-term care policies are usually governed by the following benefit eligibility requirements:

- **Pre-existing conditions.** This requires that a specified period of time must pass after a policy is effective (usually 6 to 12 months) before benefits will be paid for any condition that the covered person had during a specified period before the coverage went into effect (usually 6 to 12 months before).

Table 10.2
Premium Rates for U.S. Policies

Issue Age	Monthly Premium for $80 Daily Benefit
25	$ 6.40
40	14.00
50	26.40
60	61.36
70	174.16

- **Elimination period.** This provision defines the number of days the covered person must be confined in a facility, or the number of days of home care service days the covered person must have received, before policy benefits begin. These periods usually range from 15 to 120 days.

- **Prior hospitalization.** Long-term care plans require a minimum number of hospital days (usually three), before a beneficiary qualifies for coverage; and also may require the hospitalization to occur within a limited number of days the start of such coverage.

- **Exclusions.** Policies generally do not pay for services that are related to suicide, confinements outside of the country, war or an act of war, mental or nervous conditions, alcoholism, mental retardation, or certain other health conditions. However, Alzheimer's disease and other organic mental disorders generally are covered.

(3) Design Considerations

If long-term care coverage becomes prevalent in Canada, employers will have to consider several issues in designing the program. Perhaps the most important is whether or not sufficient long-term services will be available in the community to provide the benefits that have been purchased. Another consideration is whether or not the coverage is necessary, in light of provincial health insurance programs. Other considerations include: employee interest, possible government mandates, employee pressure for employer contributions, and tax regulations.

(c) CHILD CARE

Child care would seem to be a natural benefit for inclusion in a flexible benefit program, because it would make the benefit program more attractive to many employees. Employers might also benefit from the introduction of child care, because it could reduce absenteeism and improve the hiring and retaining of employees. However, few, if any, flexible programs include child care for a simple reason: there are no tax advantages to including this benefit within a flexible benefit program. Therefore, the employee is no better off arranging child care through the employer's flexible program than outside it—unless, of course, the employer subsidizes the cost.

Contrast this to the situation in the United States, where an employee may have his or her salary reduced by up to $5,000 per year for reimbursement of child care (or other dependent care) expenses. No tax is payable on such reimbursements.

Although child care is not offered as a flexible benefit option, the changing demographics of the workplace, which have helped flexible plans flourish, have also encouraged some employees to address the child care needs of employees.

(1) Types of Child Care Benefits

The child care benefits available outside a flexible plan cover a wide range, from on-site day care to referral services.

- **On-site.** Some employers provide day care facilities in their building. This could be a major advantage to the employer in recruiting and retaining valuable employees. Employers typically provide the facility for free, so employees only have to pay for the day care staff. The employer subsidy for on-site care is not a taxable benefit to the employee. Reasons that more employers do not offer this benefit include cost, insurance and legal liability issues, difficulty in providing on-site day care in a multiple-location company, necessity of complying with local legislation (access to "green space" and so forth), and perceived inequity of subsidizing one group of employees.
- **Subsidized private day care.** Employers may subsidize the cost of private day care facilities selected by employees. The subsidy would be a taxable benefit to the employee.
- **Education and referral services.** A number of commercial and non-profit services are available to provide information to employees covering general issues among day care (types of day care available, for example) and specific information on providers. Some services provide telephone counselling where the employee calls the provider with questions. Others are computerized databases, which can be installed at the employer's offices. Employees having questions can

sign on and get a list of after-school day care facilities within five kilometres of the office, for example.

- **Flexible work schedules.** Many employers have addressed the needs of working parents by introducing flexible work hours. Others grant employees a number of "personal days" each year that can be used for looking after a sick child, doctor's visits and so forth. A few companies will pay for emergency child care to look after a sick child. Normally, there is a maximum of five days' payment per year. One company goes as far as paying the cost of overnight baby-sitting, should the employee and spouse both need to travel out of town on the same night.

(d) ELDER CARE

A growing concern of many employees is the need to look after elderly parents. As the population ages, the baby boomers are being faced with the dual concerns of looking after their children and their parents. The term "sandwich generation" has been coined to describe this phenomenon. Successful employers in the 1990s will be those who find innovative ways of addressing the needs of the sandwich generation.

The programs employers have adopted to date are very similar to those used to address child care needs:

- **Information.** Seminars or a library can help educate employees on the needs and problems of the elderly and describe what services are available.
- **Referral.** A number of commercial and non-profit services are available to provide information to employees covering types of elder care available and providing specific information on local resources. The services range from telephone counselling to computerized databases, which can be installed at the employer's offices.
- **Flexible work schedules.** Employers can help address employee needs in this area by introducing flexible work hours.

§ 10.3 FINANCIAL BENEFITS

(a) GROUP MORTGAGES

For many years, financial institutions have offered subsidized mortgages to their staff as an employee benefit. The benefit was usually tax-effective, because part or all of the subsidy was provided tax-free to the employee.

In some cases, the employer could pay 3 percent or more of the mortgage interest and not generate a taxable benefit to the employee.

The concept of tax-effective group mortgages was made available to all types of employers in the late 1980s, when several insurance companies developed group products. Under the group plans, the employee is free to negotiate the payment terms of the mortgage and the amortization period with the insurance company. The interest rate charged by the lender is usually a competitive current rate. If the employee leaves the company, the mortgage is converted to an individual mortgage.

(1)   Tax Considerations

As discussed in Chapter Eleven, the value of any benefit provided to an employee by an employer is taxable to the employee, unless there is a specific exemption in the Income Tax Act. One of the few exemptions is for an employer subsidy of an employee mortgage. The subsidy is only taxable to the employee to the extent that it reduces the effective interest rate below a government prescribed rate. For example, if an employee secures a mortgage at 12 percent and the prescribed rate is 10 percent, then the employer could pay 2 percent, without this subsidy being taxable income to the employee. If the employer paid 3 percent, then 1 percent would be taxable income and 2 percent would be tax-free. The prescribed rate, which the employer can subsidize without creating a taxable benefit, is based on the 91-day Treasury Bill rate at the beginning of the preceding quarter. The prescribed rate is changed every three months and cannot exceed the prescribed rate on the date the mortgage is issued. If the rate decreases in the future, the employee receives a larger tax-free benefit.

A recent history of five-year mortgage rates and the prescribed rate is shown in Table 10.3.

To ensure the employer subsidy is not taxable if it falls between the gross and prescribed rates, the employer must pay it directly to the lending institution.

(2)   Plan Design Features

The employer needs to decide upon several design features when installing a plan, including:

- **Eligibility.** The plan could be extended to all employees, or it may be limited to a group, such as all salaried employees.

Table 10.3
History of Five-Year Mortgage and Prescribed Rates

Date	Prescribed Rate (91-Day Treasury Rate)	Five-Year Mortgage Rate	Tax-Free Benefit
January 1986	9%	11.50%	2.50%
April 1986	11	11.25	2.25
July 1986	10	11.25	1.25
October 1986	9	11.25	3.25
January 1987	9	11.00	2.00
April 1987	8	10.75	2.75
July 1987	8	11.25	2.25
October 1987	9	12.25	3.25
January 1988	9	11.50	2.50
April 1988	9	11.00	2.00
July 1988	9	11.25	2.25
October 1988	10	11.75	1.75
January 1989	11	12.25	1.25
April 1989	12	12.50	0.50
July 1989	13	11.75	N/A
October 1989	13	11.75	N/A
January 1990	13	12.00	N/A
April 1990	13	13.25	0.25

- **Waiting period.** The plan might require a 6- or 12-month waiting period before the employee can make use of the plan.
- **Direct subsidy amount.** An employer needs to decide whether or not to subsidize the mortgage. Most employers, not in the financial sector, do not want to add on the additional cost of paying part of an employee's mortgage.
- **Other sources of subsidy.** An alternative would be to allow the employee to direct credits from the flexible benefit program to subsidize the mortgage. Credits should be considered as a company-paid subsidy by Revenue Canada and not generate a taxable benefit, unless the net employee rate falls below the prescribed rate. Before adding this system to a flexible plan, the sponsor should review the available credits to determine if they would be sufficient to provide a meaningful subsidy.

Another source of subsidy could be the employee's agreeing to forgo a future salary increase in exchange for an equivalent mortgage subsidy. Although Revenue Canada has stated that it will not accept such an arrangement and will apply the doctrine of constructive receipt, many tax experts believe the approach is defensible as long as the irrevocable election is made before the employee becomes entitled to the salary increase.

(b) REGISTERED EDUCATION SAVINGS PLAN

Other than Registered Retirement Savings Plans, Canadians have few tax-effective investment options available. One of the options is a Registered Education Savings Plan or RESP. This type of plan, which permits earnings on investments made for education to grow tax-free, has been available for many years as an individual arrangement. Recently, a number of RESP sponsors have designed group plans to be offered to employees through an employer. An RESP could be an attractive option in a flexible or traditional employee benefit program. It meets most of the criteria listed in § 10.1 for a valuable option—it has tax advantages, is paid by payroll deduction, fills a gap in coverage and makes the process easy for the employee, because the employer selects the provider.

(1) How Does an RESP Operate?

The rules governing RESPs are contained in Section 146.1 of the Income Tax Act. A typical group plan works as follows:

- **Deposits.** The employee contributes to a qualified RESP in the name of a beneficiary. The deposit can be a single lump sum or periodic payment. Beginning in 1990, the maximum payment is $1,500 per year.
- **Beneficiary.** The beneficiary is normally the employee's child. However, the beneficiary could be a grandchild, niece, nephew, godchild or someone unrelated. In fact, the beneficiary could be an adult. All RESPs allow the contributor to change the beneficiary. Some plans only allow a change prior to the beneficiary's 13th or 14th birthday. Most plans, however, have no age restriction.
- **Price.** In some plans, the contributor purchases one or more "units" in the RESP fund. The price of the unit depends on the age of the beneficiary when the unit is purchased—the younger the beneficiary, the lower the cost. In this way, a unit will mature for the same amount at age 18, regardless of the child's age when the RESP was started. In other plans, the contributions are deposited in a mutual fund.
- **Payroll deductions.** Premiums are paid by after-tax payroll deductions. The contributor is not entitled to a tax deduction for the premium.

- **Investment earnings and forfeitures.** No tax is payable by the employee, the beneficiary or the trust on any investment earnings or forfeitures in the trust. However, the beneficiary pays tax on investment earnings when they are paid out as educational assistance payments.

- **Investments.** Some RESPs invest in balanced pooled funds. Others allow the contributor to select from a number of mutual funds or, in some cases, to have self-directed investments.

- **Maximum deposit.** Revenue Canada limits the total deposit on behalf of a beneficiary to $31,500 in 1990. This amount is generally increased each year in line with changes in the Consumer Price Index. Beginning in 1990, an annual maximum contribution of $1,500 per beneficiary is in effect.

  (The above information is based on new rules proposed in the February 1990 Budget. When these rules become law, they will have retroactive effect. After February 20, 1990, annual contributions to one or more RESPs on behalf of a particular beneficiary may not exceed $1,500.

  There will also be a ceiling of $31,500 for total RESP contributions for a particular beneficiary. This ceiling ties in with a 21-year limit on the lifespan of a plan, as annual contributions of $1,500 for 21 years will amount to $31,500.)

- **Maturity.** The total deposits are refunded to the contributor when the plan matures. Investment earnings are retained in the plan for payment to the beneficiary. Some plans mature on the child's 18th birthday. Others have more liberal restrictions, such as a requirement that the plan mature no later than 21 years after the first deposit (under 1990 proposed changes to the Income Tax Act, a plan will not be permitted to continue after 21 years). Interest is not paid at this point. Since the deposits were made with after-tax payroll deductions, they are paid tax-free to the employee. The maturity date is designed to coincide with the beneficiary's first year of post-secondary education, although the employee is under no legal obligation to use the refund of contributions for the beneficiary's education.

  Effective in 1990, a plan in existence for more than 21 years will cease to be a registered plan.

- **Forfeitures.** If the beneficiary does not go on to university or other eligible post-secondary institution, the interest earned on the investment is forfeited by the employee. Depending on the plan, there are two ways the forfeited funds can be handled. In some plans, forfeitures remain in the pool and are eventually paid out to other beneficiaries in the same maturity year. In other plans, the forfeited amount is contributed to a post-secondary institution designated by the contributor. Earnings on the investments are also forfeited if the contributor stops participating in the plan.

The original investment, less administrative fees, where applicable, is never forfeited. It is always paid back to the employee.

- **Educational assistance payments.** Typically, one-third of the interest and forfeitures (if any) that the investment has earned is paid out at the beginning of each of the next three years following maturity of the plan. To be entitled to a payment, the beneficiary must be in the second, third, and fourth years of post-secondary education at the beginning of Years 2, 3, and 4, respectively. Scholarships are taxable income to the student in the year received.

- **Portability.** If the employee terminates, the RESP can be continued on an individual basis. Instead of payroll deductions, the premium would be paid directly to the issuer by the former employee.

- **Post-secondary education.** To qualify for a scholarship, the student must attend a recognized university, community college, or technical institute in Canada or any other country. Under 1990 budget proposals applying to plans established after February 20, 1990, beneficiaries will be eligible to receive payment only if they are full-time students enrolled in a "qualifying educational program" at a "designated institution" as defined for purposes of the education tax credit.

- **Postponement.** RESPs sometimes allow the student to skip a year or two of education. The scholarship would continue to be paid if the beneficiary returned to complete studies.

(c) FINANCIAL PLANNING

Few flexible benefit programs offer financial planning options. However, some form of financial planning can complement the choices within the choice-making program. Like many other benefits described in this chapter, those in a wide range of financial planning services available. They include:

- **Group seminars or lectures.** These are frequently offered at lunch time and would cover topics such as RRSPs, life insurance, investments, estate planning, and so forth. Topics related to the choices within the flexible plan (such as life insurance) could be scheduled to coincide with the annual flexible plan enrollment.

- **Individual counselling.** One-on-one sessions between an investment or financial counsellor and the employee can be scheduled. Typically, these sessions are limited to executives, because of the high cost.

  There are two important considerations in setting up financial counselling sessions. First, the cost is generally a taxable benefit, if paid for by the employer. (There are some exceptions—preretirement counselling, mental and physical health counselling and reemployment counselling are not taxable.)

  Second, the employer should ensure the counsellor is independent and not merely a representative of a financial institution looking for ways to sell commissionable products.

- **Computer software.** Interactive, touch-screen computer software is in its infancy. During the next decade, it will become widespread, and its cost will decrease dramatically. Already, employees at some companies can enroll in their flexible benefit program using this software. First, they try different benefit considerations by using the interactive enrollment program for modelling possible choices. Only when they have selected a package that meets their needs do they enroll. As choices within retirement plans become more common, employers will provide interactive software so employees can see the long-term impact of their choices.

(d)   GROUP UNIVERSAL LIFE INSURANCE

Universal life insurance evolved in the early 1980s in response to critics of traditional whole life insurance, who argued that individuals would be better off buying term life insurance and investing the premium savings over the cost of whole life. The theory was that the individual would be better off, because the investments would exceed the cash value of the whole life insurance policy. A universal life policy achieves the same result, because it allows the individual to "buy term and invest the rest" in one product and earn new money rates of interest, not the average portfolio rate of whole life.

Under universal life, the insurance premiums are deposited into an investment account with the insurer. Once a month, the insurance charges, along with administration charges and premium taxes are removed from the account. Investment earnings, at a current rate of interest are credited to the account. Cash withdrawals are permitted at any time. This is illustrated in Figure 10.1.

Although individual universal life policies are quite common, group plans have not yet become popular in Canada. Only a couple of

Figure 10.1   Monthly Cash Withdrawals

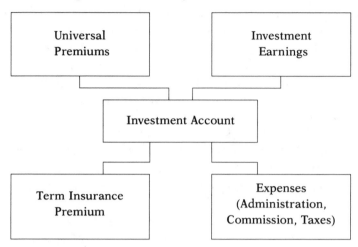

insurance carriers now offer these programs. The existing plans offer the following features:

- If there are flexible premiums, the policyholder decides on the amount and timing of premium payments.
- The policyholder chooses between a level death benefit and an increasing benefit. The increasing benefit equals the original coverage plus the value of the investment account.
- On termination, the employee can continue the plan or take the cash value.
- On retirement, the employee can either continue the coverage for as long as the cash value will pay the insurance premium or reduce the coverage so the insurance protection will last longer. A third option is to cash out the cash value of the policy.
- Any premium paid by the employer directly or using flexible credits is taxable income to the employee.

§ 10.4   OTHER BENEFITS

(a)   HOME AND AUTO INSURANCE

Most employees have home and auto insurance through their broker or insurance agent. Does it make sense for an employer to offer group coverage as an option within a benefit plan? Many employers believe so and include these plans as part of a benefit program (flexible or otherwise). Group home and auto plans offer the convenience of payroll deductions, company selection of the insurer and, in some cases, lower rates for employees.

Under these plans, employees are free to use the group insurance plan or to continue with their personal arrangements. Most eligible employees request a group quotation before the expiry of their own coverage to determine if the group plan offers any savings. The following features should be considered in designing a plan and in selecting an insurance carrier:

- **Cost.** Employees may have high expectations that their premium for group home and auto insurance will be significantly lower than what they are currently paying. However, in many cases, the savings will be smaller than expected or non-existent. In many provinces, insurers are prohibited from offering lower rates to employers, than they do to the general public. Because of this, the "household name" insurers do not offer group insurance, because they cannot undercut their individual premiums. Instead, insurance is offered through specialized insurers that only offer group coverage. For this reason, the name of the group carrier may be unknown to employees.

  (The reason for the prohibition on offering lower rates to groups is unclear; after all, there is no similar prohibition on group life insurance premiums. A cynic might suggest that the home and auto insurance agents were more effective lobbyists than were life insurance agents.)

- **Tax effectiveness.** There are no tax advantages to employees of buying home and auto insurance through their employers, either through payroll deductions or flexible credits. If the benefit is purchased with credits, the cost will be a taxable benefit to the employee.

- **Enrollment date.** Home and auto insurance does not easily fit into an annual flexible benefit enrollment cycle. Since individuals' personal coverage comes up for renewal throughout the year, it is common for group coverage to continue this practice. So the enrollment is spread throughout the year, instead of being concentrated on one date, as is the rest of the flexible program. Therefore, it is very difficult to integrate the coverage fully with the rest of the flexible program—and, as a result, credits freed up from other benefits, cannot easily be used to pay for home and auto coverage.

To overcome this, some employers require all home and auto policies for their employees to mature on a common date. This allows
the benefit to be coordinated with other plans. Insurance carriers
generally resist a common anniversary date, because it makes it too
easy for the employers to compare insurance rates, and, if appropriate, change carriers in the future.

- **Location of employees.** Most or all insurance companies offering
  group coverage will claim to provide services in all provinces (unless provincial auto insurance eliminates the need for private coverage). A national employer should ask for references from the insurer
  to determine how consistent the administration is across Canada,
  and how well the insurer serves rural areas.

- **Policy provisions.** If home and auto is offered in conjunction with a
  full flexible benefit program, it is imperative that the coverage be
  flexible. For example, in auto insurance, employees should be given a
  range of deductibles from which to choose, a range of liability limits
  and so forth. For home insurance, replacement cost coverage, coverage on seasonal residences and boats and motors, and so on should
  be available.

- **Administration/claims payment.** Many employees elect not to introduce group home and auto insurance, because of the fear that
  poor administration will cause the plan to backfire. If claims are
  rejected by the insurer, or take a long time to be paid, employees will
  complain to the employer. The best advice is to ask other companies
  what their experience has been with the particular insurer.

(b)   GROUP LEGAL

The Canadian Auto Workers (CAW) negotiated a group legal services
plan for its members in 1984. Despite much publicity, few organizations
outside the auto industry have adopted legal plans.

Where plans are provided, the employee may have specified legal
services—wills, home purchases, marriage contracts, and so forth—
performed by a legal panel. Normally, the employee is not permitted to
use the plan to sue the employer.

The structure of a group legal plan is similar to that of the capitation dental plan described in Chapter Five—the employer pays a fixed
fee per employee to the provider and the employee must use the services of specified provider (lawyer or dentist). The reaction of the legal
profession to group legal plans has been similar to that of the dental
association to capitation plans; they don't like the concept and argue

that it removes an employee's freedom of choice. An obvious advantage of such plans, however, is the potential for lower than average fees, which larger employers are able to negotiate.

One reason legal plans have not become more popular is that the employer premium for the coverage is taxable to the employee—so any credits used to purchase group legal coverage would be taxable income to the employee. Therefore, unlike dental, there is no tax advantage to providing legal benefits through a flexible program. Another difficulty in including group legal in a flexible program is adverse selection—any employees who anticipate having legal expenses in the coming year will purchase the coverage. The cost of coverage would, therefore, escalate and could become prohibitive.

(c) CAR LEASING

Firms offering fleet leasing policies to employers claim they offer significant savings to employees due to group purchasing power. Typically, the employee decides on a car and options and then places an order with the fleet operator. Normally, there is a minimum number of months of installments (six is common) that the employee must make before the balance can be paid off.

The 7 percent Goods and Services Tax (GST) scheduled to begin in 1991 may make group car leasing less attractive than an individual borrowing money from the bank to buy a car. That's because interest charged by a bank does not attract the GST, whereas the full lease payment on a car (principal and interest) is taxable.

(d) SMOKING CESSATION AND OTHER HEALTH-RELATED COUNSELLING

The cost of enrolling in a stop smoking program could be paid out of a health care expense account as a permitted medical expense. Similarly, the cost of tobacco, drug, alcohol, and stress management consulting could be paid from an account.

(e) FITNESS CLUB

This is usually restricted to specialized fitness centres and would exclude sports and social clubs, such as golf and curling clubs. Any employer subsidy of the cost (either a direct subsidy or through flexible credits) is taxable income to the employee unless there is a business purpose for the membership.

Part Three

Legal and Regulatory Environment

Eleven

Taxation of Flexible Benefits

§ 11.1 INTRODUCTION: THE LEGAL FRAMEWORK

Like any other employee benefit plan, there is a legal framework or set of rules within which flexible benefit plans must operate.

Flexible benefits means basically that employees are allowed to choose among different forms and levels of benefits. Each of the separate benefits included within a flexible benefit program must comply with the set of rules applicable to that particular benefit. For example, if a dental program is included as one of the choices in a flexible benefit program, the dental plan will be subject to the same Revenue Canada rules that apply to a stand-alone plan. Similarly, if group term life insurance is a choice, laws governing the maximum employer-paid benefits that can be provided on a non-taxable basis must be reflected. The point is that a separate set of rules applies to each separate benefit within a flexible benefit program.

Another part of the framework governs choices between taxable and non-taxable benefits. The rules permitting this kind of choice making comprise a relatively new part of the legal framework and apply to the flexible benefit program as a whole, rather than to the separate benefit components within the program. This portion of the legal framework establishes the conditions under which choices between taxable and non-taxable benefits may be made.

If a plan permits choices between non-taxable benefits only, or between taxable benefits only, no special legal framework is applicable to the choice-making mechanism. (In these situations, however, the rules applicable to each separate benefit still need to be considered.) Choices between taxable and non-taxable benefits would normally trigger a tax doctrine called "constructive receipt." Essentially, the doctrine of constructive receipt provides that if an employee has the right to income, the employee will be taxed as if the employee actually received that income, whether or not the right is exercised.

The doctrine of constructive receipt will not be applied by Revenue Canada in all cases, however. This will be discussed in more detail later in the chapter.

The legal framework, then, consists of two parts: the taxation of each individual benefit in a flexible benefit program and the tax consequences arising from the choice between taxable and non-taxable benefits. The laws and policies of Revenue Canada make up this legal framework and determine how benefits are taxed.

The information in this chapter has been obtained from a variety of sources. Aside from an examination of basic references such as the Income Tax Act and Revenue Canada Interpretation Bulletins, information has also been obtained from advance rulings on specific flexible benefit plans and a series of meetings with Revenue Canada over the course of several years. Despite an extensive review of these sources, there are still areas of flexible benefit taxation that remain unclear. These areas undoubtedly will be clarified in coming years as the popularity of flexible benefit plans continues to grow.

§ 11.2 REVENUE CANADA: LAWS AND POLICY

Five sources must be examined to determine the tax consequences of flexible benefit programs:

- The Income Tax Act
- Interpretation Bulletins published by Revenue Canada
- Advance rulings and opinion letters of Revenue Canada
- The doctrine of constructive receipt
- Court decisions.

(a) INCOME TAX ACT

The Income Tax Act specifies that all employment benefits be included in an employee's taxable income. Paragraph 6(1)(a) states that an employee's employment income shall include:

> the value of board, lodging and other benefits of any kind whatever received or enjoyed by him in the year in respect of, in the course of, or by virtue of an office or employment . . .

Paragraph 6(1)(a) also lists exceptions to this rule. Benefits excluded from an employee's employment income are those:

> derived from his employer's contributions to or under a registered pension plan or fund, group sickness or accident insurance plan, private health services plan, supplementary unemployment benefit plan, deferred profit sharing plan or group term life insurance policy . . .

Although the exceptions listed above do not address flexible benefit plans specifically, it should be noted that the mere act of granting flexible credits to an employee does not trigger tax consequences. If flexible credits were taxed when granted, flexible benefit programs would be at a competitive disadvantage to other benefit arrangements. The non-taxable employer premium for benefits, such as dental insurance, for example, would become taxable under a flexible benefit program. To eliminate this concern, the taxation of flexible benefits is determined only after the employee makes his or her election. If the employee fails to make an election within the time period stated by the plan, the appropriate tax rules will be applied to the default election specified by the plan. If the default election is a taxable benefit, the employee will be taxed accordingly.

These basic rules form the basis of benefits taxation. We must turn to other sources, however, for a detailed explanation of these rules.

(b) INTERPRETATION BULLETINS

Although the Income Tax Act contains the broad provisions relating to the taxation of benefits, most of the detail is found in the various Revenue Canada Interpretation Bulletins. Interpretation Bulletins set out the administrative policies of Revenue Canada. Although they do not have the force of law, they are applied, for the most part, as if legally binding. Interpretation Bulletin IT-339R, for instance, sets out the criteria for a

"Private Health Services Plan." Health plans not meeting the criteria contained in IT-339R would be prohibited from claiming the special status afforded such qualifying health plans in paragraph 6(1)(a) of the Income Tax Act.

Other Interpretation Bulletins deal with other benefits available to employees under a flexible benefit program. These will be discussed in the analysis of specific benefit options later in this chapter. It should be noted, however, that the Interpretation Bulletins do not cover the taxation of every benefit. In those situations, the general principles of statutory interpretation (in this case, of the Income Tax Act) prevail.

(c)   ADVANCE RULINGS AND OPINION LETTERS

When the meaning of the Income Tax Act and the various Interpretation Bulletins published by Revenue Canada is unclear, an individual or company can apply for an advance ruling by Revenue Canada on the application of the Income Tax Act to a specific flexible benefit program. Such rulings are binding on the plan sponsor and participating employees. The only means of challenging such a ruling is by way of a court application.

Because flexible benefit plans are relatively new in Canada, advance rulings on flexible benefit programs have not been challenged in court. However, several companies have received advance rulings on flexible benefit plans. Such rulings have confirmed the various points discussed in this chapter. Revenue Canada also has responded to inquiries of a general nature by way of opinion letters, which are not binding but state the position Revenue Canada likely would take, if it were to rule on the provisions of a specific program. These opinion letters have been taken into consideration in the discussion of issues in this chapter. As flexible benefit programs become more prevalent in Canada, the tax consequences will become more clearly defined.

(d)   DOCTRINE OF CONSTRUCTIVE RECEIPT

The doctrine of constructive receipt is a common law principle applied by Revenue Canada in the interpretation of the Income Tax Act.

As discussed earlier, the doctrine of constructive receipt provides that if an employee has the *right* to income, the employee will be taxed as if the employee actually received that income, whether or not the right is exercised.

Consider the doctrine of constructive receipt as it would apply to a choice between taking flexible credits in cash or putting the money into a health care expense account. The doctrine would require that even though the employee chose health care benefits (which are not taxable), the employee is taxed because of the *right* to receive cash (which is taxable).

Appropriately, Revenue Canada has not applied the doctrine to such routine flexible benefit elections as described previously. Unlike the United States, however, Canada has no comprehensive legislation that specifically exempts flexible benefit programs from many constructive receipt situations. Consequently, it is unclear how Revenue Canada intends to apply the doctrine. The doctrine could be applied by Revenue Canada, for instance, in cases in which an employee chooses to take a salary reduction, or forgo a scheduled salary increase, and elects a non-taxable benefit in its place. In such cases, the employee would be taxed as if he or she had received cash. Such situations could also be subject to the salary-deferral-arrangement rules discussed in § 11.4.

From discussions with Revenue Canada, one general rule concerning constructive receipt does emerge. As long as the employee cannot manipulate salary or salary increases to fund non-taxable benefits, it is unlikely that Revenue Canada will apply the doctrine of constructive receipt. This means that employees must choose their individual benefits prior to the plan year and *cannot change or revoke* their choices mid-year.

Exceptions will be made if the employee experiences a mid-year change in family status—for example, the birth or death of a dependent, marriage or divorce, and so forth. In these cases, changes in elections are permitted by Revenue Canada. Until a comprehensive set of rules is developed, however, the doctrine of constructive receipt will be applied on a case-by-case basis.

(e)   COURT DECISIONS

To date, there have been no decisions of universal application to flexible benefit programs. As such plans become more common, challenges will undoubtedly be made in the tax court. Such decisions will be binding on both Revenue Canada and the plan sponsors.

§ 11.3   TAXATION OF SPECIFIC FLEXIBLE BENEFITS

(a)   HEALTH CARE BENEFITS

A key component of almost every flexible benefit program is choice making in the area of health care benefits. Health care benefits typically include dental expenses, supplemental medical plan coverage, prescription drugs, vision care, semi-private hospital, and other related health care expenses. These plans are normally structured as Private Health Services Plans to receive favourable tax treatment. As discussed previously in this chapter, Interpretation Bulletin 339R sets out the criteria for qualification as a Private Health Services Plan.

The five basic elements are as follows:

1. It must be an undertaking of one person
2. To indemnify another person
3. For an agreed consideration
4. From a loss or liability in respect of an event
5. The happening of which is uncertain.

Qualification entitles an employer to deduct premiums as a business expense (with no deemed benefit to the employee) and allows tax-free reimbursement to employees for covered expenses.

(1) Supplemental Medical Plans

Most employees are familiar with traditional supplemental medical plans. Typically, after paying a variable deductible amount, employees are reimbursed for medical expenses not covered by provincial health insurance, up to certain annual or lifetime maximums. Such coverage is of less importance in Canada than in the United States, where public health insurance is restricted to very low-income earners. However, expenses in Canada can still be considerable.

Virtually all supplemental medical plans meet the five criteria described above to qualify as Private Health Services Plans. As such, employers can deduct the amount of all premiums and employees are reimbursed on a tax-free basis.

(2) Dental Plans

Because there is limited public dental insurance coverage in Canada, dental care is a high priority for most employees. Dental plans operate much like supplemental medical plans. In order for employees to receive tax-free reimbursement of expenses, and for the employer premium to be non-taxable to the employee, dental plans must meet the criteria of a Private Health Services Plan. Virtually all dental plans meet these criteria.

(3)   Vision Care Plans

Vision care plans must also qualify as Private Health Services Plans to receive favourable tax treatment. Although employees generally have more control over vision care needs than dental and medical needs, there is still enough uncertainty associated with eye care to equate vision care plans with insurance.

Thus, qualification as a Private Health Services Plan is fairly straight-forward. The tax implications of vision care plans are identical to those for medical and dental plans.

(4)   Health Care Expense Accounts

Health care expense accounts are designed to cover minor health care expenses or the deductible or coinsurance amounts required under traditional medical plans. Employees can elect to allocate flexible credits to their health care account. Throughout the year, employees are reimbursed out of their accounts for covered expenses. When the money in the health care account is used up, the employee will receive no further reimbursement for that year.

To qualify as a Private Health Services Plan, a health care account must contain the five criteria mentioned previously. This includes the criterion of some uncertainty that the risk covered will actually occur. In other words, there must be some chance that the employee will have to forfeit the "premium" allocated to the account. The health care account must resemble true insurance to qualify. If the insured event does not occur, the premium (or in the case of a health care account, the account balance) is lost. This was how such health care expense accounts were traditionally set up.

Revenue Canada has stated (unofficially), however, that it may be possible to refund unused health account dollars at the end of a plan year or to roll over unused amounts for an unspecified period of time, perhaps several years. There would still be some element of risk to the employee, but this would lessen the chances of the employee having to forfeit account funds. In essence, the only way an employee would lose his or her health care expense account dollars is if the employee terminated employment mid-year and had "rolled over" dollars still in the account from the prior year. The employee would still be able to have his or her current-year dollars refunded. In addition, when unused health care expense account dollars are rolled over, they will be deemed to be used first when a claim is made the following year. This "first-in, first-out" principle again minimizes the chance of an employee having to forfeit funds. Since Revenue Canada's position on roll-overs and refunds has not been officially stated, we do not know at this time what the scope of the roll-over provisions will be.

Other health care plans that do not qualify as Private Health Services Plans are subject to the normal tax rules. The premiums paid on behalf of employees, or the amounts allocated to their health care accounts, are considered taxable benefits.

(b) LIFE INSURANCE

(1) Group Term Life Insurance

Most employers offer some form of group term life insurance insuring the lives of their employees. Group insurance plans, like Private Health Services Plans, are an exception to the normal rule that all benefits be included in an employee's income. To qualify for this special tax status, the insurance policy must pay a benefit only upon the death or disability of the insured employee. The policy cannot be restricted to accidental death. The detailed qualifications for such policies are contained in Section 248(1) of the Income Tax Act and Interpretation Bulletin 227R.

If a policy meets the above qualifications, the premium paid by an employer on behalf of an employee is not considered a taxable benefit to the employee, if the employer-provided insurance coverage is $25,000 or less.

Because premium payments attributable to employer-provided coverage above $25,000 are included in the income of employees, a method of determining the taxable benefit is needed. The cost of insurance to an individual employee is based on the cost of insurance to the group as a whole.

The following example assumes a net premium cost to the employer (reflecting any experience rating refund) of $100,000 and a total amount of term life insurance of $20,000,000:

$$\text{Average cost per \$1,000 of insurance:}\quad \$100,000 \times \frac{\$1,000}{\$20,000,000} = \$5$$

If an employee were insured for employer-provided coverage of $60,000, the premiums attributable to $35,000 of insurance ($60,000 − $25,000) would be included in income and taxed accordingly. Thus,

$$(\$35,000 \times \frac{\$5}{\$1,000}) = \$175$$

would be included in the employee's income. The employer must withhold tax on this amount.

Any additional group insurance above the $25,000 threshold, purchased by an employee with flexible credits, is considered company-paid and will, therefore, generate a taxable benefit. Although these tax consequences may discourage many employees from purchasing additional insurance using credits, there are incentives for certain employees to purchase insurance.

For example, if the cost of a company's group term insurance is graded according to the age of the insured, then it is advantageous for older employees to purchase additional insurance with credits, if the flexible benefit program permits. If, as in the above example, the average group cost of insurance is $5 per $1,000 of insurance, and the actual insurance premium for an older employee is $8 per $1,000 of insurance, the older employee will only be taxed on premiums based on the group average of $5. Conversely, a younger employee might only have to pay $2 per $1,000 of insurance, but will be taxed on premiums at the group rate of $5 per $1,000. The group-average-cost concept will be of great advantage to an older employee in such circumstances, but will penalize a younger employee who wishes to buy additional insurance with his or her flexible credits. The younger employee would be better off buying the coverage using payroll deductions.

(2)   Survivor's Income

If employer-paid survivor's income benefits (paid on a periodic basis rather than as a lump sum) are provided under the flexible program, the lump-sum value of the benefit must be calculated for purposes of determining the amount of insurance provided. This lump-sum amount would then be added to the lump-sum amount of company-paid group life insurance payable upon the employee's death to determine the taxable benefit to the employee.

(3)   Dependent Life Insurance

In addition to insuring their own lives, employees often wish to take out additional insurance on the lives of their spouse and children. Dependent life insurance, however, is granted no special tax status. If dependent life insurance premiums are paid with flexible credits, the cost will be considered a taxable benefit and included in the employee's income according to Section 6(1) of the Income Tax Act. Even though the insurance covers the spouse or child of the employee, Revenue Canada has taken the position that it is still a benefit enjoyed by the employee by virtue of his or her employment, and thus is taxable. The flexible credits used to purchase additional insurance will be included in the income of the employee. Therefore, the employee would be better off buying this coverage with payroll deductions and using the credits to purchase more tax-favourable coverage, such as dental insurance.

(4)   Whole Life and Universal Life Insurance

There are no employee tax exemptions for employer-paid whole life or universal life insurance premiums. Paragraph 6 of Interpretation Bulletin 227R states that any policy with a cash surrender value is not a term life insurance policy and is thus not eligible for special tax treatment. Employees who purchase whole life or universal life insurance with flexible credits will have the value of the premium included in their taxable income for the year.

(5)   Accidental Death and Dismemberment

Accidental death and dismemberment (AD&D) insurance provides lump-sum payments to covered employees in the event of accidental injury or death. The lump-sum payments complement the periodic payments that might be paid to employees under a wage loss replacement plan. The taxation rules associated with AD&D insurance are relatively straightforward. Such insurance falls under section 6(1)(a)(i) of the Income Tax Act as a "group sickness or accident insurance plan." Like disability insurance, the premiums paid to purchase AD&D insurance are not included in the income of the employee. Unlike group term life insurance, there is no maximum coverage rule limiting the tax-free benefit to the employee. In addition, lump-sum payments received by an employee are excluded from the employee's income by virtue of Section 6(1)(a)(i) of the Income Tax Act.

Therefore, even if AD&D insurance is purchased with employer-provided credits, the benefits are received by employees tax-free.

There may be a concern that the accidental death portion of the insurance falls under the definition of group term life insurance and is subject to the $25,000 maximum benefit for tax-free premiums. Paragraph 3 of Interpretation Bulletin 227R, however, defines "life insurance" as "insurance payable in the event of death from any cause." Because accidental death insurance restricts payments to circumstances of *accidental* death, it may not be included in Revenue Canada's definition. Most employers consider AD&D premiums to be a tax-free benefit to employees.

There is a similar concern with AD&D insurance provided to dependents of employees. Employers have traditionally treated such insurance as a non-taxable benefit to employees, although pure dependent life insurance is taxable to the employee.

(c) SHORT- AND LONG-TERM DISABILITY

Short- and long-term disability plans are considered wage loss replacement plans by Revenue Canada. Interpretation Bulletin 428 defines a wage loss replacement plan as:

> any arrangement, however it is styled, between an employer and employees, under which provision is made for indemnification of an employee, by means of benefits payable on a periodic basis, if an employee suffers a loss of employment income as a consequence of sickness, maternity or accident.

This definition encompasses both short-term and long-term disability plans. Section 6(1)(a)(i) of the Income Tax Act excludes any employer contributions used to fund such plans from the income of employees. Unlike the $25,000 tax-free coverage limit for group term life insurance, there is no such limit on wage loss replacement plans. Generally, short-term disability plans (where employees have a certain number of sick days allowable per year) are employer-funded on a pay-as-needed basis and are not included in flexible benefit programs. Long-term disability plans, however, often form part of flexible benefit plans.

Where an employer pays for long-term disability coverage, Section 6(1)(f) of the Income Tax Act provides that any benefits received by the employee will be included in the employee's income and taxed accordingly. Long-term disability coverage purchased with flexible credits is considered employer-paid and the benefit payment is taxed accordingly. As discussed earlier, the actual credits used to purchase the coverage are not taxable. The employer has paid for the coverage (by providing flexible credits) and in such cases, all disability benefits received by the employee are taxable.

The benefits provided under employee-paid disability coverage, however, are not taxable. If the employee pays for the entire cost of insurance on an after-tax basis, any benefits payable under the plan will be received by the employee tax-free. Simply put, an employee-paid plan is not a plan within the meaning of Section 6(1)(f) of the Income Tax Act (employer-paid plans) and is not taxable as such.

There is no "best" way to pay for long-term disability coverage. Some employers pay the premium so their employees do not need to make payroll deductions. Others argue that employees should pay the premium so that any benefit payment is received tax-free. Many flexible programs leave the decision up to the employee—either pay for the coverage with flexible credits or payroll deductions. To protect the tax-free status of payroll deduction plans in these cases, employers should set up separate insurance arrangements (such as contracts or funding agreements) for employer-paid and employee-paid plans. This guarantees that no employer premium subsidy is directed to the employee-paid plan. The costs associated with maintaining such plans should develop separately over time.

(d) VACATION TIME

The buying of vacation time under a flexible benefit program is a contentious tax issue which, to date, has not been resolved. Revenue Canada is concerned this option could be used to defer or avoid income tax. For instance, an employee could buy additional vacation time with payroll deductions (in effect, taking time off without pay). If the employee doesn't use the vacation days in the year of purchase, the employee could roll unused vacation days into the following year. If the employee does not use the vacation days the second year, the employer may allow a cash-out of the unused portion. This results in a one-year deferral in the receipt of taxable income.

Revenue Canada has indicated informally its difficulty with vacation buying as part of flexible benefit programs. The potential for abuse, as just described, makes such schemes an undesirable element, according to the tax authorities. Vacation buying, however, is already entrenched as an important and popular part of many flexible benefit programs. But the option is included to offer employees flexibility; not to help them defer tax. Despite this, Revenue Canada likely will adopt rules or laws in the future to minimize the so-called abuses.

One rule likely to be adopted works as follows: if an employee normally has 10 vacation days in a year, and purchases two extra days from the employer, the two extra days would be the last vacation days he or she takes in the year. No roll-overs of these two days of purchased vacation time would be permitted. Thus, if the employee only uses 11 of the 12 available days, the one extra day would be considered one of the purchased days and it could not be rolled over. The employee would be given a refund in cash at the end of the year.

This would eliminate Revenue Canada's concern as the employee would pay the income tax within the year. In effect, the employee would have provided the employer with an interest-free loan of one day's pay for the year. The employee is, therefore, penalized if all available vacation time is not used in the year. This arrangement was adopted in the United States to prevent the possibility of salary deferral.

At present, Revenue Canada has not articulated any clear rules. It is likely, however, that restrictions will be applied at some time. Revenue Canada has indicated informally that vacation-buying options using the no-roll-over-of-purchased-days principle would be acceptable.

Vacation selling does not appear to pose any tax problems, as there is no possibility of tax loss or deferral of income. An employee making $30,000, with three weeks of vacation, might decide to sell one week of vacation for $600 (2 percent of $30,000). The employee will be taxed according to how he or she allocates the amount within the flexible benefit program. If, for instance, the employee buys $600 worth of dependent life insurance, he or she will be taxed on the $600. If, instead, the employee elects to place the money in health care expense account, no tax will be paid. In any event, Revenue Canada has suffered no loss of revenue. (The employee still earns $30,000 and will still be taxed on the full $30,000.) It is unlikely, therefore, that restrictions governing vacation selling need be adopted.

(e) CASH PAYMENTS AND TRANSFERS

In lieu of purchasing benefits, employees may, if the flexible benefit program permits, take their unused flexible credits in cash. The cash payment would be included in income and taxed accordingly.

However, other options also may be available. If employees have room in their group or individual Registered Retirement Savings Plan (RRSP), then tax can be deferred by contributing the cash to such a plan. If the employer administers a pension plan that permits voluntary employee contributions, employees also can shelter taxable income in this manner. For a pension plan or RRSP, the employee must include the transferred amount as income, but the Income Tax Act permits a corresponding deduction, up to a set maximum, which by 1995 will be adjusted annually for inflation. Money can only be contributed to such tax-deferred plans if contribution room for that year still exists in the plans. Likewise, the money may be deposited in an employer-sponsored deferred profit sharing plan. The money contributed to a deferred profit sharing plan would be characterized as an employer contribution and would not be taxable income to the employee. The income earned by the contributions accumulates tax-free—no tax is paid by the employee.

(f) PERQUISITES

The taxation of perquisites or fringe benefits is based primarily on Section (6)(1)(a) of the Income Tax Act and Interpretation Bulletin 470. The Interpretation Bulletin contains an incomplete list of perquisites. Revenue Canada may informally articulate its position on certain benefits not referred to in the Bulletin; however, not all of these positions have been officially sanctioned.

There are a variety of benefits that employers may include in a flexible benefit program, although many of these benefits are offered only to employees at an executive level. These include club memberships, financial planning, home computers, parking, day care, and car telephones. The general rule is that the value of all fringe benefits is taxable to the employee, although exceptions are made in some cases. Employee club memberships, for instance, if primarily for the benefit of the employer, are not taxable to the employee. Parking and day care facilities are not taxable benefits if facilities are provided on-site by the employer. Otherwise, the benefits are taxable. Financial planning, if provided in-house, has not been taxable in the past; however, recent changes to Interpretation Bulletin 470 state that all financial planning provided directly by the employer will be taxable beginning in 1990. Planning related to re-employment or retirement, however, is not taxable. Individual or group counselling provided by outside professionals, except for purposes of re-employment or retirement, is also taxable.

There are, however, some tax-effective alternatives to the traditional fringe benefits listed above. These may be provided through a flexible expense account, as described in Chapter Seven, or as stand-alone benefit options within the flexible program. Section 80.4 of the Income Tax Act and Interpretation Bulletin 421R provide some relief in exempting group mortgage plans from taxation. Employees can elect to use some of their flexible benefit dollars to pay a portion of their mortgage interest expense. Revenue Canada sets a prescribed rate each month. The amount by which the employee's mortgage rate exceeds the prescribed rate can be subsidized tax-free. For example, if the employee's mortgage rate is 2 percent higher than the prescribed rate the employee can pay up to 2 percent of interest with tax-free credits from the flexible benefit program. If the employee had a mortgage of $100,000, up to $2,000 could be allocated under the flexible program to the employee's mortgage account. The $2,000 is not subject to tax. The advantage, however, of group mortgage plans disappears if the market mortgage rate drops below the Revenue Canada prescribed rate.

Other fringe benefits exempt from taxation include: reimbursement of moving expenses for transferred employees, subsidized meals, and discounts on the purchase of merchandise from the employer (at cost or higher). These exemptions are outlined in greater detail in Interpretation Bulletin 470.

Revenue Canada has taken a strict position on such perquisites as home computers and car telephones. Even if these items are used exclusively for business purposes, Revenue Canada has stated they are a taxable benefit to the employee. The employee, however, may be able to claim a deduction for the cost of these items.

Instead of actually buying computers or car telephones for employees, many companies simply keep the item in the name of the company. The employee can then use the item, while never actually owning it. A taxable benefit of the book value (undepreciated capital cost) is created if he or she later leaves the company and keeps the equipment.

§ 11.4 SALARY DEFERRAL

Generally, employment income is taxed when received by the employee. The salary deferral rules found in the Income Tax Act, and the doctrine of constructive receipt, are two exceptions to this general rule. The exceptions are designed to prevent employees from delaying the receipt of earned income in order to delay or reduce tax payments. Section 248(1) of the Income Tax Act defines a salary deferral arrangement as:

> a plan or arrangement, whether funded or not, under which any person has a right in a taxation year to receive an amount after the year where it is reasonable to consider that one of the main purposes for the creation or existence of the right is to postpone tax payable under this Act by the taxpayer in respect of an amount that is, or is on account or in lieu of, salary or wages of the taxpayer for services rendered by him in the year or a preceding taxation year . . .

The issue of salary deferral arises when an employee chooses to forgo a salary increase, defer a bonus entitlement, or reduce salary in exchange for more flexible credits, which can then be channelled into non-taxable benefits. Revenue Canada has stated that it will not allow employees to elect non-taxable benefits in lieu of salary, because it views this as a salary deferral arrangement. This type of arrangement is also caught by the doctrine of constructive receipt, as discussed earlier.

Revenue Canada has stated, however, that the employer can unilaterally elect to reduce or eliminate a salary increase and give an employee or group of employees a choice between cash and benefits. As long as an employee has no decision-making power in reducing his or her salary, Revenue Canada will not consider this a salary deferral arrangement. Employers, however, must ensure the decision to use potential salary increases to fund benefits is theirs alone.

Revenue Canada's position on flexible benefits and salary deferral has not been challenged in the courts. There are circumstances that do not appear to be caught by the salary deferral wording. Although reducing your salary to buy non-taxable benefits might be prima facie evidence of salary deferral, opting to forgo potential salary increases or bonuses in advance of a plan year would hardly seem so. Employees do not generally have a right to future salary increases. The premise of a salary deferral arrangement is that employees give up their right to salary. In addition, it is not clear that one of the main reasons for forgoing an increase is to postpone taxation. This will, of course, depend on the facts of the individual case. It is almost always cheaper, for example, for an employee to purchase benefits from his or her employer than to buy benefits individually. Postponing tax may be of little or no concern to the individual.

Finally, one need only look at typical union negotiations to see that the forgoing of future salary increases to fund benefits is common practice. Typically, a monetary increase is agreed-upon between management and the union. Further negotiations then ensue to determine how this increase will be spent. Some portion will go to benefits, the rest to salary. There appears to be little difference between the traditional union negotiations and the forgoing of a salary increase in the context of a flexible benefit program. Until Revenue Canada's position is challenged, however, the scope of the salary deferral rules will remain undefined.

Employers who wish to adopt this position should consult their tax advisors, since they may need to proceed before the courts if challenged by Revenue Canada.

Table 11.1 summarizes the tax treatment of benefit plans within a flexible program. The relevant Revenue Canada Interpretation Bulletins are included in the Appendix to this book.

Table 11.1
Taxation of Flexible Benefits

Benefit	Employer-Paid (with Pre-Tax Flexible Credits)	Source	Employee-Paid (with After-Tax Payroll Deductions)
Medical/Dental/ Vision Care Insurance	Company deducts cost of premiums. Premiums are a tax-free benefit to employee. Employee not taxed on any benefits paid out.	IT-339R S.6(1)(a) *Income Tax Act*	Benefit is tax-free.
Health Care Expense Account	Company deducts amount allocated to account. Employee not taxed on amount allocated or reim-bursed for valid expenses. Roll-overs permitted to following year.	IT-339R S.6(1)(a) *Income Tax Act*	Not permitted.
Group Term Life Insurance	Company deducts cost of premiums. Premiums for up to $25,000 worth of insurance are a tax-free benefit to employee. Employee taxed on premi-ums used to buy insurance in excess of $25,000. Benefit is tax-free.	IT-227R S.6(1) *Income Tax Act*	Benefit is tax-free.
Survivor's Income Insurance	Company deducts cost of premiums. Premiums on lump sum equivalents exceeding $25,000 are a taxable bene-fit to the employee. Interest portion of benefit payment is taxable. Capital portion is tax-free	IT-227R S.6(1) S.12(4) *Income Tax Act*	Interest portion of benefit pay-ment is taxable. Capital portion is tax-free.
Dependent Life Insurance	Company deducts cost of premiums. Premiums are a taxable benefit to employee. Benefit is tax-free.	IT-227R S.6(1) *Income Tax Act*	Benefit is tax-free.
Whole Life and Universal Insurance	Company deducts cost of premiums. Premiums are a taxable benefit to the employee. Benefit is tax-free.	S.6(1)(a) *Income Tax Act*	Benefit is tax-free.

Table 11.1 (*Continued*)

Benefit	Employer-Paid (with Pre-Tax Flexible Credits)	Source	Employee-Paid (with After-Tax Payroll Deductions)
Accidental Death and Dis-memberment Insurance	Company deducts cost of premiums. Premiums are a tax-free benefit to employee. Benefit is tax-free.	S.6(1)(a) & S.6(1)(f) *Income Tax Act* IT-428	Benefit is tax-free.
Long Term Disability Insurance	Company deducts cost of premiums. Premiums are a tax-free benefit to employee. Employee is taxed on benefits paid out.	S.6(1)(a) & S.6(1)(f) *Income Tax Act* IT-428	Benefit is tax-free.
Vacation Buying	Company deducts amount used to purchase vacation. Employee not taxed on purchase price, but cannot roll over vacation days to following year.		Not applicable.
Vacation Selling	Proceeds from sale taxed according to how they are used.		Not applicable.
Perquisites	Company deducts cost of perquisite. Employee may be taxed on value of perquisite, subject to specific exemptions.	IT-470 S.6(1)(a) *Income Tax Act*	Employee may be able to deduct cost as a business expense.
Group Mortgage Plans	Company deducts amount allocated to mortgage account. Employee not taxed to extent amount allocated is used to pay interest above prescribed rate.	IT-421R	Not applicable.

Twelve

Human Rights Legislation

§ 12.1 INTRODUCTION

Compensation and benefit plans are coming under increased scrutiny by Canadian courts as individuals and interest groups focus their attention on employment discrimination issues. Employers face a difficult challenge in working through the maze of federal and provincial legislation governing employment discrimination.

§ 12.2 CANADIAN CHARTER OF RIGHTS AND FREEDOMS

The Charter has a potentially significant role to play in the development of employment discrimination issues. The Charter is entrenched as part of Canada's Constitution and can override federal and provincial government legislation that violates its provisions.

The Charter is limited in scope in that it does not apply to the acts of private individuals; it applies only to the acts of government or institutions exercising governmental functions. With regard to traditional and flexible benefit plans, the Charter could be used in a court application to strike down provincial legislation that permits discrimination in some instances. Provincial discrimination provisions are discussed in more detail in § 12.3.

Section 15(1) of the Charter states that:

Every individual is equal before and under the law and has the right to the equal protection and equal benefit of the law without discrimination and, in particular, without discrimination based on race, national or ethnic origin, colour, religion, sex, age or mental or physical disability.

The application of Section 15(1) is not limited to the grounds of discrimination listed above, but can also encompass related grounds. Marital status might be one such related ground. It should be noted that all Charter rights are subject to the limits outlined in Section 1, which states that:

The Canadian Charter of Rights and Freedoms guarantees the rights and freedoms set out in it subject only to such reasonable limits prescribed by law as can be demonstrably justified in a free and democratic society.

In order to justify a Section 15 infringement under Section 1 of the Charter, the government must show a pressing and substantial reason for the infringement and demonstrate that the scope of the discrimination is not out of proportion to that reason. For example, if a provincial government were challenged on employment standards discrimination provisions, and the discrimination were found not to be justified, the legislation would be stuck down. Employers would then have to alter any existing benefit plans to eliminate such discrimination.

12.3   PROVINCIAL LEGISLATION

The provinces have enacted laws governing discrimination in employment. The federal government has also enacted similar laws protecting federal public sector employees and employees engaged in occupations (such as banking, interprovincial transportation, and communications) within the federal jurisdiction. The legislation comes in many forms, from general "equal treatment" provisions, to equal pay for equal work and equal pay for work of equal value (pay equity), to specific prohibitions against discrimination in benefit plans. (Equal pay for equal work and equal pay for work of equal value are discussed in § 12.5 and § 12.6, respectively.)

Each province has set its own employment standards in different manners and in different pieces of legislation. In Ontario, the Human Rights Code and the Employment Standards Act contain the bulk of employment discrimination provisions; in Alberta, one must look to the *Individual's Rights Protection Act*; in Quebec, the *Charter of Rights and Freedoms.*

(a) EQUAL TREATMENT PROVISIONS

Most of the jurisdictions guarantee "equal treatment with respect to employment." For example, Section 4(1) of the Ontario *Human Rights Code* states that:

> Every person has a right to equal treatment with respect to employment without discrimination because of race, ancestry, place of origin, colour, ethnic origin, citizenship, creed, sex, sexual orientation, age, record of offences, marital status, family status, or handicap.

Equal treatment "with respect to employment" may encompass many things, such as hiring, promotion, termination, retirement, compensation, benefits, and so on. Those jurisdictions without specific provisions or regulations respecting discrimination in compensation and benefits have formal or informal policies to administer their legislation in those areas.

(b) NON-DISCRIMINATION IN BENEFITS

Ontario has the most extensive legislation governing non-discrimination in benefits. The general rule in Ontario is stated in Section 34(2) of the *Employment Standards Act:*

> Except as provided in the regulations, no employer or person acting directly on behalf of an employer shall provide, furnish or offer any fund, plan, arrangement or benefit that differentiates or makes any distinction, exclusion or preference between his employees or class or classes of his employees or their beneficiaries, survivors or dependents because of the age, sex, or marital status of his employees.

On the basis of this Section, employers are prohibited from discriminating on the basis of age, gender or marital status in providing benefits to employees. The terminology "fund, plan, arrangement, or benefits" is intended to be all-encompassing. It includes all conventional individual and group insurance plans, pension plans, savings plans, and other fringe benefits.

The regulators in Ontario, and most other jurisdictions, recognize circumstances under which distinctions based on age, gender, or marital status may be valid. For example, most provinces expressly permit employers to contribute different amounts on behalf of different classes of employees. This is permitted for benefits such as life and health insurance and pensions, where there is an actuarial basis for making a distinction. The actuarial basis would typically be related to gender (as women on average live longer than men but have higher disability and medical costs) or age (costs of most group benefits increase with age).

Other jurisdictions (notably Alberta, British Columbia, Ontario, and the federal government and its agencies) permit exceptions on grounds of marital status, as well as age and gender. For example, an employer would be able to provide health insurance coverage to a married employee and extend coverage to the employee's spouse and children. A single employee would receive individual coverage, which would be less valuable than family coverage.

Ontario's Regulation 282 to the Employment Standards Act outlines the exceptions to the general rule contained in Section 34(2) of the Act. Regulation 282 differentiates between employee-pay-all plans and plans paid for in whole or in part by employer contributions. The rules for employee-pay-all plans are generally less restrictive than the employer-paid plan rules.

(1) Employee-Pay-All Plans

Regulation 282 permits the following exceptions to the requirements of Section 34(2) of the Employment Standards Act for employee-pay-all plans.

- Group Life
  Employee contributions for group life insurance may be lower for females than for males. The regulation permits:

  A differentiation in the contributions of an employee to a voluntary employee-pay-all life insurance plan where such differentiation is determined upon an actuarial basis because of sex. (Section 5(a))

  It is also permissible either to have higher premiums for older employees or to provide lower benefits for such older employees. The regulation permits:

  A differentiation in the benefits under or the contributions to a voluntary employee-pay-all life insurance plan where such differentiation is determined upon an actuarial basis because of age. (Section 7(a))

- Disability
  The employee premium for disability coverage can differ by the sex and age of the employee. The regulation permits:

  A differentiation in the rate of contributions of an employee to a voluntary employee-pay-all short or long term disability insurance plan where such differentiation is determined upon an actuarial basis because of the age or sex of the employee. (Section 8(a))

  However, in practice, few employers reflect age in the employee premiums and very few employers, if any, use sex-distinct premiums.

- Medical and Dental
  It is permissible to have employee premium rates that depend on the gender of the employee. Although this is rarely, if ever, done, the regulation permits:

  A differentiation in the rate of contributions of an employee to a voluntary employee-pay-all health insurance plan where such differentiation is determined upon an actuarial basis because of sex. (Section 9(a))

  Section 9(c) of Regulation 282 also allows for additional dependent health insurance coverage by permitting a differentiation in benefits or employee contributions, because of marital status. This differentiation can be made to provide benefits for an employee's spouse or dependent child. The section states:

  A differentiation in the benefits under or the contributions of an employee to a health insurance plan because of the marital status of the employee where such differentiation is made in order to provide benefits for a spouse or a dependent child of the employee.

(2)   Plans Having an Employer Contribution

Regulation 282 permits the following exceptions to the requirements of Section 34(2) of the Employment Standards Act for plans partially or fully paid by the employer.

- Group Life
  The employer is permitted to pay more for older employees and for male employees in order to equalize group life benefits.

  Section 5(a) covers exceptions based on gender:

A differentiation in the contributions of an employer to a life insurance plan where such differentiation is made on an actuarial basis because of the sex of the employee and in order to provide equal benefits under the plan.

Section 7(b) covers the permitted exceptions due to age:

A differentiation in the contributions of an employer to a life insurance plan where such differentiation is determined upon an actuarial basis because of age and in order to provide equal benefits under the plan.

- Disability
  The rules for disability are similar to those for life insurance. The employer can pay higher premiums for certain categories of employees to equalize benefits. The regulation permits:

  A differentiation in the rate of contributions of an employer to a short or long term disability insurance plan where such differentiation is made on an actuarial basis because of the age or sex of the employee and in order to provide equal benefits under the plan. (Section 8(b))

- Medical and Dental
  Employers can pay more for female employees to equalize medical and dental benefit levels. The regulation permits:

  A differentiation in the rate of contributions of an employer to a health insurance plan where such differentiation is made upon an actuarial basis because of the sex of the employee and in order to provide equal benefits under the plan. (Section 9(b))

Employers must pay the same proportional cost for single and family coverage. Section 9(d) permits:

A differentiation in the rate of contributions of an employer to a health insurance plan, where there are specified premium rates and where such differentiation for employees having marital status and for employees without marital status is on the same proportional basis.

This regulation was introduced to ensure employers did not discriminate against single employees by paying, say, 100 percent of premiums and only 50 percent of the single employee premiums. However, the wording may also prohibit the reverse; paying 100 percent of single premiums and only 50 percent of family premiums.

(c) APPLICATION OF PROVINCIAL RULES TO FLEXIBLE BENEFIT PLANS

Most of the legislation governing equal treatment in employment and non-discrimination in benefits was introduced long before the first flexible benefit plan was introduced in Canada.

The legislation and regulation provide exemptions on a plan-by-plan basis and do not contemplate whether or not a benefit program as a whole is discriminatory. The plan exemptions outlined previously differ by factor; for example, marital status is a permitted exemption for an employer medical contributions but not for a employer long-term disability contribution. How are the exemptions to be applied to a flexible benefit plan, where the employee has control over the flexible credits and decides how they will be used?

A second question arises because of the distinction between employee-pay-all plans and plans to which the employer contributes. Technically, flexible credits are characterized as an employer contribution, therefore, any benefit purchased with credits is an employer-paid benefit even though in most other respects, the plans resemble employee-paid plans.

(1) Illustration

Consider an employer who offers a competitive level of supplemental medical insurance as a standard option of a flexible benefit program. Employees would receive an employer contribution (flexible credits) exactly equal to the cost of this option. Therefore, an employee with a family might receive $400 in credits (the cost of the competitive supplemental medical option for a family), while a single employee might receive, say, $200 in credits (the single employee cost). All employees would, therefore, have sufficient credits to purchase the competitive supplemental medical option. However, an employee could, instead, elect a higher or lower level of supplemental medical coverage or decide to opt out of medical altogether and use the credits to purchase other benefits such as life insurance. Some programs would permit the employee to take the credits in cash. If both the single employee and the married employee, in the above example, buy life insurance or take cash, the married employee would receive twice as much as the single employee. Is this a permitted exception to the general non-discrimination rule in Section 34(2)?

Since the permitted exceptions differ by benefit area, an employer contribution that is permissible in one benefit area could technically violate the rules if the employee voluntarily elects to spend it in another area. The employer has no way of knowing how each employee intends to spend the credits because of the concept of choice inherent in flexible benefits.

For instance, in our previous example, the single employee received $200 in credits, while the family employee received $400. This is permissible under Section 9(d) of Regulation 282, if the credits are spent to buy medical coverage. However, if the two employees elect to spend the employer contribution on disability coverage, the family employee could purchase more than the single employee. This appears to violate Section 8(b) because the benefits are not equal.

Would a flat contribution of, say, $400 per employee, regardless of family status prevent this anomaly? Probably not, because a younger employee could purchase more life insurance than an older employee, where the group life contribution depends on age. This appears to violate Section 7(b), because the resulting company-paid life insurance benefits are unequal.

(2) Proposed Clarification for Flexible Plans

The previous illustration indicates that virtually any credit/pricing structure would be technically at odds with the rules, because it would violate at least one section of the regulation. This result is clearly illogical and arguably contrary to public policy. If one takes a narrow interpretation of the rules out of context, one can conclude that it is impossible to design a non-discriminatory flexible benefit plan.

How should this be clarified? The best solution would be for the regulators to add a regulation specifically dealing with flexible plans.

To illustrate how such a proposed regulation would work, assume there is a standard set of benefit options that the employer wishes to pay for fully by allocating sufficient credits so each employee can provide for his or her own premium. Under a special flexible benefit regulation, this structure would be permitted, assuming the employer contribution was non-discriminatory if every employee elected this standard set of benefits. The program would not become discriminatory merely because some employees voluntarily elected to spend the company credits on a different set of options.

(3)   Minimizing Risk of a Successful Challenge

In the absence of such a regulation, however, what can an employer do to minimize the risk? The first step is to discuss the situation with its counsel. Although many of the provincial authorities have been adopting narrow interpretations of the legislation, many employers interpret the regulations more liberally. The regulations concerning employer-paid plans use the term, "rate of contribution of an employer for a disability (or health or group life) plan." The *employer contribution* to a disability plan, which is part of a flexible program, could be interpreted as the number of flexible credits designed to allow the employee to purchase a specified level of disability benefit. If an employee spends the employer disability contribution elsewhere, this does not change the employer disability contribution and the fact that it was allocated in a non-discriminatory manner consistent with the regulations.

Furthermore, the 1975 Task Force report, which was used to develop the Ontario regulations, contains wording that would justify the pricing/credit structure described earlier. The report states:

> One approach to employee benefit plans which has attracted a great deal of discussion, but which has not yet been widely accepted, is the "cafeteria approach." Under this approach, an employer would provide each employee with a given benefit plan contribution, which the employee could allocate to the various types of benefits as he or she saw fit. The amount of each type of benefit which a given employee would receive would necessarily be determined on a money purchase basis; i.e. the amount of each benefit would be whatever could be purchased from the portion of the contribution allocated to that benefit by the employee, on the basis of actuarial cost factors corresponding to that employee's age and sex. The main advantage of this cafeteria approach is that each employee can tailor the benefit package to suit his or her own particular circumstances, taking into account such factors as state of health, nearness to retirement, number of dependents, and other financial considerations. However, this approach suffers from the same drawbacks as the employee-pay-all approach, since a contribution level that produces adequate benefits on the average will not necessarily produce adequate benefits for the high-cost employees.

The problem outlined in the last sentence—high-cost employees not having sufficient credits to buy adequate coverage where the contribution level buys adequate benefits on average—was also identified by employers as a shortfall of flexible programs. Therefore, instead of calculating an average contribution level for all employees, flexible plans typically grant more credits to higher cost employees (families, for example), so they have enough to purchase an adequate level of benefits. Therefore, the Task Force encouraged the growth of flexible credit structures that recognize that the cost of providing adequate benefits differs by employee.

Employers may decide to prohibit the purchase of group life benefits with flexible credits to minimize the risk of a discrimination challenge. A major concern of Ontario regulators is that older employees would not have sufficient credits to purchase company-paid life insurance. By making life insurance fully employee-paid, this concern is eliminated.

(4) Summary

Unfortunately, there is no definitive answer to this question and it is likely to remain unresolved for a number of years for at least three reasons:

- Some jurisdictions permit some degree of age, sex and marital discrimination in determining the employer contribution to traditional benefit plans. However, as described, their rules do not cover flexible plans.
- Other jurisdictions prohibit marital discrimination. Therefore, even traditional medical and dental plans may technically violate human rights legislation in these areas because the employer pays more for family coverage than for single coverage.
- National employers must deal with different jurisdictions, each having a different set of rules.

Employers with flexible benefit plans may run a risk of not complying with provincial anti-discrimination laws. The legislation, however, is enforced based on employee complaints. To date, the regulators have not received any complaints concerning flexible plans. Because of the uncertainty, plan sponsors should review these issues with their legal counsel.

§ 12.4   EQUAL PAY FOR EQUAL WORK

Equal pay for equal work is commonly understood to refer to legislation that specifically redresses gender discrimination in pay practices. In actual fact, the more general "equal treatment provisions" described in § 12.3 effectively disallow pay discrimination on all the listed prohibited grounds. For example, an employer would be prohibited from providing different amounts of pay solely based on an employee's race, marital status, age, and so forth.

Some jurisdictions, within the framework of "equal treatment" legislation, have enacted specific provisions directed at gender discrimination. For example, Section 33 of Ontario's *Employment Standards Act* states:

33.-(1) No employer or person acting on behalf of an employer shall differentiate between his male and female employees by paying a female employee at a rate of pay less than the rate of pay paid to a male employee, or vice versa, for substantially the same kind of work performed in the same establishment, the performance of which requires substantially the same skill, effort and responsibility and which is performed under similar working conditions, except where such payment is made pursuant to,

    (a) a seniority system;

    (b) a merit system;

    (c) a system that measures earnings by quantity or quality of production; or

    (d) a differential based on any factor other than sex.

(2) No employer shall reduce the rate of pay of an employee in order to comply with subsection (1).

(3) No organization of employers or employees or its agents shall cause or attempt to cause an employer to agree to or to pay to his employees rates of pay that are in contravention of subsection (1).

(4) Where an employment standards officer finds that an employer has failed to comply with subsection (1), the employment standards officer may determine the amount of moneys owing to an employee because of such non-compliance, and such amount shall be deemed to be unpaid wages. (R.S.O. 1980, c. 137, s.33.)

The basic objective of the legislation is that if two jobs in an establishment are considered substantially the same, then an employer is not entitled to differentiate pay on the basis of gender. The jobs would be evaluated on the basis of skill, effort, responsibility, and working conditions.

The concept of equal pay for equal work will not have an impact upon the provision of benefits nor the design of flexible benefit plans, except in so far as benefits are considered part of "pay." The value of benefits should be factored in to any equal pay for equal work analysis. This is, of course, subject to any recognized exemptions in providing benefits in a discriminatory manner.

§ 12.5 PAY EQUITY

Equal pay for equal work deals only with gender discrimination in substantially similar jobs. Pay equity goes one step further to address gender discrimination in any jobs of equal value—the concept of equal pay for work of equal value. Ontario's pay equity legislation is the most extensive, covering all public and most private sector employees in Ontario.

The legislation is designed to bring the pay of women in traditionally undervalued female-dominated job classes to the same level as men in comparable male-dominated job classes. The comparable jobs can vary widely. When the jobs are compared, so too are the compensation levels of each job. For purposes of pay equity legislation, compensation includes benefits.

Employers should be aware of pay equity legislation when developing or evaluating their flexible benefit plans. Although it is unlikely that a flexible benefit plan on its own would violate pay equity legislation, the value of all benefits for which a value can be ascertained will be included in the compensation of employees when comparing jobs for pay equity purposes.

Part Four

Structure and Financing

Thirteen

Prices and Credits

§ 13.1 INTRODUCTION

If flexible benefits were viewed as a car, the pricing and credit structure would be recognized as the engine. It is the pricing and credit structure that puts the program in motion—or brings it to a standstill. Employees choose from their "menu" of options by comparing the prices for the benefit choices to the dollars available to spend and matching the various alternatives to their individual needs. If the pricing and credit structure is not well thought through, excessive employer costs or too many employees electing the same option could result. These types of results defeat the purposes of a flexible benefit program. Employer costs should be controlled, not unbridled. Employee selections should be those that best meet individual needs. The typical employee workforce has diverse needs, and those needs should manifest themselves by employees selecting a wide variety of benefit options.

The two components of the structure—prices of the options and credits (or benefit dollars) available to employees—often are considered the same thing. In reality, they are like two sides of a coin, different but closely interrelated. For example, program prices may actually encompass a portion of the credit allocation in terms of a price subsidy. Nonetheless, a company will find the task of developing a pricing and credit structure more manageable if the two components are viewed separately.

Accordingly, this chapter discusses the two components separately, but with frequent reference to their interdependence. The chapter is organized as follows.

223

The first section examines the setting of objectives for the financial structure of a flexible program and demonstrates how objectives influence the pricing of options and the allocation of credits. The next section explores the pricing of program options, focusing first on pricing short-term benefits (medical, dental, and vision) and then on pricing long-term benefits (life insurance and long-term disability). (See also the separate chapters within Part Two for a brief discussion of pricing and credit generation for other benefits—namely, vacation, retirement, and other types of death and disability coverage.) Subsequently, the discussion moves on to the derivation and allocation of credits under a flexible program. The chapter concludes with ways to analyze the total structure for purposes of determining feasibility.

It should be noted that although the focus of the chapter is on first-year pricing and credit allocation, the same processes and procedures apply for subsequent-year changes in the financial structure of a flexible program. (See also Chapter Twenty-One on financial analysis for additional discussion of subsequent-year pricing.)

§ 13.2 SETTING OBJECTIVES

(a) FOUR PRICING AND CREDIT OBJECTIVES

After an organization has developed the basic design of a flexible benefit program, the next step is to price the options and determine the sources, amount, and allocation of credits. Neither of these steps can be accomplished, however, without examination of employer objectives for the financial structure of a flexible program. Experience shows that employers frequently have four goals or objectives they want to accomplish through the pricing and credit structure. These objectives may be summarized as follows:

- **Option prices should be set realistically, based on anticipated experience.** That is, the prices of the benefit options should fully support the claims those options are expected to experience. Using realistic prices will enhance employee understanding and appreciation of program costs and allow benefit choices to be made freely without the influence of incentives or disincentives.
- **Flexible credits should be allocated equally.** That is, each employee should receive an equal dollar amount or percentage of pay in flexible credits. If benefit dollars are to be considered another

form of compensation, allocating credits based on age, number of dependents, and so forth, represents an inappropriate allocation of employer dollars—akin to awarding pay increases on factors other than merit.

- **There should be no losers under the program.** That is, to prevent negative employee perceptions of the new program, each employee should be able to repurchase prior coverage (or if unavailable, the most comparable coverage) with no increase in costs.

- **There should be no additional employer cost.** That is, a reason for adopting a flexible benefit program is to enhance the organization's ability to control costs. In keeping with this goal, the employer should not incur additional cost for benefits due to implementation of the flexible benefit program.

(b) FOUR PRICING AND CREDIT APPROACHES

As desirable as each of these four objectives might be, it is generally impossible to achieve all four simultaneously under a flexible program. The primary reason is that most organizations currently do not allocate employer dollars for benefits equally to all employees. That is, most benefit programs today contain subsidies. One example appears in life insurance, where all employees may be charged a flat rate per $1,000 of insurance regardless of age, resulting in a subsidy of older employees by younger employees. Another area is supplemental medical and dental coverage, where employees with dependents may not pay the full value of the dependent coverage, resulting in a subsidy of employees with families by the employer.

Consider an example of the pressures created for a flexible program structure when medical benefits for dependents currently are heavily subsidized. In a typical situation, an employer might have medical claims costs that average $200 for a single employee, and $500 for an employee with dependents. As illustrated in Example 13.1, the employer might require a $100 contribution from the family employee, but employer cost still would amount to $200 for the single employee and $400 for the family employee, even though average cost for the covered group might be $300.

The employer wants to implement a flexible program offering options in supplemental medical. One option will be the current plan (Option A), but the two new options will be lesser-valued plans—Option B which is valued at 70 percent of the current plan and Option C which

Example 13.1
Current Supplemental Medical
Plan Claim Costs (per Employee)

	Employee Coverage Status	
	Single	Family
Annual supplemental medical claims cost	$200	$500
Employee contributions	0	(100)
Employer cost	$200	$400
Percent of employees in status group	50%	50%
Average cost	$300	

carries 40 percent of the current plan's value. Claims cost under each of the options is expected to be as shown in Table 13.1.

The issue for the employer is how to structure the pricing of the options and allocate credits to employees for the purchase of those options, but in a manner that achieves all four of the objectives cited earlier—realistic option pricing, equal allocation of credits, no losers under the program, and no additional employer cost. In general, an organization has four basic approaches or alternatives to choose from for the structuring of prices and credits. These include allocating credits on the basis of (1) family coverage costs, (2) average cost for all employees, (3) an actuarially determined amount, or (4) the cost of single employee coverage. But as is explained next, each approach will achieve only three of the four employer objectives—none will achieve all four objectives.

Table 13.1
Expected Supplemental Medical
Claims under Flexible Program Options
(per Employee)

	Single	Family
Option A (current plan)	$200	$500
Option B		
(valued at 70% of Option A)	140	350
Option C		
(valued at 40% of Option A)	80	200

Table 13.2
The Family Credit Approach

	Single	Family
Option A (current plan)	$200	$500
Option B	140	350
Option C	80	200
Credits	400	400
Average cost per employee	$400	

(1) Family Credits

The first approach is the *family* credit allocation (see Table 13.2). This approach involves allocating enough credits so the most costly employee (in this case, the employee covering a family) will incur no additional cost.

Objectives Achieved

1. **Experience-based (realistic prices)**
2. **Equal credits**
3. **No losers**
4. No additional employer cost

With this approach, the first three objectives are attained. Prices are based on expected claims. Each employee receives an equal amount of credits—$400 worth. No employee need incur any additional cost.

The employee covering a family under this approach must pay $100 for Option A—which is no change from the prior plan. However, the single coverage employee experiences a windfall of $200 at the expense of the employer, raising average employee cost from $300 to $400 per employee. Objective 4 is not achieved.

(2) Average Credits

The second approach simply calculates average cost of the current plan per covered employee and allocates that amount in credits to each employee (see Table 13.3).

Table 13.3
The Average Credit Approach

	Single	Family
Option A (current plan)	$200	$500
Option B	140	350
Option C	80	200
Credits	300	300
Average cost per employee	$300	

Objectives Achieved

1. Experience-based (realistic prices)

2. Equal credits

3. No losers

4. No additional employer cost

Again, prices are based on expected claims, and the credit allocation is equal for all employees. Also, by definition, this approach produces no additional employer cost—the credits equal the average cost of the prior plan. However, the approach produces both winners and losers. That is, there are employees who are better off *and* employees who are worse off relative to the coverage they had under the prior plan. For instance, the employee covering a family under Option A will now pay $200 versus $100 under the prior plan. Objective 3 is not reached.

(3)   Actuarial Credits

The third alternative is referred to as the *actuarial* approach (see Table 13.4). This method allocates credits based on the average cost of each employee to the employer prior to the flexible benefit program. The allocation takes into account the differing cost of employees based on whether or not they cover dependents.

Objectives Achieved

1. Experience-based (realistic prices)

2. Equal credits

3. No losers

4. No additional employer cost

Table 13.4
The Actuarial Approach

	Single	Family
Option A (current plan)	$200	$500
Option B	140	350
Option C	80	200
Credits	200	400
Average cost per employee	$300	

There are no winners and losers because employees can choose Option A and receive the same coverage at the same cost as under the prior plan. However, some employees—that is, those not covering dependents—may feel it is inappropriate that those covering dependents receive an additional $200 in benefit value from the employer. Benefit value equity (Objective 2) is not achieved.

(4) Single Coverage Credits

The fourth alternative is the *single coverage* credit approach (see Table 13.5). Credits are allocated to all employees at a level equal to the average cost of the employee-only (single) coverage.

Objectives Achieved

1. Experience-based (realistic prices)
2. **Equal credits**
3. **No losers**
4. **No additional employer cost**

Table 13.5
The Single Credit Approach

	Single	Family
Option A (current plan)	$200	$300
Option B	140	210
Option C	80	120
Credits	200	200
Average cost per employee	$300	

In order to meet the objective of no losers, prices for Option A, family coverage, are adjusted downward from $500 to $300, so the out-of-pocket cost to employees remains $100. The average company cost for all employees remains at $300—$200 in credits for everyone and a $200 subsidy of the price for the 50 percent of employees with families. Prices for Options B and C, family coverage, were set equal to 150 percent of single prices to parallel the Option A relationship. The result, of course, is in contradiction to Objective 1. Prices for family coverage now are unrealistically low, with each option priced at 60 percent of the expected cost. Also, the relationship between family status levels is inaccurate. For instance, Option C for family coverage costs $40 more than Option C for single coverage. In reality, the option is worth $120 more. Finally the out-of-pocket cost to employees selecting family coverage under Options B and C is too high. The out-of-pocket cost for Option B is $10, for example ($210 price less $200 credit). Under the actuarial credit structure, this election would produce $50 of excess credits ($350 price less $400 credit). Thus it is more difficult for employees to make reasonable decisions when prices do not reflect true cost or value.

(c) ADOPTING A STRATEGY

The pricing and credit structure for a flexible program creates the potential for a dilemma although it is one that can be remedied by setting priorities. Addressing key issues, such as those that follow, can help an organization establish a strategy for the structure of a flexible program.

- What broad organizational goals should be reflected in the pricing and credit structure?

    Addressing this question will surface organizational attitudes toward benefit value equity (Objective 2) and its appropriateness within an organization's culture. That is, are benefits viewed primarily as protection for employees, which may indicate that differing credits may be appropriate for employees with greater need for protection? Or do benefits represent a portion of an employee's total compensation, which may argue against differentiation by family status or age? Concerns about competitive position may also arise, both in terms of employee recruitment and cost control. Moreover, how this question is answered will lead to decisions on the importance of each of the other objectives.

- What are the objectives for the flexible benefit program?

  If future cost management is a goal, the employer may insist on experienced-based prices (Objective 1) where the cost is effectively severed from the form of benefits, and no hidden costs exist in the form of price subsidies. The use of realistic prices effectively forces the employer's cost to be equal to the credits allocated to employees. Thus the employer cost is more easily identified and managed. If immediate cost containment is a goal, no additional cost (Objective 4) at the program's genesis would likely be a requirement.

  If immediate cost reduction is a goal, by definition, some employees will be losers (Objective 3), either through reduced coverage or increased employee contributions. The employer may also want to enhance the employee's appreciation of benefit value which would incline the organization toward a realistic pricing structure (Objective 1) to give employees the most accurate indication of that value.

  The preceding discussion focuses on only a few of the possible program objectives and their implications for pricing and credit allocation. The point is that these objectives should be considered when adopting a strategy for the structure of a flexible program.

- What is the current employee mood or morale?

  The success of a flexible benefit program will vary depending on employee reaction to the organization's pricing and credit strategy. For example, the idea of benefit losers (Objective 3) may or may not be acceptable, depending upon the organization's financial situation and the benefit programs of competitors. On the other hand, benefit value equity (Objective 2) may not be an issue. The current employee mood should be taken into account when the organization develops its price/credit strategy.

After considering questions such as these and setting priorities, an organization's strategy will begin to form. The strategy may include all four of the basic approaches discussed earlier, a combination of several, or some variation as will be discussed later in this chapter. What the objective-setting process will certainly do, though, is crystallize a price/credit strategy that is consistent with the organization's desires and set the stage for the making of decisions on prices and credits.

§ 13.3 PRICING PLAN OPTIONS

When pricing options in a flexible program, it is helpful to separate benefits into two categories: short-term benefits and long-term benefits. Short-term benefits are those where claim frequency is high and per claim amount is relatively low. Benefits in this category include supplemental medical, dental, and vision. The plans are heavily utilized because of their nature, and plan costs are evaluated in terms of annual claims. For those many employees who do incur claims, the average claim size is typically small compared to long-term benefits.

Long-term benefits are those where claim frequency is low and per claim amount is high. Benefits in this category include life insurance and long-term disability. Most employees will never incur a claim for these benefits, but if they do, the claim is large. Claim costs can fluctuate dramatically from year to year. Costs are not evaluated in terms of annual claims, but in terms of the probabilities of claims and the expected annual costs based largely on actuarial data. The long-term contingencies being protected against are severe in nature, typically ending an employee's active working career.

The following discussion covers the pricing of short-term benefits. Although the focus is on supplemental medical benefits specifically, the methodology is appropriate for all short-term benefits. The next section covers the pricing of long-term benefits.

(a) SHORT-TERM BENEFITS

The pricing of benefit options can vary dramatically, depending on the organization's objectives for prices and the program in general. No matter what the objectives are and what pricing scheme is desired, actual or realistic prices for the benefit options should be determined first.

Realistic prices are those prices that could reasonably be expected to support the claim costs. This may be true for each option individually or for all the options under one type of benefit. Basically, the pricing process can be divided into six steps: (1) Data Collection and Analysis, (2) Option Pricing, (3) Subgroup Pricing, (4) Anticipation of Change, (5) Pricing Scheme Adjustments, and (6) No Coverage Option Pricing. The first four steps are used to determine the realistic prices.

(1) Data Collection and Analysis

The first step in pricing involves collecting data on the current plan over the past few years. This includes claims data for the covered group, administration fees, premium costs for an insured plan, and participation data (by dependent coverage category). The short-term nature of these benefits makes annual claims of the plan a reasonably good indicator of the true future cost of the plan.

For pricing decisions, it is preferable to use claims incurred for a given year rather than claims paid. Claims incurred represent all the claims attributable to a given year, including those actually incurred in one year, but paid in the succeeding year. Since covered employee data is usually tracked for the plan year, a more accurate claims per covered employee can be calculated from this amount. Also, incurred claims experience will reflect more accurately the impact of plan changes because changes tend to be made at the beginning of a year. (If available, this data also should be broken down by subgroups, as will be discussed later.)

The collection of data serves two purposes. One is that the data will serve as the basis for pricing all of the options in a benefit category. The other is that the data should provide some indication of past cost trends and which factors to use to anticipate cost increases for the coming year.

During this process, the organization should review the data that is already available and determine what additional data should be collected in the future. The employer will want to set up data-tracking mechanisms now as data will be crucial to future-year pricing, to determining the program's financial position, and to managing the program's costs.

Organizations should recognize that the reflection of a plan's claims experience in prices for future years might very well lag by one year. New prices will need to be developed at least two to three months prior to the beginning of the next plan year. Data will be available for only seven or eight months of the current year when the pricing analysis for the next year needs to be performed. Employers will be forced either to allow the reflection of experience in pricing to lag by a year or to attempt to project the experience based on partial-year data.

(2)   Preliminary Option Pricing

After claims data has been gathered and a per-covered-employee cost determined, the next step is option pricing. Option pricing consists of determining a fair price for each benefit option, based on covered employee claims experience in the current plan.

Option pricing requires that a *relative value* for each option be determined, usually based on the current plan. Using these relative values and current claims data, preliminary option prices can be calculated. For example, if the employer calculates that the current plan (Option A) is worth $500 per employee, and two new options, B and C, are worth

Table 13.6
Preliminary Option Pricing

Option	Relative Value	Base Plan Claims Per Employee	Price
A (current plan)	100%	$500	$500
B	70	500	350
C	40	500	200

70 percent and 40 percent (respectively) of the current plan, the preliminary prices would be set as shown in Table 13.6.

So far, the prices are preliminary, because they are based on claims data that is one or possibly two years old, and adjustments have not yet been made for plan changes, adverse selection, or different employee utilization patterns. A later step will involve adjusting the preliminary prices for these and other changes.

Relative values are usually calculated using insurance underwriting methodology. A value is determined for the base plan according to the characteristics—such as deductibles, out-of-pocket maximums, coinsurance percentages—of the plan. Values are then calculated for the options, and a relative value is determined by dividing the option value by the base plan value. Relative values usually are most easily calculated by the employer's insurer or consulting actuary.

(3) Preliminary Subgroup Pricing

Subgroup pricing is a method of dividing the pricing structure into smaller groups with similar characteristics. Subgroup pricing helps minimize adverse selection by creating more equitable prices for different groups of employees. The most common category is dependent coverage. The range of alternative dependent categories includes:

- Employee-only, family
- Employee-only, employee-plus-one, employee-plus-two-or-more-dependents
- Employee-only, employee-plus-spouse, employee-plus-children, family or
- Employee-only, employee-plus-one, employee-plus-two, employee-plus-three dependents, and so forth.

Other pricing subgroups might include location for organizations with employees in multiple locations or might be based on age of the employee. Geographical (provincial) pricing is becoming more common for supplemental medical benefits, particularly when the claims experience varies by location due to underlying differences in the cost of medical services. The costs may differ due to variations in local rates for services—Ontario's high semi-private hospital fees are an obvious example—or due to differences in the benefits provided by the underlying provincial plans. The differences in dental and vision costs have not been large enough to warrant making these distinctions.

Subgroup pricing is based in part on an organization's own experience if the claims data is available. However, even if the data is available, it typically is not used exclusively. This is because the number of covered employees in each subgroup may be small and, consequently, the claims data may not be as reliable as the data for the entire plan. Therefore, prices should be checked for reasonableness, based on related data from outside sources.

(4)   Anticipation of Changes

After the preliminary prices have been derived, some adjustment will be required. The preliminary prices are based on claims data a year or two old. Annual claim costs, especially medical claims, cannot be expected to remain static. There are many reasons why claims experience will likely change:

- **Medical inflation.** General increases in the cost of health care services are to be expected. One measure of medical inflation is the medical component of the Consumer Price Index. In a recent four-year period (1985–1988), the compound average increase measured 6.5 percent—versus only half that level for general inflation.

- **Technological improvements.** The cost of medical care may increase at a faster rate than medical inflation alone, because of the expense of new technology to improve diagnosis and treatment.

- **Employer cost leverage.** If features such as deductibles and out-of-pocket maximums are not indexed or periodically adjusted for inflation, the percentage of each supplemental medical claim paid for by the employer will increase over time. The effect of fixed schedules and maximums is in the opposite direction.

- **Plan changes.** Claims data from earlier periods require adjusting for any recent plan changes which affect benefit levels.

- **Adverse selection.** In a flexible benefit program, employees are given a financial incentive to choose a plan which best fits their needs.

However, if the probability of their need is too predictable, adverse selection will result. (See also Chapter Fourteen on adverse selection.)

In the late 1980s, a typical range for estimates of employer cost increases in supplemental medical has been 10 percent to 15 percent per year, excluding changes due to plan design, utilization, and adverse selection. For consistency, such an estimate should be compared to the current plan's historical cost increases.

If plan design changes were made, the cost impact can be reasonably estimated through the relative-value pricing methodology. As for utilization changes and adverse selection, their expected impact is generally not included in the prices until subsequent years when the actual results of the program can be measured. Changes in utilization after introducing a flexible program may produce reductions in cost (because employees are often moving to medical plans with greater cost sharing through deductibles and coinsurance levels), and predicting the amount of this change is exceedingly difficult. Estimating expected adverse selection is also very speculative, and reflecting an estimate in the pricing could actually exacerbate the adverse selection problem, so adverse selection estimates are also typically excluded.

(5) Pricing Scheme Adjustments

The preceding material describes how realistic prices are developed. If these are not the prices the organization prefers to use, there are alternatives. The alternatives are generally in one of two categories: carve-out pricing and subsidized pricing.

- **Carve-out pricing.** This pricing scheme is essentially a different way to communicate realistic prices. For instance, if the program is designed with a core or required minimum option, the employer may prefer to have employees see a price of $0 for this option. Alternatively, the employer may want to use this scheme to minimize the visible difference in credits (or prices) by coverage category (family versus single). For example, assume the realistic prices for supplemental medical options in a flexible benefit program are as follows:

	Price	
Option	Single	Family
A (enhanced)	$200	$500
B (current)	140	350
C (core)	80	200

If the employer believes a core option should be implied, a pricing scheme (called core carve-out) can subtract the price of Option C from Options A and B as follows:

	Price	
Option	Single	Family
A (enhanced)	$120	$300
B (current)	60	150
C (core)	0	0

Alternatively, the core could be single coverage under Option C, with the result that all of the realistic prices—single and family—are simply reduced by $80 as follows:

	Price	
Option	Single	Family
A (enhanced)	$120	$420
B (current)	60	270
C (core)	0	120

If the employer wishes to make it clear beyond a shadow of a doubt that the flexible benefit program is not a benefit reduction, the carve-out price will be Option B, the current plan, instead of C, as follows:

	Price	
Option	Single	Family
A (enhanced)	$60	$150
B (current)	0	0
C (core)	(60)	(150)

This second scheme is referred to as *opt-up-or-down* pricing because the employee pays a price for taking more coverage (*opting up*) and receives a credit for taking less coverage (*opting down*). Opt-up-or-down pricing is considered an appealing way to encourage employees to select a lower-valued option.

A variation of this opt-up-or-down approach provides equal credits regardless of family status to employees who opt down. This credit can be a blend of the credit for singles and families or it can simply be the single credit as shown on page 238.

Carve-out pricing does have drawbacks. The employee will not have as full an appreciation of the total cost of the different options,

	Price	
Option	Single	Family
A (opt up)	$ 60	$150
B (current)	0	0
C (opt down)	(60)	(60)

and it is often difficult to explain to employees what the prices represent. Future price increases may also be more difficult to explain, because they will be larger relative to the price shown. For example, if the prices for Option A rise 12 percent in one year and the prices for Option C rise 5 percent, the realistic prices for single coverage move to $224 ($200 × 1.12) for Option A and $84 ($80 × 1.05) for Option C. These may look quite reasonable to employees, but if the core carve-out approach is utilized, the price for Option A rises from $120 ($200 − $80) to $140 ($224 − $84), almost 17 percent.

The question of what to do with the $0 option will also surface. (That is, should the option always be free to the employee? When does the employer start charging for the option?) Finally, the carve-out pricing scheme is a less flexible cost-management tool, because the approach tends to bind the company to cost increases in the $0 option instead of breaking the automatic escalation with a separation of prices and credits.

- **Subsidized pricing.** Subsidized pricing represents an indirect form of credit allocation. True prices ultimately are equivalent to claims experience (or premiums charged by an insurance company in an insured situation). Prices that differ substantially from true prices are another form of credits being allocated to employees on a subsidized basis. The subsidies can take the form of across-the-board percentage subsidies (for example, prices are 80 percent of realistic prices); constant flat-dollar subsidies (for example, the price for covering dependents is $100 less than the actual cost); or simple price reductions. Whether subsidized prices reflect an added company cost will depend upon the inter-relationship of prices and credits.

  There are several reasons why an employer may opt for price subsidies. The employer may want to encourage the selection of certain options because of cost savings expected from that option. In other words, the employer may want to provide an incentive for employees to choose one option over another. Conversely, the employer may want to limit the potential for adverse selection in an option by encouraging more employees to select it (e.g., dental coverage).

Subsidies may also be necessary if the first three objectives discussed earlier have priority.

Some companies try to avoid extensive price subsidies. One reason is that subsidies tend to skew employee selection decisions by masking the value of the benefit options. Subsidies also can restrict the ability of a flexible program to serve as a cost-management tool, because some of the costs are hidden and thus more difficult to exert control over. In addition, it can be difficult to re-price consistently in future years, if prices are artificially derived from the start.

Some employers will utilize price subsidies initially, although intending to eliminate them gradually over time. This strategy allows employees to adapt and accept the loss of subsidy, but not all in one year. However, in these cases, it may be advantageous to communicate the strategy explicitly to employees, so they recognize and accept increases from the previously subsidized levels when required.

(6) No Coverage Option Pricing

The issue of whether to allow employees to waive coverage, in supplemental medical, is sometimes an area for considerable debate within an organization. One area of concern is philosophical. What is the company's responsibility to ensure that employees are protected? Does it go beyond the protection provided by provincial medicare plans? Another concern is adverse selection—the fear that only the healthiest employees will choose no coverage and, therefore, receive significantly more in credits than the program would have paid in claims. This result would increase total employer costs. As discussed in Chapter Fourteen, adverse selection concern can usually be managed through design and pricing decisions. Moreover, employees cannot know their own health situation sufficiently to risk a year without coverage. Employees who choose no coverage almost always have coverage available under another medical plan (for example, that of the spouse's employer), and there is no evidence these employees are healthier than other covered employees.

No coverage pricing is really a variation of negative pricing. The employer is trying to determine how many credits to give to someone opting out of coverage. In theory, the issue is a straightforward claims-cost question. Knowing what the average employer-paid claims would have been for these no coverage employees (assuming they had remained in the plan), would indicate exactly what the no coverage price should be. In practice, it is not possible to know the cost.

Another issue relates to the generosity of the rebate for opting out of coverage. The claims cost of these employees is no longer left to chance occurrence during the year; it is fixed by the dollars given to these employees for selecting no coverage. Moreover, the dollars are hard dollars, not the soft-dollar exchange of prices and credits evident for employees who remain in the plan. Because of the lack of margin for error, the credits given for the no coverage option are often conservatively estimated at less than the expected value.

(b) LONG-TERM BENEFITS

Pricing long-term benefits bears some relation to short-term benefit pricing, but there are also striking differences. For instance, prices are rarely based on annual claims experience, the benefits are more often insured, and the benefits are designed primarily to cover the employee with less coverage or no coverage for dependents. However, the pricing process for long-term benefits still involves consideration of the four pricing objectives and their priority (for example, realistic prices, equal credits, no losers, and no additional employer cost). Here the equal credits objective typically relates to avoiding age-based differences, (and possibly sex and smoker differences), rather than coverage-category based differences. Setting objectives for long-term benefits will help guide the organization in the pricing process.

The long-term pricing process will also follow the same six steps as pricing short-term benefits, although the manner in which these steps are addressed is quite different.

(1) Data Collection and Analysis

Although collection and analysis of employer data is usually done, the information is almost always too sketchy to be sufficient for pricing purposes. For pricing long-term benefit plans, general actuarial data considered in conjunction with the characteristics of the employer's workforce is more appropriate. Also, if the benefits are insured, the employer's cost may be predetermined by insurance company rates.

(2) Preliminary Option Pricing

Long-term benefits are typically expressed as a dollar amount of coverage or a percent of pay. Therefore, prices are expressed either on a per $1,000 basis or as a percent of pay, with the price of additional coverage relatively easy to calculate. LTD may represent an exception. In LTD, benefits are usually offset by Canada/Quebec Pension Plan (C/QPP) and Workers' Compensation benefits. The relative value of option prices will not be as directly related to the pay replaced. Consider, for example, an employee earning $35,000 per year:

Option	Benefit Formula	Pay Replacement by C/QPP	Actual Plan Pay Replacement
A	50% of pay less C/QPP	23%	27% (50–23%)
B	60% of pay less C/QPP	23%	37% (60–23%)

Cost of Option A = .5% of pay

$$\text{Cost of Option B} \neq \frac{60\%}{50\%} \times .5\% \text{ of pay or } .6\% \text{ of pay}$$

$$\text{Cost of Option B} = \frac{37\%}{27\%} \times .5\% \text{ of pay or } .69\% \text{ of pay}$$

The basis for these types of calculations tends to be more actuarial in nature and, therefore, may be more readily available from the employer's insurer or consulting actuary.

(3) Preliminary Subgroup Pricing

Long-term benefits may have more subgroup categories than short-term benefits which are applicable for pricing. Although dependent coverage is often limited and geographic differences tend to be insignificant, the categories that are applicable are age, sex, and smoker status. Long-term risks are significantly age- and sex-related. Life insurance is the most obvious example, but the same is true for LTD. In addition, the life insurance risk also depends on whether or not the insured person is a smoker.

Because of the close relationship between age and need for these long-term benefits, age-graded rates tend to be considered equitable. Rates graded by age, sex, and smoker status also decrease the potential for adverse selection by being more competitive with market rates, particularly for life insurance. For example, if a flat rate per $1,000 of coverage were charged for life insurance, younger employees, females and non-smokers could probably buy it cheaper on the open market. Older employees, especially males and smokers, however, would recognize the low price and purchase the coverage. The true cost of the benefit would then be much more than the flat rate being charged. Graded rates help eliminate this potential problem.

There are some considerations that relate to grading long-term benefit prices. Historically, if a flat rate has been charged, the new rate for
older employees—in particular, males and smokers—will be considerably higher. These older employees may not be able to purchase their
previous coverage without a significant increase in contributions. Conversely, if the credit allocation is tied to the price of the coverage, large
amounts of benefit dollars may be "given away" to older employees. In
general, however, most organizations still use age-graded rates in their
pricing structure for life insurance. Many also reflect sex and smoker
status. Although the true cost of LTD coverage is also highly age- and
sex-related, the majority of companies do not vary LTD prices by these
categories. It is not believed to be as critical an issue for LTD, due to
the lack of a large market of competitively priced individual policies (as
is the case in life insurance).

(4) Anticipation of Changes

Unlike short-term benefit prices, which are adjusted for a variety of
anticipated changes, long-term benefits are susceptible to only one
primary influence—adverse selection. However, pricing for adverse
selection in long-term benefits is extremely difficult. Adverse selection
is better addressed by age-grading prices, limiting maximum benefits,
limiting benefit increases from year to year, or including underwriting restrictions. Typically, prices are not adjusted for anticipated
changes.

(5) Pricing Scheme Adjustments

Pricing scheme adjustments are also limited in scope. Price subsidies are
one possibility. Subsidies are included in LTD prices in some plans, but
are less common for life insurance. Some employers view LTD coverage
as especially important and wish to encourage participation through
subsidized prices. Employers also recognize that insurers are less anx-
ious to cover LTD if participation is low, so they are more likely to feel
compelled to support the benefit financially. Most employers do not use
subsidized LTD prices, however, because the presence of employer contributions means the benefit will be taxable to the disabled employee.

Instead, some form of carve-out pricing is often used. For example,
if 50 percent LTD coverage is required as part of core benefits, the
employer will often pay the cost. The employer could pay for the LTD

coverage by simply giving employees enough additional credits to purchase the coverage. Alternatively, the employer could price the minimal coverage at $0, implicitly paying for it. This $0 price tag makes it very clear to employees that the benefit is employer-paid. The cost of options offering more LTD coverage would then be the incremental cost of the additional coverage.

In the life insurance area, a company may wish to introduce rates that vary by age group, and possibly by sex and smoker status, but the increase in costs for older employers who had previously paid a flat rate (e.g., $.40/month/$1,000) may be unacceptable. As an intermediate position, the company may elect to introduce a modified age-related pricing scheme, for example $.15 to $.80, rather than the full actuarial rates of approximately $.03 (younger, female, non-smoker) to $2.20 (older, male, smoker).

As part of this step in the process, some preliminary financial analysis should be done, especially if prices are not directly related to costs. The most obvious example is when benefits are fully insured. If the rate charged by the insurance company is different from the option price tags, calculations can be made to determine if the prices are supporting benefit costs in the aggregate. If life insurance options are currently available, testing can be performed based on current selections by employees. A simple alternative method of testing is to assume all employees select one times pay. Similar methods can be used for LTD testing.

(6) No Coverage Option Pricing

No coverage option pricing is not nearly the financial issue it is for short-term benefits. Claims are neither as frequent nor as predictable, so permitting no coverage is less of an invitation for adverse selection. However, the issue can be an emotional one. Considering that the contingency being covered (death or total and permanent disability) is a devastating one, employers are often reluctant to allow employees to go without coverage. Also, if credits are being allocated based on the age-related prices of the benefit, a large amount of benefit dollars can be generated for older employees. Employers may be unwilling to allow all of these dollars to be used for other purposes, especially when a lack of coverage can be very detrimental to employees and their beneficiaries. Therefore, no coverage credits are often "scaled back" to minimize the incentive to opt out and, in many cases, some core coverage is required for long-term benefits.

§ 13.4   DETERMINING FLEXIBLE BENEFIT CREDITS AND PAYROLL DEDUCTIONS

Closely related to the setting of option prices is the generation of credits used to purchase the benefits. In one sense, credits are simply the other half of the equation. For instance, prices and credits can be manipulated to net out to the desired result for each employee. However, an approach such as this, which only considers the net effect and not what prices and credits represent independently, fails to utilize the full potential of a flexible benefit program. Conversely, if prices represent the true expectation of the total cost of the benefits, employer-allocated credits represent the employer's expected cost. This approach, which fully separates the employer cost of benefits from the form of benefits provided, tends to be a highly effective means of cost management in that costs have been explicitly identified. This approach can also be readily communicated to employees, because prices and credits represent easily understandable concepts. The separation of option prices and credits (or related variations) forms the basis of the following discussion.

Three key elements must be developed to form a credit structure for a flexible benefit program. These include the sources, the amount, and the allocation of credits.

When developing credits, the points discussed next apply to the second and later years, as well as the first year of program operation. The flexible benefit program can serve as a long-term planning tool, as well as a short-term solution.

(a)   SOURCES OF CREDITS AND DEDUCTIONS

Where does the money come from? Conceptually, the sources of funds for a flexible program originate with either the employer or the employee. Practically, how those funds are derived is somewhat more complicated. The employer usually is not making an arbitrary decision about the flexible credits and their origin. Rather, funds are generated from a combination of identified sources.

(1)   Current Benefits

Current benefits that will become part of the flexible benefit program all have costs associated with them, net of any employee contributions. The fact that a benefit is included under the new flexible program creates a credit pool equal to the cost of those current benefits. This cost can be cut back, added to, or held constant, depending on the cost strategy of the organization. In any event, prior plan costs represent a source of credits. Although this credit pool is created, the amount explicitly allocated to employees will usually take into account the pricing scheme. (This concept is discussed in more detail in a later section on allocation of credits.)

(2)   Benefit Reductions

Another source of credits is benefit reductions—not necessarily reduction of the benefits included in the flexible program, but from reductions in other benefit areas. For example, an organization may conclude that retirement plan benefits (and resulting contributions) are too high and that a reduction is in order. Instead of absorbing all of the savings from cutting back future accruals to a retirement plan, some portion of the future savings may be passed on to employees in the form of credits. On the other hand, a benefit plan may be eliminated for one reason or another (for example, a minimal vision plan may be dropped), and the cost savings may flow into the credit pool.

(3)   Benefit Selling

Employees in many plans may increase their credits by trading in excess vacation entitlements. Most such vacation selling elements limit the vacation sold to a maximum of five days and will not permit employees to sell vacation if they would be left with less than the minimum vacation mandated in their province. Each day sold provides the employee with a credit of about .4 percent of pay. Some plans limit the pay in which the credit will be based to, say, $50,000 ($200-per-day credit).

Employees in Alberta and British Columbia can also increase credits by selling provincial medicare premiums, where the flexible plan permits. Companies that pay all or part of the premium in these provinces may allow employees who could be covered by their spouse to "sell" the company's provincial premium payment for extra credit. The credit is typically less than the provincial premium, which produces cost savings for the employer and more credits for the employee.

(4)   Additional Employer Money

A fourth source is simply additional employer money. The employer may want to add to the credit pool to provide dollars for a new benefit plan, to make the over-all program more attractive, to reward employees for an especially profitable year, and so forth. Of course, this avenue only applies to those employers not wishing to reduce benefit costs.

(5) Employee Payroll Deductions

Depending on the benefit levels employees select, their credit allocation may not be sufficient to cover all benefit needs. To make up the short-fall, employees can use payroll deductions to supplement the credit pool. The opportunity for employees to use payroll deductions to supplement credits is common practice. In fact, it is rare in today's environment to have a flexible program that is fully employer-paid. As discussed in Part One of this book, there are significant differences between credits (employer pre-tax dollars) and deductions (employee after-tax dollars).

(b) AMOUNT OF CREDITS

Defining the sources does not necessarily define the size of the credit pool, although identifying the sources helps set parameters for the amount. For example, one source will be the cost of the current plans, such as supplemental medical. The employer, however, may not want to incur the same cost as at present for medical coverage. As the employer examines each of the benefit plans to be included in the flexible program, the company will want to evaluate current cost levels to see how much should be used to generate credits. Using this component approach, the employer can identify how many dollars from current benefits will be available for credits.

The employer will also be identifying the amount of additional dollars from possible reductions in other benefit areas or simply how much additional benefit cost the organization is willing to support. The fourth source, payroll deductions, is largely an independent decision, because employees determine whether to use it, if made available.

After the amount of credits generated from different sources has been identified, the employer needs to view the result in terms of what the credit pool actually represents: the employer cost of the benefit program. Ultimately, equating the total credit pool to benefit costs is the concept that makes flexible benefits an efficient benefit cost-management tool.

The decision on the amount of available employer credits should be considered for future years as well as the current year, at least in a strategic sense. Conceptually, a strategy should be developed for how the credit pool is intended to increase in future years. The decision may be as flexible as a totally discretionary decision every year, or it may be as structured as the amount necessary to support a specified level of benefits. The strategy may tie credit-pool increases to salary increases, company profitability, or even some outside index. The point is to bring future strategy into focus so that the flexible benefit program has some direction for managing benefit costs.

(c) ALLOCATION OF CREDITS

The third and final task of developing the credit structure is to determine how to allocate credits to employees. There are almost as many variations in credit allocation structures as there are flexible benefit programs. However, these structures generally flow directly from only a few key considerations: the concept of equity in benefit value, the employee's ability to repurchase current (or equivalent) benefits, and organizational objectives.

(1) Equity in Benefit Value

From the outset, if an employer wants to achieve equity in benefit value (Objective 2 from the earlier discussion), prices for benefit options will be set realistically, and credits allocated on a per capita basis. Some organizations have adopted this structure in the first year. However, they have also accepted the consequences of this structure. Employees will be either better or worse off compared to their prior program. Many employers who agree with the concept of benefit value equity cannot accept these consequences, at least not all in one year. Instead, many prefer to phase in the concept over a number of years.

Some organizations also have attempted to achieve apparent benefit value equity by allocating equal credits and changing the prices to achieve the desired net result. However, a limitation of this approach is that it merely disguises in the prices the portion of the credit allocation that is not equal for all employees.

(2) Repurchase of Current Program

Ensuring each employee's ability to repurchase the current program or some other stated level of benefits was also discussed earlier as Objective 3—no losers under a flexible program. If this objective is a high priority, it will be a major factor in the design of the credit allocation structure. The most straightforward method of guaranteeing that each employee will be able to purchase a given level of benefits is through a component allocation structure.

Component allocation is a structure whereby credits are allocated to employees for each type of benefit, and the sum of the components is the employee's total credit allocation. A certain number of credits is provided for medical, dental, life insurance, vision, LTD, and so forth. In so doing, it is readily apparent where the credit shortfalls or excesses exist for each type of benefit. Component allocation is also consistent with credit source determination, because the cost of the current benefit program is determined on a component basis. A component allocation method also lends itself better to a financial analysis of each of the types of benefits individually. Expected employer cost (credits) and expected total cost (prices) are available for each benefit to compare to actual employer cost and actual total cost.

Component credit allocation can be refined beyond benefit type to subgroups of employees in much the same manner as subgroup pricing. Credits can be allocated based on dependent status, either actual number of dependents or by coverage chosen. In addition, the credit allocation may vary by age or geography. An age or geography structure may be appropriate if prices are grouped on that basis. It is highly unlikely that employers would vary credits by sex or smoker status. The component credit structure with a subgroup allocation does not necessarily mean employees will be able to purchase a given level of coverage, but it will be easier to measure and ensure the desired result for each employee.

Component credit allocation often leads to a formula type of allocation. Because of the different nature of benefits (some being pay-related and some not), the ultimate allocation may be based on a formula with a flat-dollar component and a percentage-of-pay component. For example, assume the credits allocated for each type of benefit are as shown in Example 13.2 for a given employee, age 45, and earning $40,000 per year.

Depending on the subgroup breakdown, employees will have a formula fitting their own characteristics and situation.

Component credit allocation can also be accomplished implicitly through the pricing mechanism. The carve-out pricing method can actually be a component credit allocation method. To illustrate, consider some alternatives of a simple flexible medical plan that can be priced in different ways—using realistic prices, a core carve-out method, and negative prices—shown in Example 13.3.

Using the core carve-out pricing scheme, each employee selecting single coverage implicitly receives $80 in credits, and each employee

Example 13.2
Component Credit Allocation

Benefit	Credits
Medical	$300
Dental	$500
Vision	$ 50
Death	1% of pay
LTD	.5% of pay

Formula:
$850 + 1.5% = $850 +
(.015 × $40,000) = $1,450

selecting family coverage implicitly receives $200 in addition to any direct credit allocation. Also, in the opt-up-or-down pricing scheme, the employee selecting family coverage implicitly receives $500. These examples should also help illustrate that unrealistic prices are really a variation of a credit allocation scheme. Some employers feel it is advantageous to provide credits implicitly through the prices, especially if credits are not allocated equally. In addition, implicit credit allocation tends to reduce an employer's concern over the cost of an employee selecting no coverage and taking the credits in cash. An implicit

Example 13.3
Component Credit Allocations through
Different Pricing Structures

	Option	Single	Family
Alternative 1:		Realistic Prices	
	A	$ 200	$ 500
	B	140	350
	C	80	200
Alternative 2:		Core Carve-Out	
	A	$ 120	$ 300
	B	60	150
	C	0	0
Alternative 3:		Opt-Up-or-Down Pricing	
	A	$ 0	$ 0
	B	(60)	(150)
	C	(120)	(300)

scheme locks some of the credits into the benefit selections, preventing employees from cashing in the options.

Component credit allocation is also useful for an explicit benefit-by-benefit recognition of an employer subsidy. This structure can be useful for an employer attempting to achieve an equal credit allocation in the supplemental medical plan, but doing so over a number of years. For example, an explicit subsidy can be provided which allows all employees to purchase the most valuable medical option in the first year. In future years, as prices and credits increase, however, the subsidy is held constant or even eliminated. To illustrate, using the facts from the previous example:

	Realistic Prices	
Option	Single	Family
A	$200	$500
B	140	350
C	80	200
First year credits:		
All employees	$200	$200
Family subsidy	0	300
Total credits	$200	$500

After the first year, the subsidy could be held constant or reduced, with the reduction either reallocated to employees on a per capita basis or used to reduce the cost of the benefit.

(3) Organizational Objectives

Because of their significance, employee benefit costs cannot be considered in a vacuum, and neither should the credit allocation formula for a flexible program. The organization's allocation of credits, be it an explicit allocation or implicit in the prices of the benefit options, is really an allocation of employer benefit dollars. Organizational objectives, then, will have an impact on the method of allocating those benefit dollars. Examination of organizational objectives will help illustrate this concept.

- **Cost management.** An organization may feel management of benefit costs is a top priority. This objective would lead the organization to a very explicit credit allocation structure in which credits are equivalent to employer costs and no costs are hidden in the prices.

- **Profit sharing.** Some organizations feel strongly that the sharing of successes and profits should permeate all aspects of the employee's relationship with the company, including benefits. This can be accomplished in the flexible benefit program by allocating more or less credits based on the profitability of a division or the company as a whole.

- **Service recognition.** Employers may want to recognize and reward employees who are loyal to the organization. Credits may then vary by years of service.

- **Social responsibility.** Some employers consider it a social responsibility to provide benefits to employees, independent of other benefit-related objectives. This responsibility may lead the employer to; (1) support a selected level of benefits, (2) require employees to select a minimum level of coverage, (3) limit the employee's ability to cash out credits, (4) subsidize certain benefits that should be encouraged, (5) vary credits by neither profitability nor service, or (6) limit aggressiveness in managing costs.

- **Benefit value equity.** Employers who believe equity in benefits is as important as in other forms of compensation may eventually want to allocate credits on a per-capita basis.

- **Employee performance.** Employers may wish to link a portion of the credits to employee performance. For example, an above-average performer could receive a bonus, such as an extra $100 credits or 25 percent additional credits.

- **Health awareness or other corporate initiatives.** The credit allocation system can reinforce a health awareness campaign or other initiative by the employer. One plan allocates an extra $50 to non-smokers; a further $50 to anyone who takes a health test; and a third $50 to employees who agree to buckle up while driving in the coming year.

The objectives an organization has for the allocation of credits will almost always have some internal inconsistencies. Identifying the priorities and finding the right mix of objectives can be a difficult step within the design of a flexible program.

§ 13.5 TESTING FOR FEASIBILITY OF THE PRICE/CREDIT STRUCTURE

Although the discussion has treated prices and credits as two independent components, both are intertwined. To determine the feasibility of the total structure, prices and credits must be viewed in combination. A key determinant of how the components fit together is the way employees are affected. In this regard, a winners and losers analysis can be extremely valuable.

In addition, an analysis of employer cost should be performed. The analysis will entail accumulating the credits explicitly allocated to employees, the expected value of the implicit credits (price subsidies), the hidden costs not recognized in the realistic prices, and the changes in costs due to employee selection patterns.

Finally, the structure should be reviewed with a broader perspective. Getting too close to all the "numbers" can obscure a primary purpose for a flexible program—meeting the needs of employees. Reviewing the structure for reasonableness can bring the program back into focus.

(a) WINNERS AND LOSERS ANALYSIS

Winners and losers analysis is simply comparing an employee's situation before and after implementation of the flexible benefit program. What were the benefits each employee was receiving prior to the new program? What was the employee's cost? How does this compare to the employee's cost for similar benefits purchased under the flexible approach? How many dollars are available for other uses if the employee chooses a different combination of benefits? What will the result be if the organization follows a different price/credit strategy in the future? To illustrate, a very simple first-year winners and losers analysis of a supplemental medical plan is provided in Example 13.4.

The analysis shows the additional cost (or dollars available) for employees relative to their cost for medical benefits under the prior plan. For example, the employee who selects family coverage must either pay an *additional* $100 to receive the same coverage as in the prior year or select a reduced coverage option and pay a lesser amount as in the prior year. Winners and losers analysis is an attempt to outline, in dollars, the employee's perspective of choices compared to the prior year. The analysis may surface flaws in the price/credit structure in terms of unintended impact on employees.

The out-of-pocket cost to the employee under the prior plan and the flexible plan can be compared to determine who wins and who loses under the flexible pricing structure. Under Option A, it is obvious the single employee wins $100. Under the flexible plan, this employee spends only $200 of credits to buy back plan A, leaving a $100 credit windfall. The family employee, on the other hand, is a $100 loser. This

Example 13.4
Employee and Employer Cost in Prior Plan

	Single	Family
Prior supplemental medical plan cost	$200	$500
Employee contribution	0	100
Employer cost	$200	$400

Flexible Benefit
Medical Plan Price/Credit Structure

	Prices	
Option	Single	Family
A (prior plan)	$200	$500
B	120	350
C	80	200
Employee credits	$300	$300

employee must add $200 out of his or her own pocket to the $300 credits to pay the $500 pricetag. Under the prior plan, the out-of-pocket cost was only $100, so the cost to the employee has doubled. The complete analysis is shown below:

(Winners)/Losers Analysis

Option	Single	Family
A	$(100)	$ 100
B	(180)	(50)
C	(220)	(200)

(b) EMPLOYER COST ANALYSIS

Some analysis should be performed to determine expected employer cost, especially if cost management is a goal of the flexible program. This analysis involves identifying the obvious employer costs, credits plus price subsidies, and also the not-so-obvious costs. These not-so-obvious costs include:

- **Adverse selection.** Will the plan costs rise if employees are allowed to choose their own benefits? If so, how much?

- **Dependent coverage.** Will the program likely cause employees to change their decisions on where to cover their dependents? If so, what is the likely cost impact?
- **Benefit utilization.** If employees change their benefit elections, will that change likely affect their propensity to use the services the benefits cover? If so, what might be the impact?

Although these areas of cost are somewhat nebulous, attempting to identify them and calculating an expected employer cost of the plan is an important exercise in determining the appropriateness of the price/credit structure and the ultimate success of the program. (See also Chapter Twenty-One for a broader discussion of employer financial analysis.)

(c) REASONABLENESS

It is difficult to define exactly what this final step may include for each employer. Basically, it is reviewing the program as the average employee will. The employer should be asking the same kinds of questions an employee will ask such as:

- Do I understand the options?
- Do the prices make sense?
- How does the price for one option compare to another?
- Are the choices clear, or are the options and their prices so close together as to be indistinguishable?
- Is one option an obvious choice over all others, no matter what my situation?
- Are the credits adequate for my needs?
- Is the employer paying a fair share of the cost?

At times, the employer may become too close to the plan to remain fully aware of the employee's perspective. An alternative is to test the flexible benefit program with a sample group of employees. (See also Chapter Eighteen.) Pretesting the plan with employees could bring to light subtle problems with the price/credit structure that otherwise may be difficult to identify. Pretesting may also provide a necessary measure of confidence in the program prior to implementation.

Fourteen

Adverse Selection

§ 14.1 INTRODUCTION

Few concepts are more feared—or misunderstood—in the field of flexible benefits than adverse selection. The concern arises in that any offering of choice, whether inside a flexible program or otherwise, increases the potential that "bad risks" will be drawn to certain options, thereby driving up the cost of the coverage and producing negative financial results. The misunderstanding occurs for various reasons.

One reason is the relative newness of flexible benefit arrangements. Until embarking on a flexible benefit project, few employers (or their underwriters) might anticipate the leverage that exists for controlling experience through plan design and option pricing. In effect, design and pricing operate as levers within a flexible program to contain the potential for adverse selection.

Another reason is that adverse selection within flexible programs is often confused with higher claims costs. In practice, the risk of higher claims resulting from a move to choice making is often non-existent, due to the structure of most flexible programs. In supplemental medical, for example, the pre-flexible plan is frequently offered as the highest valued option in the program. Some proportion of employees will opt down in coverage from that level, thereby lowering aggregate claims cost. Instead, the adverse selection issue in flexible programs relates more to the level of reward or incentive provided to employees (through credits or lower prices) to elect lesser-valued coverages or to opt out of the program altogether.

Finally, the adverse selection issue presumes that employees are able to predict benefit plan utilization—both for themselves and their families—with a high degree of accuracy. Except in unusual situations (such as an employee anticipating orthodontic expenses for a child), experience shows that the types of calamities covered by most benefit plans are "unknowable" in advance, particularly in family-coverage situations. Further, emotion often clouds what otherwise might be strictly economic decisions in the benefit area. In effect, security and budgeting often are more powerful influences on employee benefit plan elections than the profit motive.

The purpose of this chapter is to discuss the concept of adverse selection as it relates to flexible programs and to explain the types of approaches used to minimize the potential for unfavourable financial experience. Note that most of the discussion concentrates on the potential for adverse selection to occur in medical and dental plans, paying limited attention to other benefit areas.

§ 14.2 ABOUT ADVERSE SELECTION

To understand *adverse* selection, it may be helpful to review the general principles underlying the concept of insurance. True insurance occurs when the likelihood of a claim is completely unknown or random, but the potential consequences are so great that few people would forgo paying a modest amount to gain the coverage. Consider an illustration.

Example 14.1 shows a hypothetical distribution of claims in a given year for a supplemental medical plan covering a group of 100 employees. The price of the coverage equals $400—or the same amount as the average employee's claims. (In order to simplify, retention, reserves, administrative, and other costs are excluded from the example.)

Example 14.1
Illustration of Winners and Losers in Medical

Annual Claim Range	Number of Employees	Average Claim	Total Claims	Total Premiums	Claims Less Premiums
$0–$99	30	$ 60	$ 1,800	$12,000	$(10,200)
$100–$399	50	250	12,500	20,000	(7,500)
Over $400	**20**	**1,285**	**25,700**	**8,000**	**17,700**
	100	$ 400	$40,000	$40,000	$ 0

The majority of the members in the group incur claims that are lower than the price of the coverage. In effect, these employees are "losers" under the plan (shown in italics) in that their cost exceeded what they received in terms of benefits. A few employees are "winners" under the plan (shown in bold typeface) in that their claims exceeded the price of the coverage. Still, all of the members of the group are willing to pay the average price to protect against the risk of incurring a large medical claim. This is the principle of insurance—the risk of an event occurring is spread over a group of people with none of the members able to predict individual (or family-unit) experience.

Adverse selection is created when employees know or can reasonably predict the probability of an occurrence. For example, based on the previous illustration, if all the participants could predict their medical claims, only employees with claims in excess of $400 would purchase the insurance. Those with claims below that amount would be better off without the coverage. So the provider of the insurance would experience a shortfall in revenue to pay the cost of the claims. In the jargon of the insurance industry, employees would have "selected against" the plan.

Another way to illustrate the concern over adverse selection is in the area of vision coverage. Assume that an employer wants to cover vision expenses on an insured basis. Further, assume that the price of the insurance is $50 and the cost of frames and lenses, for example, is $200. As the need for vision care is relatively predictable, only those employees who expect to use the benefit will elect the coverage. In time, the plan will be covering only the bad risks (i.e., those who need glasses), so eventually the price of the insurance will equal the cost of the frames and lenses—$200. The principles of insurance will fail to operate.

Vision represents one of the most extreme examples of the potential for adverse selection to occur. (The other area with significant potential is dental.) The chief reason is that the risk the insurance is intended to cover is almost totally predictable. If the event the insurance protects against is less predictable, the potential for adverse selection diminishes proportionately. For example, at the opposite end of the spectrum in terms of predictability would be AD&D coverage. The incidence of an accident occurring is considerably more difficult to predict, so the potential for adverse selection to arise to such an extent as to influence plan costs is relatively minimal.

In the middle of the spectrum in terms of the potential for adverse selection is supplemental medical, long-term disability and group life. One of the reasons medical represents a medium, rather than extreme, possibility for adverse selection is the relative unpredictability of most claims, particularly for a full family. Few employees know with certainty what their level of medical plan utilization will be in a given year. Further, decisions on medical (as well as other benefit areas) often are clouded by emotion. Many employees want the best medical protection for themselves and their families, whether or not the coverage represents a good deal financially. Finally, medical plan elections often are based on factors unrelated to the specific options offered—namely, the availability of coverage through a spouse's employer. For these kinds of reasons, adverse selection often turns out not to be the nemesis it first appears simply because employees cannot make fully rational economic decisions in every case.

Another reason that the impact of adverse selection can be reasonably contained is that proper program design and option pricing further shrink its potential for occurring. For example, offering coverage for the most predictable types of expenses—such as vision, hearing, sometimes dental—through health care expense accounts—rather than on an insured-plan basis—effectively avoids any potential for adverse selection. But this type of "easy" solution is not always available (or practical). Instead, adverse selection needs to be controlled through other means. The purpose of the next section is to explore the range of solutions available to employers for controlling adverse selection through restricting choice (design) and varying costs (pricing).

§ 14.3   CONTROLLING ADVERSE SELECTION

Adverse selection is dependent on two variables. One is the availability of choice, and the other is the predictability of the occurrence. Influencing one factor influences the other. For example, if a benefit is predictable, but choice is unavailable, no adverse selection will occur (because of the absence of choice). On the other hand, if a benefit is available for selection in numerous forms and amounts, but occurrence of the benefit need is completely unpredictable (or random), again, no adverse selection will result (because of the absence of predictability). Therefore, the freer employees are to choose and the more accurate their ability to predict, the greater will be the concern over adverse selection.

If an employer's goal is to eradicate any potential for adverse selection, that objective can be achieved. But the means would involve radically restricting the choices available to employees or prohibitively inflating the prices of the options. Instead, most employers elect to tolerate some amount of adverse selection almost as a necessary evil in flexible benefit programs. That is, they will use the levers of design and pricing to control the magnitude of the potential for adverse selection, but they will otherwise accept the risk of some (modest) increase in costs, because of the advantages to be gained from choice making and the potential for savings in other aspects of the program. In medical and dental, for example, reduced utilization by employees electing options with higher deductibles and copayment amounts may offset all or most of any cost increases resulting purely from unfavourable experience.

The following material examines the control that can be exerted over adverse selection through the design and pricing of specific benefit options.

(a) DESIGN APPROACHES

As discussed previously, restricting choice reduces the effect of predictability and therefore limits the potential for adverse selection to arise. Numerous design approaches can be used to contain the potential for unfavourable experience, some of which are used more frequently in certain benefit areas than others. In general, however, these types of design approaches include the following:

- **Limit the frequency of choice.** Some employers limit the frequency under which employees may move in or out of specific benefit options (for example, every two or three years instead of annually). This type of design restriction is particularly effective in the more predictable benefit areas such as vision or dental. In effect, the longer the period of coverage (or no coverage), the more difficult it is for the employee to predict expenses or specifically influence the timing of incurring those expenses.

- **Limit the degree of change.** Many plans restrict changes to one level of coverage per year. For example, an employee electing medical Option 2 in the first year would be permitted to increase to Option 3, decrease to Option 1 or make no change for the second year. Choices above Option 3 would be off limits for the second year.

   This *staircase rule* is very common in dental plans to prevent employees from manipulating the system—without the rule, employees could elect the richest option in the first year and submit large claims; opt out in the second year and receive flexible credits; elect the rich option in the third year and so on.

   A variation of the staircase rule is the *up staircase rule* that permits one increase per year, but has no restrictions on decreases.

These staircase rules make it difficult for an employee to make major changes in benefit levels, because of knowledge of upcoming expenses.

A number of flexible benefit programs combine the two approaches just described. They use the staircase rule and add the restriction that employees electing the richest option must remain in it for at least two (or three) years. This combined approach might be appropriate in supplemental medical, for example, if the richest option contains vision coverage with a two-year maximum benefit, while the other options have no vision care.

- **Level the spread between options.** In some coverage areas (such as dental or long-term disability), it may be appropriate to minimize the difference between high and low options to avoid extremes in employee elections. Many employers offer a core coverage specifically for this reason. Core coverage promotes a larger covered employee group, thereby spreading the financial risk over a wider population. Another variation used most frequently in life insurance is including maximum benefit limitations, such as fixed-dollar amounts or percent-of-pay multiples. These types of restrictions serve to moderate the impact of adverse selection.

- **Require proof of insurability.** Some programs require proof of insurability before employees may increase coverage in long-term disability or life insurance.

  This type of restriction may apply to any increase in coverage or may be limited to increases of more than one level of coverage.

- **Group certain coverages together.** Some flexible programs package certain options; for example, dental or vision coverage with supplemental medical. This has the effect of reducing the employee's ability to predict specific benefit plan utilization, and it also causes elections to be based on factors in addition to the employee's expectation of incurring a claim. The extreme example of this approach is the modular structure for a flexible benefit plan whereby all benefits are grouped together. Another variation is to require interdependent elections; for example, the most valuable dental option is available only when choosing a lower level of medical. The popularity of these types of restrictions, however, has waned in recent years, because the trade-off for minimizing adverse selection is reduced flexibility to employees.

- **Delay full payment.** Another approach is to delay or restrict full payment of benefits. In dental, for example, lower benefits might be paid in the first six months (or one year) following a period of no coverage. In the disability area, delayed enrollment might make benefits effective only one year after the date of the election or subject to a shorter maximum duration for a disability which occurs in the first year of coverage. These types of design restrictions help prevent the possibility of a "windfall" accruing to employees inclined to move in and out of coverage—and also discourage such patterns of election.

- **Offer a health care expense account.** As mentioned earlier, some employers cover certain health-related expenses—such as vision, occasionally dental—only through a health care expense account. This strategy removes the insurance element from these types of benefits, thereby fixing the benefit cost and eliminating any potential for adverse selection.

- **Maintain parallel design.** Consistency in option design helps avoid differences in coverage that employees may be able to manipulate. For example, orthodontia coverage might be offered with each dental option and at the same level of plan payment. Similarly, vision, prescription drug coverage, and so forth might be attached to each supplemental medical plan option. If the specific coverage pertains to a predictable benefit, it typically makes sense to include it consistently throughout all like options.

- **Test the program with employees.** Although not a design restriction, many employers test preliminary program design with employees. Testing may bring to light any potential weaknesses in the design that later could produce adverse selection. Any shortcomings in the proposed program then can be corrected before implementation. Separately, testing also can provide a firmer basis for the actual pricing of flexible program options.

Well-designed plan restrictions can be tremendously effective in controlling the potential for adverse selection. Since adverse selection is predicated on the choice and predictability of benefits, employers can selectively restrict choice and thereby reduce the potential for additional costs. However, design restrictions need to be used judiciously so as not to reduce excessively the flexibility and, therefore, the usefulness of choice-making programs to employees.

Unfortunately, there are many times when design restrictions are either inappropriate or insufficient as a defence against adverse selection. The other available lever is pricing.

(b) PRICING ALTERNATIVES

As a general rule, anticipating adverse selection in the pricing of plan options is difficult to accomplish. In many respects, *pricing, employee elections,* and *experience* are interconnected to such an extent as to form almost a circular chain. That is, pricing decisions influence selection patterns, which in turn affect experience. Using experience to set prices influences employee elections so that prices are affected yet again. The circular flow—almost akin to a dog chasing its tail—is almost impossible to interrupt. However, some measure of relief can be achieved through a number of pricing strategies designed to limit the magnitude of the cost impact that may be produced by adverse selection.

One approach is to price options in a way that reflects the expected risk or cost of the benefit. Consider, for example, age-related pricing in life insurance. Life insurance coverage is often charged to employees at the same flat rate, regardless of age. However, the value of life insurance is distinctly age-related (because the risk of death increases with age). If a flat rate is charged to everyone, older employees will recognize that the price for the coverage represents a bargain, while younger employees will find the rates inflated. As a result, a disproportionate number of older employees will select higher levels of coverage, which will increase the plan costs and eventually increase the price the company needs to charge employees. Younger employees will seek coverage outside the benefit program, because better deals exist elsewhere. Age grading the prices can help minimize the potential for adverse selection costs (if having older employees elect large amounts of life insurance because of an artificially low price is viewed as adverse selection). It could also minimize adverse selection in long-term disability options; however, almost all employers use the same percentage of pay for all ages under LTD plans.

Many employers reduce the risk even further by recognizing the employee's sex and sometimes smoker status in setting group life rates. These two factors can have a dramatic impact on costs—the rate for a male smoker might be three or four times that of a female non-smoker the same age. Employers who use age, sex, and smoker status are trying to duplicate the risk categories established for individual life insurance.

Why don't all group life plans recognize sex and smoker status?

- Administering different premium schedules will increase the cost and complexity of the program.

- The risk to the employee of misrepresenting smoker status, whether deliberately or inadvertently, may be too high a price for the employer to pay. If a declared non-smoker (generally someone who has not smoked a cigarette in the past 12 months) dies and was actually a smoker, the insurance company may decide not to pay the benefit. In Quebec, the Superior Court ruled that Industrial Life Insurance Company did not have to pay $100,000 life insurance and $50,000 accidental death benefit to the beneficiary of Gilles Perron, who died in a 1985 car accident. Although the cause of death was unrelated to smoking, Perron knowingly misrepresented his status when applying for insurance. The Quebec Superior Court ruled that voided his coverage.

- Some insurance carriers are reluctant to offer smoker/non-smoker rates, because they find it difficult to determine who is a smoker. An employee who hasn't smoked in two years and elects non-smoker rates is under an obligation to change status, if he or she starts smoking again. In practice, this usually does not happen.

- Group life premiums that are different for males and females will likely be considered discriminatory and prohibited at some future date. This happened in the United States in the early 1980s.

A similar risk-related pricing structure can be adopted in medical and dental through tiered pricing of the coverage. For example, employees covering several dependents typically would be inclined to select the richer plan options, because of the greater probability of claims being incurred for a full family. To draw a cross-section of lower risks (for example, employee-only, or employee-plus-spouse) will require some differential in the pricing of the options. This is the reason many organizations use three or four (sometimes more) coverage tiers for option pricing, rather than only one or two. Tiered pricing causes the relationships between options to be more realistic and, therefore, it reduces the potential for employees to select against a particular plan based on family size.

Another relatively straightforward strategy for mitigating the effects of adverse selection is employer subsidization of the option prices. For example, an employer with two dental options (coverage or no coverage) may want to encourage broad participation in the plan. Subsidized pricing can make the coverage a "better deal" for more employees, thus encouraging participation. Higher participation will help spread the risk, thereby diminishing the potential for adverse selection.

However, even with age- or risk-related pricing or employer subsidies, an underlying difficulty with adverse selection is *anticipating* actual experience. Only rarely does "expected" experience precisely match actual utilization, especially in medical and dental. This problem is not unique to flexible programs, but it is heightened by the ability of the employee to choose levels of coverage.

Consider an example. Assume the employer offers three dental plan options: the current plan (now costing $50 per month) plus two lesser-valued coverages worth 80 percent and 50 percent, respectively, of the current plan. Pure actuarial pricing might suggest that the option price tags be set at $50, $40, and $25. One decision the employer will face is whether to anticipate the potential variance in claims experience and adjust the price tags accordingly or to operate the flexible program in the first year using these unadjusted price tags.

Adjustment of the price tags for anticipated experience can be accomplished in several ways. One approach is to reduce the reward to employees for opting down by loading the prices of the lesser-valued options. That is, instead of charging $40 and $25 for the lower coverages, the prices might be set at $50 (same as actuarial pricing), $45 and $35. This solution would diminish the potential for over-rewarding the presumably good risks who elect lesser coverage although at the expense of reduced flexibility to employees. Moreover, in practice, what is likely to happen under this approach is that more employees will remain clustered in the rich current plan (because the incentive to consider the other options is diminished) rather than moving to plans with more cost-efficient designs, thereby thwarting cost-management objectives for the program.

A second alternative would be to push all of the cost of expected adverse selection (say, 2 percent of dental cost) into the highest-valued option, but keep the prices for the other options at the same level. If half the employees are expected to remain in the high option, this might require about a 4 percent increase in the high-option prices to recoup a 2 percent total dental program cost. Prices under this strategy would be set at $52 for the current plan, and $40 and $25 for the other options. All of the cost of adverse selection has been added to the price of the highest-valued option—so employees effectively cannot buy back their prior coverage without paying more (unless the employer increases flexible credits by a like amount for all employees).

Further, to avoid paying more for the prior plan, a greater-than-expected number of employees will likely be driven to the lower-valued options, thereby escalating the price for those options. However, the net effect, most likely, will be positive in that these are the options with higher deductibles and copayment amounts. Ironically, some added cost savings are likely to have been achieved as an unintended result of the concern over adverse selection—but at the risk of employee dissatisfaction over the increased cost to purchase the prior plan.

A variation on this strategy would be to spread the cost of the anticipated adverse selection over the price of all the options (for example, increasing the price of each option by 2 percent). Here the original relative relationships between the plans have been maintained and greater equity achieved by spreading the cost of adverse selection produced by offering choice to all employees, but a similar (although diminished) problem exists with the ability of employees to buy back the former coverage.

The practical difficulties with anticipating adverse selection incline many employers to use of unadjusted pricing—at least in the first year of a flexible program's operation. The prices are set at the pure actuarial level and adjusted only after the combined effect of adverse selection costs and utilization savings are better known. Under this type of scenario, it would not be unusual to see expected versus actual experience on the order of magnitude shown in Example 14.2.

This example also illustrates another issue that arises with adverse selection. That is, the effect of adverse selection will be felt disproportionately across options, producing both positive and negative results. The actual claims experience under any one option (particularly in medical and dental) will likely vary (and perhaps dramatically) from that expected under a completely random election process. But unfavourable experience in one option (typically the highest option) will usually be offset (in full or in part) by favourable experience in other options, so the impact on the aggregate experience of the program is likely to be modest.

It should be noted also that unfavourable experience may not always be negative. That is, on occasion, an employer may want to encourage (or allow) adverse selection to occur naturally as a means of phasing out

Example 14.2
Adverse Selection

Option	Percent of Employees Electing	Actuarial Value	Actual Experience	Effect of Adverse Selection
High	60	$50	$55	+ 10%
Intermediate	25	40	36	− 10
Low	15	25	17	− 32
Average cost		$43.75	$44.55	+1.8%

an option. This might be the case in situations where the highest-valued option is considered too rich, but the employer is concerned about the employee relations impact of eliminating the option by decree. Instead, the employer might allow "option suicide" to occur by keeping the pricing of each option on a self-supporting basis. Over time, migration of the heaviest users to the option will cause the price to rise prohibitively, in which case the option will have priced itself out of the market.

To summarize, adverse selection in choice-making programs does not represent a benign influence on plan costs. It is an issue that requires careful attention and consideration. The point is, however, that numerous strategies and techniques can be employed to limit its potentially damaging effects. In combination, the levers of program design and option pricing can be activated in such a manner as to shrink most of the potential for adverse selection to a manageable level.

Fifteen

Insurance Considerations

A typical flexible benefit program is laced with benefit options that may require some involvement by an insurance carrier. Life insurance, short-term disability, long-term disability, medical, and dental options often will be underwritten for the smaller employer or administered by a carrier for the larger organization.

§ 15.1 THE INSURER'S PERSPECTIVE

(a) INSURANCE RISK CONCERNS

To understand the insurer's perspective of flexible benefit programs, some appreciation of the carrier's financial risk is helpful. To a carrier, an employer who designs a benefit program (whether flexible or otherwise) and then tells someone else to insure it is attempting to play poker with a stranger's money. The "player" organization risks little, while the stakes are high for the strangers. Although this may not be an issue for very large employers (who typically self-fund many of their benefits), it is a concern for smaller employers who insure most or all benefits.

As background, it may be helpful to discuss the three universal methods of insuring programs: pooled, experience-rated, and partial insurance.

Pooled insurance is the most familiar concept. Auto insurance is pooled. A driver is placed in a pool with others sharing similar characters. The experience of the pool influences the rates the individual is charged. At year-end, no premium is returned even if a particular driver avoided having an accident, and neither are any deficits applied to the policies of the drivers who have an accident. So the slate is wiped clean each year. In the next year, however, rates might increase if the driver is reassigned to the pool with the one-accident drivers. Pooled group insurance of this kind is typically used for organizations of 200 or fewer employees.

Experience-rated insurance requires a full financial accounting at the end of each plan year. If any premium is left after the carrier deducts all claims, allocates reserves, and recovers all expenses, the employer receives that difference. Conversely, if a deficit occurs, that amount is charged interest, carried forward, and recovered by the carrier through premium increases in future years. Although all deficits potentially can be recovered, a carrier will have two incentives to avoid deficit situations: (1) initial loss of cash flow; and (2) possible termination by the employer of the policy prior to full deficit recovery. This kind of insurance is the most common group benefits financing method.

Partial insurance is a generic term for any arrangement where the employer self-insures the coverage up to a predetermined limit, after which the carrier's liability begins. The limit might be by claim, by employee, by total-claims-expected-per-year, or some other variation. Partial insurance, for example, is quite common in long-term disability where the employer pays the claims for the first three years, say, of an employee's disability. After three years, the benefit is paid by the insurer. The risk to an insurance carrier under a partial insurance arrangement is very similar to the risk under any other insured arrangement. Large or excessive claims will trigger deficits. Under partial insurance arrangements, the deficits may or may not be recoverable in future years, depending on the terms of the policy.

In each case involving insurance then, the carrier is at risk to some degree and will seek to protect itself by influencing plan design, requiring evidence of insurability for especially risky benefits, or increasing rates to avoid deficit positions.

The three primary influences on risk are:

- Volume, or number of participants in the benefit plan
- Liability, or size of potential claim reimbursement

- Selection patterns, namely, the potential that high utilizers will tend to select the plan.

For example, a $200,000 life insurance benefit is not a high risk for a carrier insuring a 5,000-employee organization, if only 100 employees are eligible for this benefit based on pay. The total annual life insurance premium from this organization will easily absorb the one or two large claims that might occur in a year. The same benefit for a 50-employee organization with a much smaller annual premium would be considered risky.

To explain the influence of selection patterns, consider the 5,000-employee organization with a flexible benefit program under which all employees are eligible to purchase a $200,000 benefit. If only 10 people do so—who are all 64 years old and perhaps not in the best of health—and the other employees take little or no coverage, the total annual premium is far less than $200,000. This is an extreme example, but it serves to illustrate what a carrier will recognize as adverse selection and, therefore, potential risk. These and other more subtle variations are types of risk potential that appear in various aspects of flexible programs. (See also Chapter Fourteen for ways to minimize this type of risk).

(b) ADMINISTRATIVE CONCERNS

Insurance carriers provide most employers with a substantial number of administrative services: (1) participant eligibility maintenance and benefit verification, (2) life, disability and health claims processing, (3) premium/fee statement preparation, and (4) conversion policy maintenance. Administrative concerns that might result from flexible benefit programs typically would arise from the *eligibility maintenance* and *claims processing* functions.

More than a decade ago, insurance carriers began to install sophisticated computerized claims processing systems that accept eligibility information on computer tape, process claims with a minimum of manual intervention, and generate meaningful claims reports.

As a result, most major carriers have systems in place that can readily process almost any medical or dental claims that may be generated by a flexible benefit program. The function of processing claims for multiple-option medical programs, for example, should not even require a systems change. Carriers simply use the same procedures required to process different plans for different divisions of the same company—a capability built into all systems years ago.

The carrier's systems specialists are generally cooperative in making some changes to adapt to unusual plan features. Of course, the size of an organization will influence the carrier's interest in customizing systems and procedures. The 100-employee organization, for example, probably will have to accept the limitations of their carrier, simplify the plan, or attempt to select an alternate carrier with a more flexible system.

Inflexibility of a computer program, however, does not in itself void a carrier's ability to administer a particular program. Since manual intervention may be required for any client's unusual program features, this approach is available at least as a backup measure to the carrier.

A good flexible benefit program should be designed to meet a company's specific needs and objectives and should not be unduly restricted by systems limitations. However, some preliminary planning regarding possible administrative snags might reduce the amount of time-consuming carrier negotiations or the number of manual intervention situations that might be required of a carrier with a less sophisticated claims payment system.

§ 15.2 AVOIDING POSSIBLE ADMINISTRATIVE STUMBLING BLOCKS

Although an employer designs a flexible benefit program to meet organizational objectives, designing around some touchy carrier concerns can often be accomplished without major compromises. Creativity in plan design can ameliorate insurance carrier concerns in a number of areas. The following design discussion is organized by major benefit area.

(a) SUPPLEMENTAL MEDICAL

(1) Adverse Selection

In an insured or partially insured situation, the insurance carrier's objective in underwriting supplemental medical coverage is to rate the benefit plan options to anticipate any adverse selection that might occur. That is, the high utilizers may tend to pick the highest coverage possible, and the low utilizers may tend to opt out or choose the least coverage possible. If this occurs, it results in less spreading of the risk and a higher cost per employee than in a situation where all employees participate in a single plan. The carrier will typically reflect some expectation of adverse selection in the rates charged to the employer.

Methods available to the plan sponsor to minimize adverse selection are outlined in Chapter Fourteen. In addition, that chapter discusses alternative ways of developing the option prices that are communicated to employees—which may be different from those developed by the carrier.

(2) Core versus Opt-Out Provision

Insurers typically will be much more comfortable in underwriting risk when employees are provided a minimum level of coverage. Core coverage promotes a larger covered employee population, thereby allowing the insurer to spread the risk over a larger financial base. Allowing an opt-out provision in a plan could increase an underwriter's concern over adverse selection. However, if an employer's current non-flexible program requires employees to pay for coverage, introduction of an opt-out provision will probably not dramatically change employee participation under the flexible benefit program.

The core versus opt-out concern also arises in other benefit areas, but it is most pronounced in health care (medical, dental, vision).

(3) Evidence of Insurability

Occasionally, insurers will require *evidence of insurability* in the form of a health statement before covering someone who previously opted out of coverage. In these cases, coverage can be denied to employees or dependents based on their health statement responses, or a physical may be required before coverage is approved. Although this approach is an effective safeguard against adverse selection, it also restricts employee choice making and results in some administrative difficulties. This approach is rare in Canada, because the financial risk to the insurer is much lower than in the United States where requiring evidence of insurability is more common.

(4) Claims Administration

Stumbling blocks might arise in claims administration, if the employer designs an unusual option that cannot be easily programmed into the insurer's claims processing computer system. These snags are not directly related to the introduction of medical choices, but they might occur because specific medical plan provisions were changed in the flexible program design process. Simple changes made to an employer's plan in order to create options (in terms of deductibles and coinsurance, for example) typically do not affect the insurer's ability to process claims electronically.

However, other less typical changes that might require manual intervention include:

- Multiple coinsurance levels within the same plan
- Penalties or incentives applicable to certain cost-containment features such as generic drug provisions, that are not standard for the insurer
- Non-standard benefits or benefit limits
- Out-of-pocket limits in the plan. These features limit the individual's total exposure though deductibles and coinsurance to a predetermined amount, say, $500. Because they are relatively rare in Canadian plans, the insurance carrier may not have the capability of monitoring out-of-pocket limits with its automated system
- Health care expense account. Most insurers do not yet offer automated administration systems for these plans.

These administrative difficulties should not discourage employers from adopting these provisions, but employers should be aware that some slight changes in design might enable insurers to avoid manual intervention. Audits of insurance carrier claim payments show that errors are significantly greater in situations where manual intervention is used.

(b)   DENTAL

(1)   Adverse Selection

The financial effects of adverse selection on dental plans is typically greater than on supplemental medical plans, because dental costs are usually higher than medical costs and dental expenses are much more predictable.

(For a discussion of adverse selection in the dental area and ways in which an employer can minimize its effect through plan design and pricing, refer to Chapter Fourteen.)

(2)   Claims Administration

Like flexible medical options, the mere offering of choices in dental creates few inherent claims administration problems. Only in adding a unique plan provision might a stumbling block be created.

One provision that might cause administrative concern to a carrier involves a *pre-existing condition* exclusion. Some employers have attempted to limit adverse selection by requiring coverage under the flexible program for a certain period of time—such as one year—before a bridge is replaced, for example. Many carriers' systems must view this dental option as two separate benefit plans—one for pre-year 1 participants and one for post-year 1 participants. The employer, then, would need to submit eligibility information distinguishing between these two groups.

Employers might find alternative approaches to control adverse selection which are as effective (or more effective) than this type of limitation, but without the administrative difficulties.

(3) Capitation Dental Plans

Some organizations offer *capitation* or *managed-care* dental plans. These organizations have negotiated reduced fees with selected panels of dentists. Expenses are usually reimbursed in full, except for small copayments.

A capitation dental plan can be an attractive addition to choices in dental, especially in a situation where the employer has chosen to offer only one standard dental option. The capitation dental plan can result in substantially higher benefits to employees. Capitation plans are covered in detail in Chapter Five.

(c) VISION

(1) Adverse Selection

Because vision care expenses are even more predictable and discretionary than dental expenses, the risk of adverse selection is greater. As a result, some employers choose to provide employees with vision care reimbursement only through health care expense accounts.

Alternatively, employers who prefer to offer a vision care benefit may create a core vision plan or include a vision benefit in all of the medical options. Another alternative would be to include vision under several, but not all, of the medical plans. The prices of these plans should reflect the adverse selection cost. This cost is reduced by restricting movement in or out of the options. A two- or three-year enrollment will accomplish this. Or, the vision options could be packaged with dental options to reduce such movement.

(2) Prepaid Vision Plans

Employers who plan to include prepaid vision plans as a part of their flexible benefit program should be aware that providers offering these arrangements are especially sensitive to adverse selection. They will often decline to offer their arrangements as a part of a flexible benefit program without two- to three-year enrollment requirements unless a minimum participation level can be guaranteed.

(d) LIFE INSURANCE

(1) Adverse Selection

Insurers are not typically as concerned about adverse selection in life insurance as they are in health care benefits. The total costs are usually less, the predictability of claims much smaller, and the experience they have in dealing with choice-making plans in life insurance is much higher. (See also Chapter Fourteen for discussion of common ways to minimize adverse selection in the life insurance area.)

(2) Evidence of Insurability

Insurance carrier underwriters will have some concerns, although modest, in the area of life benefit selection at the initial enrollment. Under a flexible benefit plan, the employee is no longer provided with employer-paid basic life and given the opportunity to buy additional coverage. Instead, credits are allotted by the employer, and the employee is permitted to select as much coverage as he or she needs. This potential volatility in coverage may promote conservative underwriting practices, unless the program is properly presented.

In particular, a carrier usually will wish to impose evidence-of-insurability requirements for benefits exceeding a certain level. This level is typically based on employer size or total anticipated life volume. In a 1,000-employee company with a maximum $1 million lifetime benefit, employees might be required to submit evidence of insurability for amounts exceeding $600,000.

If possible, it is often preferable to avoid such an evidence-of-insurability approach. A denial of benefits may result in a re-selection of choices by the employee. The final denial might not be communicated by the carrier until after the program has gone into effect, resulting in a reprocessing of that employee's election form and possibly retroactive adjustment to payroll reductions. With some discussion, carriers are often willing to "grandfather" any large benefits being carried by employees under the current program without evidence of insurability.

(3) Dependent Life

Some insurance carriers restrict the maximum spouse's life insurance benefit to a certain percentage—for example, 50 or 100 percent—of the employee's life benefit. Most carriers, however, no longer have such a requirement.

(e) LONG-TERM DISABILITY

As in other benefit areas, insurers will want to spread the risk associated with long-term disability benefits among as large a population as possible. A typical stumbling block that occurs with disability is misunderstanding of a flexible program's credit allocation method. Without a full understanding of the over-all flexible program structure, a carrier's underwriter might see a completely voluntary long-term disability plan and rate it using large adverse selection margins, assuming the high risks will be more likely to choose the coverage. In reality, the program may be designed to provide each employee with enough credits to purchase at least a minimum level of long-term disability coverage. This mechanism does not guarantee the underwriter that all employees will opt for the coverage, but participation in the option will be substantially greater than enrollment in a purely voluntary plan, where the employee pays the full cost of the coverage.

Some insurers are concerned about their risk in plans offering taxable and tax-free long-term disability benefits. As discussed in Chapter Six, the taxable plan is funded by the employer with flexible credits, while the tax-free plan is funded by the employee using payroll deductions.

To maintain the tax-free status of the payroll deduction plan, it is important that no employer money be used to fund it. This causes a problem where the experience in this tax-free plan is poor and the insurer wants to increase the premium. If the experience in the taxable plan is favourable, the resulting premiums would be lower and this could drive many employees away from the tax-free plan and into the taxable plan. This would make it impossible for the insurer to recover the deficiency in the tax-free plan. To prevent this, the insurer may be tempted to use any surplus in the employer-paid taxable plan to offset a deficit in the employee-paid tax-free plan. Such a transfer would jeopardize the tax-free status of the employee-paid plan, since this employer-paid plan surplus is considered an employer contribution. The concern of the insurer is mitigated when a high proportion of employees elect the tax-free plan. (See also Chapter Fourteen for more complete discussion of approaches to controlling long-term disability adverse selection.)

§ 15.3 WORKING WITH THE INSURER

In order to work effectively with an insurance carrier on installation of a flexible benefit program, the employer needs to consider issues related to communication, negotiation, and implementation.

(a) COMMUNICATING WITH THE INSURER

Early notification to an insurer that flexible benefits are being considered could help avoid future complications. Carriers who have had some experience with flexible benefit programs should have insights regarding the interaction of flexible options with their own systems, procedures, and underwriting guidelines. During this initial notification and discussion, an employer might recognize the need to solicit proposals from other carriers, if the existing carrier's capabilities are insufficient.

Another objective of early notification is to create an atmosphere of openness where carrier input is sought and fostered. The carrier representatives—underwriters, systems analysts, claim supervisors, contract specialists—will begin to share in the team approach to flexible benefits, enhancing the chances for a smooth implementation.

In some situations, the line between the insurer's constructive input and inflexibility may be unclear. Employers should design flexible benefit programs to meet their needs, while recognizing that some concessions to insurance carrier underwriting or administration limitations might be necessary, particularly for the smaller employer.

(b) NEGOTIATING WITH THE CARRIER

Carrier negotiations on flexible benefit programs typically involve one or more of the following issues:

• Insurance rates
• Benefit limitations
• Administrative procedures.

As discussed earlier, insurers might view the flexible benefit program as a risk, resulting in conservative underwriting—that is, high rates. To temper the risk, the carrier might wish to limit the maximum benefits available or require evidence of insurability for some benefits. Also, carrier systems limitations or standard procedures might inhibit the flexible benefit program design or administration.

All of these issues are negotiable—to some degree. Prior to negotiating any issue, the employer should estimate the size of the "bargaining chips" involved. That is, how motivated is the carrier to accommodate the employer and retain the account? Any or all of the following factors can influence the insurer's perspective:

- **Size of organization.** A "large" client represents lower risks and higher profitability to an insurer. However, the employer's size might be viewed differently, based on the company's geographic location and on the carrier's current book of business in the office that would be handling the account.
- **Presence of a traditional benefit program.** A company having a small number of employees in a flexible plan might be very attractive to an insurer, if the company also sponsors a large traditional benefit program for a different group of employees.
- **Life insurance volume.** Life insurance continues to be a profit leader for insurance companies, so substantial life benefits make any package extremely attractive to a carrier.
- **Employer prestige.** An insurance carrier may enhance its image in a community by including as current clients the most respected local organization(s).

With this understanding of the carrier's perspective, the employer can discuss issues openly and honestly, recognizing that some concessions might be necessary.

(c) SELECTING A NEW CARRIER

Many employers can maintain their existing insurers when a flexible benefit program is adopted. However, sometimes, "irreconcilable differences" require that an employer's existing carrier be replaced. These circumstances can arise in the following kinds of situations:

- The insurer's services or rates have been uncompetitive, and a change in carriers would have been considered, regardless of the proposed program design.
- The employer learns the insurer is not committed to underwriting flexible benefit plans. Examples of a lack of commitment include unreasonable pricing of flexible options, strict adverse selection controls and high fees to administer the program. One measure of capability and commitment is whether or not the insurer provides a flexible benefit plan for its own employees.
- After some preliminary discussions with the insurer, the employer finds that the insurer's systems or services are unable to adapt to flexible benefits.
- The employer uses two or more insurers to underwrite the current benefit package and determines that consolidation of all benefits under one carrier will simplify flexible benefit administration.
- The insurer displays a lack of understanding of flexible plans. It is important that the entire insurance company team understand how flexible benefit plans operate; from the service representative to the administrative and underwriting staff. Problems have occurred, for example, when underwriters apply traditional methods to analyze flexible plan experience. Recently, an insurance company analyzed the first year's enrollment patterns under three long-term disability options and proposed the following rates:

Option	Benefit	Rate
1	50%	$.75 per $100 of pay
2	60	$.53 per $100 of pay
3	70	$.61 per $100 of pay

The underwriter reviewed the characteristics of employees enrolling in each plan separately and, since older employees tended to take the 50 percent plan, proposed a rate that was higher than under the other two plans. The result is clearly ridiculous and, if implemented, would actually increase the insurer's risk. Anyone in the 50 percent option would re-enroll in the 60 percent plan for the lower premium. Thus, the older employees would be covered for a larger benefit at a lower cost. The proposed pricing structure would cause, not prevent, adverse selection.

The flaw in logic that generated these rates was the failure to recognize that everyone has a 50 percent benefit—the employees in the 60 percent option have 50 percent plus 10 percent optional while those electing 70 percent have 50 percent plus 20 percent optional. The premium for the 50 percent plan should reflect the characteristics for all employees, while the premium for the 60 percent plan should be the cost of 50 percent plus an optional 10 percent. The optional 10 percent should reflect the demographics of those electing 60 and 70 percent.

Definitions and assumptions change from carrier to carrier. The employer must ensure that the carrier representatives have a clear understanding of the program as designed by the employer. The search for a replacement occurring in conjunction with a flexible program implementation may not be the best timing for the employer—but in certain situations may be warranted.

(d) IMPLEMENTING THE PROGRAM

Insurers have had considerable experience implementing new benefit plans under traditional benefit programs, both for existing and new clients. Except for any unusual flexible program details created by the addition of choice, the administrative work will be handled by the insurer as any other new program. Assuming that the employer and the carrier have adequately planned the implementation process and assigned project completion dates, the implementation will proceed smoothly.

However, to increase the potential for a smooth transition, following is a short checklist of carrier administrative responsibilities that need to be addressed:

Systems

- Adapt employee eligibility data to include new benefit choices.
- Program claims payment system with new benefit options and plan provisions.
- Establish the appropriate breakdowns for maintaining and reporting claims experience.

Employee Communication

- Prepare any required explanatory and enrollment materials and new identification cards.
- Deliver claim forms to the employer for any new benefits being offered.

Contracts

- Amend policies to reflect new benefits.

Final rates must be established by the insurer prior to communication of the program to employees. This timing is sometimes an issue. Because of communication, enrollment, and systems requirements, an employer might need final rates three to four months (or more) prior to the effective date. This issue of rate delivery timing should be addressed in preliminary discussions with the insurer. Rates for self-funded coverages, of course, can be developed at any time, since insurer involvement is not an issue.

Part Five

Communication

Sixteen

Communicating with Employees

§ 16.1 INTRODUCTION

Even with the most carefully crafted design and the most efficient administration system, the level of success of a flexible benefit program at last depends on one uncontrollable element: people. Benefits, after all, are for *employees*. Eventually, employees will be the judges of how well the program meets their protection needs, motivates their behaviour, or encourages them to join or remain with the company.

The reaction of employees, therefore, can determine how well a flexible program meets its objectives, and that reaction will be shaped during the implementation process. Today, most employees are aware of the concept of benefit choice making and in some environments have even lobbied employers for a flexible program. Still, when actually faced with making decisions in areas they may never even have thought about before, the mere fact of the change can trigger all the emotions associated with protecting the status quo: fear, uncertainty, suspicion, anxiety. If such potential employee concerns are not dealt with adequately, all the time, money, and effort spent designing the program might just as well never have been spent.

Flexible programs really work best when employees use them well— when their benefit choices change as their life situations change, when they use the health care expense account with minimum forfeitures, when they associate the value of their benefits with the cost of providing them. But flexible programs are used in this way only when employees have confidence in and enthusiasm for the process. Companies achieve the best results when employees are satisfied with the benefit protection available, comfortable that reasonable cost sharing is fair, and convinced that choice making increases the usefulness of benefits.

However, these results are not achieved automatically with the implementation of a flexible program. Employee satisfaction with flexible benefits cannot be created or controlled by an act of will, but it can be significantly influenced. Communication in a variety of forms can be used effectively to motivate, educate, persuade, and satisfy employees as to the value of the flexible program and their ability to make the decisions they will need to make.

(a) STEPS IN IMPLEMENTATION

Flexible benefits require a substantial commitment in time and effort from both the employer and the employee. While it is just one part of the implementation task, communication can represent the single largest hard-dollar cost, particularly for employers with few internal design or production resources. And money aside, the sheer size of the communication task can appear overwhelming before the task has even begun. Therefore, communicating a flexible program requires a strategy—a strategy designed to achieve the best results for the time and dollars spent, recognizing that employees have a significant role to play in the final success or failure of the program.

Although each flexible benefit program is unique, experience reveals there is a logical order to the information flow:

- **Step One: Developing a plan.** The company should identify an over-all communication approach consistent with the organizational environment.
- **Step Two: Announcing the program.** The program must be announced to employees in a way that will maximize positive emotions and minimize negative ones.
- **Step Three: Educating employees.** Employees need additional information to better understand the concepts and get a handle on the facts and figures.
- **Step Four: Enrolling employees in the program.** Enrollment forms, worksheets, workbooks, instructions, and other enrollment-related communication must be clear and easy-to-follow.

- **Step Five: Following up.** Follow-up communication must be considered to help keep the level of benefit understanding high for claims filing and reenrollment.

The remainder of this chapter examines these steps in more detail.

§ 16.2   DEVELOPING A PLAN

Flexible benefit communication is almost always more extensive, more technical, and broader in scope than other employee benefit communication undertakings. If a company is not used to communicating on this scale, the prospect can be daunting. However, organizations implementing a flexible program also see the potential in being able to capitalize on the communication effort as an opportunity—a chance perhaps for the first time to create significant employee interest in benefits, to strengthen awareness and appreciation of employer expenditures for benefits, and to promote greater understanding and ownership of benefit coverages.

Employees' initial reaction to change, the significant impact their decisions could have on their own personal financial security, and the diversity of viewpoints present in any workforce make a substantial communication effort almost mandatory. The investment in time, money, and effort can be significant, but planning the process carefully helps save not only time and money, but considerable effort down the road.

The result of a careful, coordinated planning effort is often a written document—a blueprint that can be followed as the communication campaign unfolds. While such a document is often changed and updated as implementation proceeds, it never fails to keep the campaign on track.

(a)   ANALYZING THE ENVIRONMENT

To get the planning started, assemble a small team including plan designers or administrators and those responsible for the communication effort. Remember that field representatives can bring a different perspective. Once the team is assembled, invest some time in reviewing the task ahead and analyzing the communication environment at the company. In short, make sure all team members are starting from the same place. To a large extent, designing the appropriate communication campaign depends on the team's conclusions on environmental issues such as:

- **Scope of the program**—which benefits are involved and what is the level of employee risk if a "wrong" decision is made; which parts of the program will change the most and require more explanation; which benefit areas have been historically "sensitive" for employees.

- **Audience**—which employee groups will be included in the program; the profile of the audience (age, sex, marital status, length of service, level of education, etc.); the need for material in English and French; how important/unimportant communicating to families might be.

- **Employee relations climate**—how employees are feeling about the company *before* flexible benefits; field morale versus morale at company headquarters; relations with unions or groups lobbying for unionization; recent history of benefit or compensation increases or cutbacks.

- **Current business environment**—both inside the company and among competitors—how the company is faring economically; how employees have seen the results (e.g., layoffs, bonuses); how the flexible program reflects the company's business strategy; any good news or bad news likely to break during the implementation of the flexible program.

- **Existing communication channels**—benefit communication that worked well and not so well in the past; other internal communication channels typically not used for benefit communication, but which might be considered; any new equipment or technology recently available to the company.

And finally, consider any particular "trouble spots" which may not be reflective of the company as a whole, but may affect how the program is received by a particular group or division, for example, rumours of a plant closing at one location. Once the planning team has a shared understanding of the communication *environment*, the focus can narrow to the communication campaign.

(b) SETTING OBJECTIVES AND CHOOSING MESSAGES

The most effective communication campaigns are designed to meet very specific objectives. "Let's just tell employees about it," is certainly a straightforward approach, but one that quickly gets mired down in a mass of detail and contradictory messages. Furthermore, it is all but impossible to communicate just the facts. Facts are always coloured by the viewpoint of the communicator; words carry connotative, as well as denotative, messages. One of the first tasks in the planning process, therefore, is for the team to decide just what they want to tell employees and how they want the message told. This is done by setting objectives, by establishing parameters that will guide the communication effort.

For example, one company may want to emphasize the value and competitiveness of the flexible program. For another company, the priority might be to introduce the concept of total compensation—tying benefits and pay together. Other broad objectives could include:

- Explaining the concept and rationale behind flexible benefits
- Demonstrating the company's interest to be an innovative employer sensitive to the needs of a changing workforce,
- Educating employees so they can make informed decisions
- Conveying the concept of managing or controlling benefit costs for the future
- Introducing the concept of an employer/employee/government partnership in providing protection and security
- Establishing a company identity in a merger, spinoff, or reorganization environment.

Once over-all objectives have been agreed upon, the planning team should list the most important messages—the central issues or ideas to convey to employees through the communication effort. Such messages might include:

- "You can tailor coverages to your own needs."
- "You can choose (not choose) your old plans."
- "You can take advantage of important tax benefits."
- "Choice is a good thing."
- "The program is unique."
- "Nobody loses."
- "The company is spending the same amount of dollars as before."
- "You and the company can manage costs better."

The unique character and environment of the organization should lead naturally to the right objectives and specific messages for the communication campaign. The planning team's study of the background and climate should tie into the objective-setting process, just as the chosen objectives and messages will be the raw material from which the communication pieces finally will be developed.

(c)   DEFINING MEDIA AND APPROACH

Once the planning team has identified *what* they want to say, they need to turn their attention to *how* they want the message delivered—the media for getting the message from the company to the employee. Clearly, every known medium for human communication can be considered from the simplest (face-to-face) to the most complex (satellite transmission to a company cable system or interactive video presentations using laser disks). The task of the planning team is to determine which vehicles make the most sense, given what they know about the company's environment.

Despite the vast array of possibilities, most flexible programs are communicated using multiple combinations of generally available types of media—employee meetings as well as print and audiovisual presentations. According to a recent survey, employers with flexible programs in place identified the media they used in the first year and subsequent years as shown in Table 16.1.

Determining the media, however, is only half the battle. Most people (particularly in office environments) receive a blizzard of paper every day. Employees must have some means to identify which information is related to the flexible program and which is not. In other words, a "communication campaign" is not a "campaign" unless it contains some unifying elements. Those elements typically fall into two categories: vocabulary and design.

Choosing a vocabulary for the flexible program can seem relatively simple. First, the planning team must decide what the program is to be called. Now that flexible benefit programs have been around for several years, it is not surprising that most, if not all, of the generic names have been devised and are in use. Here is a representative list:

Flexplan '90 ('91, '92, etc.)	ChoiceSystem
FlexAccount	FlexComp
Flex Fund	FlexChoice
SelectPay	BeneTrade
PlusPay	Flexpay
Benefits Plus	BenePlus
FlexSecurity	Beneflex

In certain circumstances, a new and unusual name readily presents itself. American Express Canada uses "Express Yourself," while a

Table 16.1
Communication Media

	First Year (%)	Subsequent Years (%)
Employee meetings	93	38
One-on-one sessions	56	50
Newsletters	74	72
Highlights brochure	63	61
Personalized enrollment material	78	83
Election confirmation report	67	78
Bulletin board notices, memos	33	28
Enrollment workbook	41	39
Benefits handbook	67	61
Hotline and/or information centre	33	22
Sound/slide show	33	17
Videotape presentation	48	6
Benefit statements	44	67
Payroll inserts	15	11
Claim kit	15	17
Interactive computer software	4	6

Source: Hewitt Associates 1989 Survey of Canadian Flexible Benefits Programs and Practices.

prominent brokerage house uses "FlexFolio." However, more and more today, employers are turning away from coining a name for their flexible program and simply referring to it as "Flexible Benefits" or "Flexible Compensation." An obvious reason is the dwindling supply of names not already in use. An alternative is to tie the campaign together with a theme or tagline, such as these being used by companies today:

". . . The Right Combination"
". . . Benefits You Can Count On"
". . . The Choice for Your Future."

Once a name or theme has been chosen and other vocabulary decisions have been made (such as what to call option prices, flexible credits, etc.), graphic designers can be called in to unify the look of the campaign with colour, type style, paper, illustrations, and other graphic design elements. Again, make sure the approach chosen is appropriate for the environment. It is probably unwise to adorn communication materials with expensive-looking graphics, if the flexible program is accompanied by benefit cutbacks. On the other hand, in a different environment, bright, interesting graphics can send a message to employees that the new program is valuable and a high priority to the company.

(d) ESTABLISHING SCHEDULES, RESPONSIBILITIES, AND BUDGETS

The planning process is incomplete until a schedule for implementation has been established, responsibilities have been assigned, and budgets have been approved. Typically an employer will need more time, more people, and more money in the first year flexible benefits are communicated than in later years.

Communication planning needs to occur well in advance of the targeted implementation date. As a general rule, an average of five months is required for planning the campaign and preparing the materials. Interestingly, the lead time for getting a campaign underway tends to vary little by the size of the organization. In effect, the planning process involves about the same magnitude of effort, regardless of the number of employees eligible for the program. A typical timetable for communication is shown in Example 16.1.

To assign responsibilities, the planning team must first consider any internal resources the organization can bring to bear, including the corporate communication staff, training department, print shop and mail room, and even graphic designers from the marketing department, if appropriate. In some companies, the staffing requirements will have been included in the prior year's budgeting process. However, the vast majority of companies must try to staff the communication effort with internal people already committed to other projects. The corporate communication staff will have the bimonthly company magazine to release, the training department will be committed to the annual sales meeting, and so on. However, once the planning team knows how much talent and time is available internally, it can fill the gaps with outside resources, up to the budget available.

It is difficult to generalize about budgets for flexible benefit communication. So many elements will vary from company to company and campaign to campaign. However, there seems to be one almost-universal truth: it is more extensive and will cost more than any other benefit communication the company has ever undertaken. During the implementation year, communication costs are driven up by the sheer volume of information and the number of individual communication pieces required to carry the communication effectively in a relatively short period of time.

Example 16.1
Sample Communication Timetable

Activity	Apr	May	Jun	Jul	Aug	Sep	Oct	Nov	Dec	Jan	Feb
				1991						1992	
Develop communication plan		▮									
Present to management			▮								
Present to human resources staff			▮								
Distribute announcement materials			▮								
Publish articles in company newspaper					▮	▮			▮		▮
Issue newsletter (twice monthly)					▮▮▮▮▮						
Pretest enrollment materials					▮						
Train meeting leaders/counselors						▮					
Conduct employee meetings/distribute election kits							▮	▮			
Staff benefits hotline							▮▮▮				
Election deadline								▮			
Send confirmation reports									▮		
Effective date									▮		

When budgeting, the planning team must consider these issues:

- The internal resources (soft dollars) available and the external support (hard dollars) that will be needed
- The complexity of the flexible program or the company environment (some companies simply have more information to send than others)
- The size of the population and the quantity of the materials needed,
- The need to produce materials in English and French
- The media included in the plan, including any design elements which will affect costs (colours, paper quality, illustrations or photographs, etc.)
- The availability and efficiency of the distribution network in place at the company for shipping and receiving materials.

As might be expected, communication costs vary by type of flexible program. For example, the numerous moveable parts within a choice-making-plus-health-care-expense-account arrangement would require a more extensive first-year communication effort than a stand-alone health care expense account. Figure 16.2 shows the average internal (soft dollar), external (hard dollar), and total costs associated with flexible programs.

On a per capita basis, the costs decrease with the size of the organization. Data collected from Canadian flexible programs cannot be used

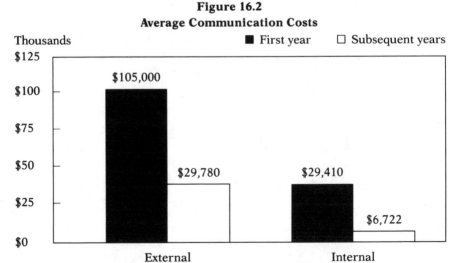

Figure 16.2
Average Communication Costs

Source: Hewitt Associates 1989 Survey of Canadian Flexible Benefits Programs and Practices.

to analyze these costs by type of program and size of employer because of the small sample size. However, U.S. data is available to illustrate these differences:

Figure 16.3
Average Communication Costs
per Employee in U.S. Program

Eligible Population	Internal	External
Full Choice-Making Plans		
Fewer than 1,000	$ 8	$50
1,001 to 5,000	7	31
5,001 to 10,000	6	26
10,000 or more	10	17
Health Care Expense Accounts		
Fewer than 1,000	$ 2	$14
1,001 to 5,000	7	17
5,001 to 10,000	3	7
10,000 or more	1	4

Source: Hewitt Associates 1989 Survey of United States Flexible Compensation Programs and Practices.

These are significant dollars. But when compared to the cost employers pay every year to provide benefits to employees, and considering the value to be gained when employees understand and appreciate a flexible program (or even their benefits for the very first time), the numbers begin to appear less overwhelming. When setting communication budgets for a flexible program implementation, therefore, it is helpful to understand upfront that the numbers will be large. But they do not have to be unreasonable; with proper planning, costs can be controlled and managed.

§ 16.3   ANNOUNCING THE PROGRAM

Once the communication plan has been completed and approved, the campaign can begin. A successful announcement phase starts where employees are and recognizes that the company will seldom have the first word. The grapevine often has taken care of that. In hallways, break rooms, and plant floors, on telephones, faxes, and assembly lines, the news about flexible benefits may be out and possibly inaccurately so. By the time the employer is ready with the big announcement, employee reactions already might have been kicked into high gear by half-truths and sheer conjecture.

In this environment, announcing a flexible benefit program can sometimes be seen as a marketing challenge. The company needs to get employees' attention and convince them that official channels are the best, most reliable sources of information. Starting with many details is usually a mistake; instead, acknowledge the turmoil employees may be in and begin there. Get managers and the human resources staff on board first, for this group will later support the communication effort with employees.

To the extent possible, announcement communication should be:

- **Straightforward.** In a general way, let employees know what they are winning and what they are losing.
- **Reassuring.** Provide evidence of management support and assure employees that more communication (more details) will follow.
- **Attention-getting.** Keep it short and simple.

Employee acceptance can pay large dividends to an employer, so many companies have chosen innovative approaches to announcement materials, approaches; they would not have considered before flexible benefits. These include highly creative campaign themes; novelty items such as buttons, T-shirts, and posters; and a wide variety of other non-traditional media. This type of unusual media blitz can be very effective, depending on the environment, but it is not always necessary. A letter from the Vice-President of Human Resources or a memo from the CEO can work just as well. What is needed is good, clear, reassuring, simple, and straightforward communication.

§ 16.4 EDUCATING EMPLOYEES

Once employees have tuned in to the company as a source of information, the channel cannot go off the air and still expect to keep the audience enthralled. A steady flow of information will not only keep employees' interest, but will begin to provide the misinformed with consistent, accurate information.

Education is an important step in achieving employee acceptance of the program, but do not give too much education at one time. If we are honest in remembering our worst educational experiences, they would probably include the nonstop lecture packed with details and the all-night study sessions before exams. Usually, we passed the exams, but forgot the content within a week. The concepts behind flexible benefits and the details of how the individual plans work need to be stored more permanently. Employees need to make this information part of their working knowledge, to build on in the months and years ahead. Employers can help by developing educational materials that:

- **Arrive in small doses.** Build understanding in the employee group by adding one piece of knowledge to another. Employees may not take the time to read a book about their benefits, but they likely will read four pages once every couple of weeks.

- **Focus on what is important.** Providing all the details during implementation is probably not only unnecessary, but self-defeating. Employees cast adrift on a sea of information will pick and choose the messages they receive (or choose none at all). Focus on what employees *must* know to enroll; save the fine print for later.

- **Offer diversity.** Different people are attracted by different media. Some read newspapers; others do not. Different company locations may have very different media needs. Communicate in different ways, at different times, and remember to provide a forum for getting questions answered.

- **Encourage learning over time.** With flexible benefits, employees are required to understand benefit messages in more than a general way. Experience indicates that for a typical full-flexible program, employees will need to devote several hours to their decision process. The volume of details alone, not to mention the importance of the decisions being required, indicates that reinforcement of the messages is critical. Communicate simply, but often.

Newsletters or regular articles in the company newspaper can be very effective vehicles for time-releasing details about the program in specific environments. One large mining company used newsletters to good effect, because employees had been trained to receive company financial information in that format. On the other hand, a large manufacturing company had less success with this method because many employees had no workspace to keep such materials, and the company was unwilling to incur the cost of sending materials home.

The key is to take the audience into account when choosing the media for the education phase. If newsletters will not work, maybe a highlights brochure sent to the home will. Or try an audiocassette. One company mounted a sales-like campaign to encourage employees to read the education materials. Local sports figures were enlisted to make 60-second "commercials" for the flexible program on audiotape. For example, one athlete talked about how he needed more protection than his teammates and compared his situation to an employee with several dependents. The audiotapes were played over the public address system in cafeterias and throughout company buildings at the end of each day. An unusual approach, certainly, but tailor-made for an employee audience unaccustomed or hesitant to read benefit materials.

Most organizations also conduct employee meetings near the end of the print communication campaign. This is usually the time when a company unveils a sound-slide show or audiovisual presentation encapsulating and to some extent "selling" the merits of the new program. In addition, employees have the opportunity for face-to-face interaction with meeting leaders who are well-versed in the program, familiar with the organization's reasons for "going flexible," and available to field any questions about the new program.

§ 16.5   ENROLLING EMPLOYEES

By the time employees have reached this stage, they should have received enough information (in small doses) to have a basic understanding of the concepts and important details of the program. They should feel satisfied that they understand how they will be affected by flexible benefits and the company's motives for implementing the program.

Enrollment communication has two goals. First, from the company's perspective, enrollment forms must be completed and returned on time and as accurately as possible. And second, from the employees' perspective, the enrollment process must be relatively easy and non-threatening. These goals are not necessarily mutually exclusive, but they often seem as if they are. In fact, the entire implementation effort can flourish or founder on this issue.

Enrollment materials must represent the joint efforts of computer systems, administration, and communication professionals. If systems issues drive the development of materials, the result is often too technical for administrators or employees to use easily. If administration issues take over, the often cumbersome result is not only complex for employees, but impossible for data entry operators to follow.

Communicators can cause problems, too. When communication issues are allowed to override systems and administration concerns, the materials may not provide enough information to allow systems and administration people to do their jobs.

Effective enrollment communication builds on the foundation laid during the education process and takes into account the needs of other disciplines. It is effective when it is:

- **Clear and easy to follow.**   If enrollment is the "final exam," make sure the test is easy to understand. Provide examples and simple instructions, directing employees from one piece to another or from one part of the form to another. Clearly identify space used only by administrators.

- **Consistent.**   Keep the anxiety level low by using terms and phrases made familiar by earlier communication. There should be no surprises here, no last-minute changes in terminology to confuse employees.

- **Complete.**   Tell employees what they need to think about and what they can ignore for now.

- **Positive.**   This is the chance to revisit the big picture, to look at the over-all goals of the program and to define a future direction for benefits and compensation at the company. After concentrating on the details for a period of time, employees will welcome the opportunity to put the pieces together.

If there is a secret to a successful enrollment phase, it can be summed up in one word: personalization. Employees learn the value of flexible benefits more quickly and completely when they see the effects on their own situations before choosing coverage. Communication materials can be personalized to varying degrees. Here are some common approaches, listed in order of increasing personalization:

- **Role-modeling** uses a number of fictional examples and allows employees to identify the ones most closely resembling their personal situations. Typically included in overview materials or audiovisual presentations, role-modeling establishes a set of demographics and life circumstances, then outlines why the fictional people chose the benefits they did. While technically not a true personalization, role-modeling does help employees become aware of the different issues they may have to think about when making their own decisions.

- **Worksheets, workbooks, and calculators** allow employees to learn something about how benefits affect them personally by entering personal information manually and doing calculations. For example, a worksheet for a health care expense account might ask employees to write down eligible expenses they had in the previous year, then estimate how much they expect those expenses to be in the coming 12 months. An additional calculation with the help of tables will show the employee the tax savings expected by using the health care expense account for those expenses.

- **Computerized reports, worksheets, and election forms** provide some basic personalized information for each employee from the company's data base. If there are restrictions on certain benefit options, these personalized materials can show just those options for which the employee is actually eligible. When benefit amounts or option prices differ by pay, sex, family status, or years of service, computer-printed materials can show employees the precise value of the benefit and what it will cost them to choose it. Not only is this information clearly useful to the employee when making decisions, but it can prevent a multitude of errors on election forms by limiting the number of mathematical steps the employee must take.

- **Interactive software and interactive video** are beginning to emerge as an effective new medium for employers to communicate with employees during the enrollment phase, and for good reason. Interactive materials offer the highest degree of personalization. Employees with access to such a system can not only find their individual benefit amounts and prices, but they can create new scenarios again and again before finally completing the enrollment form. They can watch as each change in option affects not only their coverage, but their over-all cost and their tax situation.

All the goodwill earned through the announcement and education stages can reap rewards for the employer now. If enrollment materials are personalized to some degree, are useable, and easy to understand, employee confidence and appreciation for the program will grow, and the enrollment process will meet with fewer errors over-all.

§ 16.6 FOLLOWING UP

Are employees satisfied with flexible benefits? At the time of enrollment, the final answer to that question is still probably nine to 12 months away. If the enrollment process has gone well, most employees will be fairly satisfied with the *idea* of choice making. However, the true test will come when they actually start to *use* the new program or when they reenroll. That is when follow-up communication can make a major difference.

Unfortunately, at too many companies, the implementation team disbands—officially or unofficially—after enrollment. Each discipline goes its own way, usually on to other concerns or new projects. This feeling of closure at enrollment time is natural. But if a concerted effort is not made to keep up the flow of information, companies run the risk of abandoning the field just as the game is nearly won. Ultimately, employees will judge the program by how well they remember the elections they made, how easily they can get a question answered, how efficiently claims are processed, and how willing they are to "play the game" when re-enrollment rolls around.

The follow-up communication stage is really never over, but it is probably most critical in the first 12 months after implementation. To be effective, follow-up communication should be confirming, consistent, and complete.

To be confirming, find ways to report to employees about the benefit coverage they elected individually and as a group. A computerized confirmation or benefit statement is a clear communication to employees that the "system" understood and recorded their elections accurately. It will also serve as a reminder of the coverage they have when they need to use their plans months down the road.

Use the newsletter or company newspaper to reinforce the election patterns which meet the program's objectives. And find out how employees felt about the enrollment process by the most direct approach: ask them. Do a follow-up focus-group study or ask a random sample of employees to complete a questionnaire and report the results to the employee group.

To be consistent, simply keep up the good work. If the communication approach used for implementation worked (graphics, theme, terminology, etc.), do not abandon it now. Build on what has gone before as claim forms, status-change forms, reimbursement forms, account statements, workbooks, and other communication materials are developed.

To be complete, think about filling in the gaps. Now is the time for benefit handbooks and all the detail employees could not have used effectively during enrollment. Take some time to repackage or reorganize reference materials. There may be a more logical approach for the flexible benefit environment.

Perhaps the most important job in the follow-up phase is the communication leading up to and surrounding second-year enrollments. "Reflex" provides an opportunity for the company to make things better, to learn from any mistakes made during implementation and broaden the base of employee satisfaction. Taking time to evaluate first-year communication efforts can help immeasurably when Year 2 appears on the horizon.

§ 16.7 SPECIAL CONSIDERATIONS

Ideally, this five-step approach to communication will lead to a successful implementation. Particularly if the company is offering a good news benefit package, the communication effort, although extensive, can be fairly straightforward.

However, not all companies will be serving up unleavened good news. In some cases the introduction of flexible benefits is accompanied by cutbacks. In others, employers must approach a workforce mindful of past economic or organizational problems. Even at companies where almost everything lines up in the good news column, pockets of employees may have reactions different from the population as a whole. For these companies, communication can be seen as the most unpredictable factor in a flexible benefits implementation. Many of the particular communication problems such companies will face are emotional in nature, while others are simply related to getting the job done. Either way, the successful solving of these communication problems is not only essential, but it can have a major positive effect on employee acceptance of the flexible program.

(a) EMPLOYEE UNCERTAINTY

Whether they believe flexible benefits are a good idea or a bad idea, the secondary reaction of most employees hearing about it for the first time is uncertainty. They are being asked to make decisions in an area that could have a significant effect on their financial security, but also one they know little or nothing about as yet. "The Company" has always made those decisions before. Suddenly, it seems, they have to learn a whole new language, and the risk of failure seems high.

Disarming employee uncertainty is a gradual process. It starts with the confidence projected by company representatives as they announce the program, and it usually ends once the employee has successfully enrolled and used the new benefits. The communication campaign can encourage this process by including some basic strategies:

- **Focus on personalized communication.** Provide materials that will help employees understand how their decisions affect their personal situation. Find ways to demonstrate the balance between benefit cost and risk in a *personal* way. Any opportunity employees have to try different scenarios with real numbers will help them make decisions they can feel good about.

- **Provide real life examples.**   The new program will not operate in a vacuum. It is designed for *people* to use, so provide employees with examples of how real people might elect and use their benefits.

- **Emphasize the implications.**   To be comfortable with choice making, employees need to know more than the facts and figures. They also need to understand the implications of what they are doing, the reasons why one employee might choose differently from another. Although a line must be drawn between informing and giving employees advice, even a list of issues employees should consider can help.

- **Provide an effective question and answer network.**   Employees should know about and feel comfortable approaching a designated person for answers to their questions. An effective network of this type can be crucial in resolving misunderstandings, clearing up complaints, and facilitating decision making.

(b) EMPLOYEE SUSPICION

In some environments, employees can view a flexible program as management's attempt to "sneak something past" them. One company was surprised at the high level of employee suspicion about a proposed flexible benefit program. The company was nearing the end of a three-year salary freeze and the employees feared their new program was being given to them *instead of* a long-awaited salary increase. Delaying implementation until after the freeze was lifted produced a very successful plan. An unstable business or employee relations environment is the best breeding ground for employee suspicions. This type of negative organizational background will affect *any* changes the employer makes—flexible or not. And when a flexible benefit plan is being used as an opportunity for increased cost sharing or other perceived cutbacks, negative employee perceptions can develop very quickly.

However, of all the communication problems, employee suspicion succumbs most easily to the right communication strategy. It depends, in part, on having realistic goals. It may be impossible to get all employees to embrace the program completely, but it *is* possible to help many of them understand the reasons behind the changes and to accept the business decisions as necessary, no matter how unpleasant.

The best way is to be straightforward. For employees to support the program, they must have the whole story. Companies should have confidence in their benefit design and address any trade-offs openly. Tell both sides of the story and, importantly, give employees the *reasons* behind the decisions. A high degree of management and supervisory support for the program can help here. And finally, rely on the value of choice making to help sweeten the pot. Although employers should not market the program beyond its merits, experience shows that a substantial number of employees will see cost sharing as a fair trade for the benefit of flexibility.

§ 16.8 SUMMING UP

Communication is one of the most important aspects of the implementation process. The employer simply has no other choice but to communicate and communicate well. Therefore, companies considering a flexible program might as well bite the bullet and realize it will take a major commitment of resources—both money and people—to do the communication job right. Since those resources will be required anyway— whether the communication is effective or just mediocre—companies should take this opportunity to at least think differently about how the task might be approached. Look at new media possibilities. Identify new strategies. And most importantly, plan the communication effort in detail so both time and money can be used wisely.

Experience shows that all of the resources it takes to communicate a flexible program are worth it in the end. When the communication job is done well, when employees are comfortable with the program and trust the process, the company's other objectives for flexible benefits— even cost management—are more easily attainable.

Seventeen

Training the Human Resources Staff

§ 17.1 INTRODUCTION

While often seen as two separate disciplines, employee communication and the training of the human resources staff and, in some cases,
front-line supervisors, are inextricably linked when introducing flexible benefits. Without the enthusiasm, understanding, and support of
these professionals, it is unlikely employees will receive the kind of
education and personal attention they need during the implementation phase.

In many ways, the human resources staff can be considered part of
the media for communicating flexible benefits. Regardless of the title
they use—personnel representatives, benefit administrators, human resources professionals—their potential for influencing employee behaviour (positively or negatively) is far greater than for any other
vehicle in the communication campaign. These are the meeting leaders
who will be the first to put a human face on all the printed communication employees have been reading about the new flexible program.
These are the administrators who will be staffing benefit hotlines and
otherwise answering questions employees might have about enrollment
or their specific coverages under the new flexible program. These
might also be the people who will be helping employees file claims
under the new flexible program.

Still, most companies spend more time, money, and effort preparing booklets and videotapes than they do preparing this most effective communication resource. While the level of success of the flexible program is highly dependent on the ability of these people to communicate, training them to do their job well is often an afterthought.

If personnel representatives are media, however, they are also audience. First and foremost, they are employees—with the same personal questions and concerns as the rest of the employee population. Furthermore, the satisfaction an organization hopes to generate in employees over a period of time must be achieved in them much more quickly. They have a job to do—a job critical to a successful implementation.

That job further defines the personnel representatives as audience. To meet their personal needs, they must have similar types of information as employees. But to meet their professional needs, they must have more in-depth knowledge of the program. They must have specific skills in leadership, counselling, and administration. They must have positive, realistic attitudes. And they must have it all sooner, before they become the focus of the program for employees.

For this reason, organizations implementing flexible benefits are really facing *two* communication campaigns: one for employees and one, less elaborate but nevertheless complete, for the human resources staff. The campaigns must be integrated and compatible, although unfolding along separate time lines and using different media plans.

§ 17.2 TRAINING THE TRAINER

Besides their usual administrative function, personnel representatives can be thought of as trainers—people who teach or direct the understanding and attitudes of the employee group. As trainers, they will be considered the experts by employees looking for answers, but the level of knowledge, experience, and competency will vary by role and level of experience. Managers and members of the implementation team are likely to bring more experience and skill to the training task. Local benefits representatives, on the other hand, may be less comfortable representing the program to employees.

Some representatives are newcomers who inherited whatever knowledge they have from the person who occupied the job before them. Others are old hands who may have a good grasp of how the current plans work, but they may lack a broad outlook as to why the plans function as they do. Still others have been at their jobs so long that the fundamental changes required by flexible benefits will seem almost bewildering. The larger the company, the wider the range will be.

A common mistake is for implementation teams (who typically have been studying and working on the program design for several months) to assume that other benefits professionals in the company will approach implementation with the same knowledge base. Organizations must recognize that people other than those who have been intimately involved with benefit design will be responsible for administering flexible benefit and telling employees about the program. In short, the trainers must first be trained.

The goal of training is to develop personnel representatives who are both competent to carry out the new requirements of their jobs and confident in their ability to do so. While there are no hard and fast rules for designing a training program, it is usually helpful to follow the same five steps involved in employee communication: planning, announcement, education, enrollment, and follow-up.

(a) DEVELOPING A PLAN

The training program for personnel representatives will depend in large measure on the roles they will ultimately play in the implementation and ongoing administration of flexible benefits. Like employee communication, a training program should be planned in advance to take into account the scope of the flexible program, the employee relations climate, and the current business environment. But the type of training needed will also depend on the:

- Background and experience of those being trained, including the current state of morale of the human resources staff locally and company-wide
- Roles they will be called upon to perform—the administrative function of the benefit administrator, the employee relations function of meeting leaders or election counselors, or the coordination function of managers
- Specific knowledge, skills, and attitudes required for the implementation
- Other duties they perform on a regular basis and the time they will have available to train for and carry out their implementation roles
- Geographic dispersion and local backup available; and

- Commitment of the organization to training, in terms of time, money, and effort.

(b)   ANNOUNCING THE PROGRAM

Too often, personnel representatives learn about the flexible benefits implementation at the same time employees do. Or they receive a cursory memo from the vice-president of human resources a few days before the "big announcement"—time enough for them to worry about all the questions they will get, but not time enough to prepare themselves or ask for additional details. Considering that the attitudes of these professionals will be critical to employee acceptance of the program, this type of announcement is a major tactical error. Organizations taking this approach set themselves up for problems by antagonizing the very people they must have on their side.

The solution is relatively simple. Inform and *train* personnel representatives before sending them into the line of fire. A memo from the vice-president of human resources is not a bad start, if it explains the roles human resources staff members will play, arrives well before the announcement to employees, describes the training they will receive, and provides the name and phone number of a person who can answer questions. Allay their initial concerns by providing case histories of successful implementations at other, similar organizations. If possible, involve them in testing employee communication materials and help them feel some ownership in the change by encouraging participation in the decision-making process.

By preparing the human resources staff early in the process, some information will start leaking to employees before the official announcement, but the grapevine will always be ahead of official communication channels anyway. At least the organization can head off some potential concerns by preparing personnel representatives in advance. Moreover, with an informed staff participating, chances are the information on the grapevine will be more accurate than otherwise might be the case.

(c)   EDUCATING THE HUMAN RESOURCES STAFF

Whether the communication is for employees or personnel representatives, it is important to provide the details in small doses. It is unrealistic for a company to bring together its human resources staff just before the election process starts and force them to learn everything they need to know in two days. Confronted with this scenario, they probably will not even *look* at the massive resource binders they receive, let alone *read* them.

Information should begin flowing shortly after the plan design is completed. Again, consider the time personnel representatives have available to devote to their education. Chances are, this new information will have to be absorbed in addition to the work they already are handling. Phasing in their education respects the demands on their time and increases the likelihood that they will learn what they need to know.

By the time the program is announced to employees, personnel representatives must have a working knowledge of the concepts behind the flexible program, how the plans work, and what will be required of them and of employees. As information is released to employees, the trainers need an ever-deepening level of knowledge to keep up with the questions they will be getting. When planning how to provide this information, keep in mind:

- **Variety.** Communicate in different ways, at different times. Some learn better by reading, others through face-to-face discussion, and still others from lectures. This does not necessarily mean high-cost production values (art, colour, and other design elements). Simple, black and white memos can be effective as long as they are not the only communication vehicle used.

- **Overload.** Too much at one time is never a good thing. If a groundwork of plan knowledge is laid over a period of time, formal training meetings can be used to better advantage by concentrating on skills development.

- **Examples.** Build on the benefits knowledge administrators already have. Start with the most familiar aspects, then add more information. Use examples common in their work, then illustrate the new situation. Better still, ask them to share examples of employees' questions in a formal or informal network as the program unfolds.

- **Recap and review.** Do not forget to tie it all together. Understanding the whys will be just as critical as knowing the whats and hows.

- **Role definition.** Help the personnel representatives understand what they have to do and when they have to do it. Make them feel part of the team. Even sending tidbits of "fun" information, like how the vice-president of human resources forgot to sign her election form, can reinforce the feeling of teamwork.

Finally, determine exactly how much information will be useful. People serving in different functional disciplines may need different amounts or types of information in order to be competent and confident in the roles they will play.

(d) ENROLLING EMPLOYEES

While employee questions will add to the workload of the human resources staff throughout the flexible benefit introduction, the actual enrollment phase "turns up the heat." Their normal workload must be set aside completely for anywhere from two weeks to two months, depending on the situation. Furthermore, personnel representatives must suddenly become more *proactive*. Instead of responding to employees' initiatives, they will be required to lead meetings, counsel elections, work with new administration procedures or software, or manage these activities.

To that anxiety, add the fact that they will be making their own benefit elections. They will be going through the same process as employees—discerning their protection needs, evaluating their family situations, weighing cost versus risk. All in all, enrollment time is a high-stress period for administrative staff, so the better prepared they are (in advance) the more successful they will be.

One simple, but considerate, approach might be to allow them to dispose of their personal elections before the actual enrollment period, if possible. Let them make their elections early. If that is not feasible, at least provide copies of the enrollment materials and structure exercises so they can do all the thinking and decision making in advance, leaving only the form to complete during their busy period.

With their personal situations taken care of, the next step is to help increase the confidence level of personnel representatives. In formal training sessions, provide ways for them to test their knowledge of the program and to practise specific skills needed in the final weeks before implementation. Allow representatives to practise leading meetings, handling questions, dealing with confrontational behaviour, correcting election errors, or running new administration programs, for example.

(e) FOLLOWING UP

Once all the elections are entered and confirmed, the real, everyday work begins. Although the administrative processes will continue to be fine-tuned over a period of time, three specific types of follow-up are extremely valuable but often overlooked:

- **Debrief them.** The human resources staff is in the best position to describe what went right and what went wrong with the implementation. They can explain how the employee communication materials should be improved and how smoothly the enrollment process went. For an organization looking ahead to second-year enrollments, this resource is invaluable and relatively easy to tap.
- **Say thank you.** Personnel representatives have stretched beyond their former limits to help the organization implement flexible benefits. A simple thank you—unassociated with any other task-related communication—will speak volumes.
- **Keep them informed of what is ahead.** Implementation-related issues will continue to be important for 6 to 12 months after the actual effective date. Keep personnel representatives up-to-date on enrollment patterns, status changes, and other information that could have an effect on how they do their jobs.

§ 17.3 TYPES OF TRAINING

The effectiveness of any training program will finally be judged by how successfully the personnel representatives do their implementation jobs. Success usually depends on the mastery of certain knowledge and skills used to carry out various roles. When designing a training program, then, the organization should spend some time identifying the specific knowledge, skills, and roles needed, based on the current environment and company objectives.

(a) TRAINING FOR KNOWLEDGE

Much of the earlier discussion on education applies to building knowledge. Knowledge includes the "facts and figures," plan provisions, election processes, and role definition. But while paper flow and administrative procedures need to be mastered, training for knowledge should also focus on the big picture: how each plan works in the context of the others and the organization's compensation philosophy and objectives.

The first impulse when training for knowledge is to organize a lecture or classroom setting. The classic arrangement is to fill an auditorium, set up a projector, create several hundred overhead transparencies, and watch the audience slowly sink into their chairs with glazed eyes before the first coffee break. There is a better way; in fact, there are many better ways. Time-releasing information gives the organization an opportunity to communicate knowledge in a variety of formats. Newsletter articles, audiotapes, summaries, reviews, opportunities for self-testing or peer discussion, computerized or videotape instruction—all can be effective in helping personnel representatives acquire the knowledge they need.

On the other hand, there is a value to large group meetings. Training meetings are important opportunities for administrators to meet and talk with one another, to ask questions, to get the most up-to-date information, to *build* on the knowledge they already have. But in training for knowledge, large meetings should focus on the *key* issues. The details can be sent out in advance.

(b) TRAINING FOR SKILLS

Besides acquiring a new base of knowledge about flexible benefits, the human resources staff will need to learn or improve certain skills or behaviours. The specific skills needed will depend on the roles each individual will play and will run the gamut from operating the videotape machine in an employee meeting to running a sophisticated new computer program or working one-on-one with participants who may be frustrated. Those who are experienced will already have many of the needed skills. Others will have to brush up on one or two, while still others will never have performed the skill their implementation roles will demand.

When the objective is developing or improving skills, information alone will not do the job. To *own* the skills, the personnel representative will need a chance to *practise* them. Start by providing models, demonstrations, or case studies of the skill needed. Then move on to application projects, that is, experiments the administrators can conduct on their own, in feedback sessions with small groups, or in role-playing exercises. If the skill is technical in nature, running equipment, for example, set up the equipment in an environment where they can practise and ask questions in case of trouble.

Because some people are quicker studies, they will acquire new skills faster than others. Be sure to allow enough time for the majority of personnel representatives to become confident in their ability to use the new skill or behaviour. If they feel unsure or unprepared, that uncertainty will be the primary message transmitted to the employee group.

(c)   TRAINING FOR ROLES

Everyone who will be involved in the flexible benefit implementation will require training in knowledge and skills. But how much training they need in each area—and the specific types of knowledge and skills—will depend on the actual jobs they will be doing. The most effective training programs are role-specific, providing a basic level of training for everyone with additional efforts tailored to the different roles to be performed.

The first task is to define who will be performing which task, and that is not as easy as it sounds. Depending on the people available, it may not be easy to assign one job to this person and another job to that person. Very often, members of the human resources staff will fill more than one role. Meeting leaders may also be election counselors. Benefit administrators may also be meeting leaders. Where there are limited resources, the human resources manager may wear all of these hats. There may also be some situations—for example, a small field location—where a front-line supervisor fills these human resources roles. The specific roles and how they are filled will vary from organization to organization, but there are still some role-specific training issues to consider.

(1)   Training Benefit Administrators

Benefit administrators have the responsibility for administering the program over the long term. They may supervise a staff of people who will enter data about employees' benefit elections. They usually process claims and answer employees' day-to-day questions about how the plans work. They are typically identified as professional benefits specialists, the "gurus" with all the answers.

Knowledge-building will be a crucial part of the training for benefit administrators. They will need detailed resources if they are to continue to do their jobs effectively following implementation. Administration manuals (detailed descriptions of administrative procedures) are important tools for them. Benefit administrators will ask questions on the fine points of plan design; they will need enrollment procedures defined down to the form number on the data input sheet. Usually, no one else will need the level of detail that benefit administrators require, so it is important to meet their information needs apart from the general training sessions.

Skill development will also be important, particularly if benefit administrators must use new computer systems or administrative processes. If the training involves new technology, relate the new procedures to the old way of doing things so they can get their bearings. Allow time for hands-on work (reviewing completed forms for errors, working on terminals, etc.), so they feel confident with the process once the "flood" of enrollments begins.

(2) Training Meeting Leaders

If employee meetings will be held to introduce flexible benefits or answer employee questions, meeting leaders will be needed. Leaders typically call people together, set the tone, pace, and objectives of the meeting, handle questions, distribute information, and generally act as company spokespeople and ambassadors for the new program.

Usually, meeting leaders are assigned from the ranks of benefit administrators or other benefit specialists, but they may not always be the only choice. They do bring a detailed knowledge of how the plans work, but sometimes they do not have the other skills necessary to be effective. Moreover, leading meetings is a significant commitment at the very time their administration workload is heaviest.

Another alternative might be to recruit staff from other departments for the job. Raid the recruiting, training, or communication departments. Line managers are often quite successful as meeting leaders. If it is difficult to find all of the knowledge and skills needed in one person, consider using a team or even a panel to lead meetings.

Meeting leaders do not necessarily have to be experts on the plan. They should have a basic knowledge, understand the concepts, be able to field most typical questions, and know where to send employees for answers to more detailed questions. More importantly, meeting leaders need good presentation and group discussion skills. They should look and feel confident as they welcome employees, present material, handle questions, and facilitate the meeting. They should be able to sympathize with employee concerns or confusion and be realistic about what the program will achieve. But most of all, they should be enthusiastic and *believe* what they say, for the success of the employee communication effort will depend in large part on the meeting leaders' positive attitudes.

Capable people can be found, trained, and put in front of a group of employees with great success. There are exceptions, of course, and the messages from meeting leaders are not always consistent. With reasonably good selection and training, however, there is a consistency of sincerity and enthusiasm that registers well with employees.

(3) Training Enrollment Counselors

Enrollment counselors typically answer questions and work through enrollment issues during the election process. Whether in face-to-face settings or on the telephone, enrollment counselors are the "lifeline" for confused or concerned employees. A single contact with an enrollment counselor can make the difference between an employee's positive or negative reaction to flexible benefits.

Detailed plan knowledge is not really necessary for enrollment counselors to be effective, as long as backup resources are available. Rather, they need to understand clearly how to complete enrollment forms and the issues employees should consider when making elections. Skill development for enrollment counselors should emphasize the techniques of supportive, interpersonal communication—how to ask sensitive questions, how to react responsibly to employee emotions. A counselor must be skilled at coaching employees toward decision-making and leading employees to understand how the program can work for them. The counselor must do this without crossing the line into advice-giving—a practice that could later prove inappropriate or damaging to the organization. In short, enrollment counselors must have the skills to *handle* questions and *ask* questions in a way that will lead to a positive conclusion for and by the employee.

(4) Training Human Resources Managers

Most likely, human resources managers will themselves define how much they want to be involved personally in the implementation of a flexible benefit program. At the very least, they will assign the roles to be played by people reporting to them. At the other end of the spectrum, they could choose to be meeting leaders or enrollment counselors or take direct responsibility for deciding how the program is communicated. No matter how involved they become, however, as managers of the human resources function, they will influence the behaviour and attitudes of other benefit professionals and employees with whom they come in contact.

Training for human resources managers should be planned with a sensitivity to their specific needs and schedules. Provide training materials in advance. Concentrate on background information, the organization's philosophy and objectives that led to flexible benefits, and the ways implementation will affect their departments.

§ 17.4 SUMMING UP

Experience proves that taking the time, making the effort, and spending the money necessary to thoroughly train the human resources staff makes a significant difference in the implementation process. Enrollments are bound to go more smoothly—not only in the first year but during re-enrollments as well. When administrators feel confident about their implementation role, it will infuse their normal daily tasks and continue to influence employees, as well as the entire organization, in a positive way.

Eighteen

The Role of Employee Listening

No matter what other objectives exist for introducing a flexible benefit program—whether the program involves an increased benefit expenditure, a cutback, or simply rearrangement of existing dollars—maximizing employee appeal will be a critical factor in achieving program success. Employee listening provides valuable guidance for helping to generate maximum employee satisfaction. Employee listening can be used in a variety of ways, including test marketing flexible benefits or fine-tuning design or employee communication materials.

§ 18.1 DEFINITION OF EMPLOYEE LISTENING

Employee listening is a structured process for identifying employee needs and gathering employee perceptions. There are two basic formal listening approaches: quantitative and qualitative.

Quantitative employee listening involves a written survey, typically administered to all employees or a statistically reliable random sample. Quantitative listening is aimed at defining precisely how many employees feel a certain way and whether subgroups feel differently.

Qualitative listening involves face-to-face discussions, either one on one or in group meetings, usually with only a small cross-section of employees. Qualitative listening is aimed at probing why various employee attitudes exist, how those attitudes are formed, and how the attitudes can be reinforced or changed.

An analogy may help clarify the difference between the two approaches. Quantitative surveys are similar to a telescope. They provide a broad picture of what is on the horizon. Qualitative interviewing is more like a microscope. It studies the way individual components work together to form a whole. Attitudes toward any issue are the result of a number of factors. Certainly, facts play a part, but only a part. Expectations, rumours, trust, misunderstanding, interest, apathy, and personal situations all affect employee attitudes. Quantitative listening identifies the key factors present in a particular environment; qualitative interviewing identifies how the factors work together to shape attitudes.

Neither approach is "best" for studying employee attitudes toward flexible benefits. Whether a quantitative or a qualitative approach, or a combination, should be used depends on:

- The particular information to be gathered
- What kinds of data an organization's management requires to make decisions
- Whether significant variations in attitudes are expected among different employee groups
- How important it is to understand employees' reasons for their answers
- How much attention it is desirable to call to a study
- The time frame for collecting the information.

§ 18.2   USES AND PURPOSES OF EMPLOYEE LISTENING

There are three stages in which employee listening can be of value for studying flexible benefits:

- Before program design, to identify employees' benefit preferences and priorities and to assess employee interest in choice making
- After program design, to assess reaction to the proposed plan and identify information needs
- After implementation, to measure satisfaction with program design and communication and to evaluate any appropriate changes.

(a) BEFORE PROGRAM DESIGN

Employee listening can serve several purposes prior to program design.

First, listening can provide a perspective or context for task-force decision making. As any organization that has worked on a flexible program can attest, there are times when the development process comes to a standstill because agreement cannot be reached on design issues. Often the deadlocks are based on conflicting hypotheses about employee needs, attitudes, and preferences. For example, one person states that employees will not care about more life insurance; another argues that the organization should not communicate the flexible program as being a "big deal," because all that is happening is that employees are being given choices, with no additional company dollars; another holds that only one dental option is needed, because all employees will buy the most dental coverage possible. Employee listening provides definitive information to prove or disprove such hypotheses and keep the design process moving.

A second reason for conducting employee listening prior to program development is related to the basic nature of flexible programs—the emphasis is on meeting individual employees' benefit needs. Preliminary employee listening identifies individual benefit preferences and priorities and defines what needs to be done to meet those needs. Consider the guidance provided to three different organizations from separate employee listening surveys.

Employees at each organization were asked to complete a benefit trade-off exercise. They could choose to increase, decrease, or maintain coverage in current benefit areas or choose new coverages not currently offered. But like the organization itself, they had to work within a set benefit budget, so increasing coverage in one area required decreasing coverage elsewhere. The results showed differences as illustrated in Example 18.1.

With this insight, each organization developed a very different type of flexible program. Organization A decided to offer higher-deductible medical options than originally intended, since more than one-quarter of employees expressed interest in lesser-valued coverage.

Organization B responded to the listening results by expanding the flexible program design to include a capitation dental plan and reallocated some of an existing savings plan contribution to employees in the form of additional flexible credits.

Example 18.1
Employee Benefit Priorities: Sample
Results from Different Organizations

Percentage of Employees Who Want:	Organization A	Organization B	Organization C
Supplemental medical coverage:			
Increased	6%	32%	14%
Kept the same	65	44	82
Decreased	25	20	3
Dropped	4	4	1
Dental coverage:			
Increased	29%	34%	24%
Kept the same	46	54	60
Decreased	11	8	8
Dropped	14	4	8
Life insurance coverage:			
Increased	16%	19%	24%
Kept the same	52	52	55
Decreased	19	24	11
Dropped	13	5	10
Savings plan benefits:			
Increased	39%	22%	30%
Kept the same	55	32	54
Decreased	6	42	15
Dropped	0	4	1

At Organization C, employees' heavy emphasis on current supplemental medical and dental benefits alerted management to the need for additional benefit communication. This organization had a history of providing high-value benefits, with employees consistently choosing its coverage over that available through a spouse's employer. A supplemental communication campaign was developed to explain coordination of benefits between different employer plans and to stress that electing lower coverage would generate flexible credits for use in other benefit areas.

A third potential purpose for employee listening prior to program design is the opportunity provided for building employee ownership of a flexible program. Listening to employees conveys that a major change is being considered and that employee input is valued by management as one of the factors that will be used in program-design decisions.

Later, as appropriate, communication can capitalize on the employee input and show how it was used to shape plan design.

This consideration may be particularly valuable in programs that will involve a cutback. Some organizations hesitate to ask for employee reaction in such a situation. However, the negative message of a cutback can be significantly offset by permitting employees to identify where a cutback would be most acceptable or least painful.

(b) AFTER PROGRAM DESIGN

After a preliminary design has been developed, employee listening can be used to test reaction to the proposed program and to identify employee information needs. Specifically, listening can answer five important questions about the implementation of a proposed program.

First, listening can assess how employees react to the philosophy underlying the proposed program design. Listening can probe how employees react to key design considerations, such as the equity of flexible credit allocations, the need for improved cost control, and so forth. Insights into these over-all reactions provide a valuable framework for understanding employee attitudes toward and perceptions of individual program components.

Second, listening for design purposes can determine how employees will react to the particular features proposed and answer such questions as how well the design meets employee needs, whether it has the right number of choices, and what program changes employees would make if given the chance. This information determines the perceived value of each of the various options and helps decide whether the design specifics are right from the employees' perspective.

Third, through a mock enrollment exercise, listening can be used to develop projections of choices the entire employee population might make under the proposed program. Such information on likely elections can also help assure that assumptions made regarding option pricing and adverse selection are appropriate for the particular organization.

Fourth, listening can probe whether the planned content and approach of flexible benefit communication materials are appropriate. Under a flexible approach, decision-making responsibility rests with the employee, so there is little room for misunderstanding or omissions. Listening can assess the appropriate approach and quantity of communication.

Finally, listening can determine whether there are differences in understanding and appeal of a flexible program among employee subgroups and help in fine-tuning final program design and communication.

(c) AFTER PROGRAM IMPLEMENTATION

After the program's introduction, employees must prepare for second, third, and subsequent enrollments. They will read and study the communication materials, discuss the various benefit options, review last year's expenses to estimate upcoming health care expense account deposits, assess whether they should increase their savings plan deposits, and so forth. In subsequent years, listening can be useful in probing such issues as:

- How smoothly did the enrollment process go? Many benefit managers say they hear only about the problems and feel the need for a more realistic and well-rounded picture of how the process worked.
- Are communication pieces effective? Are employees reading them? Should some materials be added or dropped? What questions or confusions still exist? Have new issues arisen?
- Are employees paying as careful attention to the process in subsequent years? Are they actively rethinking their choices each year, or do they become content to "stay" with their prior elections? Probing the reasons for employee elections can become important, particularly in situations where the employer was counting on employees opting for certain coverages in subsequent years.
- Are the enhanced levels of benefit appreciation and understanding initially associated with a flexible approach being maintained? Do employees understand and appreciate benefits more once they have experience with choice making? Or are employees settling back to pre-flexible levels of awareness?

In addition to providing this information, follow-up listening reinforces the employee-oriented nature of the flexible program and reaffirms management's interest in employee preferences and priorities.

§ 18.3 WHEN NOT TO LISTEN

There are two situations in which it may not be appropriate to seek employee input. One involves dangerous questions. The other involves dangerous answers.

An example of a dangerous question is: How will employees react to a reduction in the level of dental benefits? An organization testing this issue will alert the grapevine before it has prepared the full-scale communication campaign explaining the need for the change. If it is imperative to assess employee reaction to such an issue, an indirect method of questioning (such as probing the importance of and satisfaction with current coverage levels) usually will yield better results.

A dangerous answer is one to which an organization is unwilling to respond. Consider this situation: an organization was planning to reduce and eventually eliminate the subsidy for family supplemental medical coverage. The change was based upon a philosophical objective of equity as well as upon concern over possible future discrimination challenges. Those with dependants were obviously expected to resist such a change. Since the organization was not willing to maintain the subsidy, asking for employee feedback would have proved an empty process at best.

§ 18.4   HOW TO LISTEN

(a)   PERSPECTIVE

Before deciding to proceed with any employee listening, consideration should be given to environmental issues such as:

- The usual means of communicating with employees, and how employees are likely to react to a listening study given that prior experience
- The prevailing employee relations climate
- Management's willingness to share the study purpose with employees and to respond to the listening results with either action or communication.

Such issues can affect both the validity of the listening results and the impact of the listening exercise on over-all company/employee relations.

(b)   SETTING OBJECTIVES

To ensure that listening produces the information needed, it is important to consider the way the results are to be used. Is information on satisfaction or dissatisfaction with current benefits needed to help decide the appropriateness and value of a flexible program? Are the results to be used for a go/no go decision? Is there already a commitment to introducing a flexible program with employee input being sought only to fine-tune program design? Is plan design set and is the goal to assess communication issues and needs?

Answers to these questions will dictate when the listening should be conducted and whether quantitative or qualitative listening is more appropriate.

(c) TYPES OF APPROACHES

In deciding whether to use a quantitative or qualitative listening approach in a particular situation, the following advantages and disadvantages need to be considered.

(1) Quantitative Listening

The primary advantage of a quantitative survey is that it provides definitive statistics. The results quantify precisely how many employees agree and how many disagree with whatever questions have been asked. For example, the results can quantify how many employees are comfortable with benefit choice making, how many are not, how many express interest in various options, and so forth.

The second advantage is that detailed analyses can be performed to determine whether different groups of employees have different opinions. For example, subgroup analysis can pinpoint whether employees in different family situations have different reactions toward the way a flexible credit allowance is allocated, whether special communication needs exist at different locations, and so on.

If a standardized survey is used, a third advantage is that the results allow for valuable data base comparisons to determine if an organization's employee reactions are typical or atypical. This information can then be used to identify issues unique to that employer's environment that may require special attention.

The fourth advantage is that a written survey is a more efficient, less time-consuming way to reach a large number of employees than face-to-face meetings with the same number of employees. This is of particular benefit for organizations with a widely scattered workforce. In such circumstances, a questionnaire is perhaps the only practical way to involve employees in outlying locations and to reach such locations with a positive message of management's interest in their opinions.

Inherent in quantitative surveys, however, are also some disadvantages. Most significant is the limited opportunity provided for employee education. While a minimal problem when testing general employee benefit preferences, this is a particularly critical drawback for testing reaction to a specific flexible program design. For employees to provide well-informed reactions and opinions, in-person education with the opportunity for questions and answers is needed.

A second limitation of a quantitative survey is that the reasons for and feelings behind the opinions identified cannot be probed very well. The data will clearly determine whether employees think their new flexible benefit program is average, above average, or below average, but it will fail to explain *why* employees hold those opinions. What program are employees comparing this one with when they judge benefit quality? Are some of the benefits more prominent in their mind than others when they make that judgement? Are they less concerned about life insurance because supplemental medical is their top priority? Inability to track such thought patterns is one of the limitations of a quantitative survey.

Finally, there is an issue that can be an advantage or a disadvantage, depending upon the objectives of the employee listening exercise. A quantitative survey is very high profile; questions are in print, and a large number of employees receive questionnaires. The questionnaire makes it evident that a particular issue or benefit area is being explored. If a benefit improvement is going to be introduced, the advance notice can serve as a "plus." The survey can be the early signal that something is coming and a visible sign that the employee perspective is being taken under advisement. Feedback of the survey results can also serve as a first step in the communication campaign to build excitement about the change.

On the other hand, if there is a cutback under study, the high profile can work to the employer's disadvantage. If management is not prepared to communicate the details and answer employee questions and concerns, a qualitative listening approach is more appropriate.

(2) Qualitative Listening

The purpose of qualitative listening is to determine why employees feel the way they do, and most importantly, how those feelings developed. For testing interest in choice making, qualitative listening typically takes the form of focus group interviews. This involves gathering together a cross-section of employees in groups of 8 to 10 at a time. A trained focus group facilitator leads the discussion, making sure that the discussion stays on track, that all employees participate, and that no one dominates the discussion. The goal is to tap into or replicate the type of employee discussion that takes place in the hallways, cafeterias, and lounge areas of an organization.

Generally, focus groups are most effective with a diverse mix of participants—employees with different lengths of service, different family situations, and a mix of men and women. Such diversity tends to generate a more lively discussion. As a side benefit, a mixed group also allows participants to see that different needs and opinions exist and that management is facing the challenge of satisfying a variety of needs.

One caution, however, is that mixing focus group participants in terms of grade or pay level may create problems. Benefit discussions often generate comments about family budgets, such as the affordability of an option involving a higher medical deductible or what portion of pay can be contributed to a savings plan. In such situations, lower-income employees will feel uncomfortable with others earning more and may refrain from speaking freely. On the other hand, those at a higher-income level may feel reluctant to hurt the feelings of others who are more concerned than they are about an increased deductible. Separating group participants by income or position helps avoid these problems.

What are the advantages and disadvantages of qualitative listening? The primary advantage is that face-to-face interaction provides the opportunity to track how attitudes are formed, indicating ways to reinforce attitudes that are desirable to maintain or strengthen as well as how to change or overcome negative attitudes or employee misperceptions.

Another advantage of qualitative interviewing is that the focus-group-meeting format provides the opportunity for employee education. Employees can be provided with a presentation on a proposed flexible benefit program and have a chance to ask questions. Meeting leaders have a chance for follow-up questioning to be sure employees truly have a good understanding of the information presented and to ensure employee feedback is based on informed opinion.

In terms of disadvantages, the main drawback is that the results are not quantifiable. The emphasis is on what and why, not how many.

A second possible disadvantage is the potential for group dynamics to affect results. Someone with a very negative attitude, for example, may repeatedly voice complaints and try to dominate the group, or participants may voice only polite agreement to avoid confrontation or repercussions. The meeting leader must be well trained to respond to and balance both kinds of participation.

Finally, as is true for quantitative listening, the approach itself can offer either an advantage or disadvantage. Qualitative interviewing is relatively low profile. Only small numbers of employees are involved, relatively little is in print, and the discussion is open-ended. Qualitative listening is less likely to produce negative repercussions within the environment, but it is also less likely to generate significant employee interest.

(3) Combination Approach

Testing employee attitudes toward a particular design requires in-person education. However, it is also usually desirable to gather statistical data quantifying employee attitudes and determining likely election choices. This result can be achieved through a combination of quantitative and qualitative listening involving three parts as follows:

- An education session to give employees needed information to make decisions about the proposed flexible program.
- A benefit election exercise during which employees record their benefit choices on an election form, using a workbook which shows personalized flexible credit allowances and the pricing for each benefit option.
- A feedback session in which reactions to the proposed flexible program, election process, and communication materials are discussed. At the end of this discussion, employees complete a written questionnaire quantifying their reactions.

(d) SELECTING LISTENING PARTICIPANTS

How many employees should be included in the listening and how they should be selected depend upon two basic issues: statistical precision and employee relations or "face validity."

A random sample of employees may be sufficient to provide statistical reliability, but it may leave other employees feeling their views are being ignored. A statistically sound sample may not be necessary when a few representatives of various departments or locations can clearly articulate the opinions of the employee group.

Following is a description of four typical methods for selecting a sample of listening participants.

- A *random sample* is used if the intention is for everyone in the employee population to have an equal possibility of being selected. A simple example would be selecting every 20th name from an employee roster arranged in a *nonordered* fashion, with the starting name chosen randomly.

- A *stratified random sample* tends to be more appropriate when there are many important subgroups within the employee population. Stratifying the population by job category, for example, would assure that employees are chosen from each job category in proportion to their distribution in the population. Selection from within each stratified subgroup is made randomly. A disadvantage of a stratified random sample exists for many organizations, however, because of the geographic dispersion of their locations. Selecting a stratified random sample is likely to include only a few employees from each of a large number of locations, resulting in significant costs and difficult logistics.

- To avoid such a scattered sample while maintaining statistical projectability, a *cluster stratified sample* can be used. This involves randomly selecting a limited number of locations expected to represent many others.

- A *purposive* sample can be used if projectable statistics are not required. Employees are simply hand-selected to represent key subgroups.

In any case, the total number of employees to be sampled and the method of sample selection should be based on consideration of the trade-off involved (i.e., cost versus the degree of statistical precision and certainty required). Issues to be addressed include:

- What degree of precision and certainty about each over-all finding is required for the type of decisions to be made?
- Are there specific subgroups of employees for which statistically precise information is required? Are there any subgroups of employees or locations that can be excluded from the listening?
- What proportion of the employee population is at each location? Are different reactions expected from employees at different locations?
- Regardless of statistical considerations, how much face validity or believability will the sample size need to have for the people who will be reviewing the results?
- Regardless of statistical considerations, how many employees at how many locations need to be included for employee relations purposes?

§ 18.5   LISTENING AS COMMUNICATION

The listening process is itself a form of employee communication—an important and visible message that management cares about employee opinions. However, the listening process will raise employee questions. Why is the company asking about benefits? What will be done with the information gathered? How will things change as a result of the study?

It is impossible to avoid raising employee expectations. The key is to raise the *right* expectations. The listening exercise must make clear that, while important, employee input represents only one consideration to be reviewed in making program design decisions. The listening effort needs to include an explanation that legal, administrative, cost considerations, and so forth, will also be taken into account, and in some areas these factors may carry greater weight than employee opinions.

On the positive side, the listening process can capitalize on the employee relations value of seeking input. Even if only a small number of focus group interviews are to be conducted, an announcement of a study can be sent to all employees. After any type of listening, follow-up communication should identify ways in which employee suggestions were addressed or explain why not if that is the case. This turns the process into a two-way communication channel and provides an opportunity to explain both employees' and management's point of view.

An additional communication opportunity presents itself for employee listening on flexible benefits. A key communication message for any flexible benefit program is that a flexible approach responds to individual employee needs. The listening process can help reinforce the broader message of flexible benefits by stressing that employees are being asked to identify their needs to be sure the program suits them.

Part Six

Administration

Nineteen

Managing Administration

§ 19.1 GETTING STARTED

(a) INVOLVING THE ADMINISTRATORS

Administering a flexible benefit program usually is more complicated than administering a traditional benefit program. Administration is a major consideration, both from an implementation and an ongoing processing viewpoint. Therefore, it usually makes sense to involve key administrators as soon as possible in the plan design process. The plan design is a major factor in determining the cost and feasibility of flexible program administration.

Departments whose administrative procedures and systems typically are affected most by a flexible program include benefit administration, payroll, and data processing. The individuals who can provide the best input on the impact of a proposed program on these areas are the ones most familiar with the current procedures and systems. These include the administration of current benefit programs, payroll processing, and payroll/personnel computer systems. Without the involvement of these individuals, what may seem like a minor issue to the program designers could make the administrative task considerably more costly or, in the worst case, impossible.

If, for some reason, it is not possible to involve representatives from each administrative area in the initial plan design, it may be appropriate to refrain from finalizing design until an administrative evaluation can determine the program's full effect on administration.

(b) DEVELOPING A DETAILED PROGRAM DESIGN

Once the basic plan design is complete and approved by management, there likely will be many open design issues affecting administration. To determine which open issues need to be addressed, first look at policies, procedures, and systems associated with the current benefit program. Which existing requirements also must be met by the flexible program? Second, study each aspect of the proposed flexible program and determine its effect on each employee category (full-time, part-time, etc.) and employee status (retired, temporary, leave of absence, etc.). Third, identify new benefit administration requirements created by the flexible program (such as health care expense account claims review, annual re-enrollment, and so on).

Here are some examples of the kind of questions that may be resolved in the detailed design process:

- What data items are required (for example, date of birth, hire date, number of dependents)?
- What are the eligibility requirements for each employment category covered under the flexible program?
- How will flexible credits elected as cash be allocated to employees, and what will be the frequency of allocation (for example, lump sum at the end of the year, equal installments each pay period)?
- How will changes in compensation during the plan year affect pay-based coverage amounts and employee costs?
- What coverage, if any, will be given to employees who fail to turn in enrollment elections?
- How will employee coverages and costs change due to changes in employment status? Family status?
- How are status changes handled? What changes are permitted?
- What are the reporting requirements of the flexible program to insurance carriers? Third-party administrators? Accounting? Employees?
- How is the life insurance benefit rounded? To the nearer $1,000? Higher $1,000? What about long-term disability?

Finalize specifications for the administrative system(s) only after the detailed program design is complete. Otherwise, either the system may end up driving the plan design, instead of supporting the program, or it will be impossible to define the system because of too many open issues.

(c) ADMINISTRATIVE FUNCTIONS

Whether the flexible program is limited in scope, including only health care choices or broad in offering choice making in many benefit areas, the same basic administrative activities need to be performed. The administrative functions of most flexible programs include: enrollment in the program, ongoing coverage administration, health care expense account record-keeping, and payroll processing.

§ 19.2 ENROLLMENT PROCESSING

(a) TYPES OF ENROLLMENT

Flexible program enrollments can be classified as annual enrollment of all participants and periodic or immediate enrollment of newly eligible employees. The difference in the administrative activities involved in each enrollment type is principally one of scale. Annual enrollments usually involve all eligible participants, whereas periodic enrollments may involve only a small number of employees.

The first annual enrollment involves all eligible employees. Administering the initial annual enrollment usually begins three or more months prior to the program effective date. In following plan years, all eligible employees may be required to re-enroll as options, option prices, and flexible credit allocations change from year to year. Even though all eligible employees are involved in an annual re-enrollment, employee understanding of the flexible program is greater than in the first program year. Therefore, the annual re-enrollment effort may not require as much time to plan or execute. If no changes occur in either options or prices, annual re-enrollment may be limited only to employees wishing to change their elections.

The frequency of periodic enrollments depends on plan design. Periodic enrollments can occur semi-annually, quarterly, monthly, or even daily—such as, on date of hire.

The more often enrollment takes place, the greater the total administrative effort will be. For most employees, the concept of flexible benefits is new. Therefore, many employers try to allow enough time for employees to understand the program, including discussing options with other family members. Interim coverage in critical benefit areas may be provided to new employees until the employee is eligible for enrollment in the flexible program. This approach provides employees with basic coverage while they are considering their flexible program elections. Enrollment at specified intervals (quarterly, semi-annually) concentrates the administrative effort at each enrollment period. Daily or monthly enrollments may distribute the administrative workload more evenly. Interim coverages or longer waiting periods are used frequently by organizations with high employee turnover in the first months following employment.

(b) DATA COLLECTION AND VERIFICATION

The first step in the enrollment process is the collection and verification of participant data required by the plan design and administrative requirements for the program. Limited flexible programs may require only minimal data, such as name, employee identification number or social insurance number, and work location or home address. Broad programs covering many benefit areas usually require more extensive data such as date of birth, date of hire, number of dependents, family status, pay, and employment category.

Collection of the required data involves the identification of the data source and/or the consolidation of data to a central source. This depends on the degree to which data are already centralized, and the accessibility of the data to the enrollment system.

Verification of data is very important, especially when accuracy can affect the individual's eligibility for the program or the options and option prices available. Such data may include pay, age, length of service, employment category, employment status, and work location.

Clearly, if required data reside in one place and are reasonably accurate, this initial step of the enrollment process requires less time and effort than if data must be collected from several sources or if the accuracy of the data is unreliable.

(c) IDENTIFICATION OF ELIGIBLE PARTICIPANTS

After required data have been collected and verified, eligible participants can be identified. Eligibility is based on factors such as service, employment status, employment category, location, and possibly age. If required data are accurate, identifying eligible participants may be a simple step. This step can be more complex, however, if all benefits offered under the flexible program do not have the same eligibility requirements.

(d) PERFORMING CALCULATIONS

Once eligibility has been determined, the next step in the enrollment process is to compute the flexible credit allowance, option availability, and option prices for each eligible participant. For a limited program offering the same flexible credit allowance, options, and option prices to everyone, no individual calculations are necessary. However, a broad flexible program may allocate flexible credits based on individual participant characteristics such as pay or length of service. Prices for some options such as life insurance and paid time off may be based on pay or age. Some prices, such as supplemental medical or dental prices, may vary based on an employee's work location or employment status.

In addition to computing specific flexible credits and option prices, it may be necessary to determine which options are available to each participant for the year. For example, the plan may require participants to remain in the same medical or dental plan for a minimum number of years. In the case of life insurance or long-term disability, an increase in coverage over the current level may require proof of insurability. The system must be able to monitor these requirements.

For programs that have variations, each employee's flexible credit allowance, prices, and options will be individually calculated and communicated to the employee.

(e) ENROLLMENT MATERIAL

The scope of the program and the sophistication of the enrollment system will affect the type of enrollment materials used. Enrollment materials for a limited flexible program generally consist of an election form and a booklet describing the program. As the scope of the program broadens, additional communication and personalized enrollment material may be needed. The enrollment material for a broad flexible program usually consists of an election form, an election workbook, and a personalized statement.

The design of the election form is important to ensure easy entry of elections into the enrollment system. If the election forms will be key inscribed, column numbers may be required. If the elections will be entered on a computer terminal, the data items on the form may be designed to match the data items on the entry screen or vice versa.

A computer-posted personalized statement is often used for broad programs. This personalized statement is an individual report of each participant's available options, option prices, and flexible credit allowance. The basic participant data used for calculations may be printed on the report to provide for final verification of this data by the participant. In addition, if the participant currently is participating in the flexible program and is re-enrolling, the statement may show the participant's current coverages.

The personalized statement, election form, and workbook may be three separate communication pieces or a single combined packet. The personalized information may be computer-posted on the election form. In other cases, the election workbook is computer-posted with employee-specific credit allowances, options, and option prices.

Employee enrollment materials usually are packaged for each eligible employee and distributed prior to employee meetings where employees can discuss the program and have their questions answered. Employees are instructed to return their completed election forms to their local or central benefit office. Allow plenty of time for editing elections, correcting election errors, producing confirmation statements, and communicating elections to ongoing administration systems when setting the deadline for returning the forms.

(f) PROCESSING AND EDITING PARTICIPANT ELECTIONS

Editing participant elections is an important step in each enrollment process. Elections may be checked to ensure the participant's arithmetic is correct, that option prices are correct, and that the participant has elected options that are, in fact, available to the participant.

Editing is relatively straightforward with a limited flexible program. Forms can be designed so that participants simply circle or check the option they want. This simplifies editing to the point of simply checking that the participant made one election in each benefit area. However, in a program offering a variety of benefit options and variable flexible credits and option prices, the editing is more complex and time consuming. For this reason, editing is an automated function in most broad flexible program enrollments.

Some election errors can be corrected by the administrator. Most election errors, however, must be corrected by the participant. For example, transposition errors can occur when elections are key inscribed.

Errors of this type can be corrected simply by referring to the participant's election form. If the participant has recorded an incorrect option or option price on the election form, however, it may not be clear what option the participant intended to elect. This type of error requires correction by the participant. If an automated system is used for editing, the edit report produced by the system may be designed for use as a turnaround document and sent to the participant for correction.

The error rate for initial annual enrollment can range from 5 percent to more than 30 percent. The complexity of the plan design, the effectiveness of pre-enrollment communication, and the clarity of the enrollment material all have an effect on the election error rate. The enrollment system may provide statistical information on the types of errors employees are making. This information is helpful in restructuring communication material and enrollment forms for subsequent enrollments.

After elections have been edited and errors have been corrected, elections are recorded on appropriate ongoing administration systems. Employee after-tax payroll deductions are recorded on the payroll system. If health care expense account or savings plan or RRSP elections are included in the flexible program enrollment, required data are reported to and recorded on the appropriate record-keeping systems. In addition, health care (medical, dental, vision) elections are reported to the appropriate claims processors to ensure proper claim certification.

(g) ENROLLMENT MONITORING

A status monitoring program is an essential part of the enrollment system where large numbers of participants are involved or where the enrollment process involves multiple locations. Status monitoring reports list participants with missing enrollment forms and participants with elections that have been entered but are invalid. Reports identify the participant's name and location for easy follow-up. More sophisticated status monitoring systems may include a finer breakdown of where participants are in the enrollment process. Such systems identify how many participants have had personalized statements produced, valid elections but no signature, confirmation statements produced, and so forth.

(h) ELECTION CONFIRMATION STATEMENTS

After elections are validated, a confirmation statement may be produced to confirm the participant's elections. The confirmation statement is a personalized statement showing the elections recorded on the enrollment system for the participant.

Confirmation statements are important for several reasons. If employees are allowed to decline certain benefit coverages, the statement serves as a reminder to the employee that he or she does not have coverage during the coming year. In addition, employees are not allowed to change their elections during the year except in the event of a family status change. Therefore, confirming an employee's elections prior to the beginning of the plan year is very important. Confirmation statements also give employees a chance to catch any errors they made during enrollment or administrator errors made during election entry. Finally, if the program assigns default coverage to employees who have not returned their election forms before the deadline, the statement notifies the employee of the benefit coverage selected by default.

In its simplest form, the confirmation statement may be a copy of the participant's completed and edited election form. With broad flexible programs, it is desirable to produce a computer-posted confirmation statement, showing not only the employee's elections, but also providing information on the pay period withholding rates that will be required to pay for the employee's benefits.

Confirmation statements generally are distributed as early as possible in the enrollment period. As a practical matter, some participants will want to make changes or corrections. If changes are made before the first payroll deductions are taken, these changes are easier to accommodate.

(i) POST-ELECTION REPORTING AND ANALYSIS

After annual enrollment is completed, statistical and analytical reports may be produced for use in analyzing the impact of the program. The election analysis reports can be used to determine such things as:

- Is the program meeting the needs of employees?
- Is the program meeting management objectives? (For example, if medical cost containment is an objective, are employees electing the higher-deductible supplemental medical options?)
- What changes in the benefit program should be considered for next year?

Election analysis reports have the most value when reports from one year are compared to reports from another year. Election analysis reports typically include summary information on elections in each of the benefit areas, as well as on the over-all use of flexible credits and pay-roll deductions. Information may be broken down by age, service, pay, family status, location, and so forth.

§ 19.3   ONGOING COVERAGE ADMINISTRATION

Another area of flexible benefit administration is the ongoing adminis-tration of benefits after participants are enrolled in the program or prior to their eligibility for the program.

Ongoing coverage administration under a flexible program differs somewhat, although not dramatically, from ongoing administration un-der a traditional benefit program. In most cases, as an organization moves from traditional benefits to flexible benefits, existing ongoing administration procedures need to be modified. In some broad flexible programs, new procedures or systems need to be developed.

One requirement of ongoing administration may be to process interim coverage for new employees. This requirement depends on the design of the program. If the program does provide employees with some basic levels of coverage prior to eligibility for the flexible program, new em-ployees need to complete enrollment forms to authorize payroll deduc-tions, if any, and to make choices, if limited choices are offered. Interim coverage enrollment processing is included as a function of some flexible program enrollment systems. However, interim coverage enrollment of-ten is administered outside the flexible program enrollment system.

Coverage change processing occurs throughout the year. In general, an employee may change coverage, if the employee has a family status change, such as marriage, divorce, birth/adoption of a child. If an em-ployee terminates or transfers to an employment status which is not eli-gible for full benefits under the flexible program—for example, from full-time to part-time—the employee's coverage may change. A change in pay may mean that an employee's pay-related coverages such as life or disability insurance are increased or decreased. If this occurs, the em-ployee's cost of coverage may or may not change. Flexible credit al-lowances solely or partially based on pay or family status also may change.

Enrollment change procedures are established to process these cover-age changes. New elections and deduction rates need to be recorded on the payroll system, and in some cases new health care expense account contribution rates must be recorded on the record-keeping system.

Another function of ongoing administration is the production of group insurance reports. Periodically, the total coverage costs for each benefit option should be computed and reported. For insured plans, this would entail the calculation and payment of required premiums to the carriers. For self-insured benefits, this involves the calculation of adequate funding levels to cover expenses and maintain reserves.

Periodic health care certification reports or magnetic tapes may have to be produced for the health care claims processor(s). This information includes each participant's health care benefit election, and enables the claims processor to certify coverage. The administrative system (or, in some cases, the payroll system) produces a coverage certification report or tape for the claims processor at the end of the annual enrollment process and periodically throughout the year.

§ 19.4 HEALTH CARE EXPENSE ACCOUNT ADMINISTRATION

(a) HEALTH CARE EXPENSE ACCOUNT ENROLLMENT

A growing number of flexible benefit programs in existence today include a health care expense account. If the flexible program offers choice making in a variety of benefit areas, enrollment in the health care expense account is part of the annual enrollment in the flexible program. If the flexible program consists solely of a health care expense account, annual enrollment in the program still is required.

Chapter Seven discusses the design of health care expense accounts. In particular, it is important to recall that only employer contributions, in the form of flexible credits, can be used to fund the plan. Employees cannot use payroll deductions to fund the account.

Each year, the employee allocates a number of credits to the account. The credits may be posted to the employer's account monthly, quarterly, or once a year. Throughout the year, the employee requests reimbursement for any eligible expenses up to the current balance in the account. At the end of the year, any remaining account balance can either be rolled over to next year's account, paid out in cash or forfeited. The plan design will determine which of these applies.

(b) RECORDING EMPLOYER CONTRIBUTIONS

Employer contributions (flexible credits) are periodically posed to each participant's accounts maintained by the record-keeping system. The record-keeping system is typically designed to update employee accounts automatically with elected credit amounts on a periodic basis, such as monthly, quarterly, or annually. Updating would generally occur at the beginning of the period. The administrator then must verify that the correct amount was allocated to each employee's account and make adjustments to account balances if necessary. For example, an adjustment may be required if an employee was on an unpaid leave of absence, but was still showing a credit allocation on the record-keeping system.

(c) PROCESSING REQUESTS FOR REIMBURSEMENT

The employee completes a request-for-reimbursement claim form and attaches the required supporting documents to begin the payment processing cycle. Most programs require employees to submit covered health care expenses to the insurance carrier or claims processor before requesting reimbursement for the unpaid portion of the expense. In this case, the explanation of benefits from the claims processor provides the required documentation. A bill, receipt, or cancelled cheque may provide the required documentation for uninsured expenses. Claim submittal procedures and a list of eligible expenses should be communicated to employees during enrollment in the health care expense account along with a sample claim form.

Health care expense account claims approval may be done externally by an insurance company or other third-party administrator, or internally by program administrators. If done internally, the approval process may be centralized or decentralized. The claims approval process includes the following steps:

- Checking the employee's program eligibility. This step may be aided by an automated record-keeping system.
- Checking that expenses are incurred during the program year in which contributions were posted. In other words, 1990 contributions can only be used to reimburse expenses which were incurred during 1990 based on dates of service. As discussed later, plans allowing unused account balances to be rolled over to next year's account may allow claims made in the last three months of a year to be submitted against the following year's account.
- Checking for supporting documentation.
- Determining if expenses qualify as eligible expenses. Claims processors are provided with a detailed list of eligible and ineligible expenses.
- Checking that the form is signed by the participant.

The request for reimbursement form may be designed for easy data entry into the record-keeping system. Benefit categories may be coded to allow the system to post the expense to the appropriate account. Other information may include the dates expenses were incurred, the amount requested for reimbursement, and the name of the provider of services. Include space on the form for several expenses and benefit types to reduce claims processing administration.

Other ways to control the administrative effort are to limit the frequency of submissions (for example, once a month) and to set minimum submission and claim payment amounts (such as $50). Usually, these limits are waived during the final processing month of the plan year to accommodate year-end employee submissions.

Once the request for reimbursement is approved by the claims processor, it is processed for payment by the record-keeping system. Usually, requests for reimbursement are authorized for payment to the extent of the employee's account balance. Cheques may be produced by the record-keeping system, by another internal system such as accounts payable, by an external cheque-writer (such as an insurance company), or the reimbursement amount may be processed by payroll and included in the employee's regular paycheque as a non-taxable addition to net pay. Payments typically are made to the participant, not to the provider of services.

The frequency of reimbursement generally depends on the record-keeping system and cheque-writing system used, as well as the plan design. Payment timetables are communicated to employees during enrollment.

If the flexible expense account is based on monthly or quarterly posting of flexible credits, some claims will exceed the current account balance and may have to be resubmitted following the next updating of the account. To avoid this administrative complexity, many record-keeping systems have a *pending* feature. This eliminates the need to resubmit claims because the record-keeping system pays the claim to the extent of the account balance and automatically pends or holds the remaining claim amount for future payment, once funds are available.

The record-keeping system should produce an explanation of payment for each participant receiving a reimbursement during the processing period. The statement typically includes paid and pending amounts and the ending account balance. Year-to-date employer contribution and payment information also may be included.

(d) TERMINATED EMPLOYEES

An important issue to address in the detailed plan design phase of implementation is how to handle the expense account balance for terminating employees. The initial reaction of benefit administrators is to stop an employee's health care expense account participation on or shortly after termination of employment. Some qualify the decision to stop participation based on the reason for termination (voluntary termination versus layoff, etc.). Most cite administrative workload as the primary reason for wanting to terminate accounts prior to the end of the plan year.

Nonetheless, the majority of employers ultimately decide, for a combination of administrative and design reasons, to leave terminated employee accounts open until the accounts for active employees are closed following plan year-end.

In deciding how to treat terminated employees, consider the following questions:

- How will employee terminations be communicated to and recorded on the health care expense account record-keeping system?
- If accounts remain open beyond termination, but are closed prior to the end of the plan year, how will the record-keeping system know when to close the account?
- If exceptions to the rule are made, how will these be determined? How will the accounts be reopened?
- If the accounts are left open, how will payments to terminated employees be distributed?
- Can the cheque-writing system produce cheques for terminated employees?

(e)   YEAR-END PROCESSING

Because employees may not receive all of their year-end bills or explanations of benefits until after the plan year ends, most organizations keep accounts open for a period of time after the end of the plan year. During this period, the record-keeping system will need to maintain two sets of accounts for each participant: the current year accounts and the prior year accounts. In most cases, the grace period is from one to three months after the plan year ends. During this period, only claims for expenses incurred during the prior year may be submitted against the prior year's account balance.

This approach is particularly important in plans having a "use-it-or-lose-it" requirement, since it helps employees use up their final balances.

Health care expense accounts that do not have a use-it-or-lose-it requirement (i.e., that permit roll-over of unused year-end balances to the next year) frequently cut off claims at the end of the year. Claims incurred near the end of the plan year (usually during the last three months) may be submitted in the following plan year and paid out of the following year's account. In this way, the recordkeeper never has to maintain duplicate account balances.

At the end of the grace period, the recordkeeping system should calculate any unused balance and close out the accounts. If the plan allows this unused amount to be carried over and posted to the following year's account, it would be recorded as an additional employer contribution on the general ledger. Otherwise, the remaining balance is forfeited and the information is used to update the general ledger.

(f)   REPORTING ACCOUNT ACTIVITY TO PARTICIPANTS

Most health care expense account record-keeping systems produce an explanation with each payment. This statement usually includes a breakdown of all payment activity for the reporting period, including pending amounts as well as paid reimbursements. In addition, periodic account-activity statements are typically produced for each participant. These statements provide a beginning and ending balance, and a summary of employer contributions and claims activity.

Even if periodic account statements are provided, there will be other occasions when participants will have questions about their accounts. These questions may concern over-all account balances or specific contribution or claim activity. Administrators need access to up-to-date account information in order to respond to employee questions.

(g)   RECONCILING THE HEALTH CARE EXPENSE ACCOUNT AND THE GENERAL LEDGER

The final health care expense account requirement is reconciliation to the general ledger. Typically, the reconciliation process occurs with a frequency consistent with an organization's standard accounting cycle.

The funding of a health care expense account involves the creation of an accrued liability. This liability represents an amount of money set aside by the employer to pay for eligible expenses which will be reimbursed in the future. The liability account is increased each time a contribution is made to the account, and the account is decreased each time a payment is made or an unused balance is forfeited by an employee.

Basic journal entries are made to the general ledger accounts to correspond to each step in the administrative process. Flexible credits directed to the health care expense are accounted for as a benefit expense (the debit), which is offset by an entry to an accrued liability account (the credit). This liability account is a control account, which ties to the sum of the account balances for all participating employees. (Note that the employee is an unsecured creditor with respect to the employer for his or her account balance, until a reimbursement request has been submitted.)

At the end of the reimbursement processing cycle when payments are issued to participants, the reimbursement amount becomes payable to the employee, and another entry is made. This entry takes the total of all payable amounts, and then debits the accrued liability account and credits accounts payable. Alternatively, the payment can be charged directly to the accrued liability account.

Once reimbursement cheques are created and issued to employees, a final payment entry is made. This entry is a debit to accounts payable and an offsetting credit to cash.

The final transaction to consider is the account closure transactions. When unused funds are forfeited by employees on termination or at year-end, the total forfeiture amount is a debit to the liability account and a credit to the company's benefit expense account. The health care expense account record-keeping system, therefore, can aid the account process by providing total contributions, total reimbursements, and closing account balances for the accounting period.

§ 19.5   CHANGES TO PAYROLL PROCESSING

Whether the flexible program is broad or limited in scope, implementation of the program almost always involves some changes to the payroll system.

If a new flexible benefit enrollment system is implemented to accommodate the flexible benefit program, or if the existing benefit plan enrollment system is modified significantly, the payroll system will need to be modified to interface with the enrollment system. This is because payroll deductions for the program are reported to payroll by the enrollment system each year following annual enrollment. The enrollment system also reports deductions throughout the year for new employees and for employees who are changing their coverages.

Where the flexible program includes a health care expense account, payroll may need to be modified to interface with the record-keeping system. If the payment amounts are included in employee paycheques as an addition to net pay, the payroll system is modified to receive payment amounts from the record-keeping system for each employee. The pay stub and the net pay calculation routine then is modified to show the addition to net pay.

If the plan allows employees to purchase vacation days through payroll deductions, the net pay computation will need to be adjusted, because taxes are not applicable to these amounts. Unlike after-tax payroll deductions used to purchase benefits such as optional group life and dependent life, the deduction to buy vacation days is pre-tax. This is because employees who purchase vacation days with payroll deductions are, in effect, taking time off without pay. Therefore, they don't pay tax on earnings they don't receive.

Other questions that should be asked about changes to the payroll system are:

- Are new deduction fields required? Is room available?
- What should be shown on the pay stub? Is there room for new information?
- What changes will have to be made to the calculation routines?
- Will current benefit calculation tables have to be modified or removed?
- Will any changes be required to taxation procedures?

§ 19.6 ADMINISTRATIVE STAFFING REQUIREMENTS

The two areas that have the biggest impact on staffing requirements are annual enrollment election entry and health care expense account claims processing (if handled in-house).

(a) ELECTION ENTRY

On the average, two or three minutes per form are required to enter an election form into an online enrollment system. Entry time may vary widely based on several factors which include:

- The enrollment system's online response time
- The amount of information being entered
- If the enrollment form matches the entry screen.

(b) HEALTH CARE EXPENSE ACCOUNT CLAIMS PROCESSING

The reviewer normally checks to be sure the expense is an eligible expense under the plan and that the participant has signed the form and provided the required supporting documentation. This effort requires on average two to four minutes per claim request. When determining staffing requirements, consider the following assumptions.

- Participation in the health care expense accounts typically is 15 percent to 30 percent of the eligible employees.
- If monthly claim submission restrictions are applied, participants will submit, on average, three to five claim requests per year.
- If claims are entered into an online system, one full-time administrator is needed per 3,500 to 5,000 participants.

(c) OTHER STAFFING CONSIDERATIONS

Other functions to be considered when assessing the impact of the flexible program on staffing include:

- Administrator and employee education
- Production and distribution of personalized enrollment reports and election confirmation statements
- New employee enrollments
- Enrollment change processing
- Health care expense accounting reimbursement cheque and account statement distribution
- Employee coverage and health care expense account status inquiries.

Twenty

Administration Solutions

§ 20.1 EVALUATING ADMINISTRATIVE ALTERNATIVES

Until recently, implementing a flexible benefit program meant developing an in-house administrative system. In most cases, developing the system was the most complicated and time-consuming part of implementing a flexible program. Today, although implementation remains a lengthy and detailed process, many good alternatives to in-house system development are available. The key to the success of the implementation effort is careful evaluation of the range of administrative solutions and selection of the system that best meets the organization's program design and administrative needs.

(a) EVALUATION PROCESS

The evaluation of administration alternatives typically begins immediately following the development of the preliminary program design. Although program design is an important factor, other issues affecting the evaluation include:

- The number of eligible participants
- The degree to which administration will be centralized or decentralized

- The timing of program implementation
- The availability of internal data processing and administration re-
  sources
- The organization's long-term plans for program enhancements or
  modifications, and
- The implementation and ongoing processing budgets for the project.

Ideally, an evaluation committee should be formed to discuss each of
these factors and use them in an evaluation process. (The factors are
described in more detail in the section on selection criteria within this
chapter.) The evaluation process may take weeks or months to complete, depending on the number of alternatives under consideration and
the selection techniques used.

Many different approaches may be used to evaluate administrative
alternatives, ranging from very informal to very formal. One of the
most common approaches involves issuing a Request for Proposal
(RFP), selecting "finalists" based on responses to the RFP, and allowing
each finalist to demonstrate capabilities in a subsequent meeting with
the evaluation committee. Whether or not an RFP is issued, the committee will want to meet with each of the vendors to ensure a mutual
understanding of the needs and constraints of the organization. Actually seeing a demonstration also will help in assuring the committee of
the vendor's ability to deliver a suitable system within the required time
frame and budgets.

(b) EVALUATION COMMITTEE

As with any decision-making process, the number of people on the evaluation committee likely will have a direct relationship to the length of
time needed to make a decision. However, in order to make the right
decision, the right people need to participate in the evaluation process.
In general, it is usually more efficient in the long run to sacrifice time,
rather than short cut the process by eliminating an area that could have
significant input into the evaluation process.

A committee to evaluate flexible benefit administration alternatives
ideally consists of individuals from each of the following areas:

- Benefit administration
- Human resource information systems (or benefit systems)

- Management information systems
- Finance.

Each of these areas needs to be represented, usually by people with decision-making authority, as well as a working knowledge of day-to-day activities in the area. Again, both functional levels need to be represented, whether in the form of one person or more.

(c)   ADMINISTRATIVE ALTERNATIVES

Broadly defined, six alternatives exist for administering a flexible benefit program. Specifically the alternatives include:

- Manual administration
- Spreadsheet software
- Personal computer administration software
- Mainframe administration software
- Time-sharing services
- Third-party administration.

(1)   Manual Administration

Manual administration of a flexible benefit program may be appropriate for small organizations with simple flexible programs. One organization implemented a health care expense account for 50 participants and administered the program using three-by-five inch index cards and coloured paper clips to designate different levels of account activity. Word processing was used to produce quarterly statements for all participants.

(2)   Spreadsheet Software

Smaller organizations that have access to personal computer hardware and software have used commercial spreadsheet software to semi-automate flexible program administration. In some cases, spreadsheet software has been used successfully to administer even a broad flexible program for a small number of participants.

As with manual administration, word processing often is used to produce personalized statements for participants.

(3) Personal Computer Administrative Software

Flexible program administration systems may be developed or purchased for installation on a personal computer. In many cases, PC-based systems provide all the processing capabilities and functionality of mainframe software.

In a personal computer environment, interfaces with mainframe systems such as payroll may be facilitated through the transferring of data files between systems. Transfers of data files can be accomplished electronically or by using diskettes or magnetic tapes.

Decentralized administration is supported through the networking of multiple personal computers to the same hard-disk storage. Although technology in this area is rapidly changing, concerns still can arise in personal computer networks with data transmission speeds, the cost of the network and the cost of increased disk space.

Historically, the speed of personal computer printers discouraged some organizations from using PC-based software for flexible program administration. However, with higher speed and better quality printers increasingly available and the option of transferring high volume print files to mainframe printers, printing is no longer a major concern for most organizations.

Personal computer systems are available from a wide variety of benefit consulting firms and software vendors.

(4) Mainframe Administrative Software

Like personal-computer-based systems, mainframe software for flexible program administration may be developed internally or licensed from a vendor. Mainframe systems are especially advantageous to larger organizations with centralized data processing. In this kind of environment, additional hardware seldom is required to support the flexible program. Existing data communication networks may be used to support decentralized administration. Systems maintenance is performed by the data processing department, along with the ongoing maintenance performed for other administration systems, such as payroll and accounting.

Mainframe administration software will interface with other mainframe systems through the electronic transfer of data. Some mainframe applications can access data directly from the payroll/personnel data base, thus eliminating the need for file transfers.

Most mainframe software is built to maintain a separate participant data base to house only data necessary for administering the flexible program. Some systems, however, operate using the payroll or person-nel system's employee data base, and thus have no need to maintain their own participant data bases.

As with PC solutions, mainframe software systems for administering a flexible program are available from a wide range of benefit consulting firms and software vendors.

(5) Time-Sharing Services

In a time-sharing environment, administrators have online access to soft-ware located on a vendor's computer. Access may be limited to certain time periods or may be unlimited, depending on the time-sharing service.

An administrator gains access to the system using a terminal, mo-dem, and data communication link between the modem and the host computer. In many cases, the connection is made through a telephone line. Security prohibits the administrator from accessing the accounts of other organizations using the same service. To the administrator, a time-sharing service will provide the same functional capabilities as a mainframe system installed on the company's own computer.

Like personal-computer-systems and mainframe-based systems, a time-sharing service must interface with the organization's payroll and other administration systems. Interfaces between the administration system and the payroll system take place via magnetic tape or data file transfers over the data communication lines. Reports produced in a time-sharing environment typically are sent to the organization through the mail. Alternatively, print files may be sent over the data communi-cation lines for printing on location. Transferring large files over a data communication line is often a slow process under current technology.

There are not yet many organizations offering time-sharing services for flexible benefit administration. However, time-sharing offers many advantages over installed systems for certain organizations. The pros and cons of each type of administration approach are explored further in the selection criteria section of this chapter.

(6) Third-Party Processing

A third-party processing approach to administration takes much of the work out of the hands of the organization's administrators. This approach is used for health care expense account administration, for many flexible plans in the United States, and is increasingly being offered by vari-ous vendors for U.S. enrollment processing as well. As flexible benefit programs expand in Canada, third-party administrators (TPAs) will provide services here as well.

Third-party health care expense account administration differs from a time-sharing approach in that review and entry of claims plus payment distribution are handled by the service provider, rather than the plan administrator. Participants typically send their requests for reimbursement directly to the TPA. The TPA reviews the request and issues the payment. Users of the service seldom have on-line access to account information, thus all participant questions are directed to the TPA.

Enrollment support offered by TPAs usually is limited to annual or periodic (quarterly) group enrollments. Individual or more frequent group enrollments typically cannot be accommodated.

Third-party administration operates similarly to time-sharing in terms of interfaces between the provider of the service and the user's mainframe system. Interfaces typically are accomplished via magnetic tape.

Third-party administration services for health care expense accounts are offered primarily by insurance companies. TPA services for enrollment also are offered by benefit consulting firms.

(d) SELECTION CRITERIA

(1) Program Design

The design of the flexible program is an important factor in selecting an administrative approach. Design will have an impact both on the type of system selected (manual, spreadsheet, personal computer, etc.) and the system selected within that system type. For instance, if the plan calls for minimal choice making and no employee-specific calculations, the program may be administered by the payroll/personnel system with minor enhancements. However, if the program is broader in scope with many employee-specific components, a new administrative system may be required.

If the program offers employees the choice between paying for benefits with before-tax or after-tax dollars, the administrative system selected will need to track both before- and after-tax elections for each employee, regardless of whether the system is mainframe, time-sharing, or personal computer.

All program details need not be determined prior to the selection of the administration system. However, the system selected needs to have the flexibility to handle unforeseen changes as the program design is finalized.

(2)   Number of Participants

Manual administration and spreadsheet software may be good alternatives for organizations with fewer than 500 program participants. Larger groups typically require more sophisticated personal computer, mainframe or time-sharing solutions, if in-house administration of the program is desired.

The capacity of personal computer software is a function of the amount of data that will be stored for each participant and the hard-disk storage available on the personal computer system. As a rule of thumb, current and historical data for 1,000 flexible program participants can be stored in 10 megabytes of hard-disk storage.

As technology advances, faster processing speeds and greater data storage capacities will allow larger organizations to administer their programs using PC solutions.

Size is less of a factor when evaluating time-sharing and mainframe alternatives. The cost of the system, the desire to decentralize administration, and the availability of internal data-processing resources often are more important issues to consider.

(3)   Centralized versus Decentralized Administration

Some approaches lend themselves better to decentralized processing than others. In either time-sharing or mainframe environments, an organization can support decentralized administrator processing and still retain central control and produce summary-level reports. In a personal computing environment, maintaining central control of the system and producing summary-level reports are possible but considerably more difficult to achieve.

(4)   Implementation Timetable

The timing of program implementation has an impact on an organization's build or buy decision, as well as the type of system to implement. In almost all cases, building a system internally will take more time than buying a comparable system from a vendor.

Once a decision has been made to buy, the type of system chosen will be a factor in the amount of time required for implementation. All other factors being equal, a time-sharing service or third-party administration approach will have the least impact on an organization's internal resources and therefore may be implemented faster than other administrative alternatives. A personal computer system requires less time to implement than a mainframe system, because of the impact a mainframe system has on internal data-processing resources and the mainframe operating environment.

(5) Data Processing and Administration Resources

The availability of internal data-processing resources is an important factor when evaluating administrative alternatives. Not only is data-processing support a key issue during implementation, but it also remains a major factor in ongoing support of the system.

The importance of adequate data-processing resources obviously is key to the decision on whether to build or buy a system. Once the decision is made to buy, however, internal data-processing support is still important. A time-sharing, third-party, or even a personal computer approach to administration requires some ongoing support from data processing. However, a mainframe solution has the greatest impact on data-processing resources on an ongoing basis.

The availability of benefit administration resources also is a factor to consider in selecting the best approach.

A personal-computer-based system residing in the benefit area usually requires greater administrator support than a mainframe-based system. In a personal computer environment, the administrator often is responsible for monitoring the print process, distributing the system output, and performing system backups and other system housekeeping functions. In a mainframe environment, these functions typically are performed by computer operators.

A time-sharing service may require less administrator involvement than either a personal computer or mainframe-based system, depending on the level of service provided by the time-sharing service. Third-party administration requires the least amount of administration resources.

(6) Plans for Program Expansion

Just as the initial program design is a consideration in selecting an administrative alternative, plans for future program expansion are also important. For example, a personal computer system may be adequate to support even a large organization's health care expense account. However, if the program is expanded in a subsequent year to include broad choice making, the revised program may exceed the capacity of the personal computer system. The same problem may occur if the program is expanded to include new employee groups or additional business units.

(7) Budgets

Implementation and ongoing administration budgets are almost always factors in the selection of an administrative solution. Building an administrative system is in most cases more expensive than licensing a software package. However, given the time and internal data-processing resources, some organizations prefer the soft-dollar expense of in-house development to the hard-dollar cost of buying a system or using a time-sharing service or TPA.

When the decision is made to buy a system or service, budget constraints may be a factor in deciding what type of system to implement. When reviewing the cost of each alternative, both implementation and ongoing costs are taken into consideration.

Installable systems, both personal computer and mainframe, typically involve three types of costs: one-time planning and software preparation charges, licensing fees, and ongoing software maintenance charges.

Time-sharing services often use a two-tier fee structure, comprised of one-time planning and preparation charges and ongoing charges based on participation in the program.

Third-party administrators may structure their charges similarly to time-sharing services or charge on a per transaction basis. Transaction-based charges are commonly used for health care expense account administration. In this situation, transactions may include incoming claims or reimbursements or both.

When comparing the cost of administration systems, it is important to look at the over-all costs for each system in relation to the services provided by each vendor. Some vendors include administration and payroll consulting services, training, administration manuals, and other consulting services in their product fees. Other vendor's product fees include only the software.

(e) VENDOR ASSESSMENT

Once the type of administration system is determined and the range of acceptable systems narrowed, how does an organization assess each vendor's ability to deliver as promised?

One of the best ways to assess a vendor's qualifications is to ask for and check references. Ask for references:

- In the same industry
- With a similar program design
- Of a comparable size
- In the same geographical area
- With the same administration alternative
- Who have used the system for more than one year.

When checking references, talk to both administrative and systems personnel. Find out about both the implementation support and the ongoing support provided by the vendor. Visit a user of the system if possible. Also meet with the people who will be implementing the system or service. How much experience do they have in similar implementations?

Another factor to consider is the range of services provided by the vendor. During implementation of the flexible program, the design, communication, and administration project teams will be working closely to ensure that the administrative system supports both the plan design and the communication approach. For organizations using consultants for design and/or communication, many implementation difficulties can be reduced, if the same consultant is helping with program administration. For instance, the personalized enrollment statement produced by the enrollment system needs to use the same format and terminology as the enrollment form and election workbook designed by the communicators. The format of the enrollment form must support the agreed-upon election entry approach. And finally, the administrative system must support the detailed plan design, both during annual enrollment and throughout the plan year.

§ 20.2   IMPLEMENTING THE ADMINISTRATIVE SYSTEM

(a)   DEFINING SYSTEM SPECIFICATIONS

Regardless of whether the administrative system is developed in-house or licensed from a software vendor, the first step in implementation involves defining system specifications. During this step, the implementation project team will work to:

- Develop an implementation workplan
- Design the functional and technical specifications for the system based on the program design and administrative rules
- Identify updates to existing administrative support systems and procedures such as payroll, personnel and accounting systems
- Define the interface requirements between each applicable system, including:

  —Frequency,

  —Mode (magnetic tape, report, electronic transfer, etc.), and

  —Data requirements.

(b) PROGRAMMING AND TESTING

This step is the most difficult and time-consuming phase of implementation. The responsibility for this step depends on whether the system is being developed in-house or licensed from a vendor.

To support the initial annual enrollment in a broad flexible program, the system typically is fully tested and ready to begin enrollment processing at least three to four months before the program effective date.

(c) TRAINING ADMINISTRATORS

Administrator training is an important part of the implementation process. Enrollment training takes place prior to the initial enrollment. Health care expense account and ongoing administration training may be deferred until just prior to the program effective date. Administration or user's manuals typically are distributed to administrators and discussed during training.

The approach to training is tailored to meet the needs of the organization. If administration is going to be decentralized, training may be done at each administrative location. Alternatively, administrators may be assembled at one company location or trained at a neutral site.

Part Seven

Experience

Twenty-One

Financial Analysis

§ 21.1 CHALLENGE OF FINANCIAL ANALYSIS

Conceptually, financial analysis of a flexible program involves little more than calculating the cost (either historical or projected) of the benefit program. In practice, however, performance of a cost analysis is considerably more complex, in many ways resembling art as much as science. This is true whether the financial analysis is future-oriented—predicting future costs—or past-oriented—analyzing actual past costs.

To some extent, financial analysis of a flexible program is hampered by the same limitations that apply to conventional program structures. That is, experience data is often limited or tracked in insufficient detail; while exceptional claims experience (either positive or negative) can distort year-to-year comparisons for all but the very largest organizations.

Still other complications arise directly from the nature of the flexible program structure. For example, a flexible approach typically permits trade-offs among benefits or levels of coverage and the conversion of benefit dollars to other forms of compensation (for example, cash or RRSP/DPSP savings). The different uses of these monies, as well as the applicable tax consequences, need to be reflected in a financial analysis.

Finally, flexible programs are typically launched in concert with other organizational changes, which complicates the financial analysis. Organizations often use flexible programs as a means of integrating benefits for newly acquired divisions or units, changing or strengthening corporate culture, or responding to increased competition for new hires. In addition, companies often upgrade existing administrative systems and procedures or improve employee communication at the same time as introducing the flexible program. When multiple purposes are being served, it is often difficult to determine which portion of the over-all implementation expenses should be charged against the flexible program.

The purpose of this chapter is to outline the various types of financial analyses applicable to a flexible program, to discuss the uses of these analyses, and to provide a conceptual framework for performing financial analyses.

§ 21.2   USES AND PURPOSES OF FINANCIAL ANALYSIS

(a)   INITIAL PROGRAM DESIGN

Financial analysis is useful in helping an organization structure the design of a program. This includes deciding which benefit areas to incorporate in the program, the specific design of the options within a benefit area, the prices to charge for each option, and the amount of credits, if any, to allocate to each participant. The objective is to design the program to meet the company's financial objectives and to ensure that the financial impact on employees is reasonable and appropriate. (Financial considerations that are key to these design decisions are covered in earlier chapters on specific benefit areas and pricing and credit allocation.)

In the early days of flexible programs, initial design was relatively simple. Option designs were similar and few benefit areas were included. However, recent design studies have become more complex as employers consider new types of plan provisions (e.g., capitation plans in the dental area), and add more benefit areas for choice. Financial analysis has grown in importance in the initial design because it enables employers to focus efforts on those benefit areas where choice is financially worthwhile. In addition, analysis of pre-flexible experience contributes to effective design and pricing/credit structures in critical cost areas (e.g., supplemental medical and dental).

(b)   INCLUSION OF BENEFIT AREAS

As a general rule, it is appropriate to offer choices in benefit areas where: (a) employee needs vary, (b) costs are significant, (c) selection costs can be managed, and (d) management supports the concept. Problems with any one of these factors may be sufficient reason to exclude a benefit area from the program. Financial analysis helps employers determine the degree to which employee needs vary and the cost consequences of choice.

For example, in deciding which benefit areas to incorporate in the program an employer with a very young and healthy work force might decide that choice in the basic life and long-term disability area is inappropriate, because the financial analysis of current plan costs demonstrates that few dollars could be released for use in other benefit areas. In contrast, enrollment analysis of the prior plan might demonstrate the need for less-costly medical or long-term disability options, if enrollment in a contributory plan is so low (e.g., less than 85 percent) that the employer concludes employees are assuming inappropriate risks by "going bare." Simple retirement income projections may demonstrate that an existing savings plan provides adequate flexibility for retirement benefits, eradicating a perceived need to wrap the pension plan into the flexible program. Analysis of vacation forfeitures or carry-over patterns provides an indication of potential employee interest in vacation buying and selling, as well as potential hard-dollar costs of including time off in the flexible program.

(c)   INITIAL OPTION DESIGN

Analysis of employee demographics, prior benefit enrollment patterns, and benefit payments contribute to effective option design.

For example, analysis of prior enrollment in optional life benefits may demonstrate the appeal of a reduced core coverage, if a high share of employees (e.g., over 20 percent) waive optional coverage. Moreover, high enrollment in the maximum prior coverage might indicate the appeal of still higher life insurance options. Analysis of claim distribution patterns helps employers focus on medical option designs that result in meaningful value differences for employees. Projections of vacation buying and selling costs under several alternative design scenarios help employers focus on appropriate limits on number of days available for choice.

(d)   INITIAL OPTION PRICING

Since pricing structures for death, disability, and time off options are usually quite simple, little analysis is required to establish prices. Realistic pricing is the most common approach in each of these areas (i.e., price tags that reflect the full value of the option). However, medical and dental option pricing requires much more extensive analysis. To develop option prices that reflect real differences in value for a given employee workforce, it is helpful to conduct a detailed analysis of claims by amount and by type and location of service. Then, the impact of option features (such as deductibles and coinsurance limits) on value can be accurately determined. Projections of the impact of alternative pricing scenarios on enrollment patterns, claim patterns, and resulting costs help employers focus on the most appropriate approach.

(e) INITIAL CREDIT ALLOCATION

In the first plan year, credits are usually determined by the amount that must be given to meet the organization's goals for limiting the potential loss of value by employees. Therefore, pricing in effect controls the credits and financial analysis has little impact. However, a few employers use credits as the "balancing" item to bring cost projections into line with organizational objectives in the first plan year. This approach is most common when an employer is willing to add dollars to the system or when credits must be equal for all employees, even if it means that some employees lose value relative to the prior plan. This balancing approach is more common in subsequent years.

When credits are the balancing item, extensive analysis may be necessary. For example, assume the supplemental medical portion of the flexible plan must not only avoid losers and maintain employer cost at the same level it would have been under the prior plan, but also give equal credits. This scenario can only be met if sufficient numbers of employees waive dependent coverage. Only thorough analysis of likely enrollment scenarios, claim patterns, and resulting employer costs will reassure management that budgets can be met. This analysis will need to balance the cost of creating winners among employees who elect lower dependent coverage categories against the claims savings from those who drop coverage for dependents. The claim savings projections must reflect the fact that savings from new dependent waivers are likely to be less than average dependent costs, because those most likely to waive dependent coverage probably had primary dependent coverage.

(f) COST/BENEFIT ANALYSIS

Although introducing a flexible program may create a number of pluses for an organization and its employees, there are also significant costs involved. Senior management will often require a "dollars-and-cents" analysis of the impact of a flexible benefit program before approving plans for implementation.

A cost/benefit analysis of the financial impact of a flexible program may focus primarily on the initial year, or it may incorporate a projection of costs over a three- to five-year period.

For some employers, the financial analysis shows an increase in costs in the first year of a program (particularly if implementation costs are simply treated as a first-year expense rather than being capitalized), reaching a break-even point in the third or fourth year.

Most employers, however, absorb the implementation costs and do not try to recover them in future years. In these cases, the financial analysis would show a break-even situation in the first year. Future cost savings would be projected if the company subsidy (flexible credits) were assumed to increase slower than the claims. Otherwise, the anticipated costs of the flexible plan would equal those of the prior, non-flexible benefit program.

Occasionally, a company will use a first-year cost analysis to decide between introducing a flexible program with a variety of cost-savings features or making unilaterally deep benefit cuts. The company would analyze the savings arising from replacing an expensive set of health care benefits with a choice of options under various flexible credit situations. The financial analysis would influence the design of the flexible program in terms of accomplishing the company's cost-reduction objective. It would also help management decide whether to introduce severe benefit take-aways for employees or move to a flexible program with more palatable take-aways.

Multi-year projections are also useful in illustrating the potential impact of various inflation and health care trend scenarios on employee and employer costs under alternative pricing/credit strategies. For example, three-year projections clearly demonstrate that it is easier to justify a given "dollar" level of increase in employee costs from year to year if price tags are large (closer to realistic) than if they are heavily subsidized, or if a net pricing approach is used (i.e., no credits). If a realistic price tag for a supplemental medical option is $500 this year and the medical trend factor is 15 percent, it is relatively easy to explain a $75 increase in a price tag to employees. However, if a subsidized pricing structure resulted in a $150 price tag for the same option this year (with a hidden employer subsidy of $350), employees would be likely to question a 50 percent bump up in that price tag to $225, if the employer were forced to pass along the full increase. The leveraging effect of the hidden employer subsidy makes the same dollar increase seem unreasonable. Three-year projections under alternative scenarios help bring out the significance of pricing/credit structure decisions.

Three-year projections also help employers focus on realistic goals for future cost savings. In some situations, employers start out with unrealistic expectations for future cost increases simply because they do not know the degree to which they would have to shift costs to employees to realize long-term goals for cost savings. Continuing with the previous example, an employer might have an initial objective of holding health care costs steady for the first year of a flexible program. However, once management realizes that the net effect could mean a first-year increase of 50% in employee contributions over the pre-flexible program level, they might reassess cost savings goals (or at least restate the objective to allow greater flexibility in responding to unanticipated experience, such as an exceptional number of large claims).

(g) CASH FLOW PROJECTIONS

Separate from the issue of whether costs will increase or decrease by introducing a flexible program, an organization's cash flow patterns are likely to be altered. Although this is often overlooked (and may not be important in some organizations), a brief financial analysis of the impact on cash flow may prove to be useful.

If employees are able to take cash in lieu of certain benefits, the timing of cash payments may be accelerated. If added vacation days may be purchased but unused days are cashed out at year-end, a significant drain on cash flow could occur in December. If medical or dental benefits are reduced as an element of a flexible program, claims costs may be dramatically higher between the announcement and the effective dates.

(h) EXPERIENCE EVALUATION

Some organizations use financial analysis to measure the effectiveness of a flexible program in controlling medical, or other benefit plan, costs. For example, among the reasons one organization introduced a flexible program was its desire to freeze medical and dental plan costs. The organization offered various levels of medical coverage and found that, over time, employees gravitated toward the higher-deductible options. At the end of the program's fourth year of operation, employer costs for medical remained at exactly the same level as in the first year of operation. Moreover, the price tag to employees for only one of the options needed to be increased—and, then, only by rates comparable to inflation. The company stabilized costs without unreasonable cost sharing with employees.

(i)   FUTURE PRICING AND REDESIGN

One of the more important reasons for financial analysis is to assist organizations in making option pricing and design decisions for future years. This is especially important in medical and dental, but is relevant in other benefit areas as well.

For example, when alternative medical plans are included in a flexible program, prices need to be assigned for each option and for each coverage category (employee-only, employee-plus-spouse, and so forth) within the options. (See also Chapter Thirteen for more complete discussion of initial-pricing decisions.) Development of these prices is important to ensure that the selection process is not biased toward specific choices, that employees are not overcharged as a group, that contributions are set appropriately, and so forth. Although the experience of each option may not be the only factor incorporated in a pricing decision, clearly it will be a major determinant of next year's pricing. Even employers who are fully insured need to monitor the financial experience of each option, because their insurer will be comparing the program with others it underwrites to evaluate prices for coverage in subsequent years. In either case, therefore, the employer (and employees) will be affected financially, either directly or indirectly.

§ 21.3   COST/BENEFIT ANALYSIS

Perhaps the most important type of financial analysis conducted surrounding the design and implementation of a flexible program is that aimed at determining whether an organization should adopt such a program. In effect, is a flexible program worth the implementation effort and cost? The answer to this question will be easy to arrive at in some situations (clearly yes or clearly no), but arriving at an answer will be quite complex in other situations. Even after a financial analysis is complete, the degree to which non-financial objectives are being accomplished (or alternative problems created) needs to be considered before a final go/no go decision can be made.

In the following discussion, it is assumed that the plan design (including determination of prices and allocation of credits) has been finalized and the review of the financial impact on individual employees (evaluating winners and losers) yields satisfactory results.

(a) IDENTIFICATION OF COST VARIABLES

The first step in analyzing the cost impact of a flexible program is to determine the potential areas of significant cost changes (increases or decreases). Although certainly not a complete list, the following provides an indication of the types of items that might be considered for a broad flexible program:

Cost Savings Areas

- Specific benefit reductions such as an increase in the medical deductible, a reduction in coinsurance, and so forth
- Increases in employee contributions either initially or in future years
- Decreases in dental utilization due to higher deductibles and copayment amounts
- Decreases arising from employees dropping out of the program in dual-coverage situations
- Forfeitures from health care expense accounts (if year-end balances are not rolled over to next year's account, cashed out, or donated to charity)
- "Float" within health care expense accounts (resulting from later payment by the company)
- Potential savings in ongoing administration (due to consolidation of multiple benefit programs or computerizing previously manual processes).

Cost Increase Areas

- Implementation costs (communication, administration, legal documentation, consulting fees, staffing requirements)
- Ongoing operational costs (communication, administration, and so forth)
- Increased participation in optional, partially subsidized benefits (due to the increased communication effort or pricing and credit allocation approaches)
- Credits provided on waiver of coverage (if non-participating employees previously resulted in no company costs)
- Election experience (adverse selection)

- Improvements in specific benefits (for example, updating plan maximums) made in conjunction with the introduction of the flexible program
- Increases in Canada/Quebec Pension Plan taxes and employer medicare taxes (if benefits can be converted into cash).

Not all of these items will apply in each situation, and others that are specific only to that employer may arise. The point is that any cost factor that is significant in magnitude and can be reasonably evaluated should be included in a cost/benefit analysis. Any cost factor that is likely to be significant, but cannot be evaluated with reliability, should be included as a "best guess" or with a range of results.

(b) COMPUTATION OF COST IMPACT

The objective of this type of financial analysis is to provide the employer with an indication of the anticipated effect of a flexible program on benefit costs. As described earlier, numerous variables will produce either gains or losses, including some that defy precise measurement. At this point in the design or approval process, however, the employer needs to make a decision whether to proceed with implementation of a revised benefit program, so the estimated cost impact needs to be determined on the most reasonable basis available.

In some cases, the computation of the cost impact will be relatively straightforward and can be accomplished with a high level of precision and reliability. Certain changes are very measurable. Some examples are replacing an insured dental plan with a $200 allocation to a health care expense account, making a 20 percent increase in employee contributions to medical, or increasing a deductible from $25 to $50. Other changes may not be measurable by the employer, but the bottom-line result is known (situations in which a third party has guaranteed cost savings from a capitation dental plan, for example).

Often, however, the program will have some elements where the financial impact cannot be confidently predicted—either because of uncertainty about employee elections or about the actual experience for the year in which the elections were made. Sometimes it may not even be possible to determine whether the effect will produce an increase or a decrease in costs.

Regardless of the level of precision, the number of variables, or the length of the measurement period, the general formula in Example 21.1 can be used to compute the cost implications.

Example 21.1
Computation of Flexible Program Cost Increases (Decreases)

Cost Effect = Increase (decrease) in CLAIMS (self-insured employer), OR
                Increase (decrease) in PREMIUMS (insured employer)

      − Increase (decrease) in EMPLOYEE CONTRIBUTIONS

      + Employer CREDITS paid in cash or RRSP/DPSP deposits

      + Increase (decrease) in IMPLEMENTATION or ongoing
        OPERATIONAL COSTS

      + Miscellaneous OTHER COSTS

      − Miscellaneous OTHER SAVINGS

This formula might be applied for only one year to determine a first-year cost impact for the revised program versus the projected cost of continuing the prior program, or it may be applied for three to five years to estimate a longer-term impact. (Only rarely is a period longer than five years used to analyze the financial impact of a benefit program change.)

(c) EXAMPLE

To illustrate the operation of the formula (see Example 21.2), consider the following situation involving supplemental medical and dental plans.

Assumptions

- 5,000 employees.
- Estimated implementation costs of $150,000.
- Estimated annual ongoing costs of $60,000.
- Flexible credits increase 5 percent in year 2.

Supplemental Medical

- Average supplemental medical cost in current, non-flexible program projected to be $400, with the employee paying 25 percent ($100) and the company paying 75 percent ($300).
- Flexible program consisting of a choice of three medical plans (current and two lower options worth 75 and 50 percent of the current plan).
- Expected employee election pattern:

Option 1 (current plan): 2,500 employees
Option 2 (75 percent of current plan): 1,250 employees
Option 3 (50 percent of current plan): 1,250 employees

- The cost increase between Years 1 and 2 is 12 percent for the current plan.
- The cost increase between Years 1 and 2 for the flexible plan is:

Option 1: 15 percent
Option 2: 10 percent
Option 3: 5 percent.

Dental

- Average dental cost in current, non-flexible program is projected to be $600. This is fully paid by the employer.
- Flexible program consisting of a choice of three dental plans (current and two lower options worth 80 and 40 percent of the current plan).
- Expected employee election pattern:

Option 1 (current plan): 2,000 employees
Option 2 (80 percent of current plan): 2,000 employees
Option 3 (40 percent of current plan): 1,000 employees.

- The cost increase between Years 1 and 2 is 8 percent for the current plan.
- The cost increase between Years 1 and 2 under the flexible plan is:

Option 1: 10 percent
Option 2: 5 percent
Option 3: 3 percent.

Example 21.2 illustrates that the cost of the flexible plan in Year 1 is $150,000 higher than the cost would have been under the current plan. This is due to the implementation expenses.

By Year 2, the flexible plan costs are $195,000 less than if the prior plan had continued ($4,785,000 instead of $4,980,000). The savings come from limiting the increase in flexible credits to 5 percent, while the medical and dental costs are increasing between 3 percent and 15 percent depending on the option. If the implementation costs of $150,000 had been spread over two years, rather than being fully allocated to the initial year, the first year would have produced a $75,000 cost increase and the second year would have produced a $120,000 savings.

In order to prepare such an analysis, certain decisions and assumptions need to be made, such as:

Example 21.2
Year 1 Impact

	Current Program	Flexible Program			
		Option 1	Option 2	Option 3	Total
Medical per Employee					
1 Cost per person	$ 400	$ 400	$ 300	$ 200	$ —
2 Employee Credit	N/A	300	300	300	300
3 Net Employee Cost (1 − 2)	100	100	0	(100)	—
4 Net Employer Cost (1 − 3)	300	300	300	300	—
Total Medical					
5 Number of Employees	5,000	2,500	1,250	1,250	5,000
6 Claims (1 × 5)	2,000,000	1,000,000	375,000	250,000	1,625,000
7 Flexible Credits (2 × 5)	N/A	750,000	375,000	375,000	1,500,000
8 Net Employee Cost (6 − 7)	500,000	250,000	0	(125,000)	125,000
9 Net Employer Medical Cost (6 − 8)	$1,500,000	$750,000	$375,000	$375,000	$1,500,000
Total Dental					
10 Net Employer Dental Cost (similar calculation to above)	3,000,000	1,200,000	1,200,000	600,000	3,000,000
Other					
11 Implementation/ Operational	—	50,000	50,000	50,000	150,000
Total					
12 Total (9 + 10 + 11)	$4,500,000	$2,000,000	$1,625,000	$1,025,000	$4,650,000

Year 2 Impact

	Prior Program	Flexible Program			
		Option 1	Option 2	Option 3	Total
Medical Per Employee					
1 Increase in Medical Costs	12%	15%	10%	5%	—
2 Cost per person	$ 448	$ 460	$ 330	210	$ —
3 Employee Credit (5% increase)	N/A	315	315	315	315
4 Net Employee Cost (2 − 3)	100	145	15	(105)	—
5 Net Employer Cost (2 − 4)	338	315	315	315	315
Total Medical					
6 Number of Employees	5,000	2,500	1,250	1,250	5,000
7 Claims (2 × 6)	2,240,000	1,150,000	412,500	262,500	1,825,000
8 Flexible Credits (3 × 6)	N/A	787,500	393,750	393,750	1,575,000
9 Net Employee Cost (7 − 8)	500,000	362,500	18,750	(131,250)	250,000
10 Net Employer Medical Cost (7 − 9)	$1,740,000	$787,500	$393,750	$393,750	$1,575,000
Total Dental					
11 Net Employer Dental Cost (similar calculation to above)	3,240,000	1,260,000	1,260,000	630,000	3,150,000
Other					
12 Implementation/ Operational	—	20,000	20,000	20,000	60,000
Total					
13 Total (10 + 11 + 12)	$4,980,000	$2,067,500	$1,673,750	$ 1,043,750	$4,785,000

- What time period for the evaluation is appropriate?
- Should one-time implementation expenses be treated as first-year expenses or spread over multiple years?
- What assumptions should be made regarding employee election patterns?
- What experience is likely under self-insured options?
- What strategy will be used for future increases in option prices and credits?
- What levels of future inflation and pay increases are appropriate?

§ 21.4 CASH FLOW PROJECTIONS

(a) IN GENERAL

Most cost projections for flexible programs focus on the impact of changes on incurred claims, while the comptroller, for instance, is likely to be focusing on cash outlay for the year (i.e., paid claims). Therefore, comparisons of budgeted expense versus actual cash flow can look peculiar unless the accountants know what to expect.

Three factors affect cash flow in any benefit area where employees may elect lower coverage than the pre-flexible level—claim payments (plus expenses), credit allocations, and price tags.

For example, in the supplemental medical area, claim lags from the prior plan year typically result in relatively high claim payments under Administrative Services Only (ASO) arrangements in the first few months of the flexible program, when run-off from the prior plan is still being processed and paid. Then, cash flow for claim payments drops off, typically reflecting lower numbers of covered individuals as well as larger deductibles and copayments. After about eight or nine months, as more employees in the low-cost options meet their deductibles and out-of-pocket limits, cash flow for claim payments starts to stabilize and more closely track patterns for the prior plan.

This unusual pattern of "paid claims" makes it difficult for carriers to project medical trend factors as employers attempt to do subsequent-year pricing in July and August. Later in the year, as more experience unfolds, the trend factors may be refined.

Claims payment patterns also vary dramatically from month to month by such simple factors as the number of working days in a month. For example, November is typically an exceptionally high payment month, because there are no holidays. In contrast, a long month like July can appear low, with holiday and vacations reducing the number of working days available for claim payments. These factors combine to make simple "pro rata" claim payment projections inaccurate.

Cash flow projections also should reflect the impact of credits and price tags that are typically distributed uniformly throughout the year. For example, if employees can "opt down," fewer premiums will be collected than under the prior plan. Excess credits will be paid out, resulting in higher cash out flow to employees in their paycheques. Of course, over the course of a plan year, claim payment should be lower on average for those employees who opt down, which balances out the annual effect of decreased employee contributions.

§ 21.5   FUTURE PRICING AND REDESIGN

Once a flexible program is in operation, an employer must readdress option design, option pricing, and credit allocation issues for the next year. An important part of this annual process is financial analysis of the experience for the current year (and possibly past years). This analysis will often form the backdrop for at least the option pricing and credit allocation portions of the process and sometimes also influence option design issues.

The purposes of this financial analysis are to help answer the following kinds of questions:

- Are the actual aggregate program costs consistent with those projected for the year?
- Were the individual options fairly priced? If not, what changes may be appropriate?
- Does the experience under the program or under any specific option suggest particular design changes?
- What level of company credits in conjunction with the option prices will produce the appropriate level of company cost? What level will seem fair/reasonable to employees?

(a)   LOOKING BACK

Despite its importance, actually conducting this form of financial analysis can often be very difficult. Often, the most significant problem is lack of reliable and timely experience data. The design, pricing, and credit allocation decisions resulting from this process need to be communicated to employees, and their elections need to be recorded prior to the beginning of the next plan year, so this analysis often needs to occur at least three or four months prior to year-end.

However, at this time, the claims experience available in a self-insured situation will at best cover only the first half of the year (especially in the medical and dental areas where there is typically a one- to two-month lag between the time claims are incurred and the time they are paid by the insurance company or third-party administrator). As a result, pricing decisions usually must be made on the basis of limited data for the prior year, extrapolated forward to a full-year basis.

Employers can minimize the potential for frustration by anticipating upcoming data needs and taking steps to facilitate the early collection and categorization of results—particularly for medical and dental experience. Steps in the data collection process might include:

- Advise insurers, third-party administrators, or internal systems staff of the need for detailed analysis of elections and claims experience.
- Provide parameters for reporting actual experience—by employee group (such as, active versus retired, hourly versus salaried), location, or division.
- Request itemization of employee data by type of coverage (Medical Plan A, Medical Plan B, and so forth) and coverage category (employee-only, employee-plus-one-dependent, and so forth).
- Establish tracking systems to identify and isolate specific large claims that could potentially distort the results, particularly for options elected by a small number of employees.

Extrapolating half-year data to a full-year basis, although necessary, can be complicated by a number of factors which may make simply doubling the half-year results inappropriate. Among these are the claims lag mentioned earlier, the continuing monthly increase in costs due to inflation, and the tendency for claims to be higher in the second half of the year after more participants have met the deductible.

It is typical to see medical experience by option which is quite different from that which would be produced by a fully random selection pattern. (See Chapter Fourteen on adverse selection.) For example, the pattern of actual versus expected claims experience might be on the order of that shown in Example 21.3.

If the actual experience is substantially different in the aggregate from that which was expected, the data should be reviewed to determine

Example 21.3
Illustration of Variation in Actual versus Expected Claims Experience

Option	Number of Employees	Option Price Tag	Expected Claims*	Actual Claims	Actual as Percent of Expected
High	2,500	$400	$1,000,000	$1,100,000	110
Intermediate	1,250	300	375,000	335,000	89
Low	1,250	200	250,000	190,000	76
	5,000		$1,625,000	$1,625,000	100

* Assumes no adjustment for anticipated adverse selection or utilization changes.

whether the experience is likely to be reliable as a predictor for the future. Perhaps an unusually high (or low) number of major claims occurred during the experience period, but these are unlikely to reoccur. In a small group, for example, the average claims experience under a low option might actually exceed the average claims experience under a high option due to one or two very large unexpected claims of employees who selected the low option. This experience should be identified in the analysis, but it is probably inappropriate for full inclusion in the development of future prices.

(b) LOOKING FORWARD

After the historical experience has been accumulated, reviewed, and adjusted (if necessary), decisions need to be made regarding the future year's option prices. Again, this subject is discussed mainly from a medical and dental perspective, since these benefits are more often self-insured, and differences in option experience can be great. (Also, setting prices for the next year based on the current year's experience will require some estimate of the expected increase in medical or dental claims due to inflation. Estimates of the expected trend factor for the next year are typically available from insurance companies and other sources.)

Assuming the medical experience shown in the earlier illustration (or 110 percent of expected for the high option and 90 percent and 75 percent for the other options), the issue arises as to what degree (if any) the individual option experience should be considered in next year's option prices.

One alternative is ignoring the variations from expected, as long as over-all medical program experience is in line with that expected (as is the case in this example). Under this approach, the option prices will maintain the same approximate relative relationships from year to year, thereby achieving a sense of stability from the employee's perspective.

On the other extreme would be a full reflection of the difference actually experienced between the options. In this example, such an approach would increase the spread between the high-option and the low-option prices nearly 50 percent in a single year. This would quickly drive employees away from the highest option. In some situations, this form of "option suicide" may, in fact, be an objective—to eliminate an unduly rich medical plan through the mechanism of pricing. In other cases, this may be inappropriately disturbing to those participants who are inclined to select the highest-level medical option.

An intermediate approach is often used which reflects only a portion of the experience-based differences in option costs. This might result in nudging employees away from the high option (or at least encouraging them to consider other options) rather than driving them away.

As part of this decision, one important (and often overlooked) step should be undertaken. The prices which are to be presented to employees need to make sense relative to the coverage levels being provided. This is particularly true if the full experience difference is to be used and, therefore, the pricing spread between the options is to be dramatically increased. The price differentials between the options should be compared with the differences in benefits payable under the options to ensure that employees are being presented with reasonable choices.

For example, if the difference in deductibles under two medical options (high and intermediate) would produce no more than a $100 gain to employees in coverage, the difference in prices between the options should not exceed that amount. Employees should not be asked to pay more for an option than they could expect to receive in coverage—regardless of the actual experience (which could have been unusual in a given year). In effect, the option choices and price tags need to be reviewed for logic in the eyes of employees, as well as reflection of actual experience.

§ 21.6 DATA REQUIREMENTS

Data requirements for financial analysis are not much more extensive than most employers would wish to have for the tracking of a traditional program. Most data is readily available from standard reports from carriers. However, few employers currently request or use some of the most important information. From the start, employers should agree with carriers and third-party administrators on the data needed for effective analysis and repricing. Important data elements include:

- **Claim lag reports.** These reports lay out "claims paid by month incurred" (i.e., the dollar amount of claims incurred in January and paid in (a) January, (b) February, (c) March, etc.). Claim lag reports for each medical option are valuable for tracking and projecting cash flow. This is most significant to a company for reasonably accurate projections for accounting and budgeting purposes, because high deductibles or out-of-pocket limits in some options can trigger radically different cash flow patterns when compared with a single pre-flexible plan.
- **Aggregate claims experience.** Most employers receive periodic reports from their carriers or claim administrators that compare claims incurred and paid (plus expenses) with budgeted monthly amounts (i.e., actual experience versus expected experience). These are typically referred to as "loss ratio reports." These reports are valuable in tracking the degree of selection and for setting increases to budgeted rates (or premiums) the next plan year. It is important to clarify with the carriers or plan administrators that this data should be collected by option and coverage category. Since option enrollment patterns change from year to year, it is rarely sufficient to report only total results.
- **Incurred charges by amount.** This data has not traditionally been reported to employers by their carriers or claims administrators. However, it is very valuable in evaluating the differences in value to employees of various medical and dental options. In addition, if the data is sorted by option, employers can gain more insight into the patterns and degree of adverse selection that occur in flexible programs.
- **Incurred claims by type of service.** Most claims administrators maintain standard reports that summarize the number and dollar amount of charges incurred by type of service (hospital, vision, prescription drugs, and so on). Isolating the most costly procedures helps in analyzing adverse selection and in determining subsequent price tags.

Twenty-Two

Case Studies

§ 22.1 INTRODUCTION

The first 21 chapters of this book present the theory and technical considerations surrounding flexible benefits. This final chapter focuses on four employers who have applied the theory and solved the technical issues to introduce flexible benefits for their employees. First, the development of Canada's first full flexible plan at Cominco is examined. The six-year experience of the Cominco flexible benefit plan should provide answers to many questions from potential sponsors. The other three cases examine specific aspects of flexible benefit implementation:

- The communication campaign at American Express Canada is reviewed
- The use of employee feedback in designing the flexible plan for the Prudential Insurance Company of America is highlighted
- The administration system developed by the Potash Corporation of Saskatchewan is examined.

§ 22.2 COMINCO—CANADA'S FIRST FLEXIBLE BENEFIT PLAN

Cominco Ltd., headquartered in Vancouver, British Columbia, is the world's largest producer of lead and zinc. To benefit experts, Cominco is also known for introducing the first full flexible benefit program in Canada, in March 1984. This section will describe why Cominco introduced a flexible plan, how it was introduced, and what the experience has been.

(a) BACKGROUND

In the early 1980s, Cominco was losing millions of dollars a year due to low prices for zinc. During this period, the unions would not accept any cutbacks or concessions. Management, therefore, asked salaried, non-bargained employees to bear the brunt of the company's financial difficulties—salaries were frozen, hours of work were increased, and vacations were cut back. As Cominco began to recover in 1983, it looked for ways to repay salaried employees for their sacrifices. One of the things the company wanted to do was introduce a flexible benefit program to provide meaningful choices for employees, to be innovative, to differentiate Cominco from other Canadian employers and to differentiate Cominco's salaried employees from their unionized employees.

(b) GROUNDWORK

In mid-1983, Cominco looked at the feasibility of introducing a flexible program, using a feasibility study process similar to that outlined in Chapter Two. The study produced a tentative program design and implementation plan—which were enthusiastically approved by management.

Before the final go-ahead was given, however, the plan had to be test-marketed with employees. In October 1983, more than 225 randomly selected employees at all major locations participated in focus group sessions. Employees in the groups responded very favourably to the proposed plan with one major exception—the proposed plan included a vacation-selling option with each day sold generating 75 percent of a day's pay in extra flexible credits. The employee reaction was unanimous and very negative. "If you think I'm only worth 75 cents on the dollar, then why don't you just reduce my pay by 25 percent?" asked one employee.

Based on the results of these focus groups, management approved the introduction of flexible benefits at Cominco with one major change—employees who sold vacation would receive credits equal to 100 percent of a day's pay. Management also insisted the plan be introduced as quickly as possible—the 3 1/2 months between the go-ahead and the effective date was a challenge to all involved. But on March 1, 1984, Flex-Com was up and running. The program name had been changed from Comflex, because, graphically, the original name looked too much like Corn Flakes!

(c) PROGRAM OVERVIEW

The plan used the core plus credits approach and consisted of the elements listed in Table 22.1.

At the initial enrollment, more than 75 percent of the employees changed at least one benefit. The most common change was in long-term disability (LTD). Prior to the introduction of Flex-Com, Cominco had provided a company-paid LTD program. At the initial enrollment, more than 45 percent of the employees elected to pay the premium themselves through payroll deductions and direct the company premium to pay for other benefits.

(d) SIX YEARS OF EXPERIENCE

Flex-Com has now been operating for more than six years. The experience of the plan will be of interest to companies considering introducing a flexible benefit program for their employees. Questions that are frequently asked of Cominco include:

- **How have employees reacted to the plan?** According to Cominco, the initial reaction was very favourable—more than 70 percent of employees who participated in the focus groups felt Flex-Com would be a better benefit program than the nonflexible plan. (As a reference, 72 percent of employees viewed the non-flexible Cominco plan

Table 22.1
Flex-Com Program Overview

Benefit	Core	Options
Supplemental medical	$500 deductible; 100% coinsurance	1 choice
Dental	None	3 choices
Long-term disability	60% to $1,500 of monthly pay; 50% of excess	Pay with credits or payroll deductions
Group life	1 times pay	Up to 3 times pay
Vacation	Current plan	Can sell 1 to 5 days
Savings and stock purchase	Current plan	Unused credits deposited here. No company match

as excellent.) Fifty-four percent of the participants said the most important change Cominco could make was to introduce flexible benefits. Although no follow-up surveys have been done, the program is very well received, according to Keith Scott, manager, benefit planning and administration: "The flex plan is an attractive element in our compensation program. We still get a lot of mileage from it."

- **Has the plan design remained the same?** No—the core plus credits design has allowed Cominco to make several improvements since 1984. In 1985, spouse's life insurance and accidental death and dismemberment insurance were added. Later, premiums for life insurance were changed to reflect the smoker status of the individual. One of the attractive features of the Cominco flexible plan is that the structure is not static—introducing a new benefit or changing an existing benefit is easy.

- **Have any employees made "poor" choices that left them at serious financial risk?** (For example, has an employee with children taken the minimum life insurance benefit in order to contribute to the savings plan?) Mr. Scott is not aware of any such situations in the six years the plan has been in effect. If anything, some employees have tended to make conservative choices, electing more coverage than they need.

- **How many employees change their options each year?** This has settled down from the 75 percent who changed when the plan was introduced, to about 25 percent who now make a change at each annual enrollment.

- **How is the program communicated?** In the first year, employees received an overview brochure; attended meetings, which included a slide presentation and a question-and-answer session; and received a detailed enrollment guide, personal report, and enrollment form. For the 1990 re-enrollment, employees received an update to their benefits handbook that describes the benefits, plus a guidebook that describes changes to the program and explains how to complete the enrollment form and a personal report/enrollment form. Employee meetings are no longer necessary. In 1989, however, a special meeting was held at one location where there had been substantial employee turnover.

- **Do employees complete the enrollment forms accurately?** At the initial enrollment in 1984, about 8 percent of employees made errors in their enrollment forms—most of these errors were minor arithmetic mistakes. In 1990, only 3 percent of forms contained errors.

- **What has been the financial experience of the plan?** This is difficult to measure since it is impossible to know what the costs of the pre-flexible plan would have been if the new plan had not been introduced. However, after comparing the cost trends in the non-flexible plan for union employees with the trends under the flexible plan, Keith Scott believes Flex-Com costs are about the same as they would have been had the prior plan continued.

- **Which LTD plan is more popular—the employee-paid or company-paid benefit?** More than 53 percent of employees now elect the employee-paid plan which provides a tax-free benefit should the individual become disabled.

- **What would Cominco do differently?** If Keith Scott had to introduce flexible benefits again, the major change would be "to give myself more time."

- **What has the administrative experience been?** Cominco introduced a new Human Resources Information System at the same time their flexible benefit system was being developed. Therefore, it is impossible to isolate the impact of introducing a flexible administration system. Over-all, administration of the flexible program with the new HRIS and flex administration systems is easier and less expensive than administering the pre-flexible program using the prior systems. Much of the improvement is due to the new HRIS system. However, Mr. Scott says, "I can say that our administrative costs have not increased because of Flex-Com."

§ 22.3 AMERICAN EXPRESS CANADA—COMMUNICATING FLEXIBLE BENEFITS IN AN IMPOSSIBLE TIME FRAME

"Express Yourself . . . Exprimez-vous." These phrases greeted 2,100 employees of American Express Canada, Inc. when the Markham, Ontario-based company implemented a flexible benefit program January 1, 1988.

Introduction of the flexible program represented a new era in human resources at American Express Canada, as the company underwent dramatic growth. The company's new management team was focusing greater attention on both benefit plan design and communication, since attracting and retaining employees had been identified as top priorities. As Faye Patterson, vice-president of human resources, observed at the time: "American Express is a corporation with an extremely diverse workforce. We wanted a program that would address different employee needs—and flexible benefits seemed like the best approach for us."

Specifically, American Express Canada's objectives for the flexible program were to:

- Provide employees with a program they could tailor to their own needs
- Introduce a highly competitive benefits package
- Foster employee appreciation of company benefits
- Demonstrate the company's new employee relations approach
- Reward long service
- Produce an eye-catching, professional-looking package that shows the company's willingness to invest in employees, just as it invests in other areas such as advertising.

(a) PROGRAM OVERVIEW

The flexible program provides each employee with 150 "Express Dollars," which may be spent on a broad range of benefit choices, including medical, dental, life insurance, and AD&D. In each benefit area, American Express provides a competitive level of coverage. Employees may elect a higher level of coverage (and pay the extra cost with Express Dollars or payroll deductions), or opt for a lower level of coverage (and generate Express Dollars). Employees also have the opportunity to waive medical, dental, and AD&D coverage and generate additional Express Dollars.

In addition, employees may use payroll deductions or Express Dollars to purchase life insurance for a spouse and children; to buy up to five additional vacation days; or to purchase membership in the company's on-site fitness facility at Markham headquarters. (Employees may also use Express Dollars to join other local health clubs.)

Also under the umbrella of Express Yourself (but not as flexible benefits), the company introduced group home and auto insurance. Employees may purchase coverage through payroll deduction.

"We wanted to offer choices and let employees construct their own benefit packages to fit their lifestyles," commented Ms. Patterson. "Express Yourself presented employees with a total picture of their benefits for the first time. It encouraged employees to sit down and think about their benefit needs and, ultimately, created a higher level of understanding."

(b) COMMUNICATION OVERVIEW

Benefit communication was also a top management priority. Previous benefit communication consisted of a variety of typewritten, photocopied documents. Employee surveys indicated a low level of benefits knowledge throughout the company. The "Express yourself/Exprimez-vous" campaign was designed to communicate benefits in a comprehensive and cohesive way. By introducing a new identity for benefit communication through the campaign, the company intended to begin an ongoing communication program.

(1) Audience

The campaign presented several challenges in terms of employee demographics. Of the program's 2,100 employees, 65 percent are female with an average age of 34 and more than 70 percent fill clerical positions. About 1,000 employees are located at the company's Markham, Ontario, headquarters and the others are scattered across the country—sometimes in two- or three-person storefront operations, in addition to the seven regional offices. The majority of employees have English as a second language, having immigrated from the Far East and South America. Many have immigrated with, or brought into Canada, extended families and are raising young families themselves, as well as supporting older relatives. The 250 employees in Quebec are predominantly French-speaking. As such, all communication was prepared in French and English.

(2) Timing

An extremely tight timeframe added a twist to this project. A campaign of this scope generally takes about six months or more to complete. However, American Express Canada had only six weeks between its decision to proceed with flexible benefits in early October 1987 and its introduction of the program. The campaign started in mid-November with a letter from the president, which was mailed to employees at their homes along with an overview brochure. During the next three weeks, American Express conducted 65 employee meetings across Canada to explain the program and facilitate the enrollment process. About 20 meeting leaders from locations across the country attended a one-day training session before conducting the meetings. Since the campaign coincided with the company's busiest time of the year—the Christmas shopping season—there was considerable competition for employees' attention.

(3) Communication Goals and Objectives

The communication objectives were:

- Educate employees about benefits
- Counter a feeling of isolation among outlying offices

- Enhance company pride
- Provide a Canadian, rather than U.S., orientation in benefit communication
- Appeal to the young, multicultural, primarily female workforce
- Serve as a stand-alone benefit communication/orientation package for prospective employees and new recruits.

(4)   Communication Campaign

American Express Canada chose an upbeat, colourful, user-friendly, and top-quality approach for all the campaign materials and activities. Face-to-face communication was emphasized and the company's supervisors were trained to be resources to employees both during enrollment and on an ongoing basis.

American Express adopted a spectrum or "rainbow" graphic theme to illustrate diversity and a range of choices for employees. Colour-coding was used to aid employee understanding of the program's structure. A rainbow pen and stylized "X" served as the central graphic symbols. Along with the theme "Express Yourself," they reinforced employee choice. The theme was also paralleled well by the French equivalent "Exprimez-vous."

A highlight of the employee meetings was a nine-minute videotape. The English version featured Lloyd Robertson, CTV's national news anchorman, while Pierre Lalonde, a talk-show host and entertainer in Quebec starred in the French version. Produced in a documentary style, the video simulated a news show with "live" reports from various American Express locations—including headquarters where senior management was interviewed about the flexible program.

The campaign's phases included:

- Announcement: Introductory "teaser" posters; overview brochure and letter from president mailed to each employee's home
- Education: Training of meeting leaders; employee meetings, where employees viewed the video, received enrollment kits, discussed the program, and studied slides outlining enrollment process
- Enrollment: Reminder posters; hotlines; articles in employee newsletter personal statements and confirmation reports.

(5)   Results and Evaluation

Reaction to the campaign was unanimously positive throughout American Express Canada. Both employees and management were pleased.

Enrollment went smoothly and employees came away feeling they understood their benefits and got a good deal in the process.

Faye Patterson summed it up: "It was the first time employees saw a total picture of their benefits. The campaign was a resounding success. It was one of the most creative and well-implemented communication strategies I've ever seen."

Some of the immediate results of the campaign included:

- There was a 6 percent error rate on the enrollment forms—an extremely low percentage for a brand-new plan.
- The most frequent question on the hotline was not about the plan itself. Instead, some employees wanted reassurance that they had made the right benefit decisions. (The hotline averaged about 60 calls a day for two weeks during the height of the enrollment period.)
- Employees were eager to obtain their rainbow pens. A visit to company offices shortly after the meetings revealed nearly everybody was using one of the pens.
- The campaign sparked camaraderie among the human resources staff, who all pitched in to meet the tight deadlines and make their program a success.
- The company's public affairs department was delighted by the use of such high-profile talent in the videotapes and was eager to publicize the campaign outside American Express Canada.

(6) Ongoing Communication

In the 1990 re-enrollment, American Express decided to revamp the materials and make the transition from an introductory to an ongoing campaign. However, the "look" of the original program was to be retained. As a result, the following changes were made:

- The original workbook was divided into two elements—a brief enrollment guide covering the mechanics of how to complete the enrollment form and an information guide providing details on the benefit provisions. This information guide will form the benefits component of an extensive employee handbook.
- The video, which had become "dated" with the departure of several key employees, was replaced by a slide-transferred-to-video production (dubbed a "slideo"). This will have a longer shelf life than the video as it focuses on the program and its elements, whereas the video emphasized the change from the prior plan to the flexible plan.

§ 22.4 PRUDENTIAL INSURANCE COMPANY—A SUCCESSFUL FLEXIBLE PROGRAM THANKS TO EMPLOYEE INVOLVEMENT

The Prudential Insurance Company of America, with headquarters in Scarborough, Ontario and offices across Canada, had two important reasons for introducing a flexible benefit program in April 1988. They were to:

- Provide an alternative and innovative set of benefits to employees, which could be tailored to their individual needs; and
- Improve employee attitudes concerning benefits and to correct several problems with the existing package.

A secondary reason was to allow Prudential, as a provider of employee benefit programs, to learn about flexible benefits, by treating their employees as a pilot group. The results were expected to help Prudential become a better informed provider for flexible benefit programs.

(a) PRE-FLEXIBLE PROGRAM

Prudential had a typical employee benefit program with company-provided supplemental medical, dental, group life, and long-term disability coverages. The program had two unique features:

- Employees had to wait 10 years before being eligible for long-term disability coverage.
- Nine Personal Absence (PA) days were provided to all employees, except for agents. PA days were in addition to the vacation and holiday entitlement and could be used for any personal absences, such as doctor's visits or looking after a sick child, or could be taken as additional time off.

In 1987, Prudential conducted an opinion survey that included benefit-related issues. Only one-third of employees (34 percent) responded positively about their benefit program. This compared with an 85 percent favourable response to a similar survey of Prudential employees in the United States. Management employees responded no differently than did nonmanagement employees—only 33 percent responded favourably, compared with 76 percent in the United States.

Some of the features of the plan that caused the negative response were:

- No vision care coverage was provided
- The 10-year waiting period for long-term disability coverage meant most employees either had no protection, or had to purchase an individual policy
- Prudential did not reimburse employees for their medicare premium
- Certain items, such as oral contraceptives, were not reimbursed under the medical plan.

The response was surprising to Prudential because studies indicated the benefit costs at Prudential were high. It was obvious, therefore, that the high cost of the personal absence days did not compensate for the missing features.

(b) PROPOSED PROGRAM

A Prudential task force recommended a core plus credits flexible plan with company-paid core benefits of:

- Life insurance: One times pay
- Long-term disability after one year of service: 50 percent of pay
- Pension: Existing plan
- Medical: Out-of-country emergency coverage only
- Vacation: Existing plan
- PA days: Five.

Options which would be available included:

- Life insurance: one times pay to six times pay
- Accidental Death and Dismemberment coverage (AD&D): one times pay to six times pay
- Dependent Life Insurance: $10,000 to $100,000
- Long-term disability: 3 plans
- Major medical: 3 plans
- Dental: 4 plans
- Health care expense account
- Provincial health insurance payment
- Individual financial products

- PA days: One or two additional days
- Cash.

Employees would receive sufficient credits to buy back their pre-flexible coverage levels. All benefit areas, with one exception, offered the pre-flexible plan as one of the options. The exception was PA days where the employee could only buy back two days for a maximum of seven, including the core. Nine PA days were included in the pre-flexible plan. Employees were given flexible credits equal to the value of four days (nine current minus five in the core), but were only permitted to repurchase two of the four.

(c) PROCESS

To test the program, Prudential decided to conduct a full trial enrollment. One hundred employees at locations in Ontario and Quebec were randomly selected to participate in the sessions. The size of the sample ensured that the results of the test would be within 7 percent of the results that would have been obtained by testing with all employees, 95 percent of the time. Participants were asked to attend two sessions. On the first day, they listened, in groups of 20 to 30, to a presentation concerning the structure and mechanics of the proposed plan. The overhead material was presented by an expert on the plan design. At the end of this first two-hour session, participants received a workbook describing the plan provisions in detail. It also outlined considerations in making various choices and illustrated how to enroll in the plan. Also in their package was an enrollment form and a statement showing options and prices. The statement was personalized for each participating employee, based on age, family status, date of hire, sex, and annual pay.

Participants reviewed the material at night and completed their enrollment form. They reconvened the next day in smaller groups to discuss their reactions to the proposed plan. The discussions were led by a "listener," someone trained as a facilitator. Employee comments were recorded verbatim by a second facilitator. Toward the end of the discussion, the participants completed a questionnaire. They also handed in their completed enrollment forms.

The data collected at the meeting—individual employee comments, enrollment forms and questionnaires—were compiled and analyzed. The results were compared with those collected by other employers who had undertaken similar pilot testing.

(d)   RESULTS

The employee study group results showed:

- The employee reaction to the proposed flexible benefit program was positive—but some strong negatives were cited.
- The program's major appeal was the concept of choice—every study participant made some change in current coverage. Participants in the study-group sessions were asked to describe, in their own words, the most appealing program features. Seventy percent of the individuals cited choice making as the key feature.

    Over half (53 percent) mentioned the availability of new coverages and options. (Participants frequently identified more than one appealing feature, so the total exceeded 100 percent.)

    The appeal of choice making was confirmed in group discussions. In employees' own words:

    "I realize the old plan was very good, but to have a plan adapted to every individual's needs is a great advantage."

    "I like the concept because of the fact that it allows me to make choices based on my own needs, rather than having them made for me based on the needs of the 'average' employee."

- The majority of study group participants felt the proposed program would result in benefits better than or equal to current benefits.
- But, the majority also viewed the cutback of PA days very negatively, which seemed to limit their enthusiasm for choice making.

    A significant majority (63 percent) of employees mentioned the loss of PA days as the least appealing feature of the proposed program. Comments included:

    "I am ready to reject the whole plan if it means the number of my PA days will be reduced."

    "We shouldn't have to buy back the PA days. They shouldn't be taken away at all. We're not really getting anything. I think the new flex plan is lousy."

- Employees did not feel the plan was too complex; only 1 percent of participants felt there were too many choices. About one-third (32 percent) said the proposed plan had too few choices, while the remaining two-thirds responded that the number of choices was appropriate.
- Participants had a good understanding of the proposed program, and were comfortable with choosing their own benefits. Well over 90 percent of the participants:

— liked the idea of being able to choose their own benefits (96 percent)

— were confident they could make wise benefit decisions (93 percent)

— liked being "forced" to study details of their benefits so they could make decisions (96 percent).

- Employees appreciated Prudential's interest in their opinions, and requested feedback on how their reactions would be used.

(e) FOLLOW-UP

Prudential management reviewed the responses and elected to implement a flexible benefit program in view of the favourable response to the concept. However, they decided to delay implementation for several months so the proposed plan design could be modified to reflect the views of the participants.

The Prudential flexible benefit program was introduced on July 1, 1988 and, according to Henry Kugler, senior vice-president, was well received by employees. The major change in design between the proposed plan and the actual plan was the restructuring of how PA days were included in the plan. The Prudential flexible plan now gives employees their full allotment of nine days and permits employees to "sell" up to four days in exchange for additional flexible credits. Changes in the design and pricing of options were also made based on feedback from the focus groups. When the plan was made available to Prudential employees in 1988, an important part of the communication message was that the Company had incorporated employee views in the final design.

According to Mr. Kugler, "The flexible plan has been successful. However, if we had gone ahead without asking for the opinion of our employees, the response would have been exactly the opposite."

§ 22.5 POTASH CORPORATION OF SASKATCHEWAN— ADMINISTRATION IN A DECENTRALIZED ENVIRONMENT

Potash Corporation of Saskatchewan Inc. (PCS) is the world's largest producer of potash outside of the Soviet Union—potash is one of the key ingredients in fertilizer. Now a publicly-held company, PCS was a Saskatchewan Crown corporation when a flexible benefit program was introduced for 450 staff employees in April 1989.

(a) BACKGROUND

As a Crown corporation, PCS's compensation system was constrained because of severe losses incurred by the corporation in the mid-1980s, followed by provincial fiscal restraint in the latter part of the decade. As a result, staff wages were frozen for several years. During this period the company was losing large amounts of money each year—$68 million in 1986 and $106 million in 1987. As a result, a new management team was introduced. Charles Childers, president and CEO was hired to turn the corporation around. He and two other key members of the team came from International Minerals and Chemical Corporation, a U.S.-based corporation and a major Saskatchewan potash producer. In 1985, IMC introduced flexible benefits in their U.S. operations.

One of the key members of the new team was John Gugulyn, senior vice president of administration. Mr. Gugulyn also came from IMC where he had been involved in the successful implementation of their Canadian flexible benefit program in 1986. Mr. Gugulyn, and the rest of the new PCS management team, felt the introduction of flexible benefits would help improve employee morale, which had suffered because of staff downsizing along with the salary freeze.

In mid-1988, PCS put together a study team to investigate the feasibility of introducing a flexible program. Mr. Childers was very supportive of introducing such a program as long as it was not a cost-containment measure. He guaranteed in writing that employees would have enough credits to buy back their original benefit package. After several months' work, the team recommended introducing a program as long as employees participating in focus groups reacted favourably. The employee reaction was extremely favourable, and PCS committed to introducing a plan in early 1989.

(b) ADMINISTRATIVE CONCERNS

The biggest implementation hurdle was clearly administration. PCS is comprised of a head office in Saskatoon and four major mine sites in southeast Saskatchewan. Most administrative activities were handled at the local level. This decentralization was a result of the creation of PCS 10 years earlier. PCS was formed when the Saskatchewan government took over the operation of four separate potash producers.

Each division was responsible for administering the pre-flexible benefit programs. Divisions remitted the premium to the insurance carriers, initiated payroll deductions, handled claim inquiries for employees and so on. To complicate matters, each mine site or division had two benefit programs to administer—the common staff plan and the local union plan. (Different unions represented employees at each of the mines.)

Even payroll was decentralized. Salaried employees at three of the mines and at the corporate office were handled by separate bank payroll services. The fourth division, at Lanigan, used an internally developed payroll system. A common payroll system was used for hourly payroll at all four mines.

Executive payroll was handled manually, to preserve its confidentiality.

(c)   DIRECTION

The study group, which investigated flexible benefits, spent time discussing the administration strategy. The consensus was that administration should continue to be handled at the local level; however, systems development and support should be provided by the corporate office. The goal was to have administrators at each division responsible for producing personal reports for employees, entering elections, generating confirmation statements, dealing with inquiries, and so on. The corporate information systems group would be responsible for developing and maintaining the software to administer the plan and updating it annually to reflect new price tags and credits.

(d)   SYSTEM BLUEPRINT

After management gave the go-ahead to implement "PCS Flex," an administrative study team was created to determine the requirements of the system. During a series of meetings, administrators from each division met with systems experts from the corporate office.

(1)   Detailed Plan Design

The plan design was reviewed, relevant administrative issues discussed, and decisions made. For example, the group decided:

- How to handle employees who did not turn in an enrollment form. (Their benefits were defaulted to their prior coverages.)
- How to treat two PCS salaried employees married to one another. (Both received full credits.)

- How much time employees were to be given to change their elections, if their family status changed (30 days after the change).
- How price tags were to be calculated and rounded (to the nearest cent, which was divisible by 12, for example, a price tag of $120.50 would be adjusted to $120.48 so that system could track the cost monthly).
- How frequently credits should be deposited in the health care expense account (monthly was changed to annually for the second and subsequent plan years).
- What the plan's "year" should be. (The first plan year was only nine months—April 1 to December 31. Subsequent years run from January 1 to December 31.)

(2) Systems Issues

Technical issues were also addressed such as:

- Whether the system should be PC-based, connected by a wide area network (WAN), or be developed on the company's mainframe. (The system was developed on PCS's mainframe and terminals were installed at each division.)
- How security should be handled. (System access was restricted to specific users. Administrators in one division would not have access to information concerning another division. Some users were restricted to looking at information while others could initiate transactions. Superintendent salaries could only be accessed by the industrial relations superintendent.)
- How executives would be handled. (A separate PC-based administrative system was developed using a commercial spreadsheet program.)

(3) Insurance Carrier Administration

Meetings were held with the insurance carrier to discuss the transfer of information between PCS and the carrier. It was decided that PCS would report the benefit choices of covered employees once a month by computer produced report. A unique "division code" would be assigned to each possible combination of medical and dental options—for example, employees electing Medical Plan 3 and Dental Plan 2 were assigned to Division 32. Thus, no major changes to the carrier's administration system were necessary.

It was also decided that the PCS administration system would calculate the required premium payments. Once a month, each division would run a premium report based on the benefit elections and submit the premium directly to the insurer.

Employees were to submit claims to the Personnel Department who would forward them to the carrier. Cheques would be sent to Personnel by the insurer for distribution to employees.

(e)   SYSTEM DEVELOPMENT

The decisions made by the administrative study group formed the basis for a "requirements definition" document that was later expanded into an administration manual.

These requirements formed the blueprint for developing the system. Work began in late 1988 and was completed in the spring of 1989. According to Ross Hinther, Director Information Systems, the complete development, including testing, took two analysts just over four months. In February 1988, administrators were invited to a two-day training session where they learned to use the system.

(f)   INTRODUCTION

The administrative activities for the PCS flexible program went very smoothly during the program's introduction. Employees received their personal reports as promised and all enrollment activities were completed on schedule. The insurance carrier was astounded when it received the initial printed report in mid-March containing information on all participating employees. A final report dated March 31, 1989, was sent on that date. The insurer had assumed that systems development would delay the first data transmission for several months.

(g)   EXPERIENCE

PCS-Flex has now been operating for over a year. One of the goals in developing the system and related procedures was to minimize any extra personnel needed to administer the program on an ongoing basis. According to Mr. Hinther, this goal has been achieved: "It takes one analyst six weeks per year to maintain the system—to prepare for annual enrollment, test and implement the changes and so forth." Elaine Vetter, personnel officer in charge of benefits at the Saskatoon office, says the "day-to-day activities are minimal. PCS-Flex has not increased the workload of the administrators at our divisions." Ms. Vetter has noticed a change at PCS, however:

"Prior to PCS-Flex, the benefit programs stayed the same year after year—nothing ever happened. And that was not necessarily the way it should have been. Now, through re-enrollment, we remind people of benefits annually, and there could be changes or additions every year."

(h)   FURTHER DEVELOPMENTS

Following the introduction of PCS-Flex for staff employees, PCS introduced two more flexible programs. On January 1, 1990, U.S. employees at PCS Sales enrolled in a flexible plan. Because of the different tax and administrative requirements in the United States, a different administrative system was developed using a PC database program. Within the next year, PCS intends to incorporate the U.S. requirements in the mainframe system.

On July 1, 1990, hourly employees at the Rocanville mine were covered by the first Canadian flex plan for unionized employees. Administration is being handled by a new human resource/flexible benefit system running on PCS's mainframe. Both hourly and staff employees will be administered on this system.

In conjunction with the Rocanville plan, PCS is developing one human resource system that will work in conjunction with the flexible administration system. Before the introduction of flexible benefits, the PCS human resource system handled only salaried employees. Hourly employees' human resource information resided in a payroll system and various other systems. According to Mr. Hither, "With the hourly flex plan, we decided to replace this with two systems—a custom human resource system and a third-party payroll system."

Appendix

Interpretation Bulletins

 Revenue Canada **Revenu Canada**
Taxation Impôt

INTERPRETATION BULLETIN	BULLETIN D'INTERPRÉTATION
SUBJECT: **SPECIAL RELEASE**	OBJET: **COMMUNIQUE SPECIALE**

NO IT-227R DATE: November 10, 1980
REFERENCE:

Group Term Life Insurance Premiums

Nº IT-227R DATE: le 10 novembre 1980
RENVOI:

Primes en vertu d'une police collective d'assurance temporaire sur la vie.

Effective with the issue of IT-227R on May 26, 1980, paragraph 3 is amended to read as follows:

3. The phrase ''group term life insurance policy'' is defined in subsection 248(1) as a group life insurance policy under which no amount is payable as a result of the contributions made to or under the policy by the employer except in the event of the death or disability of the employee. An employees' group life insurance policy is a policy whereby the lives of employees are insured severally under a single contract between the insurer and an employer contracting with the insurer. The Department accepts as a life insurance policy any policy of insurance where one of the risks covered is the death of the person insured but not an insurance policy which covers death only be reason of accident.

Prenant effet avec la publication de IT-227R le 26 mai, 1980, le paragraphe 3 est modifié afin de se lire comme suit:

3. Le paragraphe 248(1) définit l'expression ''police collective d'assurance temporaire sur la vie'' comme étant une police collective d'assurance sur la vie en vertu de laquelle aucune somme n'est payable par suite des contributions faites à la police ou en vertu de la police par l'employeur, sauf en cas de décès ou d'invalidité de l'employé. Une police d'assurance collective sur la vie d'employés signifie qu'un groupe d'employés est assuré en commun en vertu d'un contrat unique qui lie l'assureur et l'employeur (ce dernier détenant le contrat). Le Ministère accepte comme police d'assurance-vie toute police d'assurance en vertu de laquelle un des risques assurés est le décès de la personne assurée à l'exception d'une police d'assurance qui assure le décès causé seulement par accident.

Published under the authority
of the Deputy Minister
of National Revenue for Taxation

Publié avec l'autorisation
du Sous-ministre
du Revenu national pour l'Impôt

Revenue Canada   Revenu Canada
Taxation   Impôt

INTERPRETATION BULLETIN	BULLETIN D'INTERPRÉTATION

SUBJECT: **INCOME TAX ACT**
Group Term Life Insurance Premiums

OBJET: **LOI DE L'IMPÔT SUR LE REVENU**
Primes en vertu d'une police collective d'assurance temporaire sur la vie

NO **IT-227R**   DATE: May 26, 1980
REFERENCE: Subsection 6(4) (also subsection 6(5) and paragraph 6(1)(a))

Nº **IT-227R**   DATE: le 26 mai 1980
RENVOI: Paragraphe 6(4) (également le paragraphe 6(5) et l'alinéa 6(1)a))

This bulletin cancels and replaces Interpretation Bulletin IT-227 dated June 9, 1975. Current revisions are designated by a vertical line.

Le présent bulletin annule et remplace le Bulletin d'interprétation IT-227 du 9 juin 1975. Les révisions sont indiquées d'un trait vertical.

1. This bulletin explains the application of subsection 6(4) which includes in the income of an officer, employee, former officer or former employee (hereinafter referred to as an employee) a part of the premium of certain group term life insurance policies.

2. Paragraph 6(1)(a) specifically excludes premiums paid by an employer under a group term life insurance policy from the benefits taxable under that paragraph, and there is no provision in the Act to include in an employee's income premiums paid by one or more employers or former employers under one or more group term life insurance policies where the total insurance coverage on the taxpayer's life is $25,000 or less. However, subsection 6(4) provides that where an employee is insured at any time in his taxation year for an amount in excess of $25,000 under one or more group term life insurance policies, part of any premiums paid by his employer(s) or former employer(s) is included in his income as income from an office or employment. The method for calculating the amount to be included in income is outlined in paragraphs (a) to (c) of subsection 6(4). Sample calculations are set out in paragraphs 16 to 18 of this bulletin.

3. The phrase "group term life insurance policy" is defined in subsection 248(1) as a group life insurance policy under which no amount is payable as a result of the contributions made to or under the policy by the employer except in the event of the death or disability of the employee. An employees' group life insurance policy is a policy whereby the lives of employees are insured severally under a single contract between the insurer and an employer contracting with the insurer. The Department accepts as a life insurance policy any policy of insurance where one of the risks covered is the death of the person insured, whether by reason of accident or otherwise. "Life insurance" means any insurance payable in the event of death from any cause.

1. Le présent bulletin vise à expliquer l'application du paragraphe 6(4), qui inclut dans le revenu d'un cadre, d'un employé, d'un ancien cadre ou d'un ancien employé (ci-après appelé employé) une fraction de la prime versée en vertu de certaines polices collectives d'assurance temporaire sur la vie.

2. L'alinéa 6(1)a) exclut formellement des avantages imposables selon cet alinéa les primes versées par un employeur en vertu d'une police collective d'assurance temporaire sur la vie; en outre, la Loi ne prévoit aucunement l'inclusion, dans le revenu d'un employé, des primes payées par un ou plusieurs employeurs ou anciens employeurs en vertu d'une ou de plusieurs polices collectives d'assurance temporaire sur la vie lorsque le montant total de la couverture de l'assurance sur la vie du contribuable est de $25,000 ou moins. Le paragraphe 6(4) stipule toutefois qu'un employé, lorsqu'il est assuré à n'importe quel moment de son année d'imposition pour un montant supérieur à $25,000 en vertu d'une ou plusieurs polices collectives d'assurance temporaire sur la vie, doit compter dans son revenu une partie de toute prime versée par son ou ses employeurs ou anciens employeurs comme revenu tiré d'une charge ou d'un emploi. Les alinéas a) à c) du paragraphe 6(4) indiquent la façon de calculer le montant à inclure dans le revenu. Les numéros 16 à 18 du présent bulletin comportent des exemples de ces calculs.

3. Le paragraphe 248(1) définit l'expression «police collective d'assurance temporaire sur la vie» comme étant une police collective d'assurance sur la vie en vertu de laquelle aucune somme n'est payable par suite des contributions faites à la police ou en vertu de la police par l'employeur, sauf en cas de décès ou d'invalidité de l'employé. Une police d'assurance collective sur la vie d'employés signifie qu'un groupe d'employés est assuré en commun en vertu d'un contrat unique qui lie l'assureur et l'employeur (ce dernier détenant le contrat). Le Ministère accepte comme police d'assurance-vie toute police d'assurance en vertu de laquelle un des risques assurés est le décès de la personne assurée, qu'il résulte ou non d'un accident. «Assurance sur la vie» signifie une assurance payable dans le cas d'un décès engendré par une cause quelconque.

Published under the authority
of the Deputy Minister
of National Revenue for Taxation

Publié avec l'autorisation
du Sous-ministre
du Revenu national pour l'Impôt

Canada

4. The calculation under subsection 6(4) takes into account any premium, premium refund or dividend in respect of the policy year ending in the taxation year of the employee, even though part or all of any of those items may have been paid or payable in another policy year or another taxation year. Ordinarily, the policy year is a twelve-month period, but subsection 6(5) provides for a shorter period to be the "policy year" where, for example, a group policy is terminated during a taxation year prior to its anniversary date in that year and the policy year is considered to have ended. Again, if a policy is a new one which has no anniversary date in the taxation year, subsection 6(5) provides that the policy year is from the date of issue of the policy to the end of the taxation year. In this case, the calculation takes into account only the premium payable for that period; any experience rating refund or dividend payable, being based on the full policy year, is considered not to be applicable, even **pro rata**, to any period forming part of that year. Where the group coverage is transferred from one insurance company to another before the end of a policy year, two calculations are required: one to the date of termination of the old policy, and one from the date of issue of the new policy.

5. Certain "paid-up" group life insurance certificates, where the whole premium is paid in the first policy year, may qualify as group term life insurance policies which are subject to the exception in paragraph 6(1)(a) and the provisions of subsection 6(4). In computing the benefit under subsection 6(4), the premium to purchase such a policy would be included in the "total premium payable on account of life insurance under the policy in respect of the policy year ending in the year", under paragraph 6(4)(a) in the year it was paid, notwithstanding that the premium could be considered to be in respect of the first policy year and all subsequent years until the employee dies.

6. The part of a premium, premium refund or dividend under an employees' group policy that is taken into account for the purposes of paragraph 6(4)(a) is limited to the part paid in respect of "life insurance" (as defined in 3 above). Accordingly any part that relates to long-term disability or accident and sickness benefits is excluded. Again where, because of the employer's contributions, a benefit (e.g. a cash surrender value) is payable under a policy other than upon the death or disability of the employee, the whole premium paid for the policy is excluded since it is not then a term life insurance policy within the meaning of subsection 248(1).

4. Le calcul selon le paragraphe 6(4) tient compte de toute prime, de tout remboursement de prime ou de tout dividende payable à l'égard de l'année d'assurance (aussi appelée «année de la police») qui prend fin pendant l'année d'imposition de l'employé, en dépit du fait que ces éléments peuvent avoir été payés ou payables en partie ou en totalité au cours d'une autre année d'assurance ou d'imposition. Habituellement, une année d'assurance correspond à une période de 12 mois, bien que le paragraphe 6(5) prévoie certains cas où une «année d'assurance» est d'une plus courte durée, par exemple lorsqu'une police collective prend fin durant une année d'imposition avant sa date d'anniversaire dans cette année et que l'année d'assurance est considérée comme terminée. Ou encore, s'il s'agit d'une nouvelle police qui ne comporte pas une date d'anniversaire dans l'année d'imposition, le paragraphe 6(5) précise que l'année d'assurance commence à la date d'établissement de la police et se termine à la fin de l'année d'imposition. Dans ce cas, le calcul tient seulement compte de la prime payable à l'égard de cette période. Toute ristourne pour surprime d'expérience ou tout dividende payable, fondé sur l'année entière d'assurance, est jugé non applicable, même réduit au prorata, à toute période formant une partie de cette année. Lorsque la couverture collective est transférée d'une compagnie d'assurance à une autre avant la fin d'une année d'assurance, deux calculs sont nécessaires: un pour la période allant jusqu'à la date d'expiration de l'ancienne police, et un autre à partir de la date d'établissement de la nouvelle police.

5. Certains «certificats libérés» de police collective d'assurance sur la vie, lorsque la prime au complet est payée durant la première année d'assurance, peuvent correspondre à une police collective d'assurance temporaire sur la vie visée par l'exception de l'alinéa 6(1)a) et les dispositions du paragraphe 6(4). Lors du calcul de l'avantage en vertu du paragraphe 6(4), la prime servant à l'achat de ce genre de police devrait être incluse dans «la prime totale payable au titre de l'assurance-vie sous le régime de la police relativement à l'année de la police se terminant dans l'année», en vertu de l'alinéa 6(4)a) dans l'année au cours de laquelle elle a été versée, même si l'on pouvait considérer la prime comme ayant été versée pour la première année d'assurance et toutes les années suivantes jusqu'au décès de l'employé.

6. La fraction d'une prime, d'un remboursement de prime ou d'un dividende en vertu d'une police collective d'employés dont il faut tenir compte aux fins de l'alinéa 6(4)a) se limite à la fraction versée relativement à une «assurance sur la vie» (au sens donné au no 3 ci-dessus). En conséquence, il faut exclure toute fraction relative à des indemnités en cas d'invalidité à long terme, d'accident ou de maladie. De même, lorsque, à la suite de contributions de l'employeur, une indemnité (par exemple, une valeur de rachat) est payable en vertu d'une police à un moment autre que lors du décès ou de l'invalidité de l'employé, la prime entière payée à l'égard de la police est exclue puisque, à ce moment-là, il ne s'agit pas d'une police collective d'assurance temporaire sur la vie selon le paragraphe 248(1).

7. In some cases, the employer may be the beneficiary of part or all of the coverage on an employee's life. If so, the relevant portion of the coverage and, if applicable, of the premiums, premium refunds or dividends is excluded from the calculation under paragraph 6(4)(a). However, the portion of the premiums applicable to the coverage on which the employer is the beneficiary in these cases is not an allowable business expense of the employer.

8. The phrase "the number of days in that period" in paragraph 6(4)(a) refers to the number of days in the calendar year that the employee is covered under the policy for more than $25,000. Where he is covered for $25,000 or less (or not at all) for part of the year, but for more than $25,000 for another part of the year, an apportionment, on a daily basis, should be made in that part of the calculation governed by paragraph 6(4)(a). Where the employee is covered for part or all of the year for more than $25,000 and the amount of that excess has changed at some time in the year, a complete calculation must be made under subsection 6(4) for each excess amount, with an apportionment being made under paragraph 6(4)(a) in each case, based on the number of days to which the specific excess applies and as if there were no excess for the remainder of the year; the sum of the amounts so calculated is to be included in income under this subsection. The example in 18 below illustrates this kind of calculation. Where there is excess coverage for part of the year with no change in the amount, only a single calculation is required.

9. In determining the "amount of life insurance in effect" at any given time, referred to in paragraph 6(4)(a), all benefits provided by a group term life insurance policy should be taken into account, whether payable on a periodic basis such as survivor income benefits, or in a lump sum. Thus the commuted value of any survivor benefits payable is added to the amount of any lump sum payable on death in calculating the "amount of life insurance in effect".

10. The "mean", or average, total term life insurance in effect under the policy, also referred to in paragraph 6(4)(a), is based only on the amounts in force at the beginning and end of the policy year. Any fluctuation in total coverage between those two dates is disregarded and no apportionment is required.

11. The amount of premium paid by the employee that is to be apportioned under paragraph 6(4)(c) is the amount he pays in his taxation year for the period during which his coverage is in excess of $25,000; this is determined on the basis of what, factually, he pays in respect of the group term life insurance policy. However, for the 1974 and

7. L'employeur peut être le bénéficiaire d'une partie ou de la totalité de l'assurance-vie de l'employé. Le cas échéant, l'alinéa 6(4)a) précise qu'il faut exclure du calcul la fraction correspondante de la couverture et, s'il y a lieu, des primes, remboursements de primes ou dividendes. Toutefois, dans ces cas la fraction des primes s'appliquant à la couverture à l'égard de laquelle l'employeur est bénéficiaire ne constitue pas une dépense d'entreprise admissible de l'employeur.

8. L'expression «le nombre de jours dans cette période» dans l'alinéa 6(4)a) désigne le nombre de jours dans une année civile pendant lesquels la police protège l'employé pour un montant supérieur à $25,000. S'il est assuré pour $25,000 ou moins (ou n'est pas assuré du tout) pendant une partie de l'année, alors qu'au cours d'une autre partie de l'année sa police le protège pour plus de $25,000, il faut établir une répartition pour chaque jour de la partie du calcul visée par l'alinéa 6(4)a). Si l'employé reçoit une protection pour une somme supérieure à $25,000 pendant une partie ou la totalité de l'année et que le montant de cette couverture complémentaire a été modifié à un moment quelconque durant l'année, il faut faire un calcul complet pour chaque montant excédentaire en vertu du paragraphe 6(4), en plus d'une répartition en vertu de l'alinéa 6(4)a) pour chaque cas. A cette fin, il faut se fonder sur le nombre de jours applicables à la couverture complémentaire en question tout comme s'il n'avait pas été question de couverture complémentaire pour le reste de l'année. Le total des montants ainsi calculés doit être inclus dans le revenu visé par ce paragraphe. Le numéro 18 ci-dessous fournit un exemple de ce genre de calcul. Lorsque le montant de l'assurance complémentaire pour une partie de l'année ne subit aucune modification, un seul calcul est nécessaire.

9. Pour déterminer à un moment donné le «montant total de l'assurance-vie en vigueur», selon l'expression de l'alinéa 6(4)a), il faut tenir compte de toutes les indemnités d'une police collective d'assurance temporaire sur la vie, qu'elles soient payables en versements périodiques, telles les indemnités de survie, ou en une somme forfaitaire. Ainsi, lors du calcul du «montant total de l'assurance-vie en vigueur», la valeur escomptée de toutes indemnités de survie payables est ajoutée au montant de toute somme payable au moment du décès.

10. La «moyenne» du montant total de l'assurance-vie temporaire en vigueur en vertu de la police, également mentionnée à l'alinéa 6(4)a), est fondée seulement sur les montants en vigueur au début et à la fin de l'année d'assurance. On ne tient pas compte des variations de la garantie totale qui pourraient survenir entre ces deux dates et aucune répartition n'est nécessaire.

11. Le montant de prime, payé par l'employé, qu'il faut répartir en vertu de l'alinéa 6(4)c) est le montant qu'il paye dans son année d'imposition pour la période où il est couvert pour plus de $25,000. C'est le montant réel versé à l'égard de la police collective d'assurance temporaire sur la vie qui détermine le montant qu'il faut répartir. Cependant, pour les années d'impo-

subsequent taxation years where an employee reimburses the employer for all or part of the premium for the coverage in excess of $25,000, his benefit under subsection 6(4) is reduced accordingly.

Multiple Policies

12. An employee may be covered under two or more group term life insurance policies for each of which his employer pays part or all of the premiums. If, for one of those policies, the separate calculation required by paragraph 6(4)(d) shows that the part of the employee's contributions as determined under paragraph 6(4)(c) exceeds the amount determined pursuant to paragraph 6(4)(b), that excess is not taken into account to reduce the amount to be included in the employee's income because of the other policies.

13. Where an employee is covered under more than one group term life insurance policy for which his employer pays part or all of the premiums, a separate computation must be made in respect of each policy, with the $25,000 "exemption" being apportioned among the policies pursuant to paragraph 6(4)(e).

14. A difficulty arises where the amount of the employee's coverage under one or more of the policies changes, since there is no one figure under each policy upon which to base an apportionment. The Department will accept the computation of a level amount of coverage under each policy, using the weighted average (based on months of coverage) of the varying amounts in force under the policy during the year, or any other reasonable method proposed.

15. A group insurance policy of any kind for which no part of the premiums is payable by the employer is ignored for the purposes of paragraphs 6(4)(d) and (e).

sition 1974 et suivantes, lorsqu'un employé rembourse à son employeur une fraction ou la totalité de la prime pour une garantie complémentaire supérieure à $25,000, il faudra réduire en conséquence l'avantage calculé en vertu du paragraphe 6(4).

Polices multiples

12. Il est possible qu'un employé soit couvert par deux ou plusieurs polices collectives d'assurance-vie temporaire, pour lesquelles son employeur verse une partie ou la totalité des primes. Si, pour l'une de ces polices, le calcul distinct exigé par l'alinéa 6(4)d) indique que la fraction des contributions de l'employé, déterminée en vertu de l'alinéa 6(4)c), dépasse le montant calculé en conformité de l'alinéa 6(4)b) on ne tient pas compte de cet excédent lors de la réduction du montant à ajouter au revenu de l'employé en raison des autres polices.

13. Lorsqu'un employé est couvert en vertu de plus d'une police collective d'assurance-vie temporaire et que son employeur verse une fraction ou la totalité des primes, il est nécessaire d'établir un calcul distinct pour chaque police et de faire la répartition de l'«exemption» de $25,000 entre les polices en conformité de l'alinéa 6(4)e).

14. Lorsqu'il y a changement du montant de la garantie en vertu d'une ou de plus d'une police de l'employé, il devient alors difficile d'établir une répartition, étant donné qu'il n'y a pas de chiffre pour chaque police sur lequel on peut se fonder. En pareil cas, le Ministère accepte qu'on calcule la moyenne du montant équilibré de la garantie en vertu de chaque police, en établissant la moyenne pondérée (fondée sur les mois de garantie) des divers montants en vigueur en vertu de la police au cours de l'année, ou en ayant recours à toute autre méthode raisonnable proposée.

15. Les alinéas 6(4)d) et e) ne s'appliquent pas lorsque l'employeur n'a pas à payer une fraction des primes relativement à tout genre d'assurance collective.

6   IT–227R

Examples

16. The two examples below show the calculations required, first, before and after 1974 where the employee's premium is in respect of his total coverage under the policy and, second, for 1974 and subsequent taxation years where the employee's premium is specifically in respect of his excess coverage.

17. In an uncomplicated case where the employee's coverage is, say $40,000 throughout the year and the mean total amount of term life insurance under the group policy is, say, $1,250,000, the two calculations under subsection 6(4) would be as follows:

Total premium for policy year (say)	$ 8,000
Less: Experience rating refund (say)	1,000
Net premium cost for policy year	$ 7,000
Average cost per $1,000 of insurance $\left(\dfrac{\$7,000 \times \$1,000}{\$1,250,000}\right)$	$ 5.60
Amount of employee's excess coverage ($40,000 − $25,000)	$15,000

Amount to be included in employee's income if no premium paid by him
$\left(\dfrac{\$15,000 \times \$5.60}{\$1,000}\right)$ 　　　　　　　　　　　　　　　　　　$ 84.00

   (i) **Premium for Total Coverage**

If employee paid, say, $50 in respect of his total coverage, the deductible portion is
$\left(\dfrac{\$50 \times \$15,000}{\$40,000}\right)$ 　　　　　　　　　　　　　　$ 18.75

Amount to be included in employee's income
($84.00 − $18.75) 　　　　　　　　　　　　　　　　　　　　　$ 65.25

   (ii) **Premium for Excess Coverage, 1974 and Subsequent Taxation Years**

If employee paid, say, $50 in respect of his excess coverage, the amount to be included in his income is
($84.00 − $50.00) 　　　　　　　　　　　　　　　　　　　　　$ 34.00

18. To illustrate a more complicated situation assume:
   (a) the mean total amount of life insurance in effect under the policy in the policy year was $1,250,000.00;
   (b) the total premium for the policy year was $8,000;
   (c) the experience rating refund for the policy year was $1,000;
   (d) an employee ("the taxpayer") was covered under the above group policy (but under no other group policy) during his taxation year as follows:

for	90	days at	$20,000	
	180		$50,000	
	95		$75,000	and

   (e) during his taxation year, the employee paid personally the following amounts in respect of this insurance:

for period of	$20,000 coverage	− $15
	$50,000	− $50
	$75,000	− $40

Calculation of the amount that is to be included in the employee's income is as follows:

(A) First calculation: Period of $50,000 coverage

IT–227R

Exemples

16. Les deux exemples ci-après démontrent, en premier lieu, les calculs nécessaires, avant et après 1974, lorsque l'employé verse une prime à l'égard d'une garantie totale en vertu de la police et ensuite le calcul pour 1974 et les années d'imposition subséquentes où l'employé verse une prime précisément à l'égard d'une garantie complémentaire.

17. Dans un cas simple, supposant qu'un employé jouisse d'une garantie de $40,000 pendant toute l'année et que la moyenne du montant total d'assurance-vie temporaire en vertu de la police collective soit $1,250,000 voici les deux calculs à faire en vertu du paragraphe 6(4):

Total de la prime versée pour l'année d'assurance (supposons)	$ 8,000	
Moins: ristourne pour surprime d'expérience (supposons)	1,000	
Coût net de la prime pour l'année d'assurance	$ 7,000	
Coût moyen par $1,000 d'assurance		
$\left(\$7,000 \times \dfrac{\$1,000}{\$1,250,000}\right)$	$ 5.60	
Montant de la garantie complémentaire de l'employé ($40,000 − $25,000)	$15,000	
Montant à inclure dans le revenu de l'employé s'il n'a pas payé de prime		
$\left(\$15,000 \times \dfrac{\$5.60}{\$1,000}\right)$		$ 84.00

(i) **Prime pour garantie totale**

Si l'employé a payé $50 à l'égard de sa garantie totale, la fraction déductible est alors de

$\left(\$50 \times \dfrac{\$15,000}{\$40,000}\right)$	$ 18.75	
Montant à inclure dans le revenu de l'employé ($84.00 − $18.75)		$ 65.25

(ii) **Prime pour garantie complémentaire à compter de l'année d'imposition 1974**

Si l'employé a versé $50 pour sa garantie complémentaire, il faut alors inclure dans son revenu le montant suivant

($84.00 − $50.00)	$ 34.00

18. Voici un exemple d'une situation plus complexe:

a) la moyenne du montant total d'assurance-vie en vigueur en vertu de la police pendant l'année d'assurance était de $1,250,000;

b) la prime totale versée pour l'année d'assurance était de $8,000;

c) la ristourne pour surprime d'expérience pendant l'année d'assurance était de $1,000;

d) un employé ("le contribuable") était assuré en vertu de la police collective susdite (mais non en vertu d'autres polices collectives) durant son année d'imposition comme suit:

pendant	90 jours, à	$20,000
	180	$50,000
	95	$75,000 et

e) au cours de son année d'imposition, l'employé a lui-même versé les montants suivants à l'égard de cette assurance:

$15 pour la période de garantie de	$20,000
$50	$50,000
$40	$75,000

Le montant à inclure dans le revenu de l'employé doit être calculé de la façon suivante:

(A) Premier calcul: période de garantie de $50,000

IT–227R

8

Paragraph 6(4)(a)

Total premium for policy year	$ 8,000
Less: experience rating refund	1,000
Net premium cost for policy year	$ 7,000

Premium cost for this period

$\left(\dfrac{\$7,000 \times 180}{365}\right)$ $3,452.05

Average cost per $1,000 of insurance for this period

$\left(\dfrac{\$3,452.05 \times \$1,000}{\$1,250,000}\right)$ 2.76164

Paragraph 6(4)(b)

Amount of excess coverage for this period

($50,000 − $25,000) $ 25,000

Average cost of insurance per paragraph 6(4)(a) $2.76164

Amount to be included in employee's income in respect of this period if no premium paid by him

$\left(\dfrac{\$25,000 \times \$2.76164}{\$1,000}\right)$ $ 69.04

     (i) **Premium for Total Coverage** −

Paragraph 6(4)(c)

If employee paid, say, $50 in respect of his total coverage for this period, the deductible portion is

$\left(\dfrac{\$50 \times \$25,000}{\$50,000}\right)$ $ 25.00

Amount to be included in employee's income $ 44.04

     (ii) **Premium for Excess Coverage** − **1974 and Subsequent Taxation Years**

If employee paid, say, $50 in respect of his excess coverage for this period, the amount to be included in his income is

($69.04 − $50) $ 19.04

(B) Second calculation: period of $75,000 coverage

Paragraph 6(4)(a)

Total premium for policy year	$ 8,000
Less: experience rating refund	1,000
	$ 7,000

Premium cost for this period

$\left(\dfrac{\$7,000 \times 95}{365}\right)$ $1,821.92

Avarage cost per $1,000 of insurance for this period

$\left(\dfrac{\$1,821.92 \times \$1,000}{\$1,250,000}\right)$ $ 1.4575

Paragraph 6(4)(b)

Amount of excess coverage for this period $ 50.000

Average cost of insurance per paragraph 6(4)(a) $ 1.4575

Amount to be included in employee's income in respect of this period if no premium paid by him

$\left(\dfrac{\$50,000 \times \$1.4575}{\$1,000}\right)$ $ 72.88

     (i) **Premium for Total Coverage** −

Paragraph 6(4)(c)

If employee paid, say, $40 in respect of his total coverage for this period, the deductible portion is

Alinéa 6(4)a)

Prime totale versée pour l'année d'assurance	$ 8,000
Moins: ristourne pour surprime d'expérience	1,000
Coût net de la prime pour l'année d'assurance	$ 7,000

Coût de la prime pour cette période

$\left(\$7,000 \times \dfrac{180}{365}\right)$ $3,452.05

Coût moyen par $1,000 d'assurance pour cette période

$\left(\$3,452.05 \times \dfrac{\$1,000}{\$1,250,000}\right)$ 2.76164

Alinéa 6(4)b)

Montant de la ristourne pour surprime d'expérience pour cette période
($50,000 – $25,000) $ 25,000

Coût moyen de l'assurance selon l'alinéa 6(4)a) $ 2.76164

Montant à inclure dans le revenu de l'employé relativement à cette période
s'il n'a pas versé de prime

$\left(\dfrac{\$25,000 \times \$2.76164}{\$1,000}\right)$ $ 69.04

    (i) **Prime pour garantie totale —**

Alinéa 6(4)c)

Si l'employé a versé $50 à l'égard de sa garantie totale pour cette période,
la fraction déductible est alors de

$\left(\dfrac{\$50 \times \$25,000}{\$50,000}\right)$ $ 25.00

Montant à inclure dans le revenu de l'employé $ 44.04

    (ii) **Prime pour garantie complémentaire — à compter de l'année
    d'imposition 1974**

Si l'employé a versé $50 relativement à sa garantie complémentaire pour
cette période, il faut alors inclure dans son revenu
($69.04 – $50) $ 19.04

(B) Second calcul: période de garantie de $75,000

Alinéa 6(4)a)

Prime totale pour l'année d'assurance	$	8,000
Moins: ristourne pour surprime d'expérience	$	1,000
	$	7,000

Coût de la prime pour cette période

$\left(\$7,000 \times \dfrac{95}{365}\right)$ $1,821.92

Coût moyen par $1,000 d'assurance pour cette période

$\left(\dfrac{\$1,821.92 \times \$1,000}{\$1,250,000}\right)$ $ 1.4575

Alinéa 6(4)b)

Montant de la garantie complémentaire pour cette période $ 50,000

Coût moyen de l'assurance selon l'alinéa 6(4)a) $ 1.4575

Montant à inclure dans le revenu de l'employé à l'égard de cette période
s'il n'a pas versé de prime

$\left(\dfrac{\$50,000 \times \$1.4575}{\$1,000}\right)$ $ 72.88

    (i) **Prime pour garantie totale —**

Alinéa 6(4)c)

Si l'employé a payé $40 à l'égard de sa garantie totale pour cette période,
la fraction déductible est alors de

$$\left(\$40 \times \frac{\$50,000}{\$75,000} \right)$$ $ 26.66

Amount to be included in employee's income $ 46.22

    (ii) **Premium for Excess Coverage — 1974 and Subsequent Taxation Years**

If employee paid, say, $40 in respect of his excess coverage for this period, the amount to be included in his income is
($72.88 − $40) $ 32.88

Total amount to be included in employee's income, (calculations (A) and (B)) if his payments in both periods were in respect of his total average $ 90.26

Total amount to be included in employee's income, for 1974 and subsequent taxation years (calculations (A) and (B)) if his payments in both periods were in respect of his excess coverage $ 51.92

$$\left(\$40 \times \frac{\$50,000}{\$75,000}\right)$$ $ 26.66

Montant à inclure dans le revenu de l'employé $ 46.22

  (ii) **Prime pour garantie complémentaire à compter de l'année d'imposition 1974**

Si l'employé a payé $40 à l'égard de sa garantie complémentaire pour cette période, il faut alors inclure dans son revenu
($72.88 − $40) $ 32.88

Montant total à inclure dans le revenu de l'employé (calculs (A) et (B)) si, au cours de ces deux périodes, ses versements visaient la garantie totale. $ 90.26

Montant total à inclure dans le revenu de l'employé, pour 1974 et les années subséquentes (calculs (A) et (B)), si au cours des deux périodes, ses versements visaient une garantie complémentaire $ 51.92

REVENUE CANADA, TAXATION   REVENU CANADA, IMPÔT

INTERPRETATION **BULLETIN** D'INTERPRÉTATION

SUBJECT: **INCOME TAX ACT**
Meaning of "Private Health Services Plan"

OBJET: **LOI DE L'IMPÔT SUR LE REVENU**
Signification de «Régime privé d'assurance-maladie»

NO. IT-339R   DATE: June 1, 1983
REFERENCE: Paragraph 110(8)(a) (also subsection 110(6) and paragraph 6(1)(a))

Nº IT-339R   DATE: Le 1 juin 1983
RENVOI: Alinéa 110(8)a) (et le paragraphe 110(6) et l'alinéa 6(1)a))

This bulletin cancels and replaces IT-339 dated August 23, 1976. Current revisions are designated by vertical lines.

1. Paragraph 110(8)(a) defines a "private health services plan" for the purposes of paragraph 6(1)(a) and subsection 110(6) of the Act.

2. The contracts of insurance and medical or hospital care insurance plans referred to in subparagraphs 110(8)(a)(i) and (ii) include contracts or plans that are either in whole or in part in respect of dental care and expenses.

3. A private health services plan qualifying under subparagraph 110(8)(a)(i) or (ii) is a plan in the nature of insurance. In this respect the plan must contain the following basic elements:

    (i) an undertaking of one person,
    (ii) to indemnify another person,
    (iii) for an agreed consideration,
    (iv) from a loss or liability in respect of an event,
    (v) the happening of which is uncertain.

4. Coverage under the plan must be in respect of hospital care or expense or medical care or expense, which otherwise would have been deductible under paragraph 110(1)(c) read without reference to the 3% limitation.

5. If the agreed consideration is in the form of cash premiums, they usually relate closely to the coverage provided by the plan and are based on some method of computation involving actuarial or similar studies. Plans involving contracts of insurance in an arm's length situation are normally assumed to contain the basic elements outlined in 3 above.

6. A "cost plus" plan is where an employer contracts with a trusteed plan or insurance company for the provision of indemnification of employees' claims on defined risks. The employer promises to reimburse the cost of such claims plus an administration fee to the plan or

---

Le présent bulletin annule et remplace le Bulletin IT-339 du 23 août 1976. Les révisions sont indiquées par des traits verticaux.

1. L'alinéa 110(8)a) définit l'expression «régime privé d'assurance-maladie» aux fins de l'alinéa 6(1)a) et du paragraphe 110(6) de la Loi.

2. Les contrats d'assurance et les régimes d'assurance-soins médicaux ou d'assurance-hospitalisation dont il est fait mention aux sous-alinéas 110(8)a)(i) ou (ii) incluent les contrats ou les régimes qui couvrent en entier ou en partie les soins ou les frais dentaires.

3. Un régime privé d'assurance-maladie admissible en vertu des sous-alinéas 110(8)a)(i) ou (ii) est un régime d'assurance. À cet égard, le régime doit comprendre les éléments de base suivants:

    (i) l'engagement d'une personne
    (ii) d'indemniser une autre personne
    (iii) moyennant une contrepartie convenue
    (iv) par suite d'une perte subie ou d'une obligation contractée à l'égard d'un événement
    (v) dont l'éventualité est incertaine.

4. La protection en vertu du régime doit porter sur des soins ou frais hospitaliers ou sur des soins ou frais médicaux qui auraient été par ailleurs déductibles en vertu de l'alinéa 110(1)c), abstraction faite de la limite de 3%.

5. Si la contrepartie convenue prend la forme de primes en espèces, ces dernières correspondent habituellement étroitement à la protection offerte par le régime et sont établies selon une certaine méthode de calcul nécessitant des études actuarielles ou similaires. Les régimes comportant des contrats d'assurance dans une situation sans lien de dépendance sont habituellement présumés renfermer les éléments de base dont fait état le numéro 3 ci-dessus.

6. Un régime «à prix coûtant majoré» existe quand un employeur passe avec un régime fiduciaire ou une compagnie d'assurance un contrat prévoyant l'indemnisation des employés qui présentent des demandes à l'égard de risques définis. L'employeur s'engage à rembourser au régime ou à la compagnie

Published under the authority
of the Deputy Minister
of National Revenue for Taxation

Publié avec l'autorisation
du Sous-ministre
du Revenu National pour l'Impôt

Canadä

insurance company. The employee's contract of employment requires the employer to reimburse the plan or insurance company for proper claims (filed by the employee) paid, and a contract exists between the employee and the trusteed plan or insurance company in which the latter agrees to indemnify the employee for claims on the defined risks so long as the employment contract is in good standing. Provided that the risks to be indemnified are those described in subparagraph 110(8)(a)(i) or (ii), such a plan qualifies as a private health services plan.

7. Where an employer himself reimburses his employees for medical or hospital care or expenses, this may come within the definition of private health services plan. This is so where the employer is obligated under the employment contract to reimburse such expenses incurred by the employees or their dependants. The consideration given by the employee is considered to be the employee's convenants as found in the collective agreement or in the contract of service.

8. Medical and hospital insurance plans offered by Blue Cross and various life insurers, for example, are considered private health services plans within the meaning of subsection 110(8)(a)(i). In addition, the Group Supplementary Medical Insurance Plan covering federal government employees qualifies as a private health services plan under subparagraph 110(8)(a)(i). Therefore, payments made by federal government employees under that plan would be considered expenses deductible under paragraph 110(1)(c) pursuant to subsection 110(6).

9. Private health services plan premiums, contributions or other consideration paid for by the employer are not deemed to be medical expenses of the employee within the meaning of subsection 110(6), nor are they considered to be employee benefits under paragraph 6(1)(a). They are however, business outlays or expenses of the employer for purposes of paragraph 18(1)(a). On the other hand, where the contributions or premiums are paid by the individual, or paid by the employer on his behalf as a result of payroll deductions from his salary or wages, in respect of himself, his spouse and members of his household with whom he is connected by blood relationship, marriage or adoption, they are deductible by him as medical expenses under subparagraph 110(1)(c)(iii) by virtue of subsection 110(6). Medical expenses are discussed in detail in Information Circular 72-12R, "Insurance Premiums Allowed as Medical Expenses" and IT-225, "Medical Expenses".

d'assurance le coût de ces demandes plus des frais d'administration. Le contrat de travail de l'employé exige que l'employeur rembourse au régime ou à la compagnie d'assurance les indemnités justifiées (demandées par l'employé) qui sont versées, et un contrat existe entre l'employé et le régime fiduciaire ou la compagnie d'assurance en vertu duquel celui-ci ou celle-ci consent à indemniser l'employé pour des demandes présentées à l'égard de risques définis tant que le contrat d'emploi est valide. Pourvu que les risques à indemniser sont ceux décrits aux sous-alinéas 110(8)a)(i) ou (ii), un tel régime est admissible à titre de régime privé d'assurance-maladie.

7. La pratique d'un employeur de rembourser lui-même à ses employés des soins ou frais médicaux ou hospitaliers peut entrer dans la définition d'un régime privé d'assurance-maladie. Il en est ainsi d'un employeur qui est tenu, en vertu du contrat de travail, de rembourser de tels frais engagés par les employés ou leurs personnes à charge. La contrepartie de l'employé correspond en général à l'engagement de l'employé en vertu de la convention collective ou du contrat de louage de services.

8. Les régimes d'assurance-soins médicaux et d'assurance-hospitalisation offerts par la Croix bleue et divers assureurs sur la vie, par exemple, sont considérés comme des régimes privés d'assurance-maladie en vertu du sous-alinéa 110(8)a)(i). De plus, le Régime d'assurance collective médicale supplémentaire dont les employés du gouvernement fédéral peuvent bénéficier est admissible comme régime privé d'assurance-maladie en vertu du sous-alinéa 110(8)a)(i). Ainsi, les versements effectués par les employés du gouvernement fédéral à ce régime sont des frais déductibles en vertu de l'alinéa 110(1)c), selon le paragraphe 110(6).

9. Les primes, cotisations ou autres contreparties versées par l'employeur à un régime privé d'assurance-maladie ne sont pas réputées être des frais médicaux de l'employé au sens du paragraphe 110(6) et ne sont pas non plus considérées comme des avantages de l'employé en vertu de l'alinéa 6(1)a). Elles sont cependant considérées comme des débours ou dépenses d'entreprise de l'employeur aux fins de l'alinéa 18(1)a). D'autre part, quand les cotisations ou primes sont versées par le particulier; ou par l'employeur au nom du particulier au moyen de retenues sur son salaire, pour lui-même, son conjoint ou un membre de sa famille avec lequel il est lié par les liens du sang, du mariage ou de l'adoption, elles sont déductibles pour le particulier à titre de frais médicaux en vertu du sous-alinéa 110(1)c)(iii), conformément au paragraphe 110(6). Plus de détails sur les frais médicaux sont données dans la Circulaire d'information 72-12R, «Primes d'assurance admises à titre de frais médicaux» et dans le Bulletin d'interprétation IT-225, «Frais médicaux».

Revenue Canada   Revenu Canada
Taxation   Impôt

INTERPRETATION BULLETIN

SUBJECT: INCOME TAX ACT
            Wage Loss Replacement Plans

BULLETIN D'INTERPRÉTATION

OBJET: LOI DE L'IMPÔT SUR LE REVENU
          Régimes d'assurance-salaire

NO   IT-428   DATE: April 30, 1979

REFERENCE   Paragraph 6(1)(f) (also paragraph 6(1)(a) and section 19 of the Income Tax Application Rules, 1971)

Nº   IT-428   DATE: le 30 avril 1979

RENVOI   Alinéa 6(1)f) (également l'alinéa 6(1)a) de la Loi et l'article 19 des Règles de 1971 concernant l'application de l'impôt sur le revenu)

1. Paragraph 6(1)(f) provides that, for 1972 and subsequent taxation years, amounts received on a periodic basis by an employee or an ex-employee as compensation for loss of income from an office or employment, that were payable under a sickness, accident, disability or income maintenance insurance plan (in this bulletin referred to as a "wage loss replacement plan") to which the employer made a contribution, are to be included in income, but subject to a reduction as specified in that paragraph for contributions made by the employee to the plan after 1967. Before 1972, such amounts received by a taxpayer were not included in income.

2. Paragraph 6(1)(f) does not apply to a self-employed person inasmuch as any amount received by such person in the way of an income maintenance payment would not be compensation for loss of income from an office or employment. With regard to "overhead expense insurance" and "income insurance" of a self-employed person, see Interpretation Bulletin IT-223.

Exemption for Plans Established before June 19, 1971

3. Transitional provisions in section 19 of the Income Tax Application Rules, 1971 stipulate that amounts that would otherwise be included in income under paragraph 6(1)(f) are to be excluded if they were received pursuant to a plan that existed on June 18, 1971 and were in consequence of an event that occurred prior to 1974. Comments on these transitional provisions, particularly with regard to admissible and non-admissible changes in pre-June 19, 1971 plans, appear in IT-54. It is to be noted that, for 1974 and subsequent taxation years, the exemption in section 19 of the ITAR is applicable only if amounts received by a taxpayer are attributable to an event occurring before 1974. In this context, the word "event" has reference to the thing that caused the disability. In the case of an accident, for example, although the effect on the taxpayer's health may not have become noticeable or serious until 1974 or a later year, the "event" would have occurred before 1974 if the accident took place before 1974 and the later disability was directly attributable to the accident. Similarly, in the case of a degenerative disease such

1. Pour 1972 et les années d'imposition suivantes, l'alinéa 6(1)f) prévoit que toutes les sommes qu'un employé ou un ex-employé reçoit périodiquement à titre d'indemnité payable pour la perte de revenu d'une charge ou d'un emploi en vertu d'un régime d'assurance contre la maladie ou les accidents, d'un régime d'assurance invalidité et d'un régime d'assurance de sécurité du revenu (désigné dans le présent Bulletin par l'expression «régime d'assurance-salaire» auquel son employeur a contribué, doivent être incluses dans son revenu, sous réserve de la réduction prévue dans ledit alinéa pour les cotisations versées au régime par l'employé après 1967. Avant 1972, les contribuables ne devaient pas inclure dans leur revenu les sommes qu'ils recevaient à cet effet.

2. L'alinéa 6(1)f) ne s'applique pas aux contribuables qui travaillent à leur compte, car les sommes qu'ils reçoivent à titre de versement en vertu d'un régime d'assurance de sécurité du revenu ne constituent pas une indemnité pour perte de revenu d'une charge ou d'un emploi. En ce qui a trait aux «assurances-frais généraux» et aux «assurances-revenu» des contribuables qui travaillent à leur compte, se reporter au Bulletin d'interprétation IT-223.

Exonération pour les régimes créés avant le 19 juin 1971

3. En vertu des dispositions transitoires de l'article 19 des Règles de 1971 concernant l'application de l'impôt sur le revenu, tous les montants qui seraient par ailleurs inclus dans le revenu en vertu de l'alinéa 6(1)f) ne doivent pas l'être s'ils ont été reçus en vertu d'un régime qui existait le 18 juin 1971, à la suite d'un événement qui s'est produit avant 1974. Le Bulletin d'interprétation IT-54 traite de ces dispositions transitoires, notamment des modifications des conditions d'admissibilité pour les régimes établis avant le 19 juin 1971. Il faut noter que pour 1974 et les années d'imposition suivantes, l'exemption prévue à l'article 19 des RAIR ne vise que les montants que le contribuable a reçus à la suite d'un événement qui s'est produit avant 1974. Au sens du présent Bulletin, «événement» désigne la cause de l'invalidité. Si par exemple, il se produit un accident qui ne semble pas avoir de conséquences visibles ou graves sur la santé du contribuable jusqu'en 1974 ou ultérieurement, mais qu'il en résulte une invalidité par la suite, l'«événement» est réputé avoir eu lieu avant 1974 si l'accident qui est la cause directe de l'invalidité est survenu avant 1974. De même, dans le cas d'une maladie de dégénérescence comme la dystrophie

Published under the authority
of the Deputy Minister
of National Revenue for Taxation

Publié avec l'autorisation
du Sous-ministre
du Revenu national pour l'Impôt

as muscular dystrophy, the "event" is the onset of the disease however much later the incapacity occurs. On the other hand, a recurring disease, such as a seasonal allergy or chronic tonsillitis, would qualify as an "event" only for the particular period of one attack.

4. For an illustration of the calculations involved where both paragraph 6(1)(f) of the Act and section 19 of the ITAR apply to a particular taxpayer, in different taxation years, see 25 below.

Meaning of a "Wage Loss Replacement Plan"

5. In the Department's view, a plan to which paragraph 6(1)(f) applies is any arrangement, however it is styled, between an employer and employees, or between an employer and a group or association of employees, under which provision is made for indemnification of an employee, by means of benefits payable on a periodic basis, if an employee suffers a loss of employment income as a consequence of sickness, maternity or accident. This arrangement may be formal in nature, as evidenced by a contract negotiated between an employer and employees, or it may be informal, arising from an understanding on the part of the employees, that wage loss replacement benefits would be made available to them by the employer. Where the arrangement involves a contract of insurance with an insurance company, the insurance contract becomes part of the plan but does not constitute the plan itself.

6. Where it is apparent that a plan was instituted with the intention or for the purpose of providing wage loss replacement benefits, the assumption will be that it is a plan to which paragraph 6(1)(f) applies unless the contrary can be established. Such a plan will be considered to exist where, for example, payments under the plan are to commence only when sick leave credits are exhausted or where benefits are subject to reduction by the amount of any wages or wage loss replacement benefits payable under other plans. A supplementary unemployment benefit plan, as defined in subsection 145(1), is not considered to be a plan to which paragraph 6(1)(f) applies.

7. A plan for purposes of paragraph 6(1)(f) of the Act and section 19 of the ITAR must be an "insurance" plan. Those provisions are not applicable, therefore, to uninsured employee benefits such as continuing wage or salary payments based on sick leave debits, which payments are included in income under paragraph 6(1)(a). It is to be noted that, while a plan must involve insurance, it is not necessary that there be a contract of insurance with an insurance company. If, however, insurance is not provided by an insurance company, the plan must be one that is based on insurance principles, i.e., funds must be accumulated, normally in the hands of trustees or in a trust account, that are calculated to be sufficient to meet anticipated claims. If the arrangement merely consists of an unfunded contingency reserve on the part of the employer, it would not be an insurance plan.

musculaire, l'«événement» se produit dès l'apparition des premiers symptômes de la maladie, peu importe le moment où l'invalidité se manifeste vraiment. Par contre, dans le cas d'une maladie rechutante comme une allergie saisonnière ou une amygdalite chronique, l'«événement» ne désigne que le moment précis d'une attaque.

4. Vous trouverez au numéro 25 ci-dessous une illustration des calculs lorsque l'alinéa 6(1)f) de la Loi et l'article 19 des RAIR s'appliquent à un contribuable pour différentes années d'imposition.

Définition de «régime d'assurance-salaire»

5. Pour le Ministère, un régime visé par l'alinéa 6(1)f), quelle qu'en soit l'appellation, désigne toute entente conclue entre un employeur et ses employés ou un groupe ou une association d'employés qui prévoit l'indemnisation d'un employé pour la perte d'un revenu d'emploi par suite de maladie, de grossesse ou d'accident, au moyen de prestations payables périodiquement. Cette entente peut être officielle, comme un contrat négocié entre un employeur et ses employés, ou officieuse, comme une promesse de l'employeur de verser à ses employés des prestations d'assurance-salaire. Lorsque l'entente prévoit un contrat d'assurance avec une compagnie d'assurance, le contrat d'assurance fait partie du régime, mais ne constitue pas le régime proprement dit.

6. Lorsqu'il est évident qu'un régime a été établi dans l'intention ou dans le but de fournir des prestations d'assurance-salaire, il est présumé que l'alinéa 6(1)f) s'applique à ce régime, à moins que le contraire ne puisse être prouvé. Un tel régime est considéré exister lorsque, par exemple, les prestations en vertu du régime ne doivent commencer qu'après l'épuisement des congés de maladie ou lorsque les prestations peuvent être réduites du montant de tout salaire ou de toute prestation d'assurance-salaire payable en vertu d'autres régimes. L'alinéa 6(1)f) n'est pas réputé s'appliquer à un régime de prestations supplémentaires de chômage défini au paragraphe 145(1).

7. Aux fins de l'alinéa 6(1)f) de la Loi et de l'article 19 des RAIR, un régime doit être un régime d'«assurance». Par conséquent, ces dispositions ne s'appliquent pas aux prestations non assurées d'employés, comme des paiements de continuation du salaire ou du traitement en fonction du solde de congés de maladie qui sont inclus dans le revenu en vertu de l'alinéa 6(1)a). Il faut noter qu'il ne doit pas y avoir obligatoirement un contrat d'assurance avec une compagnie d'assurance même si le régime doit comporter une assurance. Cependant, si l'assurance n'est pas garantie par une compagnie d'assurance, le régime doit être fondé sur les mêmes principes qu'une assurance, c'est-à-dire que les fonds doivent être accumulés, en général entre les mains de fiduciaires ou dans un compte en fiducie, et ils doivent être suffisants pour répondre aux demandes d'indemnité prévues. Ainsi, si l'entente consiste simplement en une réserve sans capitalisation pour éventualités de la part de l'employeur, elle ne constitue pas un régime d'assurance.

8. An employer may contribute to separate plans for different classes or groups of employees. For example, there may be one plan for clerical staff and another plan for administrative staff. Each plan will be recognized as a separate plan. In other circumstances, an employer may have one plan that provides for short-term sickness benefits and another plan that provides for long-term disability benefits. Each such plan normally would be considered a separate plan for all purposes but, if desired, they may be treated as one plan provided they comply with the following conditions:

(a) the same classes of employees are entitled to participate in both plans, and

(b) the premiums or other cost of each plan is shared in the same ratio by the employer and the employees.

9. An association of employers, or a health and welfare trust that is organized and managed by or on behalf of both employers and employees in a certain industry, may establish a plan with an insurer that is available to all employer-members. In these circumstances, if there is one insurance contract between the insurer and the association of employers or the health and welfare trust and the contract was entered into after June 19, 1971, there is considered to be one plan. Where employees contribute to the cost of benefits provided by a health and welfare trust, see paragraph 6 of IT-85R regarding the amount that may qualify as an employee's contribution for purposes of subparagraph 6(1)(f)(v). For plans that existed prior to June 19, 1971 see paragraph 7 of IT-54.

10. Where the nature of employment in a particular industry is such that it is usual for employees to change employers frequently (e.g. the construction industry) and the continuity of wage loss replacement benefits can be assured only if such benefits are provided under a plan administered by a union or a similar association of employees rather than directly by the various employers, the arrangement between the participating employers and the organization representing the employees is viewed as a single wage loss replacement plan.

Lump-sum Payments

11. If a lump-sum payment is made in lieu of periodic payments, that amount will be considered to be income under paragraph 6(1)(f).

12. Some contracts of employment may provide for payment of periodic benefits to employees in respect of loss of income due to disability and may also provide that employees will receive a lump-sum payment on retirement, resignation or death based on the value of unused sick leave credits accumulated under that plan. Even though these separate arrangements may be jointly funded by employer-employee contributions, it is the position of the Department that such lump-sum payments are not a periodic payment under a wage loss replacement plan to which paragraph 6(1)(f) applies but are taxable in the employee's hands by subsections 5(1) and 6(3) as remuneration received by them pursuant to their contract of

8. Un employeur peut contribuer à des régimes distincts pour divers groupes ou catégories d'employés. Par exemple, il peut y avoir un régime pour le personnel de bureau et un autre régime pour le personnel administratif. Chaque régime constitue un régime distinct. Par ailleurs, un employeur peut souscrire à un régime de prestations pour invalidité de courte durée et à un autre régime de prestations pour invalidité de longue durée. A toutes fins utiles, chacun de ces régimes constitue normalement un régime distinct, mais, toutefois, si l'employeur le désire, ils peuvent être considérés comme un seul régime s'ils remplissent les conditions suivantes:

a) les mêmes catégories d'employés peuvent participer aux deux régimes et

b) les primes ou tout autre coût afférent à chaque régime sont engagés à parts égales par l'employeur et les employés.

9. Une association d'employeurs ou une fiducie de santé et d'assistance sociale mise sur pied et gérée par les employeurs et les employés d'une entreprise donnée peut établir avec un assureur un régime à l'intention de tous les employeurs membres. En pareil cas, s'il y a un contrat d'assurance entre l'assureur et l'association d'employeurs ou la fiducie de santé et d'assistance sociale et si ce contrat a été signé après le 19 juin 1971, il est réputé n'y avoir qu'un régime. Lorsque les employés versent une partie du coût des prestations fournies par une fiducie de santé et d'assistance sociale, se reporter au numéro 6 du IT-85R pour calculer le montant admissible à titre de cotisation de l'employé aux fins du sous-alinéa 6(1)f)(v). Pour les régimes qui existaient avant le 19 juin 1971, se reporter au numéro 7 du IT-54.

10. Lorsque les employés d'une industrie donnée sont appelés, de par la nature de leur emploi, à changer souvent d'employeur (par ex., dans l'industrie de la construction) et que les prestations d'assurance-salaire ne peuvent continuer d'être versées que si elles sont fournies en vertu d'un régime régi par un syndicat ou une association semblable d'employés plutôt que par les divers employeurs eux-mêmes, l'entente conclue entre les employeurs participants et l'organisme qui représente les employés est considérée comme un régime unique d'assurance-salaire.

Paiements forfaitaires

11. Le montant du paiement forfaitaire sera considéré comme un revenu en vertu de l'alinéa 6(1)f) s'il remplace des versements périodiques.

12. Certains contrats d'emploi prévoient le versement de prestations périodiques aux employés qui subissent une perte de revenu par suite d'une invalidité, ainsi que le versement d'une somme forfaitaire au moment de la retraite, de la démission ou du décès de ces employés. Ce paiement forfaitaire est établi en fonction de la valeur du solde de crédits de congé de maladie accumulés en vertu de ce régime. Même si les employés et l'employeur peuvent verser conjointement des contributions aux régimes établis en vertu de ces ententes distinctes, le Ministère estime que de tels paiements forfaitaires ne constituent pas des paiements périodiques en vertu d'un régime d'assurance-salaire auquel l'alinéa 6(1)f) s'applique, et qu'ils sont imposables comme revenu des employés en vertu des paragraphes 5(1)

employment. To the extent that a part of the lump sum payment has been funded by employee contributions not deducted by the employee under subparagraph 6(1)(f)(v) in computing the portion of amounts taxable under paragraph 6(1)(f), the accumulated employee contributions in respect thereof (but not any interest credited thereon) would represent a return of capital to employees and need not be included as part of the taxable lump sum payment.

Employee's Contribution

13. Employee contributions that are deductible under subparagraph 6(1)(f)(v), are restricted to those that were made to the particular plan from which the benefits were received. Thus, if an employee changes employment and becomes a beneficiary under the plans of the new employer, the employee may not deduct the contributions made during the previous employment from benefits received from the new employer's plan. For this purpose, a change in employment is not considered to take place where an unincorporated business is incorporated or where there has been a merger or amalgamation. Also, the continuity of an existing plan is generally not affected by internal alterations in the plan, such as a change in the insurer or an improvement in benefits. However, for purposes of section 19 of ITAR, an increase in benefits after June 18, 1971, in a pre-June 19, 1971 plan may be viewed as the creation of a new plan as indicated in paragraph 4 of IT-54. On the other hand, where an employee, because of a promotion or job reclassification, is moved from one of his employer's plans to another, such as a move from the "general" plan to the "executive" plan, contributions to the former plan would not be deductible in respect of benefits received from the latter plan.

Employer's Contributions

14. For benefits received by an employee under a wage loss replacement plan to be subject to tax in his hands under paragraph 6(1)(f), the plan must be one to which the employer has made a contribution out of his own funds. An employer does not make such a contribution to a plan if he merely deducts an amount from an employee's gross salary or wages and remits the amount on the employee's behalf to an insurer. In these circumstances, the employee's remuneration for tax purposes is not reduced by the amount withheld and remitted by the employer to the insurer. Where the employer has made an actual contribution to a plan, paragraph 6(1)(a) provides that it is not to be included in the income of the employees if the plan is a "group sickness or accident insurance plan". It is considered that this exemption in paragraph 6(1)(a) applies to any of the three types of plans mentioned in paragraph 6(1)(f), provided that they are group plans.

15. If an employer should have a plan that is in part a wage loss replacement plan and in part a plan that provides for other types of benefits, the employer must be prepared

et 6(3) à titre de rémunération reçue conformément à leur contrat d'emploi. Dans la mesure où une partie du paiement forfaitaire a été réglée au moyen des cotisations que l'employé a versées et qu'il n'a pas déduites, en vertu du sous-alinéa 6(1)f)(v), lors du calcul de la partie des sommes imposables en vertu de l'alinéa 6(1)f), les contributions accumulées de l'employé à cet égard (à l'exclusion des intérêts versés sur celles-ci) constitueraient un remboursement de capital aux employés et de ce fait, ne doivent pas être incluses à titre de partie du paiement forfaitaire imposable.

Cotisations versées par l'employé

13. Seules les cotisations que l'employé a versées au régime donné d'où proviennent les prestations sont déductibles en vertu du sous-alinéa 6(1)f)(v). Par conséquent, si un employé change d'emploi et devient bénéficiaire en vertu des régimes du nouvel employeur, l'employé ne peut pas déduire les cotisations qu'il a versées au cours de l'emploi précédent des prestations reçues du régime du nouvel employeur. A cet effet, il n'est pas réputé y avoir changement d'emploi lorsqu'une entreprise non constituée en corporation se constitue en corporation ou lorsqu'il y a fusion ou concentration par absorption. De plus, la continuité d'un régime existant n'est généralement pas touchée par des modifications apportées à la structure interne du régime (par ex., changement d'assureur ou augmentation des prestations). Cependant, aux fins de l'article 19 des RAIR, une augmentation des prestations après le 18 juin 1971, d'un régime établi avant le 19 juin 1971, peut être réputée entraîner la création d'un nouveau régime comme il est mentionné au numéro 4 du IT-54. Par contre, lorsqu'un employé est transféré d'un régime de son employeur à un autre régime de celui-ci par suite d'une promotion ou d'une reclassification de son poste (par ex., s'il passe du régime «général» au régime «administratif»), les cotisations qu'il a versées au premier régime ne sont pas déductibles des prestations qu'il a reçues du dernier régime.

Contributions de l'employeur

14. Pour que les prestations qu'un employé reçoit en vertu d'un régime d'assurance-salaire soient imposables entre ses mains en vertu de l'alinéa 6(1)f), l'employeur doit avoir versé des contributions au régime en question sur ses propres fonds. Un employeur ne contribue pas ainsi à un régime s'il retient simplement un montant à cet effet du salaire ou du traitement brut d'un employé et s'il verse ensuite ce montant au nom de l'employé à un assureur. En pareil cas, le montant que retient et verse l'employeur à l'assureur n'est pas déduit de la rémunération de l'employé aux fins de l'impôt. Lorsque l'employeur a vraiment contribué au régime, l'alinéa 6(1)a) précise que cette contribution ne doit pas être incluse dans le revenu des employés s'il s'agit d'un «régime d'assurance collective contre la maladie ou les accidents». L'exemption prévue à l'alinéa 6(1)a) s'applique aux trois genres de régimes mentionnés à l'alinéa 6(1)f), à condition qu'il s'agisse de régimes collectifs.

15. Si un employeur souscrit à un régime combiné d'assurance-salaire et de prestations d'autres genres, il doit être en mesure de préciser la fraction des primes ou de toute autre

to identify that part of any premiums paid by him, or other contribution by him to the plan, that relates to the other types of benefits included in the plan and, similarly, the part of the employees' contributions, if any, that relate to the wage loss replacement part of the plan. This information is required to determine whether the wage loss replacement plan is one to which the employer has contributed and the relevant amount of an employee's contribution for purposes of subparagraph 6(1)(f)(v).

Employee Pay-All Plans

16. An employee-pay-all plan is a plan the entire premium cost of which is paid by one or more employees. Except as indicated under 21 below, benefits out of such a plan are not taxable even if they are paid in consequence of an event occurring after 1973, because an employee-pay-all plan is not a plan within the meaning of paragraph 6(1)(f).

17. It is a question of fact whether or not an employee-pay-all plan exists and the onus is generally on the employer to prove the existence of such a plan. It should be emphasized that the Department will not accept a retroactive change to the tax status of a plan. For example, an employer cannot change the tax status of a plan by adding at year end to employees' income the employer contributions to a wage loss replacement plan that would normally be considered to be non-taxable benefits. On the other hand, where an employee-pay-all plan does, in fact, exist and it provides for the employer to pay the employee's premiums to the plan and to account for them in the manner of wages or salary, the result is as though the premiums had been withheld from the employee's wages or salary. That is, the plan maintains its status as an employee-pay-all plan if the plan provided for such an arrangement at the time the payment was made.

18. If, under a wage loss replacement plan, the employer makes contributions for some employees, but not all, the plan will not be considered to be an employee-pay-all plan even for those employees who must make all contributions themselves. It is the Department's view that all payments out of a wage loss replacement plan to which the employer has contributed are subject to the provisions of paragraph 6(1)(f) regardless of the fact that the employer's contributions may be on account of specific employees only.

19. Where the terms of a plan clearly establish that it is intended to be an employee-pay-all plan, the plan will be recognized as such even though the employer makes a contribution to it on behalf of an employee during an elimination period (i.e. the period after the disability but before the first payment from the plan becomes due). During this period normally there would be no salary or wages from which the contribution could be deducted. Any amount so contributed by an employer should be reported as remuneration of the employee on whose behalf it was contributed in order to maintain the employee-pay-all character of the plan.

contribution versées par lui pour les autres genres de prestations du régime, et, de façon semblable, la fraction des contributions des employés, s'il y a lieu, pour la partie assurance-salaire du régime. Ces renseignements sont nécessaires afin de déterminer si l'employeur a effectivement contribué au régime d'assurance-salaire, ainsi que le montant exact des cotisations versées par les employés aux fins du sous-alinéa 6(1)f)(v).

Régimes financés en totalité par les employés

16. Un régime financé en totalité par les employés est un régime dont toutes les primes sont payées par un ou plusieurs employés. Sous réserve de ce qui est mentionné au numéro 21 ci-dessous, les prestations tirées d'un régime de ce genre sont exonérées d'impôt même si elles sont payées à la suite d'un événement survenu après 1973, parce qu'un régime financé en totalité par les employés n'est pas un régime au sens de l'alinéa 6(1)f).

17. L'existence d'un régime financé en totalité par les employés est une question de fait et il revient en général à l'employeur de prouver l'existence d'un tel régime. Il faut préciser que le Ministère n'acceptera pas que le statut fiscal d'un régime soit modifié avec un effet rétroactif. Par exemple, un employeur ne peut pas modifier le statut fiscal d'un régime en ajoutant au revenu de l'employé à la fin de l'année les contributions de l'employeur à un régime d'assurance-salaire qui sont normalement réputées constituer des avantages non imposables. Par contre, lorsqu'un régime financé en totalité par les employés existe effectivement et qu'en vertu de ce régime, l'employeur doit verser les primes de l'employé au régime et les traiter comme salaire ou traitement, le résultat est le même que si les primes avaient été retenues du salaire ou du traitement de l'employé. En d'autres termes, le régime conserve son statut financé en totalité par les employés à condition qu'il comporte une disposition à cet effet au moment du paiement.

18. Si un employeur verse des contributions pour certains employés seulement, en vertu d'un régime d'assurance-salaire, le régime en question n'est pas réputé être un régime financé en totalité par les employés, même pour les employés qui versent toutes les cotisations eux-mêmes. Le Ministère estime que tous les paiements en vertu d'un régime d'assurance-salaire auquel l'employeur a contribué sont assujettis aux dispositions de l'alinéa 6(1)f), même si l'employeur n'a contribué que pour quelques employés seulement.

19. Lorsqu'il est clairement précisé dans les conditions du régime qu'il s'agit d'un régime financé en totalité par les employés, le régime est considéré comme tel, même si l'employeur y contribue au nom d'un employé au cours d'un délai de carence (c'est-à-dire la période qui s'écoule entre le commencement de l'invalidité et la date à laquelle le premier paiement en vertu du régime est exigible). Au cours de cette période, l'employé ne touche généralement aucun salaire ni traitement; les cotisations ne peuvent donc être retenues à la source. Le montant versé par l'employeur doit être déclaré à titre de rémunération de l'employé pour lequel le versement a été fait afin que le régime puisse conserver son titre de régime financé en totalité par les employés.

20. Where an employer pays, on behalf of an employee, the premium under a non-group plan that is
    (a) a sickness or accident insurance plan,
    (b) a disability insurance plan, or
    (c) an income maintenance insurance plan,
the payment of the premium is regarded as a taxable benefit to the employee. The payment by the employer is not viewed as a "contribution" by the employer under the plan, and paragraph 6(1)(f) does not apply to subject to tax in the employee's hands any benefits received by him pursuant to the plan.

21. Whether or not the benefits an employee receives under a plan are required to be included in his income is governed both by the type of plan in effect at the time of the event that gave rise to them and any changes in the plan subsequent to that time. When a pre-June 19, 1971 plan, or an employee-pay-all plan, is changed and becomes a new taxable plan, an employee who was receiving benefits at the time of the change may continue to receive them tax-free thereafter but only in the amount and for the period specified in the plan as it was before the change. Where the new taxable plan provides any increase in benefits, whether by increases in amounts or through extension of the benefit period, the additional benefits must be included in income since they flow from the new taxable plan. Where an employee is receiving benefits under a taxable plan at a time when it is converted to a new employee-pay-all plan, the benefits he continues to receive subsequent to the date of conversion, to the extent that they were provided for in the old plan, will remain of an income nature because they continue to flow from the old taxable plan.

Claimant's Survivors

22. If the payment of wage loss replacement benefits should continue after the death of an employee who was receiving such benefits, paragraph 6(1)(f) is not applicable to such benefits paid to the widow or other dependent for the reason that the amounts received do not relate to a loss of income from an office or employment of the recipient. Such payments, however, may be viewed as being received in recognition of the deceased employee's service in an office or employment and be included in income as a death benefit if they exceed the exemption provided in subsection 248(1).

Information Returns

23. Paragraph 200(2)(f) of the Income Tax Regulations stipulates that every person who makes payments pursuant to a wage loss replacement plan is required to file Form T4A information return. The law does not require that income tax be deducted from such payments.

U.I.C. Employee Premium Rebate

24. A wage loss replacement plan may qualify the employer for a reduction in unemployment insurance premiums under subsection 64(4) of the Unemployment

20. Lorsqu'un employeur verse, au nom de l'employé, la prime exigée par un régime non collectif
    a) d'assurance contre la maladie ou les accidents,
    b) d'assurance invalidité ou
    c) d'assurance de sécurité du revenu,
la prime en question est considérée comme un avantage imposable pour l'employé. Le paiement effectué par l'employeur n'est pas considéré comme une «contribution» de celui-ci en vertu du régime et l'alinéa 6(1)f) ne s'applique pas afin d'imposer l'employé sur tout avantage reçu par celui-ci aux termes du régime.

21. Le fait que les prestations qu'un employé reçoit en vertu d'un régime doivent être incluses dans son revenu dépend à la fois du genre de régime en vigueur au moment où l'événement qui a donné lieu à leur paiement s'est produit et de toutes les modifications apportées par la suite au régime. Lorsqu'un régime établi avant le 19 juin 1971 ou un régime financé en totalité par les employés est modifié et devient un nouveau régime imposable, un employé qui recevait des prestations au moment de la modification pourra continuer de recevoir ses prestations exonérées d'impôt, compte tenu du montant et de la durée précisés dans l'ancien régime. Lorsque le nouveau régime imposable prévoit une augmentation des prestations, qu'il s'agisse d'une augmentation du montant des prestations ou d'une prolongation de la période de prestations, les prestations supplémentaires doivent être incluses dans le revenu car elles proviennent du nouveau régime imposable. Lorsqu'un employé reçoit des prestations en vertu d'un régime imposable au moment où ce régime est converti en un régime financé en totalité par les employés, les prestations qu'il continue de recevoir à compter de la date de conversion demeureront imposables car elles continuent de provenir de l'ancien régime imposable.

Survivants

22. Si des prestations d'assurance-salaire continuent d'être versées après le décès d'un employé qui recevait de telles prestations, l'alinéa 6(1)f) ne s'applique pas aux prestations versées au conjoint ou à toute autre personne à charge car les sommes versées ne comblent pas une perte de revenu d'une charge ou d'un emploi du bénéficiaire. Cependant, ces sommes peuvent être réputées être versées à titre de reconnaissance des services fournis par l'employé décédé dans le cadre d'une charge ou d'un emploi et peuvent être de ce fait incluses dans le revenu à titre de prestations versées au décès si leur montant est supérieur à l'exemption prévue au paragraphe 248(1).

Déclarations de renseignements

23. En vertu de l'alinéa 200(2)f) des Règlements de l'impôt sur le revenu, toute personne qui effectue des paiements en vertu d'un régime d'assurance-salaire est tenue de produire une déclaration de renseignements T4A. Les Règlements n'exigent toutefois pas qu'un impôt sur le revenu soit déduit de ces paiements.

Rabais de primes d'A.-C. des employés

24. Tout employeur qui souscrit à un régime d'assurance-salaire peut avoir droit à une réduction de ses primes d'assurance-chômage en vertu du paragraphe 64(4) de la Loi de

Insurance Act, 1971: This subsection also provides that five-twelfths of any such reduction must be used by the employer for the benefit of his employees. The benefit may be conferred directly by the employer, indirectly through an employees health and welfare trust or in any other manner, but it will only be tax-free in an employee's hands if it is conferred in the form of a benefit specifically exempt from taxation by paragraph 6(1)(a).

1971 sur l'assurance-chômage. Il est également précisé à ce paragraphe que les cinq douzièmes de cette réduction doivent être utilisés par l'employeur au bénéfice de ses employés. L'avantage peut être accordé directement, par l'employeur, indirectement par l'intermédiaire d'une fiducie de santé et d'assistance sociale des employés ou de toute autre façon; l'employé ne sera toutefois exonéré d'impôt à l'égard de cet avantage que si il est accordé sous forme de prestation expressément exonérée d'impôt en vertu de l'alinéa 6(1)a).

Computation of Benefit

25. The following is an example of the computation of the amount of payments received under a wage loss replacement plan that is included in income pursuant to paragraph 6(1)(f):

Assume:

(a) Employee's contributions (in addition to employer's contributions)

Year	Amounts	Cumulative Balance
1968-71	$ 110 per annum	$ 440
1972	120	560
1973	140	700
1974	140	840
1975	140	980
1976	140	1120
1977	160	1280

(b) Payments received

1972	$ 200	$ 200
1973	300	500
1974	240	740
1975	1000	1740
1976	100	1840
1977	1000	2840

(c) The plan was in existence prior to June 19, 1971 and remains unchanged.

(d) The payments received out of the plan in 1974, 1975, 1976 and 1977 are as a result of events occurring after 1973.

Amount Included in Income:
1972 and 1973 -
  none of the payments received are income because of section 19 of the ITAR

1974 - lesser of:

a) payments received in 1974		$ 240
b) aggregate of payments received after 1971	$ 740	

less:

aggregate of contributions made after 1967	840	NIL
amount to be included under paragraph 6(1)(f)		NIL

Calcul des prestations

25. Voici un exemple de la façon de calculer la fraction des prestations reçues en vertu d'un régime d'assurance-salaire à inclure dans le revenu conformément à l'alinéa 6(1)f).

Supposition:

a) Cotisations versées par l'employé (en plus de la contribution de l'employeur)

Année	Montants	Solde cumulatif
1968-71	$ 110 par année	$ 440
1972	120	560
1973	140	700
1974	140	840
1975	140	980
1976	140	1120
1977	160	1280

b) Paiements reçus

1972	$ 200	$ 200
1973	300	500
1974	240	740
1975	1000	1740
1976	100	1840
1977	1000	2840

c) Le régime existait avant le 19 juin 1971 et n'a pas été modifié.

d) Les paiements reçus du régime en 1974, 1975, 1976 et 1977 font suite à un événement qui s'est produit après 1973.

Montants à inclure dans le revenu:
1972 et 1973:
  aucun des paiements reçus ne constitue un revenu en raison de l'article 19 des RAIR.

1974 - le moins élevé:

a) des paiements reçus en 1974;		$ 240
b) du total des paiements reçus après 1971	$ 740	

moins:

total des cotisations versées après 1967	840	NÉANT
montant à inclure en vertu de l'alinéa 6(1)f)		NÉANT

1975 - lesser of:
  a) payments received in 1975 $1000
  b) aggregate of payments
  received after 1971 $1740
less:
  aggregate of contributions
  made after 1967   980   760
  amount to be included under
  paragraph 6(1)(f) $ 760

1976 - lesser of:
  a) payments received in 1976 $ 100
  b) payments received in 1976 $ 100
less:
  contributions made in 1976   140   NIL
  amount to be included under
  paragraph 6(1)(f)   NIL

1977 - lesser of:
  a) payments received in 1977 $1000

  b) payments received since
  the most recent year during
  which a benefit was taxable
  under this provision (1975) $1100
less:
  contributions made
  since 1975   300   800
  amount to be included under
  paragraph 6(1)(f) $ 800

1975 - le moins élevé:
  a) des paiements reçus en 1975; $1000
  b) du total des paiements reçus
  après 1971 $1740
moins:
  total des cotisations versées après
  1967   980   760
  montant à inclure en vertu de
  l'alinéa 6(1)f) $ 760

1976 - le moins élevé:
  a) des paiements reçus en 1976; $ 100
  b) des paiements reçus en 1976 $ 100
moins:
  cotisations versées en 1976   140   NÉANT
  montant à inclure en vertu de
  l'alinéa 6(1)f)   NÉANT

1977 - le moins élevé:
  a) des paiements reçus en 1977
  et $1000
  b) des paiements reçus depuis la
  dernière année au cours de laquelle
  une prestation était imposable en
  vertu de cette disposition (1975) $1100
moins:
  cotisations versées depuis 1975   300   800
  montant à inclure en vertu de
  l'alinéa 6(1)f) $ 800

Revenue Canada   Revenu Canada
Taxation   Impôt

INTERPRETATION BULLETIN	BULLETIN D'INTERPRÉTATION

SUBJECT: **SPECIAL RELEASE**
Employee Fringe Benefits

OBJET: **COMMUNIQUÉ SPÉCIAL**
Avantages sociaux des employés

NO.: **IT-470R**   DATE: December 11, 1989
REFERENCE: Paragraph 6(1)(a) (also sections 118.8 and 118.9, subsections 5(1), 6(3), 6(6), 118.5(1) and 248(1), paragraph 18(1)(l) and subparagraph 6(1)(b)(ix))

Nº: **IT-470R**   DATE: le 11 décembre 1989
RENVOI: L'alinéa 6(1)a) (également les articles 118.8 et 118.9, les paragraphes 5(1), 6(3), 6(6), 118.5(1) et 248(1), l'alinéa 18(1)l) et le sous-alinéa 6(1)b)(ix))

Tax Reform

This Special Release includes comments on amendments to the Act resulting from Tax Reform.

Application

This Special Release revises IT-470R dated April 8, 1988. The changes in this release are effective for 1988 and subsequent taxation years except as otherwise stated.

Bulletin Revisions

1. Paragraph 8 and its heading are cancelled and replaced by the following:

"Personal Use of Employer's Motor Vehicle

The current version of IT-63 should be consulted."

2. Paragraph 14 is amended by adding the following sentence:

"Where an employer does not control the credits accumulated in a frequent flyer program by an employee while travelling on employer-paid business trips, the comments in 3 above will not apply and it will be the responsibility of the employee to determine and include in income the fair market value of any benefits received or enjoyed."

3. The second from last sentence of paragraph 21 is deleted and replaced by the following sentence:

"To the extent that tuition fees paid by the employer for the employee's child are, by virtue of subparagraph 6(1)(b)(ix) not included in the employee's income, they may not be used in determining a tax credit for tuition fees (see the current version of IT-516)."

4. Paragraph 22 is cancelled and replaced by the following:

"22. In computing tax payable, a student may be eligible for a non-refundable federal tax credit under subsection 118.5(1) in respect of tuition fees paid by or on behalf of the student (or the fair market value of free tuition provided to the student to the extent that it

Réforme fiscale

Le présent communiqué spécial porte sur les modifications apportées à la Loi par suite de la réforme fiscale.

Application

Ce communiqué spécial modifie le IT-470R du 8 avril 1988. Les modifications que renferme ce communiqué s'appliquent à 1988 et aux années d'imposition subséquentes, sauf indication contraire.

Révisions du bulletin

1. Le numéro 8 et son titre sont annulés et remplacés par ce qui suit :

«Utilisation à des fins personnelles d'un véhicule à moteur de l'employeur

Veuillez consulter la dernière version du IT-63.»

2. Le numéro 14 est modifié par l'ajout des phrases suivantes :

«Lorsque l'employeur ne contrôle pas le nombre de crédits que l'employé accumule au programme passagers assidus grâce à des voyages d'affaires payés par son employeur, les observations du numéro 3 ci-dessus ne s'appliquent pas. L'employé aura la responsabilité de déterminer la juste valeur marchande de tous les avantages qu'il a reçus ou dont il a joui et de les inclure dans son revenu.»

3. L'avant-dernière phrase du numéro 21 est supprimée et remplacée par la phrase suivante :

«Dans la mesure où les frais de scolarité payés par l'employeur pour l'enfant de l'employé sont exclus du revenu de l'employé en vertu du sous-alinéa 6(1)b)(ix), ces frais ne peuvent pas servir à calculer un crédit d'impôt pour frais de scolarité (voir la dernière version du IT-516).»

4. Le numéro 22 est annulé et remplacé par ce qui suit :

«22. Dans le calcul de l'impôt à payer, un étudiant peut demander un crédit d'impôt fédéral non remboursable en vertu du paragraphe 118.5(1) pour les frais de scolarité versés par l'étudiant ou en son nom (ou la juste valeur marchande de la scolarité gratuite fournie à l'étudiant si elle est déclarée comme avantage imposable). Le conjoint de

Published under the authority
of the Deputy Minister
of National Revenue for Taxation

Publié avec l'autorisation
du Sous-ministre
du Revenu national pour l'Impôt

Canadä

is reported as a taxable benefit). Any unused portion of such a credit (to a maximum of $600) may be transferred to, and claimed as a tax credit by, the student's spouse under section 118.8, or the student's parent or grandparent under subsection 118.9(1) (see the current version of IT-516). For the tax implications of scholarships, fellowships, bursaries, prizes and research grants, see the current version of IT-75."

5. The last sentence of paragraph 23 is deleted since reimbursements are no longer made under the Government's Assistance Program — Workers Metric Tools.

6. Paragraph 26 and its heading are cancelled and replaced by the following:

"Financial Counselling and Income Tax Return Preparation

26. Financial counselling services or income tax return preparation provided directly (for 1990 and subsequent taxation years) or indirectly by an employer normally produce a taxable benefit to the employee who receives the benefit. However, financial counselling services in respect of the re-employment or the retirement of an employee will not result in a taxable benefit to the employee (see 46 below)."

7. Paragraph 40 is cancelled and replaced by the following:

"40. Benefits provided to an employee under a private health services plan are not subject to tax in the employee's hands. "Private health services plan" is defined in subsection 248(1). (See also the current version of IT-339, "Meaning of Private Health Services Plan" and IT-85, "Health and Welfare Trusts for Employees".)"

8. The following heading and paragraph is added after paragraph 45:

"Employee Counselling Services

46. In view of the proposed amendment to paragraph 6(1)(a) of the Income Tax Act in Bill C-28, the Department will not include in income, commencing with the 1988 taxation year, any benefit derived by an employee from counselling services provided or paid for by the employer in respect of
(a) the mental or physical health of the employee or an individual related to the employee but not including a benefit attributable to an outlay or expense to which paragraph 18(1)(l) applies,
(b) the re-employment or retirement of the employee.
The amendment will apply to such services as tobacco, drug or alcohol counselling, stress management counselling, and job placement and retirement counselling."

l'étudiant, en vertu de l'article 118.8, ou le père, la mère, le grand-père ou la grand-mère de l'étudiant, en vertu du paragraphe 118.9(1), peut demander que lui soit transférée toute partie inutilisée du crédit d'impôt pour frais de scolarité (jusqu'à concurrence de 600 $) et la demander comme crédit d'impôt (voir la dernière version du IT-516). Pour ce qui est des conséquences fiscales des bourses d'études, des bourses de perfectionnement (fellowships), des récompenses et des subventions de recherche, veuillez vous reporter à la dernière version du IT-75.»

5. La dernière phrase du numéro 23 est supprimée, car les remboursements ne sont plus effectués en vertu du Programme d'assistance — Outils métriques des ouvriers.

6. Le numéro 26 et son titre sont annulés et remplacés par ce qui suit :

«Conseils financiers et établissement de la déclaration de revenus

26. Les services de conseils financiers ou d'établissement de la déclaration de revenus fournis directement (pour 1990 et les années d'imposition subséquentes) ou indirectement par l'employeur apportent normalement un avantage imposable à l'employé. Toutefois, les services de conseil financiers offerts dans le cas du réemploi ou de la mise à la retraite d'un employé n'apportent pas d'avantage imposable à l'employé (voir le numéro 46 ci-dessous).»

7. Le numéro 40 est annulé et remplacé par ce qui suit :

«40. Les avantages dont bénéficie un employé en vertu d'un régime privé d'assurance-maladie ne sont pas imposables entre les mains de l'employé. La définition de «régime privé d'assurance-maladie» se trouve au paragraphe 248(1). (Consultez aussi la dernière version du IT-339, «Signification de Régime privé d'assurance-maladie», et du IT-85, «Fiducie de santé et de bien-être au bénéfice d'employés»).»

8. Le titre et le numéro suivants sont ajoutés à la suite du numéro 45 :

«Services de conseils financiers pour les employés

46. Compte tenu du projet de modification de l'alinéa 6(1)a) de la Loi de l'impôt sur le revenu, contenu dans le Projet de loi C-28, le Ministère n'inclura pas dans le revenu, à compter de l'année d'imposition 1988, les avantages que retire un employé des services de conseil fournis ou payés par son employeur concernant
a) la santé physique ou mentale de l'employé ou d'un particulier qui lui est lié à l'exclusion d'un avantage imputable à un débours ou une dépense auxquels l'alinéa 18(1)l) s'applique.

b) le réemploi ou la retraite de l'employé.

La modification s'appliquera aux services de conseils sur l'usage du tabac, des drogues ou de l'alcool, sur la gestion du stress, le placement sur le marché du travail et la retraite.»

Revenue Canada   Revenu Canada
Taxation   Impôt

INTERPRETATION BULLETIN

SUBJECT: INCOME TAX ACT
Employees' Fringe Benefits

NO IT-470R   DATE: April 8, 1988
REFERENCE: Paragraph 6(1)(a) (also subsections 5(1),
6(3) and 6(6), paragraph 110(8)(a) and subparagraph 6(1)(b)(ix)).

BULLETIN D'INTERPRÉTATION

OBJET: LOI DE L'IMPÔT SUR LE REVENU
Avantages sociaux des employés

Nº IT-470R   DATE: le 8 avril 1988
RENVOI: Alinéa 6(1)a) (également, les paragraphes 5(1), 6(3),
6(6), l'alinéa 110(8)a) et le sous-alinéa 6(1)b)(ix)).

Application

This bulletin replaces and cancels Interpretation Bulletin IT-470 dated February 16, 1981 and the Special Release (Revised) dated May 25, 1984 and IT-198 dated January 27, 1975. Current revisions are designated by vertical lines.

Summary

This bulletin discusses various common types of "fringe benefits" and indicates whether or not their values should be included in income. Part A of the bulletin deals with amounts to be included in income while Part B deals with amounts not to be included in income.

Discussion and Interpretation

1. The information herein refers to cases where there is an employee-employer relationship but does not necessarily apply if the employee is also a shareholder or relative of the owner of the business.

2. Except where the Act provides otherwise, taxpayers are generally taxable on the value of all benefits they receive by virtue of their employment. The more common "fringe benefits" are discussed below and have been classified generally as taxable benefits or as non-taxable privileges. In the second group there may well be a point beyond which the "privilege" concept is no longer valid, i.e., the advantage to the employee is, in fact, a form of extra remuneration. Then the "fringe benefit" is viewed as a taxable benefit.

3. Where an amount in respect of a taxable benefit should be included in income, the employer must determine its value or make a reasonable estimate of it and include that value in the box provided on form T4 Supplementary under the heading "Employment Income Before Deductions" and also in the appropriate box in the area entitled "Taxable Allowances and Benefits".

Application

Le présent bulletin annule et remplace le Bulletin d'interprétation IT-470 du 16 février 1981 et le Communiqué spécial (révisé) du 25 mai 1984, ainsi que le IT-198 du 27 janvier 1975. Les révisions courantes sont indiquées par des traits verticaux.

Résumé

Le présent bulletin porte sur divers genres d'«avantages sociaux» et indique si leur valeur doit être comprise dans le revenu. La partie A du présent bulletin traite des montants à inclure dans le revenu, tandis que la partie B traite des montants à ne pas inclure dans le revenu.

Discussion et interprétation

1. L'information fournie dans le présent bulletin se rapporte aux cas où il existe une relation d'employeur-employé et ne s'applique pas nécessairement si l'employé est également un actionnaire ou un parent du propriétaire de l'entreprise.

2. Sauf indication contraire dans la Loi, les contribuables sont, en général, imposables sur la valeur de tous les avantages qu'ils reçoivent en vertu de leur emploi. Les «avantages sociaux» les plus répandus sont examinés ci-dessous et sont classés soit parmi les avantages imposables soit parmi les privilèges non imposables. Dans le second groupe, il peut fort bien exister un point au-delà duquel le concept de «privilège» ne vaut plus, c'est-à-dire où l'avantage revenant à l'employé ne présente plus un caractère fortuit ou traditionnel par rapport à l'emploi, mais devient une forme déguisée de rémunération supplémentaire. Dans de telles circonstances, l'«avantage social» est considéré comme étant un avantage imposable.

3. Lorsque la valeur d'un avantage imposable doit être incluse dans le revenu, l'employeur doit la déterminer ou en faire une estimation raisonnable et l'inscrire dans la case de la formule T4 Supplémentaire intitulée «Revenus d'emploi avant retenues» ainsi que dans la case appropriée de la section intitulée «Avantages imposables».

Published under the authority
of the Deputy Minister
of National Revenue for Taxation

Publié avec l'autorisation
du Sous-ministre
du Revenu national pour l'Impôt

Canada

2   IT-470R

PART A
AMOUNTS TO BE INCLUDED IN INCOME
Board and Lodging

4.   The Income Tax Act refers specifically to board and lodging as a benefit derived from employment. This includes board and lodging regularly furnished as a perquisite of the employment, as is common for hotel employees and domestic and farm help. The value placed on this benefit should approximate its fair market value. Where subsidized board and lodging is provided to an employee the value of the benefit for "board" is determined on the basis described for subsidized meals (See 28 below); the "lodging" benefit will be valued at the fair market value of the accommodation less the amount charged to the employee.

5.   However, by virtue of subsection 6(6), an exception to the above rules is made in respect of board and lodging received by an employee whose duties are performed at a remote location or, in some circumstances, at a special work site. This exception is discussed in IT-91R3, "Employment at Special or Remote Work Sites".

Rent-Free and Low-Rent Housing

6.   Where an employer provides a house, apartment, or similar accommodation to an employee rent-free or for a lower rent than the employee would have to pay someone else for such accommodation, the employee receives a taxable benefit. The employer is responsible for reasonably estimating the amount of such a benefit, which would normally be considered to be the fair market rent for equivalent accommodation had the employee rented from a third party less any rent paid. However, in computing taxable income for the 1987 and subsequent taxation years, section 110.7 provides a deduction in respect of living accommodation for an individual who resides in an area that is a prescribed area (e.g., the far north). To be eligible for this deduction for a taxation year an individual must have resided, throughout a period of not less than 6 months commencing or ending in the year, in an area that was a prescribed area for the year or for one of the 2 preceding taxation years. To obtain this deduction, the individual must file a claim on prescribed form T2222 when filing the return of income for the taxation year for which the deduction is claimed.

Travel Benefits

7.   An amount received, or the value of a benefit received or enjoyed, by virtue of employment in respect of travelling expenses incurred by an employee, the employee's family or both is a taxable benefit unless the amount is an allowance which falls within the exceptions in paragraph 6(1)(b) or is an amount described in subsection 81(3.1) or otherwise excluded from income under subsection 6(6). However, in computing taxable income for the 1987 and subsequent taxation years, an individual eligible for the

PARTIE A
MONTANTS À INCLURE DANS LE REVENU
Pension et logement

4.   La Loi de l'impôt sur le revenu mentionne expressément la pension et le logement comme étant un avantage découlant de l'emploi. Cela comprend la pension et le logement régulièrement fournis comme un à-côté de l'emploi, par exemple, comme cela se pratique couramment dans le cas des employés d'hôtel, des domestiques et des ouvriers agricoles. Normalement, la valeur attribuée à cet avantage doit se rapprocher de façon raisonnable de sa juste valeur marchande. Lorsqu'un employé bénéficie de pension et de logement subventionnés, la valeur de l'avantage de la «pension» est déterminée selon la méthode applicable aux repas subventionnés (voir le numéro 28 ci-dessous). La valeur de l'avantage du «logement» correspond à sa juste valeur marchande, moins toute somme payée par l'employé.

5.   Toutefois, en vertu du paragraphe 6(6), une exception aux règles susmentionnées existe relativement à la pension et au logement qu'un employé reçoit lorsqu'il doit accomplir ses fonctions dans un chantier particulier ou en un endroit éloigné. Cette exception est traitée dans le IT-91R3, «Emploi sur des chantiers particuliers ou éloignés».

Logement gratuit ou à loyer peu élevé

6.   Lorsqu'un employeur met à la disposition d'un employé une habitation, un appartement ou un autre logement semblable sans exiger de loyer ou moyennant un loyer plus faible que ce que l'employé serait obligé de verser à quelqu'un d'autre pour un logement semblable, l'employé reçoit un avantage imposable. Il incombe à l'employeur de faire une estimation raisonnable du montant d'un tel avantage qui serait normalement considéré comme étant la différence entre le loyer versé et la juste valeur marchande d'un logement équivalent si l'employé l'avait loué d'un tiers. Toutefois, en ce qui concerne le calcul du revenu imposable pour les années d'imposition 1987 et subséquentes, l'article 110.7 prévoit une déduction relative au logement d'une personne qui habite une région désignée (par exemple le Grand Nord). Pour avoir droit à cette déduction, une personne doit avoir habité, pendant une période d'au moins 6 mois commençant ou se terminant dans l'année d'imposition visée, une région qui a été désignée cette année-là ou l'une des deux années d'imposition précédentes. Pour obtenir cette déduction, la personne doit remplir la formule prescrite T2222 et la produire avec sa déclaration de revenu de l'année d'imposition pour laquelle elle demande la déduction.

Avantages relatifs aux déplacements

7.   Un montant reçu par un employé, ou la valeur d'un avantage qu'il a reçu ou dont il a joui, en vertu d'un emploi relativement à des frais de déplacement engagés par lui ou par sa famille ou par les deux, est un avantage imposable, sauf si le montant est une allocation qui est comprise dans les exceptions prévues à l'alinéa 6(1)b) ou que le montant est visé par le paragraphe 81(3.1) ou est par ailleurs exclu du revenu en vertu du paragraphe 6(6). Toutefois, dans le calcul de son revenu imposable pour les années d'imposition 1987 et suivantes, un particulier qui a droit à la

deduction described in 6 above may also be entitled to a deduction within prescribed limits, in respect of certain travel benefits received by the individual or the individual's family from an employer who deals at arm's length with the individual, to the extent the value of the benefits is included in the individual's income for the taxation year from employment and not otherwise deducted. The deduction applies with respect to trips made in the year for the purpose of obtaining necessary medical services not available locally. In addition, a deduction may be claimed with respect to travelling expenses incurred in connection with not more than two other trips made in the year. To obtain this deduction, the individual must file a claim on prescribed form T2222 when filing the return of income for the taxation year for which the deduction is claimed.

Personal Use of Employer's Automobile

8. IT-63R2, "Benefits, Including Standby Charge for an Automobile, from Non-business Use of an Automotive Vehicle Supplied by an Employer", should be consulted.

Gifts (Including Christmas Gifts)

9. A gift (either in cash or in kind) from an employer to an employee is a benefit derived during or because of the employment. Where the value of a gift commemorating a wedding, Christmas or similar occasion does not exceed $100 and where the employer does not claim its cost as an expense in computing taxable income, the gift is not required to be reported as income of the employee. This practice will only apply to one gift to an employee in a year except in the year an employee marries in which case it will apply to two gifts.

Holiday Trips, Other Prizes and Incentive Awards

10. Where an employer pays for a vacation for an employee, the employee's family or both, the cost thereof to the employer constitutes a taxable benefit to the employee under paragraph 6(1)(a). Similarly, where a vacation property owned by an employer is used for vacation purposes by an employee, the employee's family or both, there is a taxable benefit conferred on the employee under paragraph 6(1)(a) the value of which is equivalent to the fair market value of the accommodation less any amount which the employee paid therefor to the employer. In any case, the taxable benefit may be reduced if there is conclusive evidence to show that the employee was involved in business activities for the employer during the vacation.

11. In a situation where an employee's presence is required for business purposes and this function is the main purpose of the trip, no benefit will be associated with the employee's travelling expenses necessary to accomplish the business objectives of the trip if the expenditures are reasonable in relation to the business function. Where

déduction décrite au numéro 6 ci-dessus peut aussi avoir droit, sous réserve des limites prescrites, à une déduction pour certains avantages relatifs aux déplacements reçus par lui ou sa famille d'un employeur avec lequel il n'a aucun lien de dépendance, dans la mesure où la valeur des avantages est incluse dans le calcul de son revenu d'emploi pour l'année d'imposition et n'est pas par ailleurs déduite. La déduction s'applique aux voyages effectués pendant l'année pour obtenir des soins médicaux nécessaires qui ne se donnent pas dans la région du particulier. En outre, un particulier peut demander une déduction pour les frais de déplacements engagés à l'occasion d'au plus deux autres voyages dans l'année. Pour obtenir cette déduction le particulier doit remplir la formule prescrite T2222 et la produire avec sa déclaration de revenus de l'année d'imposition pour laquelle il demande la déduction.

Utilisation à des fins personnelles d'une voiture de l'employeur

8. À ce sujet, veuillez vous reporter au IT-63R2 intitulé «Avantages, y compris les frais pour droit d'usage d'une automobile, qui découlent de l'usage non commercial d'un véhicule automobile fourni par l'employeur».

Dons (y compris les cadeaux de Noël)

9. Un don (en espèces ou en nature) fait à un employé par un employeur est un avantage obtenu dans le cours ou en vertu de l'emploi. Lorsque la valeur d'un cadeau offert à l'occasion d'un mariage, de Noël ou d'un évènement semblable ne dépasse pas 100 $ et que l'employeur n'en déduit pas le coût comme dépense dans le calcul de son propre revenu imposable, il n'est pas nécessaire de déclarer le don comme revenu de l'employé. Cela s'applique à un seul cadeau fait à un employé au cours d'une année, sauf s'il s'agit de l'année où l'employé se marie, auquel cas cela s'appliquera à deux cadeaux.

Voyages de vacances, autres prix et primes d'encouragement

10. Lorsqu'un employeur paye les vacances d'un employé, de la famille de l'employé ou des deux, les frais que l'employeur engage à cette fin constituent un avantage imposable pour l'employé en vertu de l'alinéa 6(1)a). De même, lorsqu'un employé, sa famille ou les deux utilisent une propriété de villégiature appartenant à l'employeur pour prendre des vacances, l'employé reçoit un avantage imposable en vertu de l'alinéa 6(1)a) dont la valeur équivaut à la juste valeur marchande de ce service moins tout montant que l'employé paye à l'employeur. En tout état de cause, l'avantage imposable peut être réduit lorsqu'il existe des preuves suffisantes que l'employé a, au cours de ses vacances, participé à des activités commerciales pour le compte de l'employeur.

11. Si la présence de l'employé est jugée essentielle aux affaires et si la conduite des affaires est le principal objectif du voyage, aucun avantage ne sera lié aux frais de déplacement de l'employé pour l'atteinte des objectifs commerciaux, si ces dépenses sont raisonnables par rapport aux fins commerciales du voyage. Lorsqu'un voyage d'affaires est prolongé pour donner un voyage

a business trip is extended to provide for a paid holiday or vacation, the employee is in receipt of a taxable benefit equal to the costs borne by the employer with respect to that extension.

12. There may be instances where an employee acts as a host or hostess for an incentive award trip arranged for employees, suppliers or customers of the employer. Such a trip will be viewed as a business trip provided the employee is engaged directly in business activities during a substantial part of each day (e.g., as organizer of activities); otherwise it will be viewed as a vacation and a taxable benefit, subject, of course, to a reduction for any actual business activity.

13. Where an employee receives a prize or other award related to sales or other work performance from his or her employer, the fair market value of such an incentive is regarded as remuneration to be included in income under section 5 of the Act. Similarly, the fair market value of any award not regarded as remuneration that is received by an employee
    (a) in respect of,
    (b) in the course of, or
    (c) by virtue of
the employee's office or employment is also included in income from an office or employment by virtue of paragraph 6(1)(a). (See also IT-75R2, "Scholarships, Fellowships, Bursaries, Prizes and Research Grants".)

Frequent Flyer Program

14. Under this program, which is usually sponsored by an airline, a frequent air traveller can accumulate credits which may be exchanged for additional air travel or other benefits. Where an employee accumulates such credits while travelling on employer-paid business trips and uses them to obtain air travel or other benefits for the personal use of the employee or the employee's family, the fair market value of such air travel or other benefits must be included in the employee's income.

Travelling Expenses of Employee's Spouse

15. Where a spouse accompanies an employee on a business trip the payment or reimbursement by the employer of the spouse's travelling expenses is a taxable benefit to the employee unless the spouse was, in fact, engaged primarily in business activities on behalf of the employer during the trip.

Premiums under Provincial Hospitalization and Medical Care Insurance Plans

16. Where an employer pays all or a part of the premiums or contributions that an employee is otherwise required to pay to a provincial authority administering a provincial hospital insurance plan, a provincial medical care insurance plan, or both, the amount paid is a taxable benefit to the employee.

---

ou des vacances payés, l'employé reçoit un avantage imposable qui correspond aux coûts que l'employeur a subis pour offrir cette prolongation.

12. Dans certains cas, l'employé agit comme hôte ou hôtesse dans le cadre d'un voyage servant de prime d'encouragement qui a été organisé pour les employés, les fournisseurs ou les clients de l'employeur. Un voyage du genre sera considéré comme un voyage d'affaires si l'employé participe directement à des activités commerciales pendant une partie considérable de la journée (comme organisateur des activités, par exemple); sinon, le voyage est considéré comme des vacances et est un avantage imposable assujetti, évidemment, à une réduction proportionnelle aux activités commerciales réelles.

13. Lorsqu'un employé reçoit de son employeur une prime ou un autre genre de prix lié aux ventes ou à son rendement de travail, la juste valeur marchande de cette prime d'encouragement est réputée être une rémunération devant être incluse dans le revenu en vertu de l'article 5 de la Loi. De même, la juste valeur marchande de toute prime qui n'est pas considérée comme une rémunération que l'employé reçoit
    a) à l'égard de,
    b) dans le cadre de ou
    c) en vertu de
sa charge ou de son emploi est également incluse dans le revenu tiré de la charge ou de l'emploi en vertu de l'alinéa 6(1)a). (Voir aussi le IT-75R2, «Bourses d'études, bourses de perfectionnement (fellowship), prix et subventions de recherches»).

Programme passagers assidus

14. Selon le programme passagers assidus, habituellement parrainé par un transporteur aérien, un passager aérien assidu peut accumuler des crédits qu'il peut ensuite échanger contre des voyages par avion ou d'autres avantages. Lorsqu'un employé accumule de tels crédits grâce à des voyages d'affaires payés par son employeur et les utilise pour obtenir des voyages par avion ou d'autres avantages pour l'employé ou pour sa famille, il faut inclure dans le revenu de l'employé la juste valeur marchande de ces voyages par avion ou autres avantages.

Frais de voyage du conjoint de l'employé

15. Lorsque le conjoint d'un employé l'accompagne dans un voyage d'affaires, le paiement ou le remboursement des frais de voyage du conjoint par l'employeur représente un avantage imposable pour l'employé, sauf si, au cours du voyage, le conjoint s'est en réalité adonné principalement à des activités commerciales pour le compte de l'employeur.

Primes versées en vertu de régimes provinciaux d'assurance-hospitalisation et d'assurance-soins médicaux

16. Lorsqu'un employeur verse la totalité ou une partie des primes ou des cotisations que l'employé est tenu de verser à une administration provinciale gérant un régime d'assurance-hospitalisation, un régime provincial d'assurance-soins médicaux ou les deux, le montant versé est un avantage imposable de l'employé.

17. Where an employer pays an amount to an employee in respect of the employee's premium under a provincial hospital or provincial medical care insurance plan, the amount paid is a taxable benefit to the employee.

Tuition Fees

18. Where an employer has paid tuition fees on behalf of an employee or has reimbursed an employee, in whole or in part, for tuition fees paid by the employee personally, the amount paid should be reported as income of the employee for the year in which the payment was made.

19. An exception to this rule can be made where the course for which the fees were paid was undertaken on the employer's initiative and for the benefit of the employer rather than the employee. This is usually presumed where a course is taken during normal working hours with the employee being given time off with pay for that purpose. On the other hand, if the course is taken on the employee's own time, the presumption is that the course is primarily for the employee's benefit and the amount paid by the employer is a taxable benefit to the employee.

20. Where an educational institution which charges tuition fees provides tuition free of charge or at a reduced amount to an employee of the institution, or to the spouse or children of the employee, the fair market value of the benefit will be included in the employee's income.

21. For 1984 and subsequent taxation years, any reasonable allowance (including tuition fees) received by an employee from the employer to cover the away-from-home education of a child will not be included in the employee's income by virtue of subparagraph 6(1)(b)(ix), so long as the child is in full-time attendance at a school which primarily uses for instruction the official language of Canada primarily used by the employee and the school is in a community not farther from the place where the employee is required to live than the nearest community in which there is a school having suitable boarding facilities and providing instruction in that language. To the extent that tuition fees paid by the employer for the employee's child are, by virtue of subparagraph 6(1)(b)(ix) not included in the employee's income, they may not be deducted by the child in computing income (see IT-82R3, "Tuition Fees"). Before 1984 the allowance was excluded from income only if the school was the closest available providing instruction in that language without regard to the suitability of accommodation.

22. Tuition fees (including the fair market value of free tuition to the extent that it is reported as a taxable benefit) may be claimed as a deduction in computing income under paragraph 60(e),(f) or (g), whichever may be applicable but any such deduction can only be made by the student by whom or on whose behalf the fees were paid or to whom the free tuition was provided (see IT-82R3). For the tax implications of scholarships, fellowships, bursaries, prizes and research grants, see IT-75R2.

17. Lorsqu'un employeur verse un montant à un employé pour la prime de l'employé en vertu d'un régime provincial d'assurance-hospitalisation ou d'assurance-soins médicaux, le montant versé est un avantage imposable de l'employé.

Frais de scolarité

18. Lorsqu'un employeur a payé les frais de scolarité d'un employé ou qu'il a remboursé à un employé la totalité ou une partie des frais de scolarité que l'employé a payés lui-même, le montant payé doit être déclaré comme revenu de l'employé pour l'année dans laquelle le paiement a été fait.

19. Une exception à cette règle peut se produire dans le cas où les études, dont les frais ont été payés, ont été entreprises à la demande de l'employeur et où elles profiteront plus à l'employeur qu'à l'employé; on présume ordinairement qu'il en est ainsi lorsque les études ont lieu durant les heures normales de travail et que l'employeur accorde à cette fin du temps rémunéré à l'employé. En revanche, si l'employé poursuit ses études dans son temps libre, on présume que les études doivent profiter surtout à l'employé lui-même, et le montant payé par l'employeur est un avantage imposable de l'employé.

20. Lorsqu'un établissement d'enseignement qui perçoit des frais de scolarité fournit des cours à un employé, au conjoint ou aux enfants de l'employé gratuitement ou à un prix réduit, la juste valeur marchande de l'avantage sera incluse dans le revenu de l'employé.

21. Pour 1984 et les années d'imposition subséquentes, toute allocation raisonnable (dont des frais de scolarité) reçue par un employé de son employeur pour couvrir les frais d'instruction de son enfant à l'extérieur de sa localité ne sera pas incluse dans le revenu de l'employé en vertu du sous-alinéa 6(1)b)(ix), tant que l'enfant fréquente à temps plein une école qui fournit l'instruction principalement dans la langue officielle du Canada principalement utilisée par l'employé et que l'école se trouve dans une localité qui n'est pas plus éloignée du lieu où l'employé doit demeurer que l'agglomération la plus proche dotée d'une école et offrant l'enseignement dans cette langue et des possibilités de pension adéquates. Dans la mesure où les frais de scolarité payés par l'employeur pour l'enfant de l'employé sont exclus du revenu de l'employé en vertu du sous-alinéa 6(1)b)(ix), ces frais ne peuvent être déduits par l'enfant dans le calcul de son revenu (voir le IT-82R3, «Frais de scolarité»). Avant 1984, cette allocation était exclue du revenu seulement si l'école était la plus proche pour la langue officielle visée sans égard aux possibilités de logement.

22. Les frais de scolarité (y compris la juste valeur marchande des frais de scolarité gratuits, s'ils sont déclarés comme avantage imposable) peuvent faire l'objet d'une demande de déduction en vertu de l'alinéa 60e), f) ou g), selon celui qui s'applique, lorsque le revenu est calculé; toutefois, seul l'étudiant qui verse les frais, ou au nom duquel ils ont été versés, ou à qui la scolarité gratuite a été fournie, peut jouir d'une telle déduction (voir le IT-82R3). Pour ce qui est des conséquences fiscales des bourses d'études, des bourses de perfectionnement (fellowships), des récompenses et des subventions de recherche, voir le IT-75R2.

Cost of Tools – Reimbursement

23. Where an employer makes payments to its employees to offset the cost of tools that the employees are required to have in order to perform their work, the amount of the payment must be included in the employees' incomes. However, where an employee is reimbursed by the Government of Canada for the cost of tools under the Government's Assistance Program – Workers Metric Tools, that reimbursement is not included in income.

Wage Loss Replacement Plans

24. Refer to IT-428, "Wage Loss Replacement Plans".

Interest-Free and Low-Interest Loans

25. Refer to IT-421R, "Benefits to Individuals, Corporations and Shareholders from Loans or Debt".

Employee Counselling Services

26. The fees paid by an employer to provide services such as financial counselling, counselling upon retirement or discharge or income tax return preparation are considered to produce a taxable benefit to the employee who receives the service. It is not considered that a similar benefit arises where the service is provided on an in-house basis by the employer's staff.

PART B
AMOUNTS NOT TO BE INCLUDED IN INCOME
Discounts on Merchandise and Commissions on Sales

27. Where it is the practice of an employer to sell merchandise to employees at a discount, the benefits that an employee may derive from exercising such a privilege are not normally regarded as taxable benefits. However, this does not extend to an extraordinary arrangement with a particular employee or a select group of employees nor to an arrangement by which an employee is permitted to purchase merchandise (other than old or soiled merchandise) for less than the employer's cost. Furthermore, this treatment does not extend to a reciprocal arrangement between two or more employers whereby the employees of one can exercise such a privilege with another by whom the employees are not employed. A commission received by a sales employee on merchandise acquired for that employee's personal use is not taxable. Similarly, where a life insurance salesperson acquires a life insurance policy, a commission received by that salesperson on that policy is not taxable provided the salesperson owns that policy and is obligated to make the required premium payments thereon.

Subsidized Meals

28. Subsidized meals provided to employees will not be considered to confer a taxable benefit provided the employee is required to pay a reasonable charge. A reason-

Le coût des outils – remboursement

23. Lorsqu'un employeur rembourse ses employés du coût des outils nécessaires à l'exercice de leurs fonctions, le montant du remboursement doit être compris dans le revenu des employés. Toutefois, lorsque le gouvernement du Canada rembourse à un employé le coût de ses outils en vertu du Programme d'assistance – Outils métriques des ouvriers, le montant du remboursement n'est pas compris dans le revenu.

Régimes d'assurance-salaire

24. Se reporter au IT-428, intitulé «Régimes d'assurance-salaire».

Prêts à intérêt réduit ou nul

25. Se reporter au IT-421R, intitulé «Avantages consentis aux particuliers, aux corporations et aux actionnaires sous forme de prêts ou de dettes».

Services de conseils aux employés

26. Les honoraires versés par un employeur pour fournir à un employé des services comme des conseils d'ordre financiers, l'orientation au moment de la retraite ou d'un licenciement, ou encore, l'établissement de la déclaration d'impôt, sont réputés apporter un avantage imposable à l'employé. Il n'en est pas de même lorsque le service est assuré à l'intérieur de l'entreprise de l'employeur par son personnel.

PARTIE B
MONTANTS À NE PAS INCLURE DANS LE REVENU
Remises sur les marchandises et commissions sur les ventes

27. Lorsqu'un employeur accorde à ses employés un rabais à l'achat de sa marchandise, les avantages que peut retirer un employé de l'exercice d'un tel privilège ne sont pas considérés comme étant des avantages imposables. Cependant, cette règle ne vaut pas dans le cas d'un arrangement extraordinaire conclu avec un employé donné ou un groupe choisi d'employés, ni dans le cas d'un arrangement qui permet à l'employé d'acheter des marchandises (autres que les marchandises désuètes ou défraîchies) à un prix inférieur à leur prix coûtant pour l'employeur. Cela ne s'applique pas non plus à un arrangement réciproque conclu entre deux ou plusieurs employeurs qui s'engagent à laisser les employés de l'un se prévaloir d'un tel privilège auprès de l'autre qui n'est pas leur employeur. Une commission touchée par un employé préposé aux ventes sur des marchandises qu'il achète pour son usage personnel n'est pas imposable. De même, lorsqu'un vendeur d'assurance-vie acquiert une police d'assurance-vie et qu'il touche une commission sur cette police, celle-ci n'est pas imposable pourvu que le vendeur soit propriétaire de la police et qu'il soit tenu de verser les primes exigées à l'égard de cette police.

Repas subventionnés

28. Les repas subventionnés fournis aux employés ne seront pas considérés comme un avantage imposable à condition que l'employé soit tenu de payer une somme raisonnable. Une

able charge is generally defined as one that covers the cost of food, its preparation and service. Where less than a reasonable charge is paid, the value of the benefit is that cost less the amount paid by the employee.

Uniforms and Special Clothing

29. An employee who is supplied with a distinctive uniform which is required to be worn while carrying out the duties of employment or who is provided with special clothing (including safety footwear) designed for protection from the particular hazards of the employment, is not regarded as receiving a taxable benefit.

30. Payments made by an employer to a laundry or dry cleaning establishment for laundry or dry cleaning expenses of uniforms and special clothing, or directly to the employee in reimbursement of such expenses, do not constitute a taxable benefit to the employee.

Subsidized School Services

31. In remote or unorganized areas employers frequently assume, initially at least, responsibility for essential community services of a kind normally borne by a municipal organization. Where the employer provides free or subsidized school services for children of the employees, a taxable benefit is not considered to accrue to the employees. This does not extend to a payment of an educational allowance directly to the employee by the employer, which is a taxable benefit unless excepted by subparagraph 6(1)(b)(ix) as described in 21 above.

Transportation to the Job

32. Employers sometimes find it expedient to provide vehicles for transporting their employees from pick-up points to the location of the employment at which, for security or other reasons, public and private vehicles are not welcome or not practical. In these circumstances the employees are not regarded as in receipt of a taxable benefit. However, a reimbursement or allowance paid to the employee for transportation to and from the location of employment must be included in income. Subsection 6(6) provides an exception to this latter rule. See also IT-91R3, "Employment at Special or Remote Work Sites".

Recreational Facilities

33. Where employees generally are permitted to use their employer's recreational facilities (e.g., exercise rooms, swimming pools, gymnasiums, tennis, squash or raquetball courts, golf courses, shuffle boards) free of charge or upon payment of a nominal fee, the value of the benefit derived by an employee through such use is not normally taxable. The taxable benefit received by an employee who is provided with board, lodging and accommodation is discussed in 4 to 6 and 10 above.

somme raisonnable peut être définie, de façon générale, comme une somme englobant le coût de la nourriture, de sa préparation et du service. Lorsque la somme payée est moins que celle jugée raisonnable, la valeur de l'avantage correspond au coût déterminé, moins le montant payé par l'employé.

Uniformes et vêtements spéciaux

29. Lorsqu'un employé reçoit un uniforme distinctif qu'il est tenu de porter dans l'exercice des fonctions de son emploi ou lorsqu'on lui fournit des vêtements spéciaux (y compris des chaussures de sécurité) destinés à le protéger des dangers propres à son emploi, cet employé n'est pas réputé toucher un avantage imposable.

30. Les paiements qu'un employeur verse à une blanchisserie ou à un établissement de nettoyage à sec pour le blanchissage ou le nettoyage à sec d'uniformes ou de vêtements spéciaux, ou qu'il verse directement à l'employé en remboursement de dépenses à ce titre, ne constituent pas un avantage imposable pour l'employé.

Services scolaires subventionnés

31. Dans des régions lointaines ou non organisées, il arrive souvent que les employeurs se chargent, du moins au début, de dispenser des services collectifs essentiels du genre de ceux qui sont normalement dispensés par un organisme municipal. Lorsque l'employeur fournit des services scolaires gratuits ou subventionnés à l'intention des enfants des employés, ces derniers ne sont pas réputés bénéficier d'un avantage imposable. Cela ne s'applique pas à une allocation scolaire que l'employeur verse directement à l'employé, laquelle est un avantage imposable à moins d'être exemptée d'impôt par le sous-alinéa 6(1)b)(ix) tel qu'indiqué au numéro 21 ci-dessus.

Transport au lieu d'emploi

32. Les employeurs trouvent parfois commode de fournir des véhicules pour le transport de leurs employés à partir de certains points de rassemblement jusqu'au lieu d'emploi où, pour des raisons de sécurité ou autres, il est interdit ou peu pratique de se rendre au moyen de véhicules publics ou particuliers. Dans ces circonstances, on n'estime pas que les employés bénéficient d'un avantage imposable. Toutefois, un remboursement ou une allocation versée à l'employé pour le transport aller-retour au lieu d'emploi doit être inclus dans le revenu. Le paragraphe 6(6) fournit une exception à cette dernière règle. Voir également le IT-91R3 intitulé «Emploi sur des chantiers particuliers ou éloignés».

Services de récréation

33. Lorsque l'employeur met à la disposition des employés en général, à titre gratuit ou moyennant un droit nominal, des installations récréatives (par exemple salle d'exercice, piscine, gymnase, court de tennis, de squash ou de racketball, terrain de golf, terrain de jeu de galets), la valeur de l'avantage qu'en tire l'employé n'est pas ordinairement imposable. L'avantage imposable que reçoit un employé auquel sont fournis le gîte et le couvert est l'objet des numéros 4 à 6 et du numéro 10 ci-dessus.

34. Similarly, where the employer pays the fees required for an employee to be a member of a social or athletic club the employee is not deemed to have received a taxable benefit where the membership was principally for the employer's advantage rather than the employee's. See also IT-148R2, "Recreational Properties and Club Dues".

Removal Expenses

35. Where an employer reimburses an employee for the expenses incurred by the latter in moving the employee and the employee's family and household effects either because the employee has been transferred from one establishment of the employer to another or because of having accepted employment at a place other than where the former home was located, this reimbursement is not considered as conferring a taxable benefit on the employee.

36. In addition, where the employer pays the expense of moving an employee and the employee's family and household effects out of a remote place at the termination of the employment there, no taxable benefit is imputed.

37. In ordinary circumstances, if an employer reimburses an employee for a loss suffered by the latter in selling the family home upon being required by the employer to move to another locality or upon retirement from employment in a remote area, the amount so reimbursed is not income of the employee if it is not greater than the actual loss calculated as the amount by which the cost of the home to the employee exceeds the net selling price received for it. Similarly, where an employer guarantees to give to an employee an amount equal to the amount by which the fair market value of the home (as independently appraised) exceeds the actual selling price obtained, the amount so given is not income in the hands of the employee. Should the employer buy the home from the employee, no taxable benefit is included in the employee's income if the price paid by the employer does not exceed the greater of the cost of the home to the employee and the current fair market value of comparable homes in the same area.

38. An employee who is not reimbursed, or is only partly reimbursed, for removal expenses may be able to claim certain of the expenses incurred as a deduction from income under section 62 of the Act. See also IT-178R2, "Moving Expenses".

Premiums under Private Health Services Plans

39. Where an employer makes a contribution to a private health services plan in respect of an employee, no taxable benefit arises to the employee.

40. Benefits provided to an employee under a private health services plan are not subject to tax in the employee's hands. "Private health services plan" is defined in paragraph 110(8)(a). (See also IT-85R2, "Health and Welfare Trusts for Employees".)

34. De même, si l'employeur verse les cotisations requises pour qu'un employé soit membre d'un club social ou athlétique et si c'est principalement l'employeur, et non l'employé, qui bénéficie de cette situation, on n'estime pas que l'employé a reçu un avantage imposable. Se reporter également au IT-148R2, intitulé «Biens récréatifs et cotisations d'un club».

Frais de déménagement

35. Lorsqu'un employeur rembourse à un employé les dépenses que ce dernier a engagées pour son propre déménagement, celui de sa famille et de ses effets, que ce soit parce que l'employé a été muté d'un établissement de l'employeur à un autre ou parce que l'employé a accepté un emploi dans une localité autre que celle où était son ancien lieu de résidence, ce remboursement n'est pas réputé conférer un avantage à l'employé.

36. De plus, lorsqu'un employeur acquitte les frais de déménagement de l'employé, de sa famille et de ses effets d'une région éloignée lors de la cessation de l'emploi de l'employé à cet endroit, lesdits frais ne constituent pas un avantage imposable.

37. Dans des circonstances normales, si un employeur rembourse à son employé une perte qu'il a subie lors de la vente de sa maison parce que l'employeur l'a obligé à s'installer dans une autre localité, ou parce qu'il a abandonné un emploi dans une région éloignée, le montant ainsi remboursé ne constitue pas un revenu de l'employé s'il n'est pas supérieur à la perte effective qu'il a subie, c'est-à-dire l'excédent de ce que lui a coûté la maison sur le prix de vente net qu'il a touché. De façon similaire, lorsque l'employeur garantit qu'il versera à l'employé un montant égal à l'excédent de la juste valeur marchande de la maison, selon une évaluation indépendante, sur le prix de vente effectivement obtenu, le montant versé ne constitue pas un revenu de l'employé. Si l'employeur lui-même achète la maison de l'employé, aucun avantage imposable n'est inclus dans le revenu de l'employé si le prix payé par l'employeur n'excède pas le plus élevé des deux montants suivants : le coût de la maison pour l'employé ou la juste valeur marchande de maisons comparables dans la même localité.

38. Lorsque l'employé n'est pas défrayé de son déménagement ou qu'il ne l'est que partiellement, il se peut qu'il puisse demander la déduction de certains de ses frais de son revenu, en vertu de l'article 62 de la Loi. Se reporter également au IT-178R2, intitulé «Frais de déménagement».

Primes en vertu de régimes privés d'assurance-maladie

39. Lorsqu'un employeur paie des cotisations à un régime privé d'assurance-maladie à l'égard d'un employé, l'avantage dont ce dernier bénéficie n'est pas imposable.

40. Les avantages dont bénéficie un employé en vertu d'un régime privé d'assurance-maladie ne sont pas imposables comme étant son revenu. La définition de «régime privé d'assurance-maladie» est donnée à l'alinéa 110(8)a). (Voir aussi le IT-85R2, «Fiducie de santé et de bien-être au bénéfice d'employés».)

Employer's Contribution under Provincial Hospitalization and Medical Care Insurance Plans

41. Where an employer is required, under a provincial hospital insurance plan, a provincial medical care insurance plan, or both, to pay amounts to the provincial authority administering such plan or plans (other than with respect to the contributions or premiums that an employee is required to make under the plan), the payment of such amounts does not give rise to a taxable benefit to employees.

Transportation Passes

42. Airline passes available to airline employees will become taxable only if the employee travels on a space-confirmed basis and is paying less than 50 per cent of the economy fare available on that carrier for that trip on the day of travel. The value of the benefit will be the difference between 50 per cent of the economy fare and any amount reimbursed to the carrier for that trip.

43. Employees of bus and rail companies will not be taxed on the use of passes.

44. Retired employees of transportation companies will not be taxed on pass benefits under any circumstances.

Public Office Holders

45. A public office holder may be required to incur the costs of establishing, maintaining or dismantling a blind trust set up to enable that person to comply with the Conflict of Interest and Post-Employment Code for Public Office Holders. Where such costs are reimbursed to that person by the Government of Canada in accordance with that Code, no taxable benefit is considered to arise for income tax purposes, since the person is obliged to incur the expenses only by reason of his or her office or employment. The above comments will also apply to such costs incurred, and any reimbursement thereof, under any substantially similar arrangements affecting public office holders at the provincial or municipal level.

Cotisations versées par l'employeur à des régimes provinciaux d'assurance-hospitalisation et d'assurance-soins médicaux

41. Lorsqu'un employeur est tenu, en vertu d'un régime provincial d'assurance-hospitalisation ou d'un régime provincial d'assurance-soins médicaux, ou des deux, de payer à l'administration provinciale qui gère ce ou ces régimes des sommes autres que des sommes à l'égard des cotisations ou des primes qu'un employé doit verser au régime, les sommes ainsi payées ne constituent pas un bénéfice imposable pour ses employés.

Laissez-passer de transport

42. Les laissez-passer fournis aux employés de lignes aériennes ne sont imposables que si la place de l'employé a été retenue et confirmée et que celui-ci paye moins de 50 pour 100 du tarif établi par la ligne aérienne pour le voyage, en classe économique, le jour où l'employé voyage. La valeur de l'avantage correspond à la différence entre 50 pour 100 du tarif en classe économique et les montants remboursés à la ligne aérienne pour le voyage en question.

43. L'utilisation des laissez-passer par des employés de compagnies de transport par autobus et par chemin de fer n'est pas un avantage imposable.

44. Les employés retraités de compagnies de transport ne seront, en aucune circonstance, tenus de payer l'impôt à l'égard de l'utilisation des laissez-passer de transport.

Titulaire de charge publique

45. Un titulaire de charge publique peut avoir à engager les frais nécessaires à la mise sur pied, aux opérations ou au démantèlement d'une fiducie sans droit de regard pour respecter les exigences du Code régissant la conduite des titulaires de charge publique en ce qui concerne les conflits d'intérêts et l'après-mandat. Si le gouvernement du Canada, conformément au dit code, rembourse ces frais au titulaire, il n'en découlera aucun avantage fiscal aux fins de l'impôt sur le revenu, car le titulaire doit engager ces frais uniquement en raison de son emploi ou de sa charge. Les observations ci-dessus s'appliquent aussi aux frais, et au remboursement de ceux-ci, engagés en vertu de tout arrangement substantiellement semblable qui vise les détenteurs d'une charge publique provinciale ou municipale.

Glossary

Accidental Death & Dismemberment A form of insurance which provides a lump-sum payment in the event of accidental death or injury. The payment due to injury is a percentage of the death benefit, with the percentage based on the severity of the injury.

Administrative Services Only (ASO) Plans that are not underwritten by an insurer. The employer sets aside a fund from which the administrator pays claims. No premiums are paid; the employer simply provides funds to pay the claims incurred under the plan.

Adverse Selection (Anti-Selection) Created when employees elect certain insurance coverages because of a high likelihood of a claim. A terminally ill employee selecting more life insurance is an extreme example of adverse selection.

Adverse Selection Controls Elements of a plan design that are intended to minimize the chance an employee will elect coverage because of the high likelihood of a claim. Examples include:

- Before employees increase their life insurance coverage, they must provide evidence of good health;

- Employees must remain in a dental coverage option for two years before being allowed to change to another option.

Beneficiary A person named by an employee who will receive benefits from an insurance plan or pension plan if the employee dies.

Buy Back In a flexible benefit program, refers to the ability of an employee to repurchase the level of benefit coverage he or she had in the previous benefit program.

Canada Pension Plan (CPP)—1966 Provides a retirement benefit of 25 percent of adjusted average earnings to those who contribute to the Plan during their working lives. This Plan also provides disability pensions, survivor's pensions, orphan's benefits, and death benefits.

435

Canada Health Act—1984 Replaced the Hospital Insurance and Diagnostic Services Act of 1957 and the Medical Care Act of 1966. The Act sets out the principles of the health care system, including universality, portability, outlawing extra billing and user fees, and administration by provincial public authorities. Provinces control the health care system, but receive federal subsidies only if they comply with the conditions of the Act.

Carve-Out Pricing A pricing system which sets a base price of $0 for the core option level and sets prices of other options according to their incremental value.

Cash Value The amount an individual is entitled to receive on termination of a whole life or universal life insurance policy. Essentially the cash value equals the premiums paid by the employee plus interest less expenses, such as commission and insurance costs.

Change in Family Status Employees are generally permitted to change their flexible benefit choices between enrollment periods (i.e. mid-year), if they have a change in family status. Examples include marriage, divorce, birth or adoption of a child, loss of a spouse's coverage through death or loss of employment, or change in a child's full-time student status.

Child Care Refers to a benefit plan whereby employers subsidize child care services. These may include:

- On-site day care centres;
- Payments to employees which subsidize private child care arrangements;
- Provision of child care referral services, either in-house or through an outside provider.

Children's Life Insurance A group life insurance policy covering an employee's children, generally those under age 19 or 23 if full-time students. Typically, children's life insurance options are for a flat amount (unrelated to employee pay), and are priced independent of age, gender or number of children.

Choice Making Refers to a benefit program that allows employees to choose among a number of options.

Claims A request to the insurance carrier by the insured person for payment of benefits under a policy.

Cluster Stratified Sample A method of randomly choosing employees for a survey or an employee focus group. A limited number of locations expected to represent many others is randomly selected and employees are then randomly chosen from each location.

Coinsurance The sharing of medical and dental expenses between the plan and the employee. Coinsurance is typically the percentage paid by the plan. For example, 80 percent coinsurance means 80 percent is reimbursed by the plan, and 20 percent is paid by the employee.

Component Credit Allocation Flexible credits are given to employees for each type of benefit, and the sum of the components is the employee's total credit allocation.

Constructive Receipt A legal concept referring to a situation where a taxpayer is taxed on amounts he or she did not actually receive merely because the taxpayer had the right to take the payment in cash. The income is taxed whether or not the taxpayer actually exercises the right to receive this income.

Consumer Price Index (CPI)   An index published monthly by Statistics Canada which measures the relative cost of a selected group of goods and services over time.

Conversion   Refers to a provision in a group life insurance policy which allows an employee to change from group coverage to an individual policy upon termination of employment. Generally, conversion does not require evidence of insurability.

Coordination of Benefits   A provision in a group insurance policy describing which insurer pays a claim first when two policies cover the same claim. The total payment is no more than 100 percent of the claim.

Core Level of Benefits   A basic level of benefits required by the employer. This benefit level is frequently fully employer-paid.

Core Plus Credits (Core Plus Options, Cutback Approach)   A pricing structure for a flexible benefit program. A basic or core level of coverage is provided to all employees, typically at no cost to them. The difference in costs between the prior plan and the core is distributed to employees as flexible credits. Additional options beyond the core level may be purchased with flexible credits and payroll deductions.

Cost-of-Living Adjustment (COLA)   An increase in wages, pension benefits, or disability benefits according to the rise in the cost of living. This adjustment is usually calculated using a percentage of the annual increase in the Consumer Price Index, often with a maximum. In flexible benefit programs, this is frequently a provision in optional LTD plans.

Credits (Flexible Credits)   The annual allowance of employer money received by each employee to spend on benefits. One flexible credit is generally equal to one dollar.

Deductible   The amount an individual must pay out of pocket for medical and dental expenses before any benefits are available from the plan.

Default Coverages   A set of coverages assigned to employees who do not return enrollment forms.

Deferred Profit Sharing Plan (DPSP)   A type of defined contribution plan where employer contributions are based on profits. The contributions and investment earnings are tax protected while in the plan.

Defined Benefit Pension Plan   A retirement plan that provides a specified benefit defined by a formula. Employees may or may not contribute to the plan. The employer's contribution is calculated to be sufficient to provide the promised benefit.

Defined Contribution Pension Plan   A retirement plan that provides an individual account for each participant. Some defined contribution plans provide for both employee and employer contributions, while others allow contributions by one or the other. The benefit amount depends on the amount contributed to the account.

Dental Capitation Plans (DMOs, Managed Dental Care)   An organization providing a broad range of dental care services for a fixed prepaid monthly fee (per capita). These services are provided by a specified group of dentists.

Dental Fee Guide   Each year, the dental association publishes a list of reasonable and customary charges for dental services in the province. Dentists are free to charge more, less or the same as the fee guide.

Dental Plan   A plan which provides benefits for dental care. Typically, these plans include coverage for preventive and basic work (examination, cleaning, fillings, X-rays), major restorative work (crowns, inlays, bridges) and may also include orthodontia.

Dependent   Generally an employee's spouse and children, as defined in a contract. Under some contracts, parents or other members of the family may be dependents.

Dependent Life Insurance   A group life insurance policy covering an employee's spouse and/or children. Typically, flat coverage amounts are provided for the spouse and children.

Elder Care   A benefit program that provides a variety of care services for an employee's elderly relatives. Elder-care programs can provide health services, day care, home support, educational programs, and other services to elderly people. An elder-care plan may include:

- Direct subsidies to elder-care facilities

- Payment to employees to subsidize private elder-care arrangements

- Provision of elder-care referral services, either in-house or through an outside provider.

Election Confirmation Statement   A personalized statement showing flexible benefit elections recorded on the enrollment system for a participant. Generally sent to employees after they have enrolled, but before the effective date of coverage.

Employee Listening   The process of collecting information on employee attitudes and perceptions concerning a proposed company initiative. Often used to test the appeal of flexible benefits with a random sample of employees.

Enrollment   The annual process by which employees choose options under the flexible benefit program.

Evidence of Insurability   Usually a health statement required by insurers before covering someone who previously opted out of coverage. May also be required when increasing level of coverage in life insurance or LTD, for example.

Experience-Rated Insurance   A way of financing insurance with a carrier that requires a full accounting at the end of each plan year. The employer receives any surplus or pays any deficit between premiums charged and claims and expenses paid out.

Family Allowances Act—1973   Provides flat-rate payments on a per-child basis to families with children under 18. This benefit is wholly or partially taxed back above certain income levels ($50,000 in 1989).

Flexible Benefit Program (Flexible Compensation, Cafeteria Benefits)   A benefit program that allows choice making and gives the employee control over how some of the company benefit premiums are to be spent.

Flexible Expense Account   A special fund set up by an employer from which an employee can draw to pay certain expenses. Typically, these accounts are used for health-related expenses (health care expense account) and other expenses. Payments from the health care expense account are non-taxable income to employees. Payments from a non-health account are generally taxable.

Focus Group A group of employees brought together to discuss their attitudes and perceptions toward a proposed company initiative. Focus groups are often used to test a flexible benefit program.

Forfeiture (use-it-or-lose-it) Describes the insurance risk element imposed on flexible expense accounts by Revenue Canada. Funds allocated for use during a plan year are lost if not spent by the end of the year. Recently, however, Revenue Canada has allowed the rolling over of unused balances to the next year, and the cashing out of unused balances. The employees must make the cash-out or roll over election at the beginning of the plan year.

Group Plans Employer-sponsored benefit plans providing coverage to a group of employees.

Guaranteed Income Supplement A benefit payable under the federal Old Age Security Act to those whose income is below a threshold—that is, a means test.

Health Care Expense Account Employees deposit flexible credits in this account to be drawn out during the plan year for reimbursement of health care expenses. Expenses that can be covered by this account include those that could be covered by a private health services plan (as defined in the Income Tax Act), but not covered by other private or provincial health insurance plans.

Hearing Care A health care plan which provides reimbursement for hearing aids. Usually included as a part of a supplemental medical plan.

Hospital Insurance and Diagnostic Services Act—1957 Provided the framework for the Canadian health care system. Provinces complying with federal standards received subsidies of about half the cost of providing hospital benefits. Replaced by the Canada Health Act in 1984.

Interpretation Bulletin IT-339R A Revenue Canada document that sets out the criteria for a "Private Health Services Plan" as defined in the Income Tax Act.

Interpretation Bulletin IT-421R A Revenue Canada document that provides a description of taxation of group mortgage plans. Generally, it describes taxation of benefits to individuals, corporations and shareholders from loans or debt.

Interpretation Bulletin IT-428 A Revenue Canada document that describes the taxation of wage loss replacement (disability) plans.

Interpretation Bulletin IT-470R A Revenue Canada document that describes the taxation of perquisites or fringe benefits.

Leave of Absence Time off from work that lasts for an extended period of time. Examples include educational leave, sabbatical leave, and maternity/adoption leave. Typically, these types of leave require management approval.

Long-Term Benefits Benefits having a low claim frequency and high per-claim amount. These include life insurance and long-term disability.

Long-Term Care An insurance plan that provides a benefit if an employee requires medical and support services for an extended period of time. This is usually a flat dollar amount provided per day, and can include nursing homes, home care, day care and respite care.

Long-Term Disability (LTD)   A plan which provides income protection in the event of time lost due to sickness or accident of a long-term nature. Benefits typically begin after six months and continue to age 65, and provide from 50 percent of pay to 70 percent of pay.

Maintenance of Benefits   A coordination of benefits approach in which deductibles and copayment amounts are preserved when the plan is secondary. This is because the secondary plan defines its payment as the difference between what it would pay if it were the sole plan and what the other plan actually pays.

Medical Care Act—1966   Extended the Hospital Insurance Act by allowing federal subsidies for medical benefits. Replaced by the Canada Health Act in 1984.

Medicare   A common term which refers to provincial government health insurance plans. These plans generally cover hospital ward care, hospital services, and physicians' fees.

Modular   A design structure for a flexible benefit program. Modules are created which include specific coverage levels in several benefit areas. For example, a rich set of options, a moderate set of options, and a core set of options. Employees must choose one module.

Money Purchase Pension Plan (MPPP)   A type of defined contribution retirement plan. Employee contributions are typically expressed as a percent of salary, with the employer making matching contributions. Contributions are accumulated with interest and used to purchase an annuity at the employee's retirement.

No-Coverage Pricing   The process of determining how many credits to give to someone opting out of coverage.

Old Age Security Act (OAS)—1952   Provides a monthly pension to qualified Canadian residents regardless of past earnings or current income. This pension is indexed to the Consumer Price Index. This benefit is taxed back wholly or partially for those with incomes over a certain level ($50,000 in 1989).

Opt-Up-or-Down Pricing (Rearrangement Approach)   An employee receives a credit for taking lower-coverage option, pays nothing or a modest amount for receiving a standard option, and pays a price for taking a higher-coverage option. Considered a good way to encourage employees to select a lower-valued option.

Opt Out   Refers to an employee choosing not to be covered for a certain option—for example, dental.

Options   Refers to the choices available within each benefit area of a flexible benefit program.

Out-of-Pocket Expense   Refers to payments by an employee for expenses not covered under a group insurance plan.

Partial Insurance   An arrangement where the employer self-insures the coverage up to a pre-determined limit, after which the carrier's liability begins.

Payroll Deductions   When an employer deducts after-tax dollars from an employee's paycheque; can be used to pay for benefit coverages.

Pension Adjustment (PA)   The value of pension benefits accruing to a plan member during a year under proposed Income Tax Act changes. The PA is subtracted from the member's comprehensive retirement contribution limit (18 percent of pay, subject to specified dollar limits) to determine the maximum RRSP contribution allowed for the following year.

Perquisites   A benefit tied to a specific executive-level job. Examples include a company car for personal use, a car phone, financial counselling, or use of a company fitness facility.

Personal Benefit Statements (Personal Benefit Reports)   A statement included in flexible benefit enrollment materials that lists an employee's options, price tags, and credits. The statement is personalized, because the items are calculated based on factors such as the employee's age, pay, date of hire, family status and sex.

Pooled Insurance   Insured groups are placed in a pool with others sharing similar characteristics. The experience of the pool influences the rates the group is charged.

Premium   The amount of money paid by an employer to an insurance company for an insurance policy or annuity.

Price Tag   The dollar value paid by employees for a certain level of benefit coverage. May be different from the premium.

Pricing   The process of determining the price tags paid by the employee for a benefit and the flexible credits the employer allocates to the employee.

Private Health Services Plan   As defined by the Income Tax Act, a health care plan with the following elements:

1.   It must be an undertaking of one person

2.   To indemnify another person

3.   For an agreed consideration

4.   For a loss or liability in respect of an event

5.   The happening of which is uncertain.

Qualification entitles the employer to deduct the premiums as a business expense. Benefits under this type of plan are tax-free to the employee.

Purposive Sample   A method of selecting employees for a survey or focus group if reliable statistics are not required. Employees are hand-selected to represent key subgroups.

Qualitative Employee Listening   A method of gathering employee perceptions and identifying employee needs that involves face-to-face discussions. These occur either one-on-one or in group meetings, usually with only a small cross-section of employees. Used to determine why employees have certain views or opinions. Does not produce reliable statistics on what portion of the group holds a specific viewpoint.

Quantitative Employee Listening   A method of identifying employee needs and gathering employee perceptions that involves a written survey. Typically administered to all employees or a statistically reliable sample. Designed to produce statistics on what portion of a group holds a specific viewpoint. Does not explain why the employees have certain opinions.

Quebec Pension Plan (QPP)   A retirement plan for Quebec residents that is almost identical to the Canada Pension Plan. The most notable differences in the QPP are that the maximum monthly surviving spouse's pension is significantly higher than the CPP, and the children's supplement is significantly lower than the CPP.

Registered Education Savings Plan (RESP) An arrangement under which interest earned on an investment for education can be accrued tax-free. At maturity, the principal amount is payable to the contributor, but the investment income is paid out over three years to the student as taxable income.

Registered Pension Plan (RPP) A pension plan which is registered with Revenue Canada and the applicable provincial pension commission. Registered plans are regulated by the Income Tax Act and provincial pension legislation.

Random Sample An unbiased method of selecting employees for a survey or focus group, usually accomplished by choosing a name randomly from a name roster and then selecting, say, every 20th name after that.

Realistic Prices Prices that can reasonably be expected to support claims costs.

Reenrollment A basic principle of a flexible benefit program is to allow employees to make new benefits choices periodically. Typically, the enrollment process is repeated each year. This is termed reenrollment.

Registered Retirement Savings Plan (RRSP) An arrangement between an individual and an authorized insurer, trust company, or corporation for the purpose of providing a retirement income for the individual. These are covered under Section 146 of the Income Tax Act. At the plan's maturity, an annuity is purchased or the plan assets are transferred to a registered retirement income fund (RRIF). Subject to certain maximums, the individual's contributions to an RRSP are deductible for income tax purposes and the investment income is tax-deferred.

Relative Values A method of comparing option values to a base plan value:

$$\text{relative value} = \frac{\text{option premium}}{\text{base plan premium}}$$

This method compares characteristics of optional plans to a base plan using actuarial methodology and assists in setting option prices.

Role Modelling A communication technique using fictional sample employees and allowing employees to identify the ones closest to their personal situations.

Roll-Over Describes the insurance risk element imposed on health care expense accounts by Revenue Canada. Funds must be used to reimburse expenses incurred during the year. Otherwise, the funds will be rolled over to the next year's account. Alternatively, if the employee so elects at the beginning of the year, the unused balance can be cashed out.

Sabbatical Leave An extended period of paid time off (more than six months), frequently for the purpose of study or pursuit of personal interests. Typically, an employee defers a portion of salary each year (subject to Revenue Canada rules) in order to draw upon it while on sabbatical leave.

Salary Reduction A U.S. mechanism in which employee contributions for benefits are treated as employer payments, thus escaping federal income tax and most state and local taxes. Salary reduction is prohibited in Canada.

Section 6(c) A section of the Income Tax Act stating that employer contributions to medical and dental plans are not taxable income to the employee.

Section 125 A section of the U.S. Tax Code that permits choice making between taxable and non-taxable benefits.

Section 248(1) A section of the Income Tax Act that, along with Interpretation Bulletin 227R, sets out the detailed qualifications for group insurance plans exempt from inclusion as taxable income. It also defines salary deferral arrangements.

Section 401(k) A section of the U.S. Tax Code which permits trade-offs between cash and deferral of compensation into a retirement income vehicle.

Self-Insurance A special fund set up by an employer to provide benefit coverage. The employer pays claims and administers the fund directly. In this arrangement, the employer assumes the risks and liabilities of an insurance carrier.

Short-Term Benefits Benefits which have a high claim frequency and low per-claim amounts. Some examples include supplemental medical, dental, and vision.

Short-Term Disability (STD) A benefit plan which provides payment to a disabled person for the period of the disability before long term disability benefits are payable. Typically covers first six months of an employee absence and is paid by the employer.

Sick Leave Time off from work due to illness.

Spousal Life Insurance A life insurance plan which covers an employee's spouse. The amount of coverage is typically a flat amount, but may be related to the employee's pay. Price tags for spousal life may be a flat premium amount expressed as dollars per thousand dollars of coverage, or may be graded according to age, gender, or smoker status of the spouse and/or employee.

Stop-Loss Limits An insurance contract provision which limits the out-of-pocket expenses paid by an employee during the period of coverage.

Stratified Random Sample A method of choosing an employee sample for a survey or focus group in which employees are arranged by a factor such as job category and chosen randomly with each category.

Subgroup Pricing A method of dividing the pricing structure into smaller groups with similar characteristics. The most common category is dependent coverage, for example, employee, employee-plus-one, employee-plus-two-or-more dependents.

Subsidized Pricing This pricing method refers to any difference between premiums determined by claims experience and the price tags charged the employee. This is a form of indirect flexible credit allocation.

Supplemental Medical Plan A medical plan that provides benefits not included in the various provincial health insurance plans. Typically, these plans include coverage for semi-private or private hospital rooms, prescription drugs, certain medical equipment, and health care practitioners not covered under the provincial plans.

Task Force (Study Group) A group of employees, generally representing various work groups and personal situations, who work as a group in designing a flexible benefit program.

Term Life Insurance Life insurance payable to a beneficiary when the insured person dies. No cash value is developed.

Third-Party Administration (TPA)   An administrative alternative for flexible benefits by which an outside organization administers the program.

Time-Sharing Services   A system in which flexible benefit administrators have on-line access to software located on a vendor's computer.

Universal Life Insurance   A life insurance policy under which the policyholder may change the death benefit from time to time, and vary the amount or timing of premium payments. A policy account is set up from which premiums and expense charges are deducted and to which interest is credited.

Utilization   The extent to which a group uses a service—for example, a medical or dental plan. Typically expressed as a number of claims per 100 or per 1,000 plan participants.

Vacation Banking   A system in which employers allow employees to save unused vacation time for use at a later date.

Vacation Buying   An option that allows employees to use flexible credits or payroll deduction to purchase vacation days. Typically, a vacation day is priced at the value of one day's salary for the employee.

Vacation Selling   An option that allows employees to exchange a vacation day for flexible credits. Typically, a vacation day is priced at the value of one day's salary for the employee.

Vesting   An employee's right to receive a pension benefit, whether or not the employee stays with the employer providing the benefit. Employee contributions to a pension plan are immediately vested, but employer-paid benefits may be vested after a number of years of service or plan participation.

Vision Care   A health care plan that provides coverage for eyeglasses and/or contact lenses. May be included in supplemental medical plans or as a stand-alone plan.

Wage Loss Replacement Plan   An arrangement between an employer and employees under which benefits are provided if an employee loses employment income, as a result of sickness, maternity or accident, for example.

Waiver of Coverage   Occurs when a plan allows employees to elect no coverage in certain benefit areas.

Weekly Indemnity   A weekly payment provided under an insurance policy to reimburse an employee for loss of earnings due to disability. Also known as disability income insurance. These plans pay a periodic cash amount such as 60 percent of normal earnings for a limited period such as six or twelve months.

Whole Life Insurance   Insurance payable to a beneficiary at the death of the insured person whenever that occurs. A cash value builds up over time. Premiums may be payable for a specified number of years or for life.

Winners and Losers Analysis   Comparison of benefit coverage before and after implementation of a flexible benefit program. Winners are those employees who have more than enough credits to buy back the pre-flexible options. Losers have too few credits.

Workbook/Enrollment Guide   A booklet which explains the options, price tags, and credits available in a flexible benefit program. This communication material is developed to assist employees in enrolling in the flexible benefit program.

Index